Below Stairs

400 years of servants' portraits

GILES WATERFIELD
ANNE FRENCH
WITH MATTHEW CRASKE

Foreword by Julian Fellowes

NATIONAL PORTRAIT GALLERY, LONDON

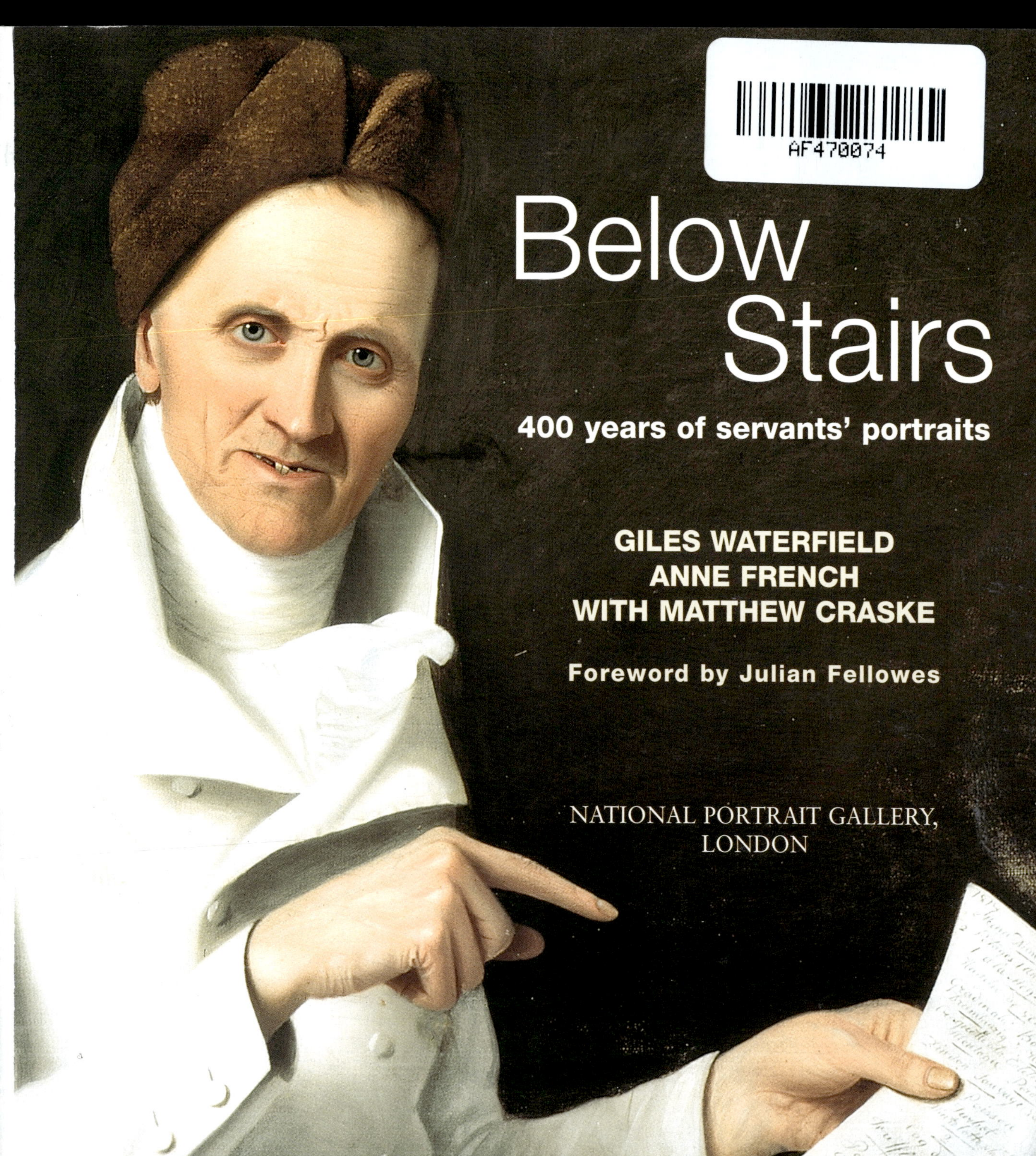

Published in Great Britain by National Portrait Gallery Publications,
National Portrait Gallery, St Martin's Place, London WC2H 0HE

To accompany the exhibition *Below Stairs: 400 years of servants' portraits* at the
National Portrait Gallery 16 October 2003–11 January 2004
Scottish National Portrait Gallery 11 February–31 May 2004

For a complete catalogue of current publications, please write to the address above, or visit
our website at www.npg.org.uk

ISBN 1 85514 509 X Paperback
ISBN 1 85514 512 X Hardback

A catalogue record for this book is available from the British Library.

Senior Editor: Anjali Bulley
Project Editor: Marilyn Inglis
Production: Ruth Müller-Wirth
Additional Picture Research: Catherine Ford
Design: Karen Stafford
Printed by BAS Printers

FRONT COVER: Detail of cat.61 **The Kitchen**, Harold Gilman, *c.*1908
BACK COVER: Detail of cat.54 **Heads of Six of Hogarth's Servants**, William Hogarth, *c.*1750–55
TITLE PAGE: Detail of cat.32 **Joseph Florance**, John Ainslie, 1817

We are grateful to the owners and lenders to the exhibition and the copyright holders who have kindly agreed to make their images available in this book. Any omissions are inadvertent and will be corrected in future editions if notification is given to the publisher in writing.

Contents

Foreword *Julian Fellowes* 4
Director's foreword *Sandy Nairne* 5

Introduction *Giles Waterfield* 7

1 Jesters, champions and pipers *Anne French* 21
2 Stewards to scullery-maids *Anne French* 37
3 Loyal servants *Anne French and Giles Waterfield* 57
4 Servants in institutions *Giles Waterfield* 77
5 Life in service *Giles Waterfield* 93
6 Servants as artists' models *Anne French* 105
7 The ambiguous servant *Anne French* 121
8 Black servants *Giles Waterfield* 139
9 In the realm of nature and beasts *Matthew Craske* 153
10 Social critique *Giles Waterfield* 167
11 The tradition disintegrates *Giles Waterfield* 183

List of illustrations 196
Acknowledgements 203
Notes 204
Bibliography 209
Index 210

Foreword

When we were making the film *Gosford Park*, I was lucky enough to be able to rely on the help and experience of some remarkable individuals who had been in service during the 1930s, the period in which the film was set. At that time Arthur Inch was a footman for the Londonderrys, both at Wynyard in the north of England and at Londonderry House in Park Lane, Violet Liddle was a housemaid for Sir Winston Churchill and Ruth Mott had been a kitchen-maid for the Countess of Iveagh at Elvedon in Norfolk. Naturally enough, their advice in almost every scene was invaluable and filled with detail that no history book could hope to supply.

At first, when talking to them, I was constantly struck by how recent the servant-motored life had been. This world, as remote now as the Planet Zog, was fully operational less than a lifetime ago. Then I noticed that, when each of them described their early working years, they would invariably conform to the same pattern. They would start to list the positions they had achieved: 'I was a hall boy to begin with and then I was fourth footman for so-and-so, then I was second footman at such-and-such ... and then the war came.' Or 'I began as a tweeny, then I was a vegetable-maid, then first kitchen-maid, then under chef ... and then the war came.' Every time it was the same; the war drew a line under everything. Of course, there were servants after the war. All three of my helpers had returned to service in some guise and I received tremendous assistance from Ron Puttock, the present Keeper at Luton Hoo. Indeed, in rare households quite large staffs survive into the present day but nevertheless I realised, as I listened to my helpers, that after 1939 the pyramid structure of promotion, the logic of a career in service as a nationwide employer, had gone. Presumably it has gone forever. As my late father once said, when challenged for his views on the continuing blight of the class system, 'What class system? All we have now is class prejudice. The *system* has been destroyed.'

Only a fool does battle with his own times and our age has declared against anything that smacks of hereditary privilege. We may rub along with a little of it, but we must not ever be thought to consider birth a useful method of selection. An inevitable consequence of this has been the discomfort engendered by the whole question of the servant-supported way of life that obtained in these islands as a natural law for a thousand years. This is more than a simple unease with the notion of humiliating work practices or a put-upon working class. Obviously, there are many far more degrading ways of earning a living than being a trusted servant in a large country house but it is a complicated question. Our generation supports the concept that there are tasks that human beings ought to do for themselves and it is therefore not just demeaning but downright *wrong* to perform such tasks for them. Washing pigs' entrails for sausages is acceptable while washing someone else's bath is not. You may serve in a bar but not at a private dinner table. Being a waiter is part of growing up but a holiday job as a footman would seem a bizarre departure. Some of the distinctions are curious. There is no stigma to being a dresser in a theatre but it is lowering to work as a lady's maid, it is a good career to cook in a restaurant but sad to cook in someone else's home. I do not seek to overturn these prejudices, only to observe them and to suggest that they have, for some time now, created a barrier between us and our immediate forebears, most of whom, lest we forget, were engaged in this exchange, whether as servants or employers.

Theirs was a convoluted world. The hierarchies below stairs were, if anything, more severe and unforgiving than those above. The ladder of promotion was laid down and had to be observed with no steps missed. In fact this led to a constant uprooting of the ambitious servant, which explodes the cherished myth of ancient retainers remaining with families for decades on end. This may have happened in some cases but the vast majority were forever on the move. In the 1880s the average time for a footman to remain in a London house was eighteen months. When one considers that few housemaids stayed beyond their mid-twenties (when they left to marry), one can understand why almost every letter of the period is filled with enquiries about decent cooks and competent ladies' maids, where to find a still-room maid or a reliable footman or an assistant chef. On and on the entreaties go until one has a glimpse of the burden that maintaining a large household must have become – which was, of course, one of the reasons for its eventual demise.

Despite the insistence of many ancient aunts, the situation cannot often have conformed entirely to their rose-tinted vision of loyal retainers grabbing at their forelocks and reeling with delight at the return of the young master but nor, I think, was it the black hole of injustice that our modern televisual media would have us believe. Although both these viewpoints were represented in the film, I attempted to convey in the script what I truly feel: that for the most part, being a servant was a job like any other, with its merits and its disadvantages. Generous employers existed as well as mean ones, kind as well as cruel, although for most servants the personalities of the butler, the cook and the housekeeper were of more immediate relevance than those of the family upstairs and tyranny in the Servants' Hall certainly existed. Arthur Inch left a job as the Duchess's Footman at Blenheim because of an intolerable butler and there are many such stories. I suppose in the end we must come back to the ancient truth that there are good and bad people on this earth and they are sprinkled in pretty even proportions throughout all classes, nationalities, periods and societies.

Perhaps it is this simple thought that will enable us to enjoy this exhibition and book without prejudging the system they commemorate too harshly. Perhaps, too, we may applaud the National Portrait Gallery for daring to mount a serious and illuminating exhibition about a subject that has been taboo for far too long.

JULIAN FELLOWES

Director's foreword

This is a book that charts new ground. While histories of domestic service have developed over recent years, there have been few occasions until now to look at the painted portraits and photographs of those who might otherwise remain anonymous. In charting this field across four hundred years, the curators and authors have discovered some extraordinary gems: portraits that give a vivid sense of that particular person, as well as insight into their duties and the relationships with their employers, whether as servant or slave.

The commissioning of a portrait of a servant was an exceptional matter, and speaks in many instances of affection and loyalty, or in other cases of a special pride in the skills involved in their work. However exceptional, there are enough common types for comparisons to be drawn, for the idea and status of portraits of those below stairs to be examined in some detail. I hope that this book will lead to more research, locating further examples of the servant portrait, and encouraging the fullest mapping of portraiture as an important element of social history.

I should first like to thank Anne French and Giles Waterfield, who had the insight to see this as a subject of importance, and have developed this project with such determination and energy. I should also like to thank Matthew Craske for his fascinating contribution to the catalogue, Julian Fellowes for his delightful reflections on the world recreated so tellingly in *Gosford Park*, and Kate Newman for her research and assistance. Many staff have contributed to the project, amongst them Peter Funnell, Anjali Bulley, Ruth Müller-Wirth, Robert Carr-Archer, Denny Hemming, Marilyn Inglis, Karen Stafford, Pim Baxter, John Haywood, Hazel Sutherland, Stephen Allen, Jan Cullen, Sophie Clark, Beatrice Hosegood and Kathleen Soriano, to all of whom I am very grateful. Thanks are also due to Karl Abeyasekera for his excellent work on exhibition design.

There are many generous lenders who have parted with precious works, and I am very grateful to them. I would like to acknowledge the special help of the National Trust, with whom we work closely on our regional partnerships, and who have been exceptionally helpful in offering advice on loans for the exhibition, particularly Merlin Waterson and Alistair Laing. It is also a pleasure to be collaborating again with our colleagues at the Scottish National Portrait Gallery, and I would especially like to thank Nicola Kalinsky and James Holloway.

SANDY NAIRNE

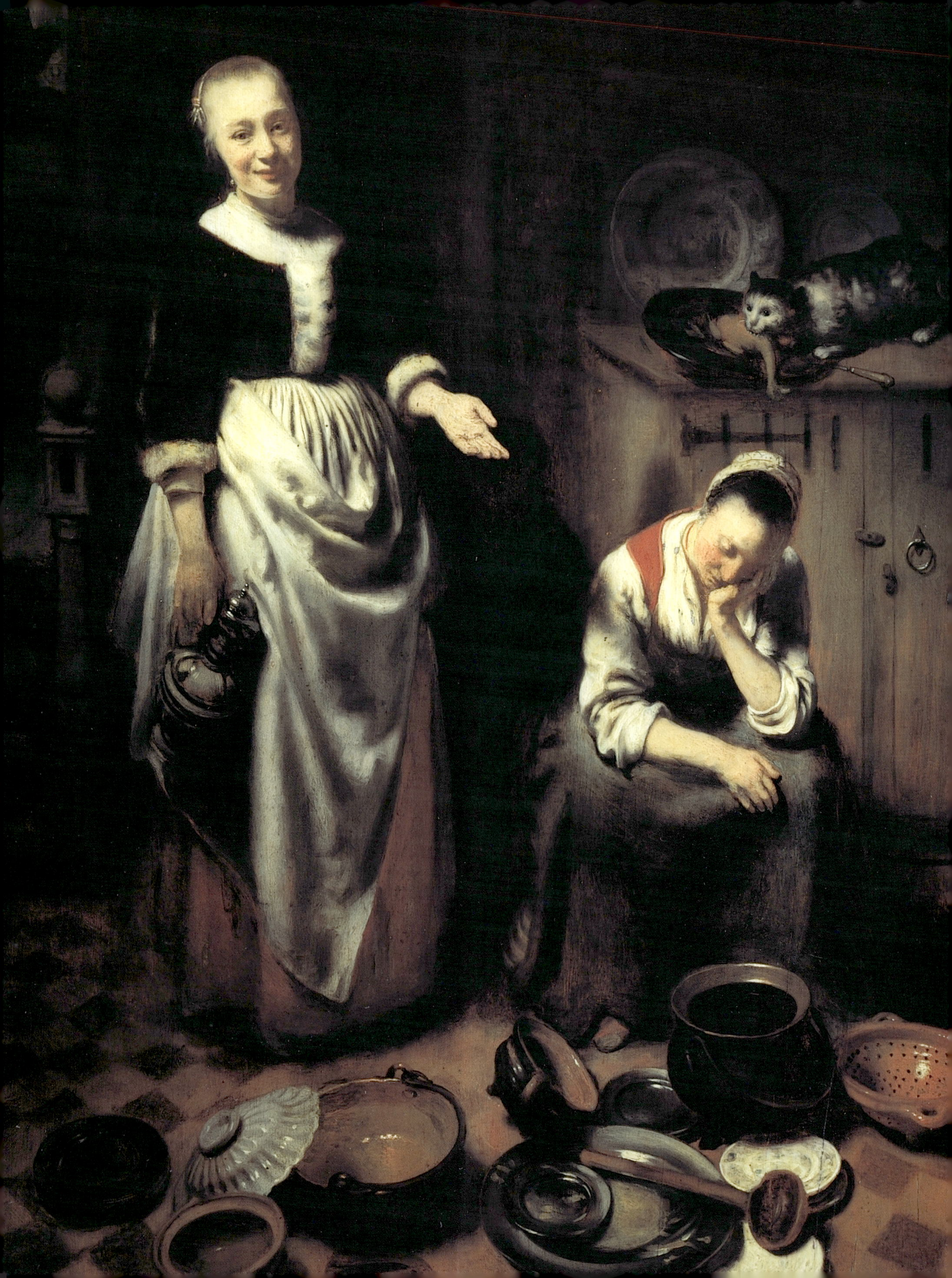

INTRODUCTION

Giles Waterfield

THIS IS A BOOK ABOUT PORTRAITS of ordinary people. Few of them were wealthy, or privileged, or distinguished. If it were not for their portraits, almost all of them would be wholly forgotten. But the group of images shown here represents a huge number of people, from the seventeenth century to the present, who for one reason or another were thought to be worth recording. The aim of this book is to study a type of painting which has generally been ignored, and to try to understand the complex and changing attitudes that fostered the portrait of the servant.

In a sense the very idea of a servant's portrait is an anomaly. At least until the development of photography, portraits were executed for people or institutions of wealth and influence – something that hardly applied to domestic servants. None of these portraits, for example, was commissioned by the sitter when he or she was working as a servant. This is not a subject that has been much studied, since it has generally been assumed that servants were hardly ever portrayed. As recently as 1993 the author of an important radical study of portraiture made this claim.[1] The most substantive study of the subject is a survey of the United States, Elizabeth O'Leary's *At Beck and Call: the Representation of Domestic Servants in Nineteenth-century American Painting* (which emphasises the notably important role of black slaves as well as the unease felt in this rapidly changing society over the concept of white servanthood). In this country, only one recent book has looked at servants' portraits, Merlin Waterson's *The Servants' Hall* (1980), which revealed the affection felt by the Yorke family of Erddig in the Welsh Marches, for the people who worked for them, and their long-standing interest in portraying these individuals in verse, painting and photography. Today the servants' portraits at Erddig are still the best-known examples of this genre. But servants' portraiture continues to be excluded from mainstream consideration. In the National Portrait Gallery

OPPOSITE Detail of Fig.2 **Interior with a Sleeping Maid and Her Mistress**
Nicolaes Maes, 1655

there is hardly a servant to be seen. They qualify for inclusion only in a secondary, generally anonymous role as the attendants to a great person or serving a beverage on the periphery of a conversation piece, or occasionally when through their ability they rose, like the footman Robert Dodsley (cat.110), the royal attendant John Brown (cat.82) and the gardener Joseph Paxton (cat.33), to national prominence.

What this book establishes is that servants were regularly commemorated in portraits of individuals or of groups. Various patterns have emerged, such as the importance of sporting pictures, serial portraits associated with a particular family, the theatrical tradition and the development of sympathetic genre paintings in the nineteenth century. The history of black servants and slaves is complex and sometimes disturbing. The images that emerge are extremely rich and varied, painted by famous artists such as Hogarth, Stubbs, Zoffany, Gainsborough, Frith and Landseer, and by people whose names are now forgotten.

The subject of domestic service itself has attracted considerable interest, particularly since the Second World War, when traditional domestic service almost ceased to exist as a result of people's unwillingness to take on such work with the development of more congenial alternatives. Such works as Dorothy Marshall's brief study *The English Domestic Servant in History* (1949) and Jean Hecht's *The Domestic Servant Class in Eighteenth-century England* (1956) initiated a series of books by academic historians and by former servants. The academic works in particular, often inspired by a rising interest in women's studies, are generally critical of domestic service: Bridget Hill's *Servants: English Domestics in the Eighteenth Century* (1996) is a vigorous example. Popular interest in servants and how they lived and worked was stimulated by the public opening at several historic houses, particularly those belonging to the National Trust, of the kitchens and other service quarters. To the generation of James Lees-Milne (who pioneered the opening of these houses for the Trust in the 1940s and 1950s) these offered no interest since houses were seen as documents of art history rather than social history. Since the television series *Upstairs Downstairs*, which was first broadcast in 1971, both television and film have found in domestic service a fertile field for comedy and intrigue, most recently in the film *Gosford Park* (2001) and the BBC series *The Servants* (2003).

The number of servants working in Britain from Roman times (as slaves) to the mid-twentieth century was very high. In the medieval and Tudor periods, the occupation was not defined as clearly as became possible in the seventeenth and eighteenth centuries. This was partly because large households, exemplified by the six hundred liveried retainers who accompanied the Earl of Warwick to Parliament in the mid-fifteenth century,[2] contained hundreds of people (mostly men), with men and women of gentle birth acting as servitors to great nobles (in a way that today has totally disappeared

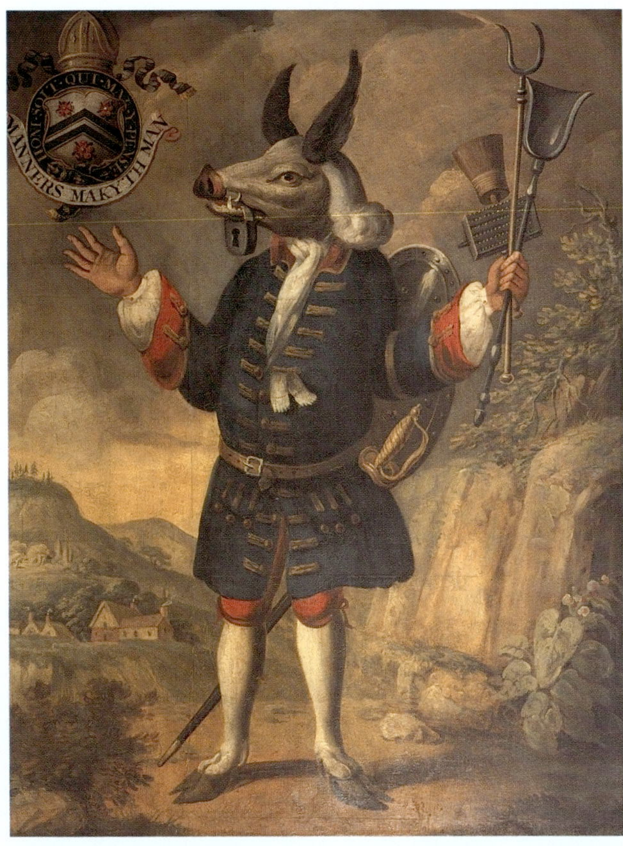

Cat.1 **The Trusty Servant**
William Cave, 1809

This extraordinary painting epitomises the aspirations of masters and mistresses over the centuries to find the perfect servant, and lists the qualities required. It ironically suggests the difficulty of achieving this ambition, as well as the dehumanising process to which servants might be subjected.

The Trusty Servant is an old image, going back to medieval literary sources. It is also an international one: comparable images exist in Poland and France. The original version of this painting was created in the early 1580s at Winchester College, at the instigation of John Hoskyns, then a schoolboy at Winchester (and later a prominent legal figure, famous for his wit and learning). It was possibly based on a print (now lost) of the same subject dating from 1577. Flanked by Hoskyns's explanatory verses in Latin (now also in English), the picture was placed in the lobby next to the college kitchens, presumably as an admonition to the college servants.

This first version was reworked, and possibly modified, on a regular basis (it had already been done three times by 1647). The image was reworked as a print in 1682 (under the ironic title *The Ages Rarity*), with the figure in a quite different pose and dress. The last major reordering was carried out in 1809 by the Winchester painter William Cave, who changed the costume and pose to please contemporary tastes. In Cave's version the figure is put into the Windsor uniform or livery devised by King George III for members of the royal household, and was chosen to honour the King.

Hoskyns was so pleased with his image that, John Aubrey tells us, in retirement in the 1620s he installed paintings of 'the old fellowe that made the fires' and of his gardener, respectively in the gatehouse and the garden of his house in Herefordshire, accompanied by appropriate verses.

A Trusty Servant's Portrait would you see,
The Emblematic Figure well Survey;
The Porker's Snout, not Nice in Diet shews,
The Padlock shut, no Secrets He'll disclose,
Patient, the Ass his Master's wrath will hear.
Swiftness in Errand, the Staggs Feet declare;
Loaded his Left Hand, apt to Labour saith;
The Vest, his Neatness – Open Hand his Faith.
Girt with his Sword; His Shield upon his arm;
Himself & Master, He'll protect from harm.
(from the panel at Winchester College)

except in the royal household). In more modest farms or small businesses, people worked both as domestic helpers and within the farm or shop, without the rigid demarcations that applied later. In the eighteenth century, as the country became richer and the middle classes expanded, the demand for servants increased: in the 1770s it was estimated that an eighth of the total population of London worked in this capacity.[3] By this time households were becoming more formal with the development of a service hierarchy in larger establishments, while the proportion of men was dropping, men being both more expensive to employ and more difficult to keep under control. By 1851 the national census listed 905,000 female and 134,000 male domestic servants in Britain; by 1911 there were 2.6 million people in service. As late as 1931 – partly under the influence of the Great Depression, which drove many people back into occupations they would have preferred to leave – over 1.3 million women (and almost 80,000 men) were still in domestic service. Only in the Second World War did the figures drop dramatically. Thus, for hundreds of years the number of servants was enormous, even though, as many life histories make clear, for many people servanthood was not a lifetime occupation. It might be a job one could drift into and out of, as did that raffish seducer of women the eighteenth-century footman John Macdonald, who worked for one easy-going gentleman after another. For many women, domestic service was the most suitable occupation for early adult life, making it possible to put together the dowry that was obligatory for marriage. The traditional idea of the household to which the old retainer was attached all their life is strongly reflected in this publication, but as Julian Fellowes says in his foreword, it represented a small fraction of the whole. The usual pattern – about which employers complained over generations – was for people to take a position for perhaps two years before moving to another position higher up the career ladder. Few portraits emerged from such behaviour as that.

How can 'the servant' be defined? Even the word is difficult, since it was not in general use for this purpose until the eighteenth century, and today is seldom applied. For this publication, we have identified two principal categories. The first group covers domestic servants – people working for families (including the royal family) in cities or in the countryside, as indoor staff or in the grounds and stables. These individuals range in status from kitchen-maids and labourers to tutors, governesses and land agents. The question of status was as important below stairs as it was above. Although people in the latter role would not have thought of themselves as servants, their employment as members of households qualifies them for inclusion. The second category includes people working for public or semi-public institutions – colleges (mostly at Oxford and Cambridge), the Bank of England, cultural institutions and London clubs. This is a smaller but interesting group of patrons with a history of commissioning portraits of their employees, generally to celebrate their loyalty.

Many recent writers on domestic service have concentrated on small households, reflecting the fact that the bulk of servants worked in one- or at the very most two-servant households, often in the most disagreeable and lonely conditions. These are not the servants shown in portraiture. In the eighteenth and still more the nineteenth century, it was generally young girls and even children, with no training, who became maids of all work or general servants in small urban or suburban households for lack of any alternative – though if they were at all talented they generally moved on very rapidly. This was an occupation particularly associated with the young, partly because employers tended to prefer young servants, and partly because those in service often left as soon as they could.[4] Most of their employers were unlikely to have themselves painted – though in due course they might be photographed – and would not have dreamt of obtaining an image of individuals whom they often exploited outrageously, and employed partly to establish their own membership of the middle class. *Maids of All Work* (cat.84) is a rare depiction of servants of this type, shown here as rather more cheerful and sociable than such solitary employees could often be.

The role of the servant was not an easy one. In the eighteenth and nineteenth centuries servants were often looked on with coldness and contempt by their employers, and with suspicion and even hostility by other working people. In the eighteenth century women servants tended to be regarded as little better than prostitutes; in the early twentieth, their relations and friends would beg them to conceal their occupation when meeting strangers.[5] As the male franchise was extended, servants were among the last men to be given the vote. Comparable doubts about their inclusion within society have extended to scholarly studies: in his magisterial work *The Making of the English Working Class*, E.P. Thompson hardly mentions this huge section of the working population.

To be a servant was to belong neither to the middle nor, altogether, the working classes – servanthood could carry negative associations with it, so when people were employed domestically by members of their own family, they tended to be thought inferior. On the other hand, domestic service offered a degree of security and a higher standard of living than many people could have hoped for elsewhere. Many families, at all levels of society, were clearly concerned about their employees, and manuals on servants from the eighteenth century onwards frequently urged that they should receive kind treatment from their masters. One significant indication of the way in which households could function at their best is the use of the word 'family' to indicate an entire household – though 'family' did not necessarily imply intimacy.

Costume is a particularly revealing indication of the servant's unusual and ambiguous social status. If they worked in a wealthy household, the upper servants were often better dressed than their relations who were not in service. In the eighteenth century at least they inherited or were given the cast-off clothing of their masters and mistresses, or wore specially designed clothes intended for display, though the extravagantly colourful and opulent dress of a footman, a symbol of their employers' wealth, could be a focus for popular derision. (Sticking pins in the calves of footmen was a favourite activity of street urchins, and an Edwardian footman described in his memoirs having old fish thrown at him in a pub because he was wearing livery.)[6] In the Victorian period a butler wore the clothing of a gentleman but cut in a deliberately old-fashioned way, so as to include a deliberate solecism in order to illustrate his inferior status.[7] In large households, servants were generally better fed than they would have been in the outside world – though unless they belonged to the upper echelons of the servant hierarchy, their accommodation in attics or basements, even in the kitchen, was frequently very poor. Above all, in large households, they were constantly exposed to a style of life and a set of attitudes unlike anything they would have been accustomed to, and were expected to show close loyalty to their employers. In many households, large or small, most particularly in the nineteenth century, a servant was often deprived of individuality, expected to wear uniform, not allowed (particularly if female) to have a relationship with the opposite sex or get married, and called not by his or her own name but by the name associated with their position.

There were further problems for the servant, which are reflected in this publication. In the seventeenth and eighteenth centuries, maidservants were often regarded as legitimate sexual prey by their masters – a theme that was explored in visual art and most notably in Samuel Richardson's famous novel *Pamela*, published in 1740 (cat.63). In Victorian times this threat receded to some extent as strict discipline was introduced, and employers became concerned with their servants' morals, with daily family prayers assuming critical importance. At the same time, interest in the physical comfort of servants remained low until late in the nineteenth century, when a new concern with employees' accommodation and health emerged in literature as in the design of houses. We know from a number of accounts how men and women who found themselves in this role reacted. Some, like the eighteenth-century footman Robert Dodsley, who, with the support of his employers and their friends, rose to become one of the best-known printers and publishers of the eighteenth century, recorded the conditions of 'Servitude' (as an early poem by him was titled) uncomplainingly, even though he soon abandoned this life (cat.110). Generally the life was easier for men, who were better paid and less likely to be victimised. But the memoirs of servants from the mid-nineteenth century onwards are often more complex and negative. It might be Hannah Cullwick (cat.81), recording in her diary[8] her fascination and frustration with the humiliation involved in domestic service, or writers in the twentieth century, from Monica Dickens and Margaret Powell[9] onwards, writing from their

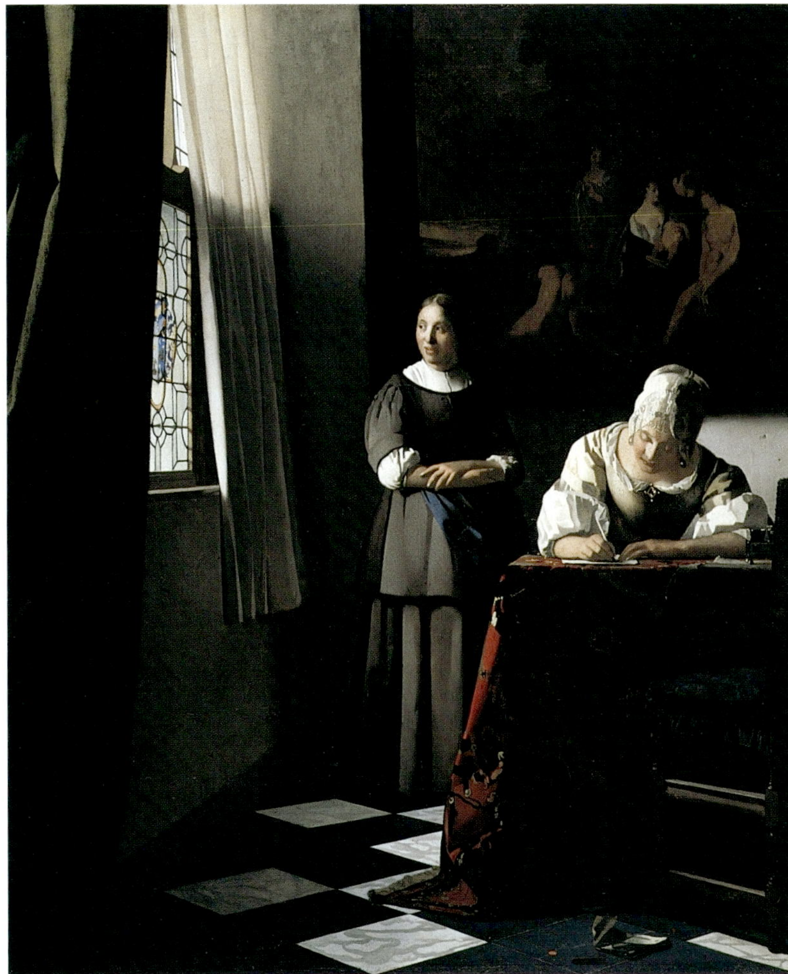

Fig.1 **A Lady Writing a Letter with Her Maid**
Jan Vermeer, 1670

personal experience, who give a vigorously disloyal view of their employers from the underside.

It is, however, too easy to be negative about the history of domestic service. This is not only a story of exploitation and class hostility; many portraits, historical and indeed modern, illustrate the more genial aspects of the relationship between master and servant. This applied particularly in rural communities in a pre-industrial age, where socially vertical loyalties and affections survived before the development of the class system as characterised by Karl Marx in the nineteenth century. Often these relationships were tender, as the numerous epitaphs written by employers for the gravestones of their servants testify. Such people as Bridget Holmes, who cleaned out the chamberpots at Windsor Castle (cat.27), or Fulke Harold, Sir Robert Walpole's gardener at Houghton Hall (cat.10), were clearly highly esteemed by employers who were the most powerful people in the country. The great majority of individual servants were painted either because (in a few instances) their employers had a tradition of commemorating their staff and chose to commission serial portraits, or because an individual servant had reached a remarkable old age in the service of one family or institution. In both instances the portraits illustrated the crucial theme of loyalty, which was thought to be the model quality for a servant.

This is not a representative publication about domestic service – the material would not allow that – but it does aim to cover as many aspects of the subject as the visual material permits. The great household (of which there was only a very limited number in England in the eighteenth century with fewer than two hundred peers) is the most strongly represented type of establishment in this book. Within the large houses, it was generally the upper servants – steward, butler, housekeeper – and the leading outdoor servants, who often enjoyed a particularly privileged and close relationship with their male employers, and who were chosen as sitters. Smaller households are hardly recorded except in satirical illustrations of the late nineteenth century and in one other case: servants painted by their artist-employers. In these images, and most famously in Hogarth's study of his servants (cat.54), considerable intimacy and affection are often expressed. These domestic studies merge into the use of servants as models within still-life studies, especially around 1900.

As we have suggested, in the eyes of their employers, servants frequently appeared to belong to a different caste. This view applied particularly to black people, some of whose images feature as a section of this book. This publication is, to a considerable extent, concerned with social and racial attitudes which are no longer familiar or indeed acceptable to us today. Over the centuries attitudes have altered greatly, particularly as a result of the Industrial Revolution when the old social system was succeeded by a much more stratified and mutually antagonistic class structure. In spite of these changes, in this country as elsewhere in Europe, people continued to be judged not just by their wealth but by whether they were aristocrats (i.e. titled) or of 'gentle' birth (that is, they belonged to the gentry, had the right to a coat of arms and did not earn their living through trade or manual labour). If they were not 'gentlemen' or 'ladies', they might belong to what was seen as a lower status – which could be broadly divided into the 'middling sort' and the 'lower orders'. These notions were of great importance over many centuries. Class is a human construct, and ways had to be invented to identify those who belonged to these lower orders, particularly when – as in the domestic household – different social groups came into regular contact with one another in a way they hardly did elsewhere. In imaginative literature and in practical written material, servants are often described in disparaging terms, as dishonest, immoral, stupid and uneducated, or at best comically incompetent: already in the early eighteenth century Daniel Defoe (cat.45) and Jonathan Swift (cat.107) are vigorously developing these themes. How far did these attitudes affect portraiture? Are sitters shown as inferior creatures? Did a specific style of presentation come into existence for servants' portraits, did these works sometimes diminish the sitter, and how far did they resemble fashionable portraiture?

This book concentrates on Great Britain – partly because the number of images has already made it necessary to exclude numerous interesting paintings and (still more) photographs, and partly because the British story has a particular character. Britain is by no means alone in its portrayal of servants, both in paintings and in literature, and it is worth considering the tradition of servant portrayal in continental Europe to put Britain in context. While depictions of household members in fifteenth-century Italian paintings were generally limited to the attendants shown in such quasi-domestic subjects as *The Birth of the Virgin*, the large-scale works of Venetian artists including Paolo Veronese (*c.*1528–88) often show the principal characters attended by a large retinue. But it is not only in the field of 'high art' that images of servants should be sought: already in 1517 the first Italian cookbook, by Rosselli,[10] was printed with its frontispiece depicting a kitchen filled with busy cooks. The focus on humbler people develops in northern Europe: successive German cookbooks and popular engravings from the sixteenth to the nineteenth centuries depict domestic life, though they seldom if ever record the likenesses of identifiable individuals.

Fig.2 **Interior with a Sleeping Maid and Her Mistress**
Nicolaes Maes, 1655

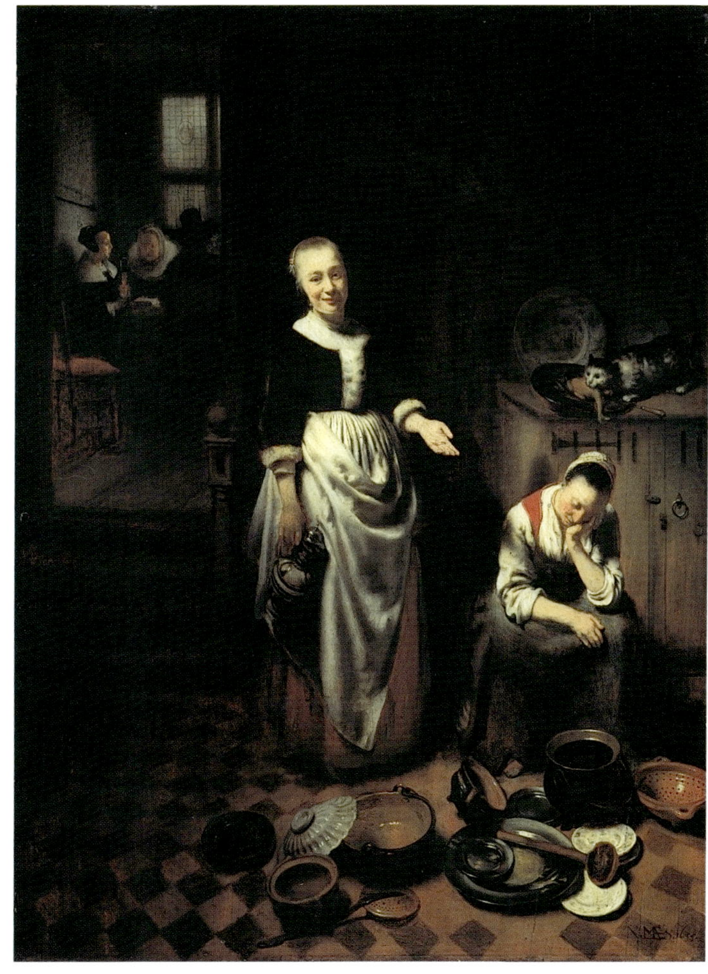

A new interest in 'low life' characters for their own sake, rather than as figures in the background, emerges in the Netherlands in the seventeenth century, in parallel with contemporary literature. In one type of image a maid is depicted engaging in domestic duties as part of a study of an interior or exterior, or acts as an assistant or messenger to her master or mistress. The most famous examples of this approach are a number of paintings by Vermeer (fig.1), in which maidservants are shown either on their own, engaged in domestic activities, or as attendants to their mistresses. A further category embodies the idea of the emblematic painting in which an allegorical figure personifies a moral message. In *Interior with a Sleeping Maid and Her Mistress* by Nicolaes Maes

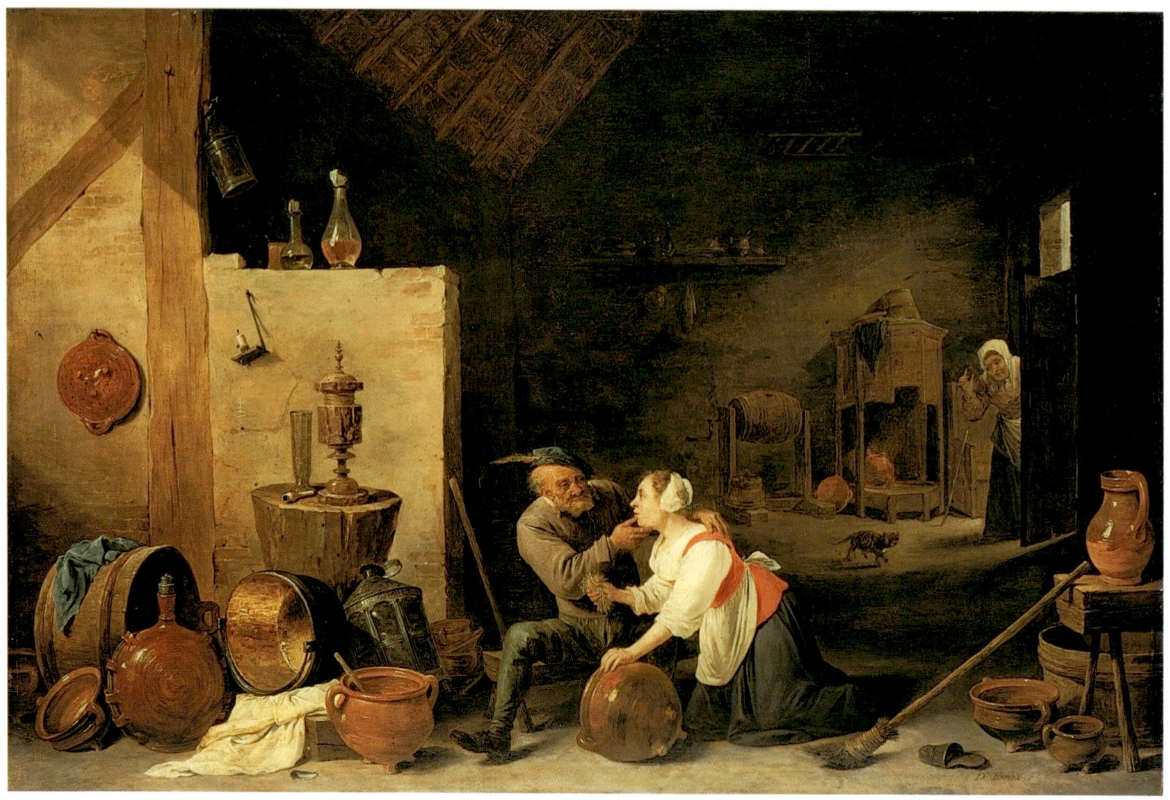

Fig.3 **An Old Peasant Caresses a Kitchen Maid in a Stable**
David Teniers the Younger, *c.*1650

(1634–93, fig.2), the mistress looks at the spectator and points, apparently with amusement, at her dozing maid surrounded by unwashed dishes while in the background a cat devours a fowl. Here established homely images of indolence and negligence reinforce, by implication, the importance of cleanliness. The rather different theme of sexuality – an important and often difficult aspect of the lives of serving women – emerges in the work of such popular artists as David Teniers (1610–90). In his *An Old Peasant Caresses a Kitchen Maid in a Stable* (fig.3), the libidinous activities of the principal characters are interrupted, characteristically for such pictures, by an old lady appearing through a door at the back. Other favoured images depict well-endowed cooks or maidservants in domestic settings, often presiding over great quantities of food – a theme enthusiastically followed by the seventeenth-century English painter Sir Nathaniel Bacon (1585–1627, fig.10). All these ideas are reflected in British painting, though such imitation is not as frequent as might be expected given the long-standing British enthusiasm for Dutch art.

Not all these images are domestic or earthy in character. A further important type was developed by Flemish artists Sir Anthony van Dyck (1599–1641) and Sir Peter Paul Rubens (1577–1640) from the vocabulary of Venetian painters, notably Titian, showing a soldier, statesman or aristocrat accompanied by an attendant. This attendant may be a professional person, for instance a secretary or clerk; the classic image is Van Dyck's portrait of the Earl of Strafford (fig.4), itself inspired by Titian. In other instances the attendant is more obviously decorative, such as a dwarf or page (sometimes black). In many instances the supporter is an identified person. Their identity is important and introduces the image of the principal subject whose status is affirmed by a supporter symbolising loyalty. A number of these images – notably the Van Dyck – became popular exemplars in British art and are crucial to this narrative.

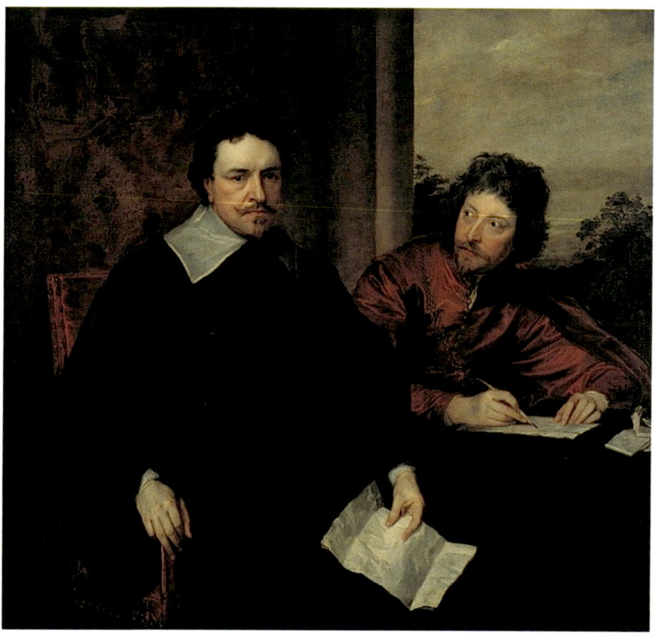

Fig.4 **Thomas Wentworth, 1st Earl of Strafford with Sir Philip Mainwaring**
Sir Anthony van Dyck, *c.*1639–40

During the eighteenth century, servants continued to play an important part in genre paintings, appearing as attendants of various sorts in fashionable portraits all over Europe. In France, where Dutch cabinet painting was widely collected, the interest in domestic portrayals was marked. In his poetic depictions of maidservants engaged in domestic labour, Jean-Baptiste Siméon Chardin (1699–1779), often compared by contemporaries to Teniers and other Netherlandish artists, invests scenes of everyday life with a dignity and gentleness hardly paralleled in Western painting (fig.5). By contrast, the bustling and more apparently aristocratic works of François Boucher (1703–70) and Jean-François de Troy (1679–1752) deploy maids as a counterpoint to their mistress in mildly titillating depictions of intimate interiors. The pastels of the internationally admired Swiss artist Jean-Etienne Liotard (1702–90), include such works as the *Chocolate Maid* of around 1744 (fig.6), an example of the genre in which servants are shown as anonymous models like elements in still-life painting. But in a close parallel to literature, servants are also depicted as active participants in contemporary life, as in the scenes of high and low Venetian society by Pietro Longhi (1702–85), and the vigorous portraits of outdoor servants by Jean-Baptiste Oudry (1686–1755). With the exception of Joseph Highmore's illustrations after *Pamela* (cats 65 and 64) and works by Henry Robert Morland (1730–97, cat.72), seventeenth- and eighteenth-century genre paintings which include servants are rare in Britain, and the Dutch moralistic tradition finds almost no followers here.

While the depiction of the servant was evidently a regular feature of the western European tradition, the continental European images we have considered tend to show the servant type, rather than the individual. An exception can be made for a group of Swedish portraits, notably a series of images by the seventeenth-century court painter David von Ehrenstrahl (1629–98). These suggest that it may be legitimate to associate likenesses

Fig.5 **The Governess**
Jean-Baptiste-Siméon Chardin, 1739

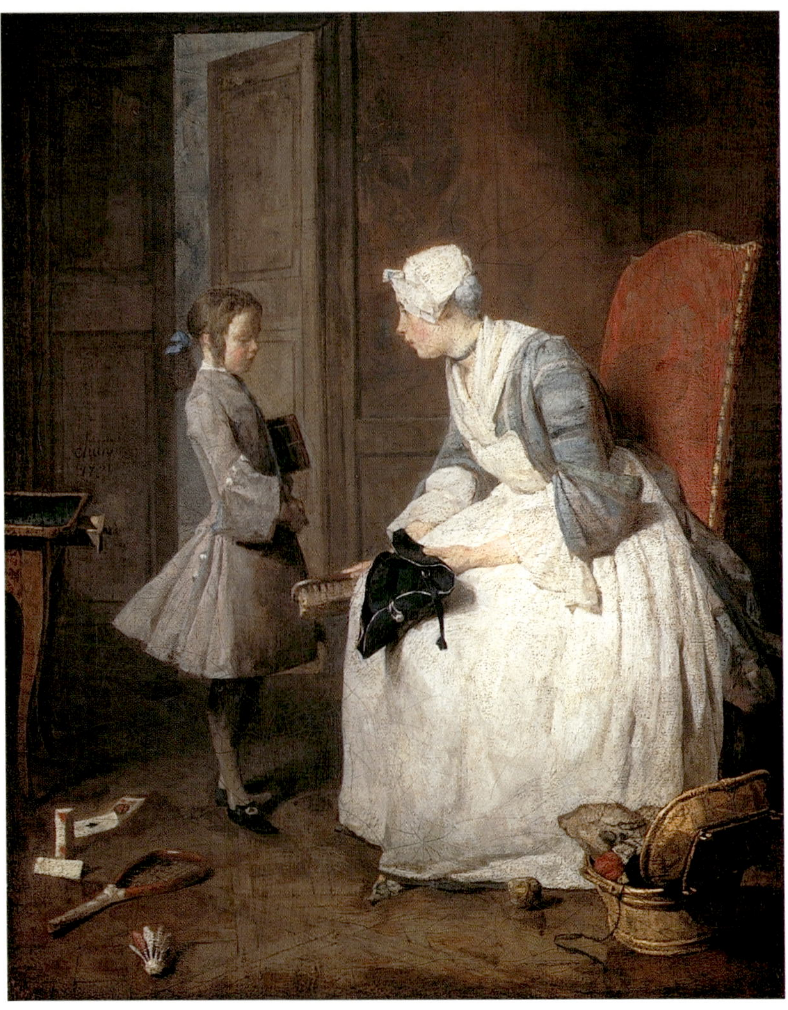

of known servants with the work ethic of Protestant countries. Further research needs to be done on European images in this genre, but our suggestion is that this is a type of portrait which survives in particular strength in Britain – either because it became a recognised tradition, or because country-house collections have had a better chance of survival in Britain than in other countries where portraits of little-known sitters may not have been preserved.

The history of the servant type in painting may be compared with a similar approach in literature. From classical times the servant has featured in high literature as well as in comic drama and fiction, particularly in certain set roles which have developed over the years. The most frequently recurring type goes back to the Greek plays of Menander (fourth century BC, and to the Latin plays of Plautus (third century BC) and Terence (second century BC). Here the impudent manservant, attached to but generally cleverer than his master, first makes his appearance. This type carries right through the tradition of European literature, including Sancho

Panza, the squire in Cervantes' *Don Quixote*, the servants in Shakespeare's *The Comedy of Errors*, and notably the plays of Molière, English Restoration comedy, and the calculating valet created by Beaumarchais and developed by Mozart and da Ponte in *The Marriage of Figaro*. This literary trope appears not to have survived the demise of the traditional service system – nor does it seem to have thrived in British art.

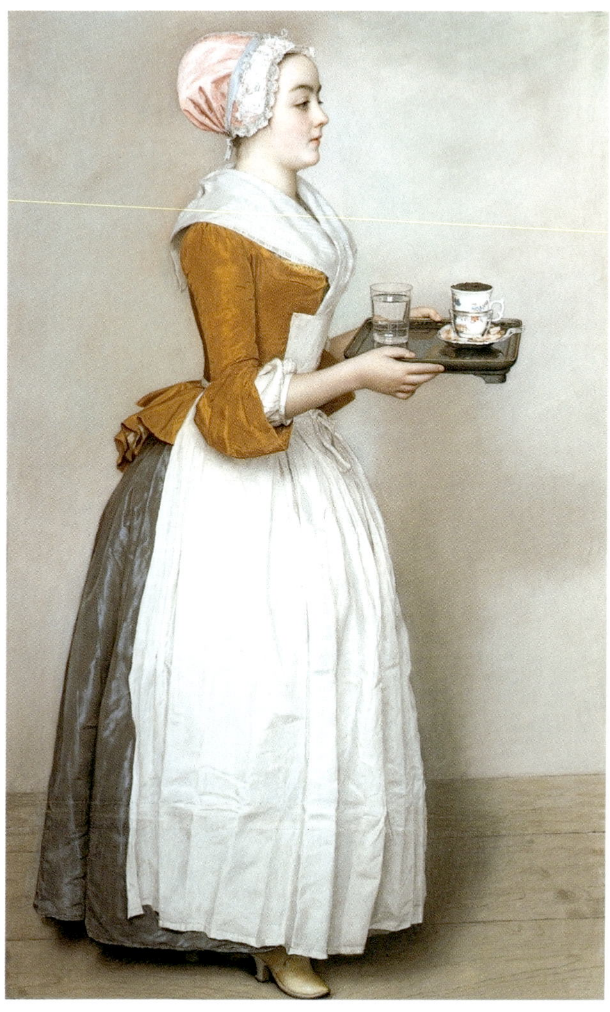

Fig.6 **Chocolate Maid**
Jean-Etienne Liotard, *c.*1744–5

A further recurring servant type is the plain-speaking frank character, often a woman, one of whose roles in drama is to speak as the voice of the audience. Emilia in *Othello* and the maid-servant Nicole in Molière's *Le Bourgeois Gentilhomme* belong to this tradition. In the very different genre of classical tragedy, the body servant, the personal attendant on a great person, acts as their confidant and often as an agent in the action, as in the tragedies of Racine. Other recurring types, notably the female servant as the victim of sexual aggression or material exploitation, will be discussed below. In this history, the literature of various European countries – which were more closely interrelated in the sixteenth and seventeenth centuries than they are today – combined to produce favourite literary types that were adaptable to a wide range of literary genres. But one has to ask how far these portrayals could be classified as portraits of servants. Certainly they were not intended to show actual individuals. It is equally doubtful (as Sarah Maza has convincingly argued in her study of servant literature in eighteenth-century France)[11] that the relationships depicted between master and servant closely reflected real relationships. Equally the logical conclusion of the frequently expressed theme of the clever servant – that since the servant was more able than his master, he was at least the master's equal – was probably only a literary convention. It was the idea of the brilliant servant, rather than the image, which entertained a sophisticated audience.

This book brings together images of generally forgotten people, a few of the enormous proportion of the population of Britain over the years whose names and faces would otherwise be unrecorded. However mediated by the views of employers or of artists, these personalities speak as directly over the centuries as do the images of the wealthy and famous – more directly, perhaps, since they are generally presented without flattery and conceit.

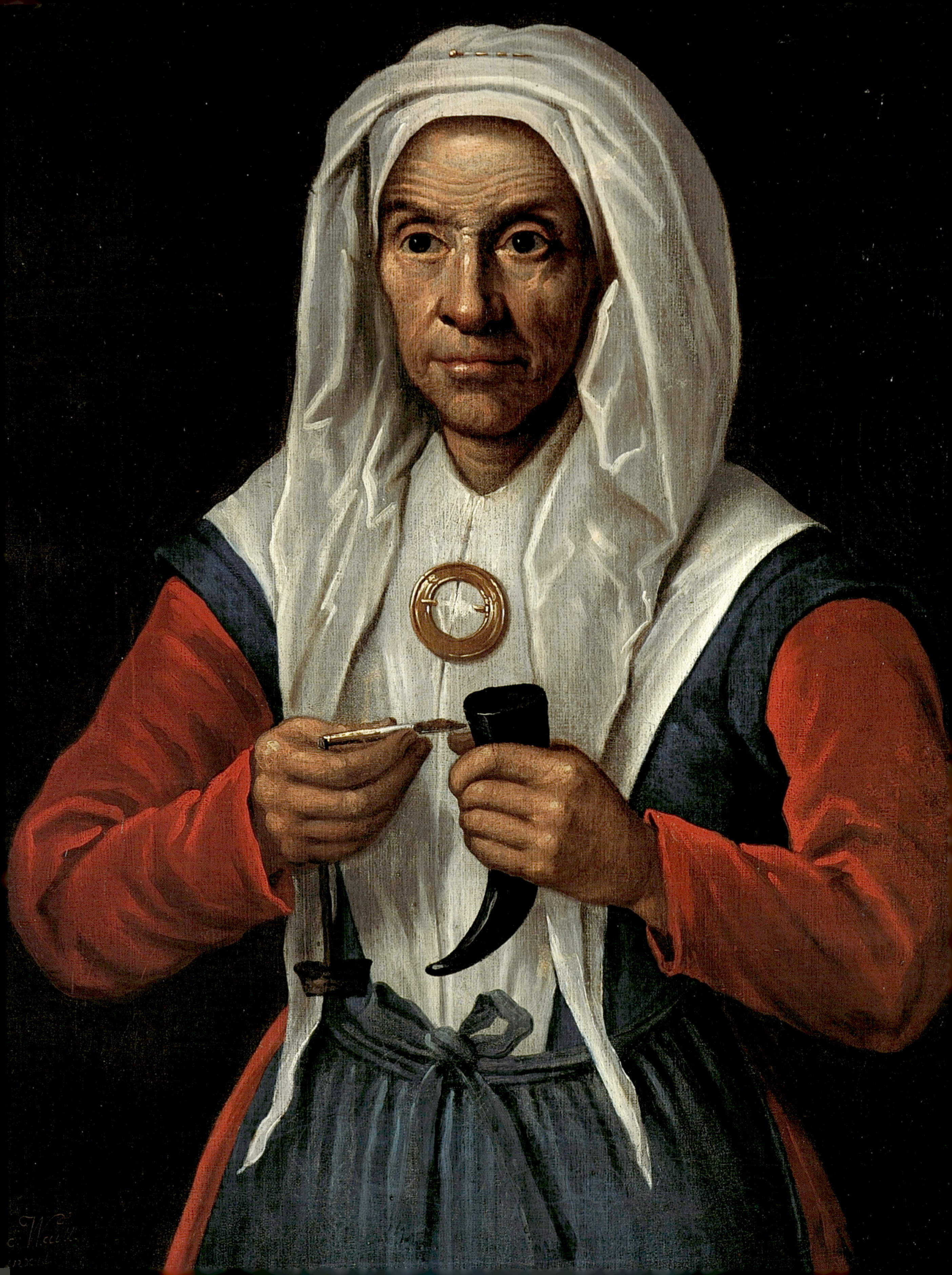

1 JESTERS, CHAMPIONS AND PIPERS

Anne French

ALTHOUGH THE ORIGINS of many positions within later households lie in the medieval great house, the noble household in the Middle Ages was very different from its seventeenth- and eighteenth-century successors. Before the Tudors imposed a firm framework of law and order on English life, secular society was still largely organised into social groups headed by earls and barons with members banding together for protection. Such a grouping, which included members of all social classes, from the lord's kinsmen and gentlemen servants down to menial servants who might be his tenants or have passed into his service through inheritance or marriage, is directly opposed to the later division of society into classes. Loyalty was to the lord and to other members of the group.

Life in the medieval noble house was full of pomp and ceremony: the lord and lady were waited on by 'gentle' servants only; three separate servants (cat.100) were required simply to serve the lord's meat and wine. The household was fully communal until around 1350, centred around the Great Hall, where everyone in the household ate; although there were placings 'above' and 'below' the salt, there were none of the separations represented much later by the concept of 'below stairs'. In an age before privacy was considered desirable, servants were involved in every aspect of household life. The word 'family', which had yet to take on its narrower modern meaning, referred to everyone in the household, including servants, powerfully expressing the cohesion of the medieval noble house. Servants were expected to swear loyalty to their lord on appointment – later concepts of loyalty derive from this early and powerful bond (see pp.57–75).

Other fundamental differences separated these households from their successors. With its origins in male war bands, the medieval noble household was, at least until the fifteenth century, almost exclusively male. Apart from her daughters, the lady of the house was attended only by her 'gentle' companions, with female 'chamberers' (later ladies' maids) to

opposite Detail of cat.7 **Nic Ciarain, the Henwife of Castle Grant**
Richard Waitt, 1726(?)

assist them. In the nursery, 'wet' and 'dry' nurses carried out other duties such as 'rocker' to the cradle. There were also laundresses, usually permitted only as far as the castle gates, and it is not accidental that one of the earliest portraits of a female servant is of a laundress (fig.16).

The medieval noble household also differed from its successors in size and organisation. As the house also acted as 'office, barracks, court and hotel',[1] and its members formed the core of a fighting force for use in times of trouble, aristocratic households could an astonishing 500 people. Even in the later Middle Ages, an average great household numbered between 100 and 200 members. Service in this period was not the menial concept it later became; instead it offered the chief route towards advancement for those of gentle birth. At the top of this broadly pyramidal structure was the steward and his deputy, the comptroller, whose role in administering the estates makes him the ancestor of today's land agent. Below these were officers in charge of the principal departments, such as the marshal of hall, chamberlain, master of horse and treasurer, as well as the highly important chaplain. The pyramid then descended in each household department, through servants of gentle birth who were the lord's personal attendants, to yeomen, grooms and finally pages who were at this point simply junior staff, not the decorative servants they later became. As these upper servants all had attendants of their own, this was a multi-layered household unlike any of its successors. Smaller households were organised in a similar way, except that in these more modest circumstances servants combined several of the above roles.

None of these household members was portrayed in paint with the exception of great household officers such as the steward who, wearing his gown, chain and staff of office, is familiar to us from Tudor portraits of officials within the royal household. It is, however, from the ranks of the lord's personal entertainers, such as his harpers, pipers and fools, that the first British servant portraits emerge.

The sixteenth- and seventeenth-century household

By the late sixteenth century, the great household had changed. From the mid-sixteenth century a gradual process of reduction in size began as life became more settled and secure; this trend would continue for the next two hundred years. Life within the household became very different. As the gentry no longer required protection from a great magnate, they withdrew from service, which was now perceived as demeaning, and were replaced in household offices by those from lower down the social hierarchy. Upper servants or 'officers' were now the sons of merchants, army officers or clergymen, and by the seventeenth century most personal servants were grooms or pages, recruited from the lower social strata of society.

As a result of these changes, the status of servants declined, and the gap between them and their employers widened, with potentially disastrous consequences for relations between them. The numbers of women employed increased: even in the later Middle Ages, their role in lower household offices had become increasingly important, and by the seventeenth century there was a preponderance of women servants, now occupying the roles of cooks and cleaners, which they would retain in future. By now the housekeeper had emerged as the key female employee, supervising the cleaning, linen and comestibles.

The new interest in privacy had an equally great impact on servants' lives. Once the family began to live in designated parts of the house where only personal servants were needed to attend them, other servants began to be restricted to specific areas of the house. By 1650 this had been located in the basement – an expression of servants' new, lower place within the hierarchy. Shortly afterwards, subsidiary wings hived off the kitchen, stables and offices. As the hall developed into a ceremonial entrance, servants no longer had a role there and they now ate in a separate chamber designated as a servants' hall, while the introduction of the 'back stairs' tidied servants away, delivering them invisibly only to those parts of the house where they were needed.

Jesters and dwarfs

The fool or jester, with his or her origins in classical times, was a significant and prominent member of British royal households from William the Conqueror onwards. From Henry II to Edward II, some early royal fools were also huntsmen; one of these, John le Fol, remained in royal service for thirty-seven years.[2] By the reign of Edward I, fools at court were probably buffoons on the model of the later Renaissance jester, enjoying grants of land and clothing and the recognised status of 'king's fool and minstrel'. They subsequently went out of fashion, but the Renaissance saw the revival of the court fool across Europe. 'Artificial' jesters assumed this role professionally, while 'natural' fools (cat.2) were of a much lower status. Technically considered insane, they had no legal rights and were treated and even given away as chattels.

These Tudor and Jacobean entertainers in royal or aristocratic households now began to feature, not simply in account books, but in literature, sometimes even writing their own memoirs.[3] Given their privileged positions as close personal servants of the monarch and his consort, it is not surprising that jesters or fools at the Tudor and Stuart courts provide the first portraits of household entertainers and servants in England. At the same time, the royal family also recorded their succession of dwarfs and black servants in what forms part of a centuries-long fascination for those with physical disabilities or of exotic appearance.

The ending of the Wars of the Roses witnessed the proliferation of fools at the courts of the early Tudors. Even the parsimonious Henry VII retained a fool, while the more lavish Henry VIII employed at least four,

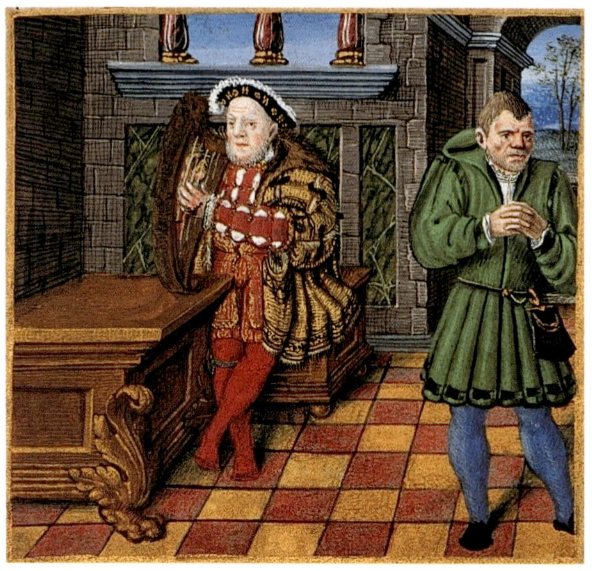

Fig.7 **Henry VIII with a Harp as David, with Will Somers**
Unknown artist, 1540

This illustration of Psalm 13, 'The fool has said in his heart/There is no God!' shows Somers turning his back on the King, who represents the psalmist David playing the harp. The portrait is redolent of the relationship between master and fool, who capped rhymes together, and provides an accurate description of Somers: 'Leane was he, hollow eyed ... and stoop he did, too'.

including the first really famous fool at the English court, Will Somers (d.1560). This 'natural' fool's portrait of 1540 with his ageing royal master survives in a Psalter made for Henry's own use (fig.7). As Lord Lumley is known to have owned a picture of Somers, this fool was probably one of the earliest household employees to sit for his portrait, and the tradition of painting court entertainers may have begun in this reign.

During the rule of Queen Elizabeth I, household fools began to be replaced by the new breed of professional theatrical clowns familiar to us from Shakespeare's *As You Like It* and *Twelfth Night*. This trend, however, was reversed with the accession of James I in 1603, and the first surviving portraits of jesters and dwarfs on the scale of life date to this period when court revelry was more unrestrained than previously. Two portraits – one of which survives in an engraving by Cecill in the British Museum – are known to have existed of the 'artificial' fool Archibald Armstrong, jester to James I and Charles I, whose boastfulness and meddling in politics created considerable tensions during these reigns. It is, however, the portrait of another court fool, the 'natural' fool Tom Durie (Derry), jester to James I's queen, Anne of Denmark, painted in 1614 by her favourite artist, Marcus Gheeraerts the Younger, which survives (cat.2). Until recently, this remarkable painting appeared to have no antecedents in British portraiture, and it was regarded as so unusual to find a portrait of a jester at this early date that it masqueraded for centuries as the King's aristocratic cup-bearer David, 1st Viscount Stormont. However, it was re-identified by Sir Oliver Millar as the 'picture of Tom Durie, Queen Anne's fool, holding a silver bowl with both his hands wherein red wine' recorded in the inventory of Charles I's collection.[4] Durie's wistful expression and lined face represents a poignant record of this 'simpleton'. He must have been a much-loved servant, as the Queen also commissioned a full-length portrait of him from Paul van Somer.

Two dwarfs at the Stuart court also feature prominently in portraiture. Jeffrey Hudson (1619?–82) made a spectacular entry into the lives of the royal family when as a child: 'Hee was presented in a cold baked pye to King Charles at an entertainment' given by the Duke of Buckingham,[5] serving as dwarf or page to the Queen until he killed an opponent in a duel. This pampered court favourite is the subject of Daniel Mytens' full-length portrait of *Jeoffry in a Wood* painted for Charles I around 1630.[6] Hudson also appears twice with his employers: in the large-scale Mytens portrait *Charles I and Henrietta Maria Setting Out For the Hunt* (*c.*1630–32), and in Van Dyck's incomparable *Queen Henrietta Maria with Her Dwarf*

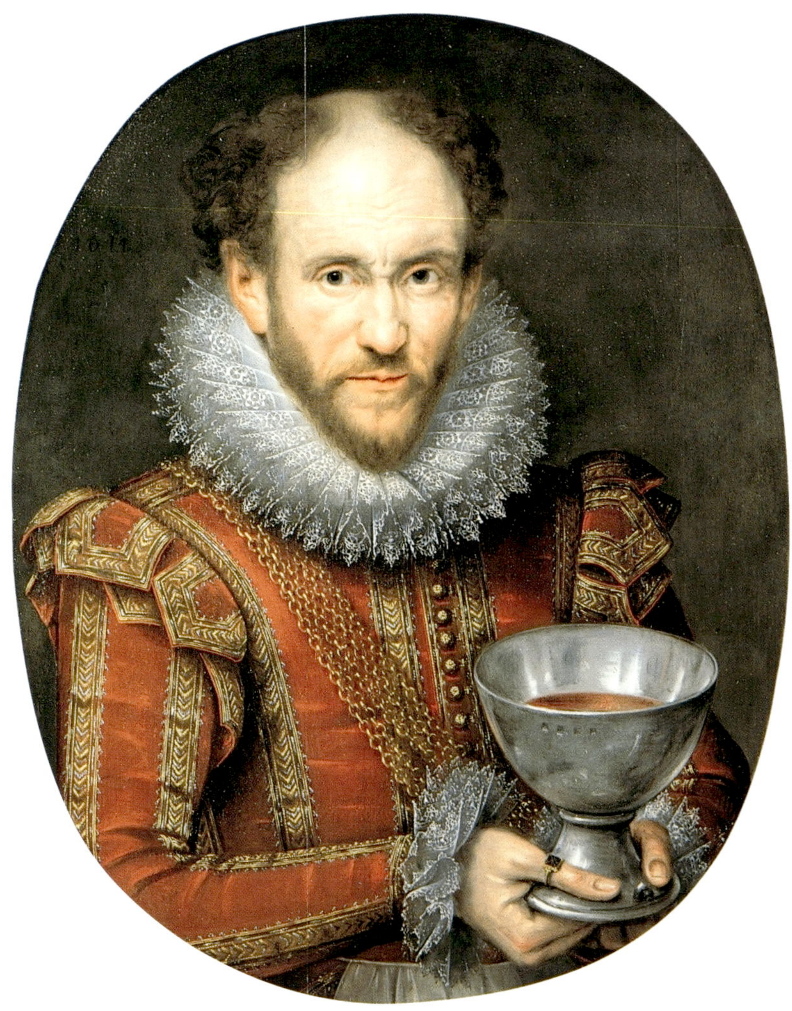

Cat.2 **Tom Derry, Jester to Anne of Denmark**
Attributed to Marcus Gheeraerts the Younger, 1614

Durie (Derry) is richly clad in a red doublet embroidered in gold and silver, with an apron to protect his clothing from wine stains. The gold chain and thumb ring may have been presents from the Queen. Durie appears to have been 'better used ... than anie servant the late Queene left behind her ...', and had a servant of his own. The cup is probably a hospitality cup, although illustrations of other fools showing them carrying similar round shapes such as a football, globe or cake, apparently refer to the 'impious fool' who denies God in Psalm 13.

Jeffrey Hudson and an Ape (1633). As the Queen was herself of diminutive height, Hudson's inclusion no doubt added 'several cubits to her stature';[7] to contemporary eyes he would also have provided a touch of the strange and exotic, a reminder of the reflection these servant portraits cast on the status and on the portrait icons of their royal employers.

The career of Richard Gibson (1615–90) was influenced initially, like Hudson's, by the fashion for employing dwarfs as pages in court circles in the first half of the seventeenth century (cat.4). Gibson was, however, not only a dwarf but a painter of miniatures whose talent, recognised by his employers, led to a life outside service. By the time he became a royal page – probably serving both Charles I as Page of the Backstairs, and the Lord Chamberlain, the great art patron Philip, 4th Earl of Pembroke – his reputation was established, and the King is known to have handed a miniature copy of Titian's *Venus and Adonis* to 'Dick my Lord Chamberlain's dwarf to copy'.[8] Gibson maintained close relations with the Pembrokes

The Fool of Muncaster

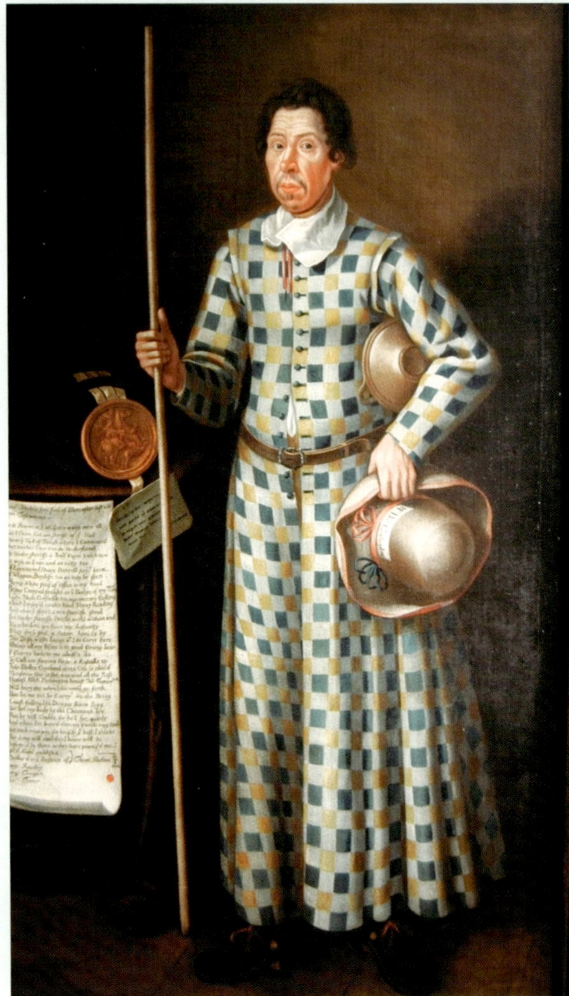

Cat.3 **Thomas Skelton, 'The Fool of Muncaster'**
Unknown artist, *c.*1659–65

Little documentary evidence survives on jesters outside court circles. Some fools seem to have been little more than drudges, although jesters in great Tudor and Stuart households probably lived lives comparable to those of their court contemporaries. Like them, they were also portrayed in paint, as is confirmed by an exceptional full-length portrait of *Thomas Skelton, 'The Fool of Muncaster'*.[9] Skelton was fool to the Pennington family of Muncaster Castle, Cumbria, but in 1659 he probably accompanied William Pennington (1655–1730), later 1st Baronet, who inherited the estate as a minor, to live in the household of his uncle and guardian Roger Bradshaigh at Haigh Hall near Wigan. Although folklore connects Skelton strongly with Muncaster, the portrait itself was undoubtedly painted at Haigh, since the mock 'Last Will and Testament' inscribed on the portrait refers repeatedly to residents in this area of Lancashire where Skelton died in 1667 or 1668. A second version in the Shakespeare Institute, Stratford, was probably painted for the Bradshaighs between 1676 and 1686 after William Pennington returned to Muncaster in adulthood, taking the portrait of his jester with him.

This portrait of Skelton represents a deliberate spoof of early seventeenth-century aristocratic portraits, in which sitters hold their rod of office and display other accoutrements of wealth and power. The painting's provincial origins presumably account for the survival of the Jacobean style in mid-century. Skelton's unfounded claims in his 'will' to have held important offices in the Wigan area are deliberately undercut by his dress. The chequered coat is a fine example of 'motley', whose variegated pattern reflecting the fool's perceived disposition meant that by 1600 the phrase 'motley fool' had become common. The jocular nature of the 'will' can be compared with the later servant portraits at Erddig (cats 20, 21), which also feature scrolls testifying humorously to a servant's life and character. However, several of Skelton's 'bequests' have a distinct edge, and may represent attempts to pay off old scores, attacking local businessmen and lawyers for their sometimes less than honest dealings with the Bradshaighs.[10] The facetious assertion 'That I Tom fool am sheriffe of ye Hall/I mean ye Hall of Haigh where I command' is a reminder of the communal entertainment of the medieval hall. It seems likely that at Haigh, as at Muncaster (both near, or on, remote stretches of the coast in Cumberland and Lancashire), earlier notions of hospitality still obtained, and that jesters remained in such households longer than in those nearer London.

Skelton's prominence in Cumbrian folklore testifies to the fame of a 'fool', who, like Archy Armstrong (p.24), appears to have been a prime example of the malignant jester who could cause serious disruption in a household. Although the grisly tale of his cutting off the estate carpenter's head, which exists in more than one version, is clearly apocryphal, stories in which he acted as unofficial hangman for the lord of the manor may relate to the notorious lawlessness of the area in the seventeenth century. The portrait itself certainly suggests a harsh and self-willed character rather than a jovial and benign one. The scant surviving documentary evidence suggests that portraits of notable jesters may have been prized possessions in some great houses, so this fact, rather than his being a beloved employee, may account for Skelton meriting a portrait on the scale of life.

throughout his life and as late as 1677 was still receiving an annuity from them. Although this may have been granted to him as an artist not as a former servant, Gibson's wife, the Queen's dwarf Anne Sheppard, also had connections with this family, almost certainly appearing in Van Dyck's portrait of Pembroke's daughter-in-law *Lady Mary Villiers*.[11] The Gibsons were later painted in a double portrait by Sir Peter Lely, also commissioned by the Pembroke family; although they are presented like Lely's usual fashionable sitters, this may commemorate their earlier service with the family.

More intriguing is the portrait by Lely of Richard Gibson asleep (cat.4). In this portrait, Gibson appears, not as a fashionable sitter, nor the successful miniaturist he had now become, but as a sleeping dwarf; the parallels with Dutch genre painting, pointed to by Millar, are evident.[12] Gibson was appointed 'picture maker' to the King in 1672 and later became

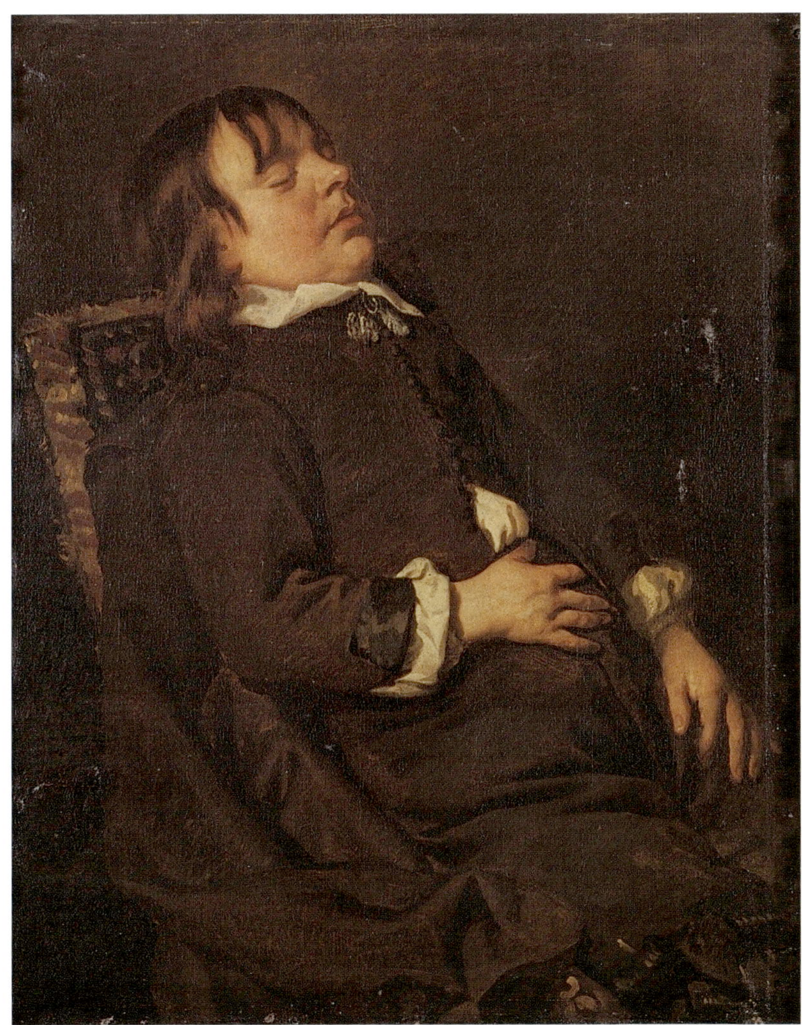

Cat.4 **A Sleeping Dwarf: Richard Gibson**
Sir Peter Lely, late 1640s

Gibson was a friend of Lely's, and this portrait of him asleep is among the artist's most arresting and informal images. The sitter's identity is confirmed by comparison with the double portrait of him and his wife, and by an early copy after a lost Lely portrait of Gibson now in the National Portrait Gallery.

drawing master to the future Queen Mary II. However, with this exception, the Civil War and execution of Charles I marked the end of fools and dwarfs at the royal court and their appearance in portraiture.

Pipers, harpers and other household entertainers

Minstrels, like jesters, had their origins in classical times, but were prevalent in Britain from well before the Norman Conquest to the reign of Henry VIII. Contrary to popular supposition, most were not wandering entertainers, but men (and sometimes women) attached to royal or aristocratic households. Early court minstrels were often highly versatile entertainers who could 'speak and rhyme well, be witty, know the story of Troy, balance apples on the point of knives, juggle, jump through hoops, play the citole, mandora, harp, fiddle, psaltery'.[13] They also occupied essential roles on the hunting field and in battle as heralds, trumpeters or pipers. Such men were often of low social status. However, in the later Middle Ages, royal minstrels often occupied positions of responsibility, and appointments frequently descended from one generation to the next in the pattern of long service replicated in later periods. The Celtic and Saxon bards, in particular, playing on a small, portable harp, had long occupied an important position as their 'lord's memory, the keeper of his genealogy and of the valiant deeds of his ancestors'.[14] From the twelfth to the fourteenth centuries, these harpers ruled supreme as entertainers in almost every British household from the manor house upwards, until their pre-eminence was challenged by increasing literacy and a shift away from their repertory of Arthurian legends.

Given that minstrels, like jesters, were drawn from among the king's or lord's retinue of personal entertainers, it might be expected that they, too, would offer subjects for the production of early servants' portraits. Pipers and harpers are indeed well represented in portraiture but with the exception of those painted in Scotland (see pp.30–35) most of these portraits are associated with a revival of interest in the medieval entertainer during the eighteenth century rather than representing a continuous tradition.

The Northumberland pipers

In Scotland, the piper was a key member of the chieftain's retinue, ranked next to the Chief or Laird, but in England the situation was very different. Although no early portraits survive, the well-documented lives of the pipers employed by the future 1st Duchess of Northumberland from the 1740s probably give an accurate impression of their position as privileged household retainers, not only in this but, by extension, in many other great households around the country.

Described by Horace Walpole as someone in whom 'the blood of all the Percies and Seymours swelled in her veins and in her fancy' and who was 'familiar with the mob, while stifled in diamonds',[15] Elizabeth Seymour became heiress to the vast Northumberland estates in 1744. Married to the Yorkshire baronet Sir Hugh Smithson, later created 1st Duke of Northumberland, she took an almost obsessive interest in her illustrious pedigree, and in maintaining old-fashioned customs she considered due to her dignity and position. Not only did the family maintain a jester with cap and bells until 1789, but the Duchess also revived the Percy custom of employing pipers, drummers and other minstrels.

This, then, was a conscious revival of the ceremony associated with the medieval house, by a family seeking to reforge its links with its own illustrious past. The most notorious of the 1st Duchess's pipers, who all played on the Northumbrian 'small pipes', was James Allan (cat.5), subject of the book *The Life of James Allan, the Celebrated Northumberland Piper.* Allan's colourful career is perhaps representative of a type of minstrel who, from the Middle Ages onwards, lived on the fringes of society, and whose integration as a favoured servant into a great household often caused considerable difficulties. The son of a tinker, he joined the future Duchess's retinue in 1746 or 1747 aged about eighteen and on the Countess's elevation to Duchess in 1766, was appointed her own piper.

Over the following decades Allan was constantly dismissed and reinstated; although the Duchess and her staff became horrified by his 'debauchery', she considered that his reformation was more likely under her roof than by 'following the life of a wandering minstrel'.[16] Although he accompanied her to the coronation of George III in 1760, he was finally dismissed for stealing and forbidden to enter Alnwick Castle again. Allan's later life reads like parts of Daniel Defoe's picaresque novel *Moll Flanders*, involving murder, a sensational life of crime with 'Morpeth Mary' and death in Durham gaol in 1810.

Not only did the 1st Duchess of Northumberland employ pipers, she initiated a tradition at Alnwick of recording her employees in paint. Despite Allan's peccadillos, he presumably sat for his portrait, as the frontispiece to *The Life of James Allan* reproduces an engraving by A. Dick 'from an original painting' (cat.5). However, it is the portrait by Francis Lindo (*fl.*1755–65) of Allan's contemporary, *Joseph Turnbull of Newburn* (*c.*1765)[17] playing an ivory set of Northumbrian pipes, which survives. The son of a miller, Turnbull was taken into the Duchess's household as a child, and later became her first official piper. His status within the household, more assured than Allan's, is suggested by his marriage to the castle housekeeper, and perhaps also by the portraitist chosen to paint him. Although Francis Lindo (*fl.*1755–65) had geographical links to the family's two principal seats at Alnwick and Syon House and painted a number of portraits for the family, the Duke himself sat to Reynolds at around the time his wife's piper was painted.

The tradition of maintaining pipers continued in the Percy family until the twentieth century. Two later portraits of Northumberland family pipers survive: one of *William Thomas Green*, piper from 1849 to three

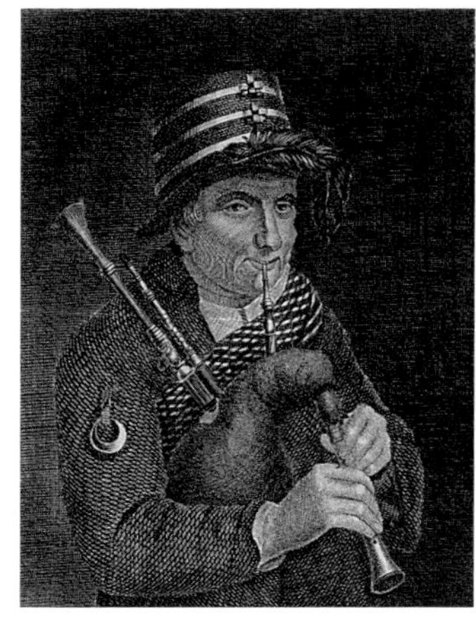

Cat.5 **The Life of James Allan, the Celebrated Northumberland Piper**
A. Dick, 1818

The frontispiece to this racy account of Allan's life depicts him playing the Northumberland pipes and wearing the silver crescent Crusader badge of the Percys, which formed an important part of their pipers' livery. The Northumberland pipers were not only painted as favourite servants; they also played the area's indigenous music and had a key role in household ceremony. Allan was also briefly one of the town waits at Alnwick; service with towns or cities was a recourse open to minstrels from the Middle Ages onwards.

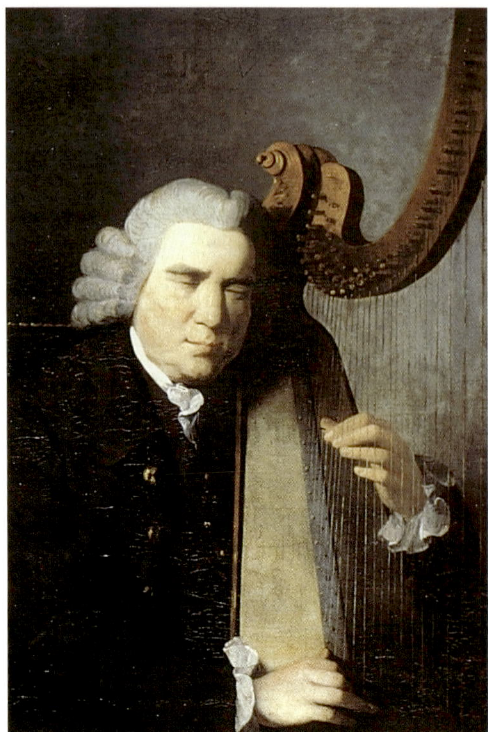

Fig.8 **The Blind Harpist John Parry**
William Parry, *c.*1760–80

This fine study of John Parry, absorbed in his playing, is by his son William. Like his father, William Parry worked extensively for Sir Watkin, who paid for his study in Italy. The original of this portrait formerly hung at Sir Watkin's seat at Wynnstay.

OPPOSITE Cat.6 **Alastair Mor Grant, the Champion of the Laird of Grant**
Richard Waitt, 1714

This iconic portrait focuses on the Champion's clothing and accoutrements, not his personality. His tartan livery corresponds to that prescribed by Alexander Grant for his followers in 1710. The Champion is armed with a scimitar-bladed sword, a pistol, dirk, long-barrelled musket and *currach* or shield. Behind him is Castle Grant, the headquarters of the clan.

successive dukes and duchesses, and of *Jack Armstrong*, appointed piper in 1949. This ancient office is currently held by Richard Butler.

Welsh and other harper portraits

Harpers were the other principal type of medieval household entertainers to be painted in later centuries. Most of the surviving images are of blind harpers, who had often been favoured servants of the Crown; both Richard II and Henry VIII employing long-serving blind harpers. Probably the earliest surviving portrait is the *Blind Harper* attributed to Lely at Althorp which almost certainly portrays a household servant rather than being intended as a genre scene. Undoubtedly the most important of these portraits is that of *The Blind Harpist John Parry* (1710?–82), harper to the great Welsh art patron Sir Watkin Williams Wynn of Wynnstay, and also to George III, painted by his son William Parry (1742–91) (fig.8). It seems likely that William Parry's portrait of his father owes much to ideas current in the 'close-knit ... circle of gentry patrons, intellectuals and artists in which he moved both in Wales and London'.[18] The intensity created by the blind harper's absorption in his playing caused the image to become famous, and it was long attributed to Sir Joshua Reynolds, under whom Parry had once studied.

The majority of harper portraits are, however, of Welsh sitters, and date from the late eighteenth and early nineteenth centuries. Although stimulated by a desire to record men who were both famous musicians and long-serving family retainers, these portraits of performers on the Welsh national instrument form part of the widespread revival of interest at this period in ancient Welsh music and poetry, stimulated by Thomas Gray's *The Last Bard* (1757), and by the Eisteddfod movement. It is therefore no coincidence that portraits of real-life harpers were painted alongside genre paintings depicting their mythical Celtic predecessors, for example William Jones's *The Last Bard* (1819).

A Scottish champion and piper

The survival of the extended medieval household in isolated parts of the country accounts for a number of seventeenth- and early eighteenth-century servant portraits (cat.3). Nowhere is this more evident than in Scotland where the survival of the clan system meant that feudal retainers such as champions or pipers, who did not form part of the 'standard' eighteenth-century aristocratic household, endured long enough to be recorded in paint. Between 1713 and 1726 two successive chiefs of Clan Grant commissioned from Richard Waitt (*fl.*1708–32) a series of around thirty portraits of them-

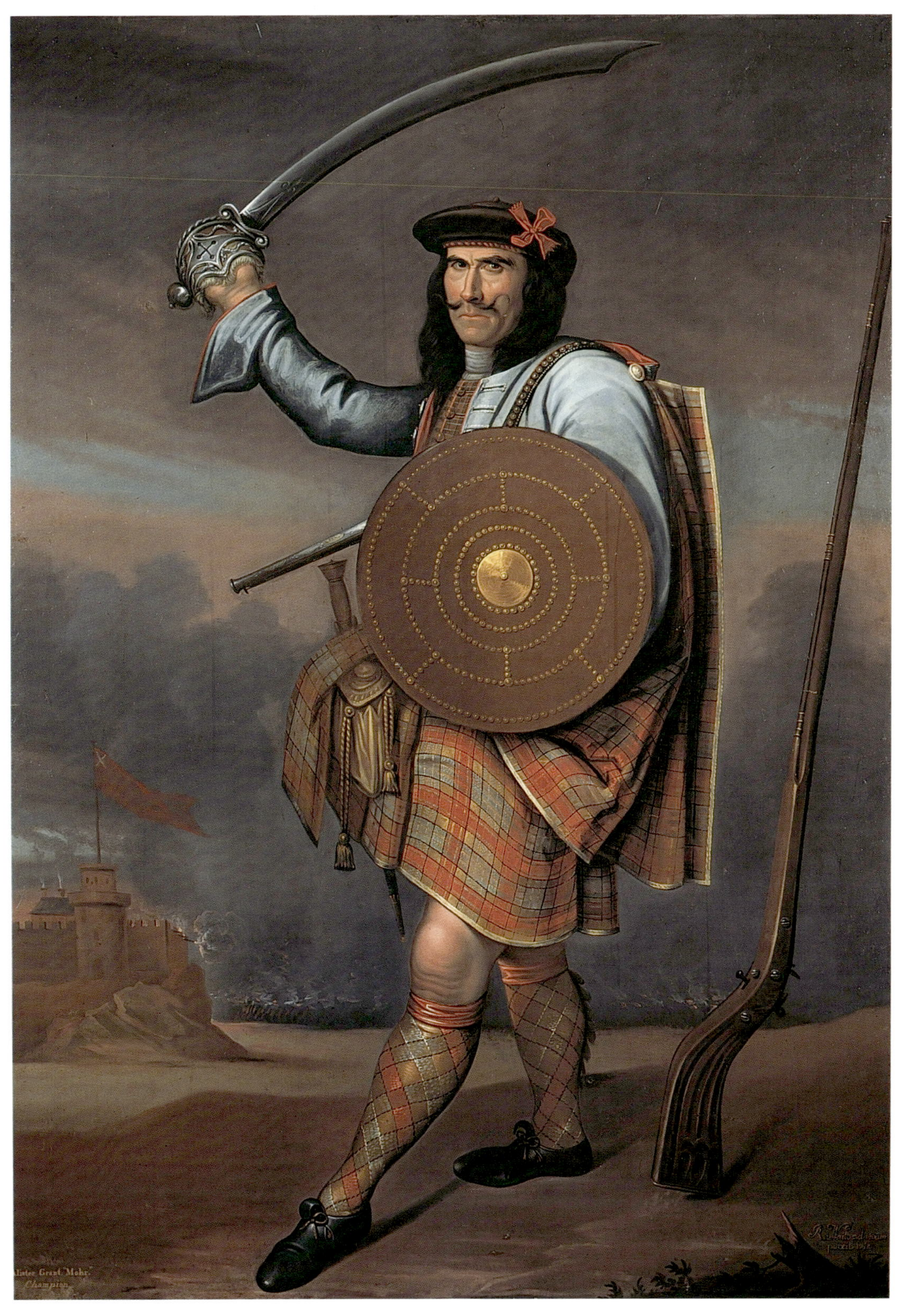
lister Grant Mohr
Champion

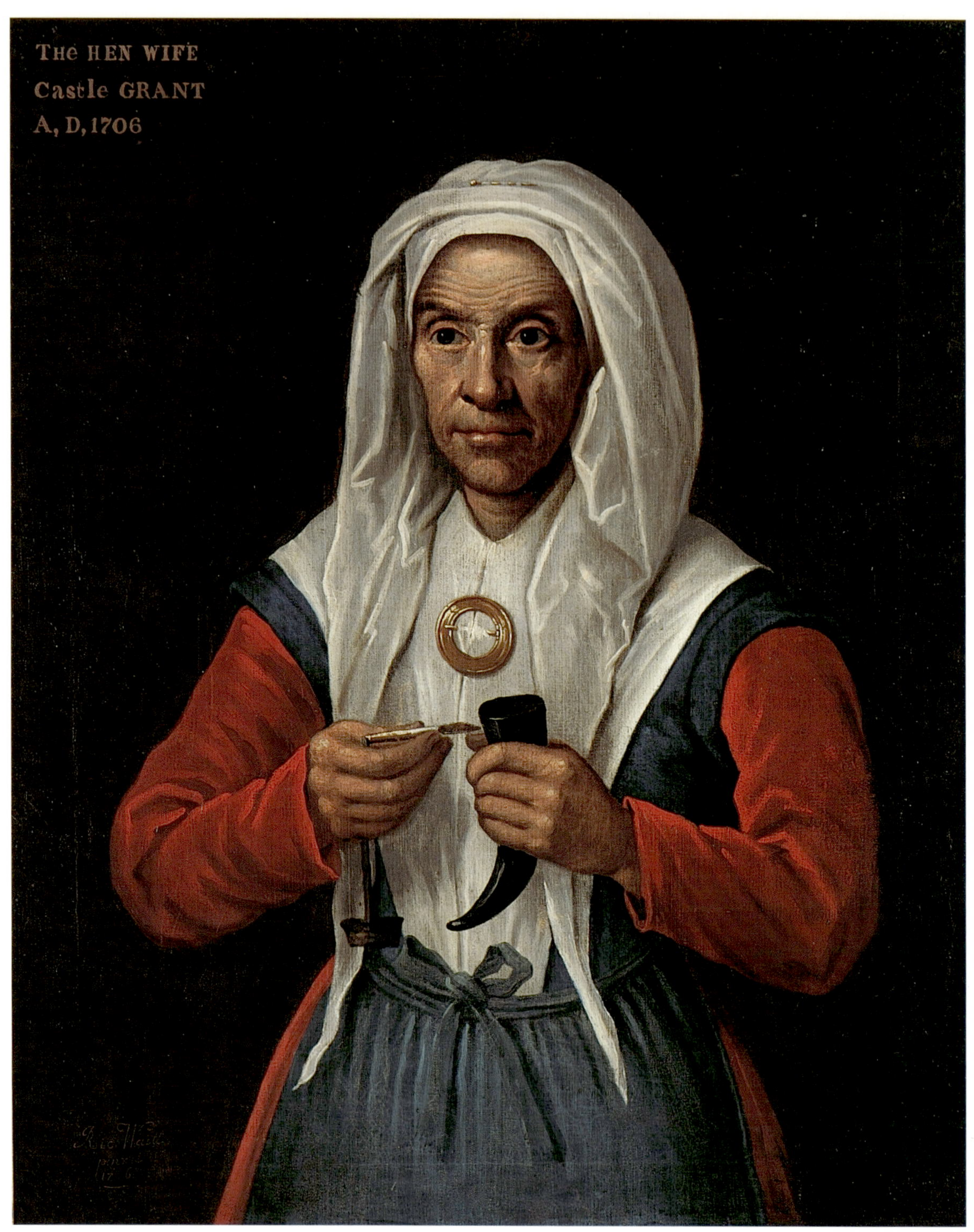
The HEN WIFE
Castle GRANT
A, D, 1706

selves, their families, kin and tenants, which included four members of their retinue. These remarkable images, unique in European portraiture, were painted just before the 1715 and 1745 Jacobite rebellions, and the abolition in 1747 of the Heritable Jurisdictions (which had given clan chiefs a quasi-regal jurisdiction), destroyed the basis of this social order. The series therefore offers a unique insight into Scotland's 'own peculiar form of feudal landownership adulterated with aboriginal Celtic imperatives of name and kinship',[19] in which the chief's 'castle was their fortress; his approbation was their pride; his protection was both their duty and their interest. In his safety their own fate was involved'.[20] Given this bond of mutual self-interest, the Grants' decision to record, not their 'lineage and exalted connections', but 'a chief and his people', is unsurprising.[21]

Not only did clan leaders enjoy feudal rights no longer extant elsewhere in Britain, they also still maintained Celtic courts at which the arts flourished, supported by a retinue of poets and musicians. By 1600 the bagpiper had replaced the harper as the principal exponent of Gaelic music; in a country still plagued by frequent warfare, the piper retained a key role in battle, calling the clan to arms. The Cummings (Cummines), who served the Grants over seven generations from around 1624 to 1785, were one of several families of hereditary Scottish pipers. An even more important and also often hereditary official was the Champion, a gentleman not an upper servant, whose role in England, prominent under the Tudors as the man who at tournaments defended the monarch's title to the crown, had now diminished, but who in Scotland remained near the apex of the clan. In 1713 Brigadier Alexander Grant singled out these two 'servants' for special treatment: *Alastair Mor Grant, the Champion of the Laird of Grant* (cat.6), and *William Cummine, Piper of the Laird of Grant* appear in full-length companion portraits, resplendent in a form of tartan livery probably paid for by their chief, and under arms. Also recorded was Grant's standard-bearer, although other members of his retinue, including his bard, armour bearer and gillies, were not. Richard Waitt also produced portraits of Alexander Grant himself and three of his siblings; at one guinea, these were modest productions, compared with the £5 each lavished on the portraits of his Champion and Piper.

Two key events provide a context for Brigadier Grant's commission. Firstly, the Grants, unlike most Highland clans, were Protestants and Hanoverians, and were rewarded in 1694 with a royal charter creating them Lairds of Grant. Their house became Castle Grant and their lands the Regality of Grant – a recognition of the almost royal rights enjoyed by the chief, who could call out his retainers for 'hosting or hunteing', when they came armed with 'gun, sword, pistol and durk' as the Champion is here.[22] Sixteen years later, a review of the clan was held when Ludovic Grant made over the leadership to his heir in 1710. Alexander ordered that 'all the gentlemen and commons of his name wear whiskers, and make all

OPPOSITE **Cat.7 Nic Ciarain, the Henwife of Castle Grant**
Richard Waitt, 1726(?)

With its vibrant colours and bold shapes, this is a remarkable record of a working woman and clan retainer. The portrait shows her taking snuff, and wearing Highland dress with a 'kertch' headdress. Her shawl is fastened with a Highland brooch. There is no attempt to idealise, patronise or sentimentalise the Henwife, and her strongly characterised and dignified lined features make this portrait unique in Scottish art.

Note the inaccurate date inscribed in the top right of the painting which may have been added later.

their plaids and tartan of red and green', and 'appear before him ... in that uniform, in kilt and under arms', just as the Champion and Piper do in these portraits painted only three years later.[23] The power and purpose of these iconic images is further explained by their original location. Together with Waitt's other portraits, they formed part of the decoration of the Hall at Castle Grant. Looking back to earlier portraiture, Waitt's figures are presented almost as cut-outs, and the focus is on clothing and the accoutrements of office rather than personalities. Although Waitt's earliest known work is a coat of arms (1708), this almost heraldic approach was probably dictated by the specific demands of the Grant commission. The clan armoury occupied a comparable role in the Hall, at once functional and decorative; the military connotations of both portraits, paid for in the very year of the 1715 rebellion, would be hard to overestimate.

Cat.8 **A 'Gillee Wet Feit' or Errand Runner**
Attributed to Paul Sandby, *c.*1749

A very different type of clan servant, who had his equivalent in the English 'Running Footman', was the 'Gillee Wet Feit' or 'Errand Runner' who could cover up to sixty miles bare-footed a day. In the seventeenth and eighteenth centuries this servant ran ahead of his employer to announce his or her arrival. This gillee wet feit's colourful striped trousers and patterned waistcoat announce his employer's identity, and also reflect the need to be seen after dark. The stave he carried is also standard. He was the ancestor of the more stationary footman of later times.

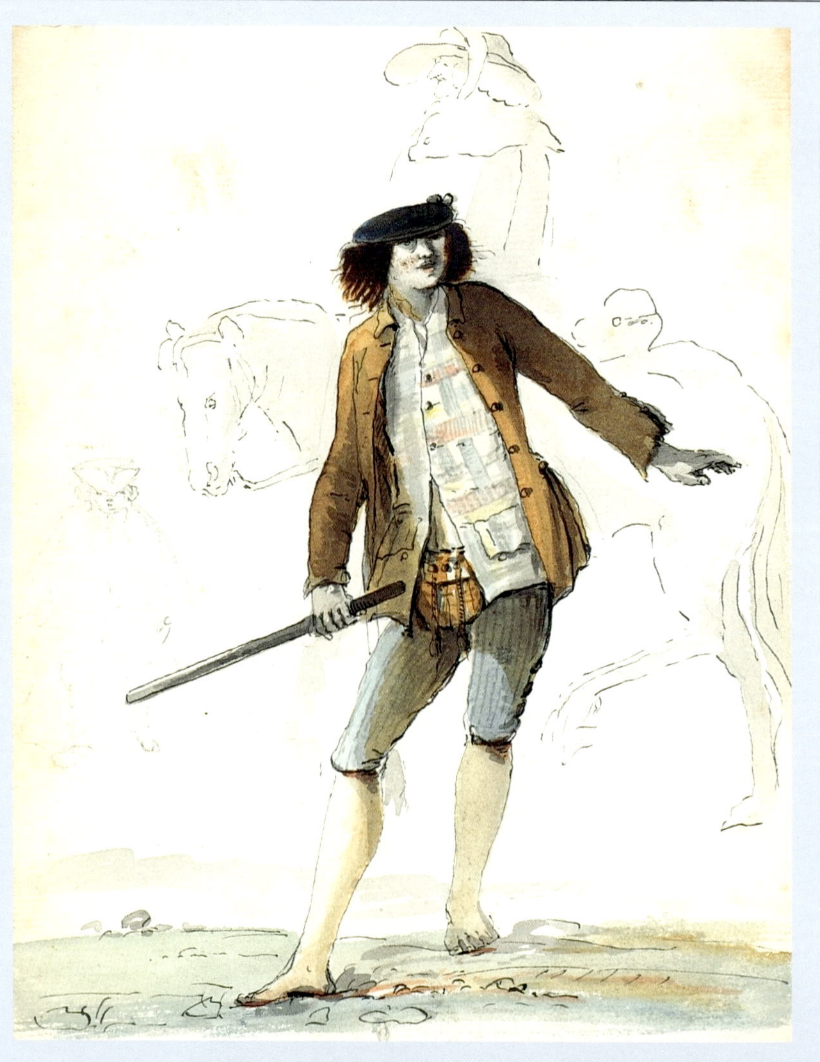

Alexander Grant died in 1718; his brother Sir James Grant, MP for Inverness-shire, succeeded him as chief, and in 1726 ordered further portraits of his family and clan from Richard Waitt. This commission, too, was a mixture of portraits of the Grants themselves, of cadet branches of the family and of (one) retainer: *Nic Ciarain, the Henwife of Castle Grant* (cat.7). The henwife was an outdoor servant of lowly status, and, unlike the Piper and Champion, was probably singled out for representation on account of her age, character, and (presumed) long service rather than her position in the clan: even Waitt's bill, 'For old Naikairn her picture',[24] reflects this. The fact that Scottish households were still predominantly made up of men – apart from henwives, women were employed as nurses, chambermaids and washerwomen – may provide another reason for singling out this retainer. A fourth servant portrait by Richard Waitt of 1731, now in the Scottish National Portrait Gallery, possibly represents the Laird's 'feel', a well-known figure at Gaelic courts, who acted as the laird's counsellor as well as fool.

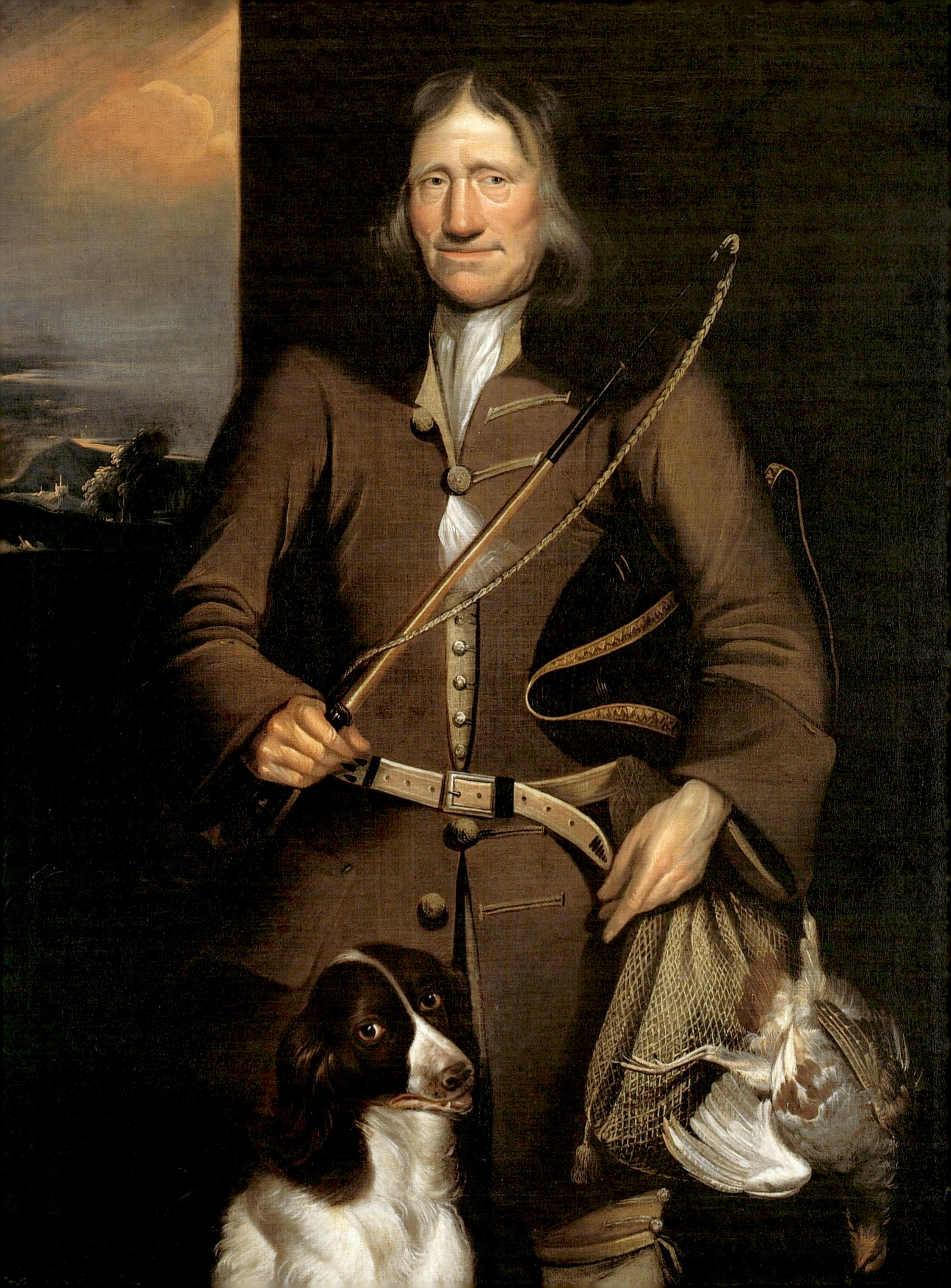

2 STEWARDS TO SCULLERY-MAIDS

Anne French

THE RISE OF THE MIDDLE CLASS, allied to growing industrial and commercial expansion, created an ever-increasing demand for servants who in the 'long' eighteenth century from 1700 to 1825 formed one of the largest groups of employees. Estimates in 1695 and 1806 respectively, suggest figures of around 560,000 and 910,000 out of a total population of around 10.4 million at the latter date. One in eight Londoners may have been a servant in 1775, and by 1796 this had risen to one in 4.5. Despite this, although great households might still employ numerous staff, most other households were much reduced, ranging from the twenty or so employed by the wealthier gentry, down to modest households with one or two employees. The loyalty of some of these humbler servants is recorded in epitaphs, but it is once again the servants of the aristocracy and the upper gentry who appear in portraiture.

By 1725 the simplification of the household structure under the house steward and housekeeper, and replacement of 'gentlemen' servants by those lower in the social scale, was effectively complete. Especially in great households, there was a wide division between upper and lower servants, reflected in the fact that upper servants were better educated, ate separately, did not wear livery, could hire, fire and discipline their subordinates and were fully conscious of these differences – one commentator referring to the 'domineering aristocracy below stairs'.[1] However, recent historians such as Bridget Hill have concluded that this hierarchy was often less rigid than has been supposed; and that it did not become codified until the Victorian era, when production of 'loyal' servant portraiture declined. Her analysis of the gentry household of Nicholas Blundell from 1702 to 1728 confirms that jobs at different levels were often interchangeable[2] and servants frequently combined their roles with work on their employers' farms.

Although social historians argue that service was already feminised by the late seventeenth century, in great households between 1750 and 1800,

opposite Detail of cat.13 **The Dudmaston Gamekeeper with Spaniel and Dead Partridge**
English School, *c*.1720

men still outnumbered women. As Hill points out, even as late as 1814 contemporaries assumed that such households contained many menservants. This may be one reason why, even at the height of servant portraiture from around 1780 to 1825, when the shift to employing women in most households was almost complete, far more portraits of menservants survive. It is noticeable that servant portraiture did not long outlive the largely female households of the nineteenth century, although servants now became a subject in genre painting.

The century saw a hostile reaction of the privileged classes to a new and to them unsatisfactory type of employee, who now moved position perhaps every two or three years, demanded what they saw as excessive wages and was considered to be insubordinate, extravagant, and abused his or her position in a number of ways. The painting of loyal servants as exemplars can be seen as part of this debate and perhaps as a result servant portraits became more numerous from around 1745.

The household hierarchy

At the top of the hierarchy in great households was the land steward or agent, whose role was to manage his employer's estates. Many were already professionals, not servants, and very few portraits of them survive. The bailiff, who managed the home farm, was a senior servant connected with the estate; among Paul Sandby's sketches at Windsor is one said to be of the Duke of Cumberland's bailiff Voules.

The senior domestic servant throughout the 'long' eighteenth century was the house steward, who had taken over from the chamberlain and ruled supreme in households where no land steward was employed, which accounts for the number of portraits of stewards that survive from the period between 1745 and 1825. The steward supervised the duties of the entire household, hiring and firing other servants, paying their wages and controlling expenditure. A man of education, the steward had his own room and dined at the head of the upper servants' table. His role as the key male employee survived well into the nineteenth century, as the serial portraits at Bramham of the 1820s confirm (cats 25, 26), and only later was he replaced by the butler. In smaller households the roles of steward and butler were often combined.

An upper servant, the *valet de chambre* was considered the master's senior personal servant, responsible for his appearance. Since valets accompanied their masters everywhere, they were expected to be 'master of every sort of politeness'.[3] French valets were often preferred; at Knole, both the Duke's valet, the Frenchman Monsieur Villette (1783) and Andrew Coronin, valet to the 3rd Duke's mistress, the dancer Giovanna Baccelli (1775), were painted by Arnold Almond. The only valet (and butler) to be painted by a major artist was Ignatius Sancho (1729–80), who in 1768 sat to Gainsborough while still in the service of the Duchess of Montagu (fig.28).

COOKS

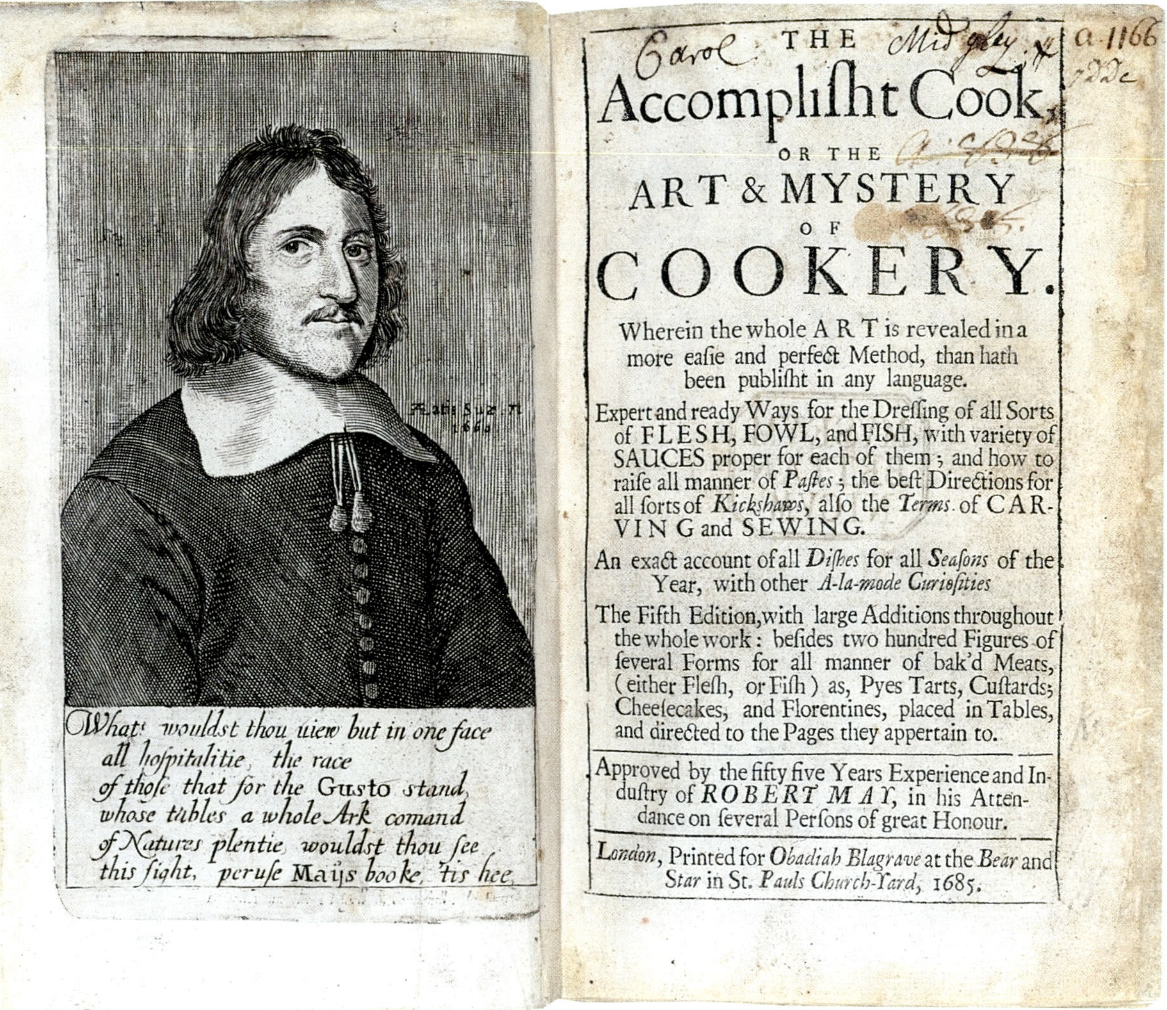

What? wouldst thou view but in one face
all hospitalitie, the race
of those that for the Gusto stand,
whose tables a whole Ark comand
of Natures plentie, wouldst thou see
this sight, peruse Maijs booke, 'tis hee.

THE
Accomplisht Cook,
OR THE
ART & MYSTERY
OF
COOKERY.

Wherein the whole ART is revealed in a more easie and perfect Method, than hath been publisht in any language.

Expert and ready Ways for the Dressing of all Sorts of FLESH, FOWL, and FISH, with variety of SAUCES proper for each of them; and how to raise all manner of *Pastes*; the best Directions for all sorts of *Kickshaws*, also the *Terms* of CARVING and SEWING.

An exact account of all *Dishes* for all *Seasons* of the Year, with other *A-la-mode Curiosities*

The Fifth Edition, with large Additions throughout the whole work: besides two hundred Figures of several Forms for all manner of bak'd Meats, (either Flesh, or Fish) as, Pyes Tarts, Custards; Cheesecakes, and Florentines, placed in Tables, and directed to the Pages they appertain to.

Approved by the fifty five Years Experience and Industry of ROBERT MAY, in his Attendance on several Persons of great Honour.

London, Printed for *Obadiah Blagrave* at the *Bear* and *Star* in St. *Pauls Church-Yard*, 1685.

Cat.9 **The Accomplisht Cook**
Robert May, 1685

In all but the largest households, the next senior male servant to the steward was the cook, who enjoyed a high profile, particularly if he was French. Joseph Florance (cat.32), chef to three Dukes of Buccleuch, exactly fits the profile of a leading male chef employed by the aristocracy. A much earlier celebrity chef was Robert May (cat.9), whose *The Accomplisht Cook* (1685) is the most important English cookery book of the seventeenth century. May was trained in Paris and London, and was chef to the Dormer family of Ascott Park, Buckinghamshire. He regarded himself as an artist and 'never weighed the Expence'. This portrait showing him aged seventy-one, when still in service, acts as the frontispiece to the first edition of his book in 1660.

In larger households specialist bakers, pastry chefs or confectioners assisted the head chef; a drawing by Charles Linsell of *Old Jack Faulkner*, baker (and trumpeter!) at Nuneham in Oxfordshire, is the only surviving image of these more menial kitchen servants. At the bottom of the kitchen department were kitchen-men, who brought in produce from the estate's gardens and fields, while the seventeenth-century scullion had now largely been replaced by the scullery-maid.

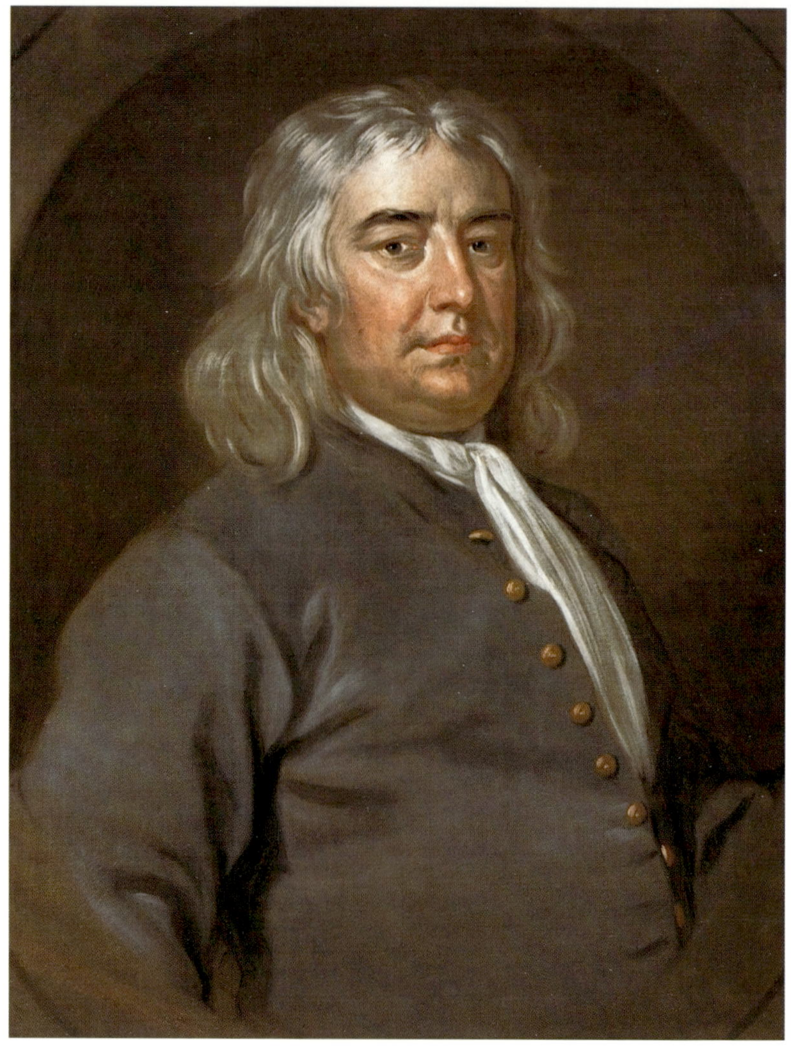

Cat.10 **Fulke Harold, Gardener**
John Ellys, *c.*1736–44

Fulke Harold had been Sir Robert Walpole's gardener at Houghton Hall since around 1718, helping him to landscape the park. In 1744, Ellys's portrait of this elderly but robust employee hung in the below-stairs breakfast parlour at Houghton, among family pictures. Harold is shown as a gentleman, with no visible sign of his profession.

In the eighteenth century the butler had yet to overtake the steward as the principal male servant except in those more modest households where his role was combined with that of steward or valet. He was responsible for wines and other liquors, and for the household glass and plate, and was required to have a 'becoming carriage'[4] as well as some knowledge of vintages. Perhaps reflecting his slightly lower role in the hierarchy, fewer images survive, although in Scotland two butlers to the Wemyss family were painted successively by Sir John de Medina (1702) and by William Aikman (*c.*1712–23).

In the age of the landscape garden, the gardener's work was of vital importance to his employer. Only a proportion of employers called in experts such as 'Capability' Brown or Humphry Repton, and in many instances the household gardener was expected to execute his employer's garden designs and ideas. This must account for the large number of portraits of gardeners that survive. The head gardener planted and maintained the flowerbeds, the kitchen garden, hothouses, greenhouses and orangeries. In larger households head gardeners, as at Knole where the head gardener John Holt, his foreman and a labourer in the garden were all painted by Arnold Almond, often had a team of assistants (see pp.64–5).

The lower male servants, including the footman, coachman and grooms, all wore livery. Chief among these was the coachman, who headed the stables, consisting of postillion, grooms and stable hands, and was expected to have an extensive knowledge of farriery. Like other servants in frequent contact with their masters, coachmen appear in a number of portraits from around 1760 until the advent of the railways (cats 11, 30). They also appear in paintings such as *The Prince of Wales's Phaeton* (1793) by George Stubbs (1724–1806). The groom belonged to the next level of the hierarchy, and countless images survive of this particular servant type.

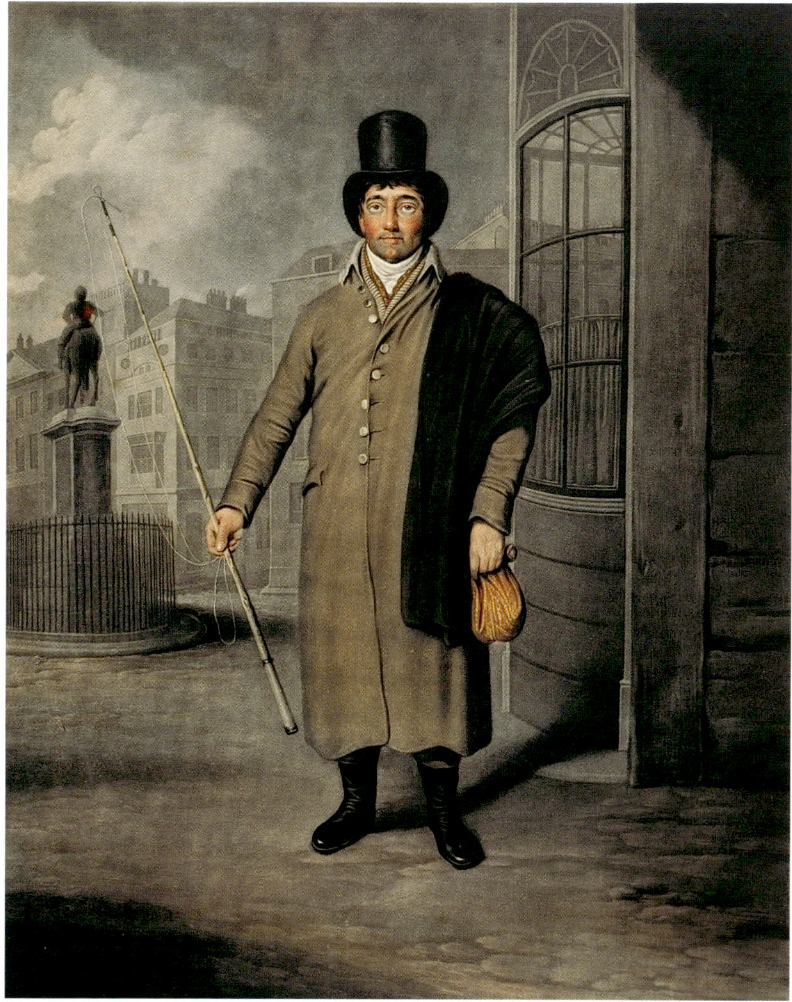

Cat.11
Robert Pointer, Coachman to Mr Boulton
Richard Earlom after Samuel de Wilde, 1811

Robert Pointer was 'many years coachman to Mr Boulton'. He is shown in this mezzotint wearing the coachman's distinctive livery of greatcoat, top hat and boots, and carrying the most potent symbol of his profession, his whip. Coachmen were usually recruited directly by the master for their ability at the reins.

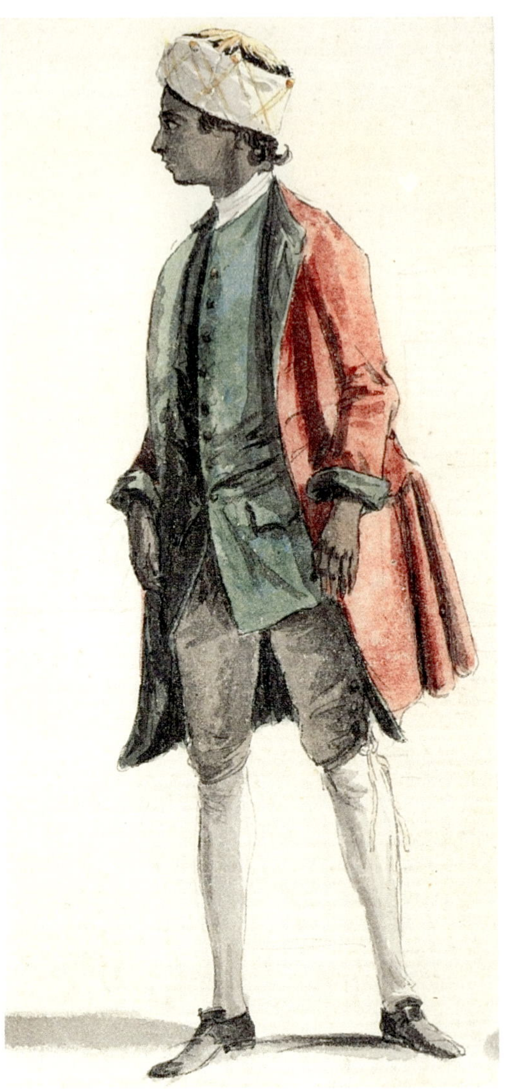

Cat.12 **Servant to the Duke of Cumberland**
Paul Sandby, *c.*1750s

In the 1750s Paul Sandby made a group of informal watercolour studies of the servants of William, Duke of Cumberland, his brother's employer, at Great Lodge, Windsor. These included the Duke's keeper or gardener, running footman, coachman, postillion and this black servant, who must have been a page or a footman. Most of the sitters, as here, wear the Duke's livery of crimson coat with green facings, green waistcoat and breeches.

Although belonging to a low level in the hierarchy, the footman was a key servant with multiple roles, waiting at table, serving tea, cleaning cutlery and glass, carrying coals and acting as escort or messenger outside the household. However, the footman's chief value lay in advertising 'the extent of his master's wealth'; his livery emphasised his 'remoteness from productive labour', and the more splendid his physique, the more he 'proclaimed the waste of time and energy of his unproductive routine'.[5] As a number of elaborately liveried footmen grouped together reinforced this visual proclamation, employers vied with each other in the numbers of footmen they employed. Perhaps the footman's very visibility – or his regular change of jobs – accounts for the fact that very few portrayals in paint were deemed necessary.

In smaller households, the footman's role was often combined with that of the valet or the steward; hence the 'gentleman's gentleman' of Sheridan's *The Rivals* or the generic 'manservant' who is the ancestor of P.G. Wodehouse's astute Jeeves (cat.118). Such employees might range from the *Servant to the Duke of Cumberland* (cat.12) to the rural manservant who combined waiting at table with work in the garden or hayfield, and are often difficult to identify in portraiture; like footmen, they were not usually painted on their own. However, two portraits – of *Jenkin Dinsdale* by Julius Caesar Ibbetson (1759–1817) and *Richard Elliott* by Charles Henry Schwanfelder (1773–1837), 'servant to B. Goodman for 27 years' – may represent the poorly paid rural manservant as general factotum, while George Morland's manservant Gibbs shared his poverty (cat.55).

One of the lower servants most frequently portrayed was the porter, who guarded the halls of town houses and institutions (cats 38, 39) and gate lodges in the country, controlling all entrances and exits. The series at Knole contains two porters, *William Hayes* and *John Hulbert*, while the Bramham gatekeeper, touching his forelock as a carriage drives up the avenue behind him, welcomes the viewer to the world of the estate.

Apart from the coachman and gardener, the key outdoor staff, notably the gamekeeper and park-keeper, were all connected with its sporting life (see chapter 9 for a detailed analysis). As organised shoots had yet to develop, gamekeepers probably spent much time rough shooting with their masters, and the close rapport between them makes the gamekeeper the subject of some of the earliest servant portraits (cat.15), and one of the most portrayed of all servants, both on his own and with his employer.

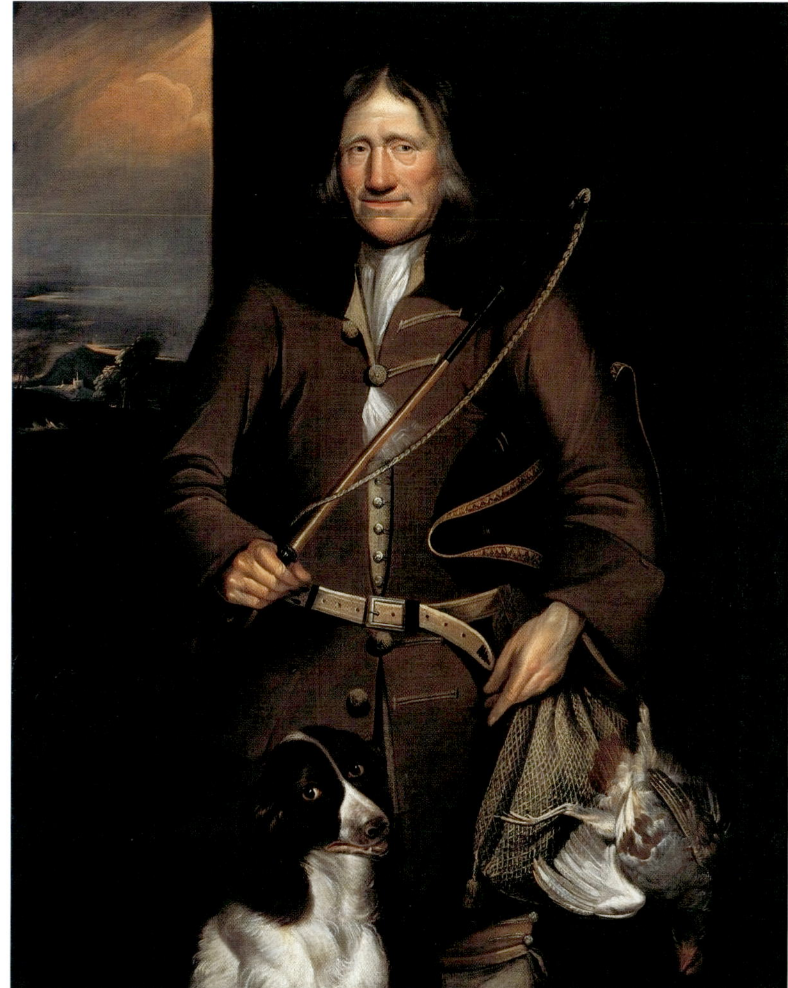

Cat.13 **The Dudmaston Gamekeeper with Spaniel and Dead Partridge**
English School, *c.*1720

This very early servant portrait shows a gamekeeper in livery with a tricorne hat and riding crop. He stands with his spaniel and game bag before a stormy sunset landscape in a composition similar to those used for aristocratic sportsmen. However, his skin is toughened by outside work, and signs of ageing in the gnarled hands and greying hair are unthinkable in fashionable portraiture.

Substantial numbers of other outdoor employees worked on the larger estates, with some of their duties shading off into farming. The Erddig series records a blacksmith and two successive holders of the office of house carpenter (cats 20, 21), while employees represented elsewhere in paint include a cowper brewer (cat.58), a woodman, cowman, bricklayer, waterman, labourer and shepherd.

At the bottom of the hierarchy of male servants was a boy variously called a yard boy, footboy or provision boy, one of whose number appears in *Heads of Six of Hogarth's Servants* (cat.54). In smaller households these positions were combined into a general factotum. The page boy was a special kind of footboy; far from being a menial servant, he was often the pampered escort of his master or mistress.

The roles of gentlemen servants such as tutors or secretaries brought them into close contact with their employers and a number of portraits of these often highly educated employees survive. Whereas early tutors such as the philosopher Thomas Hobbes, tutor to the 2nd and 3rd Earls of Devonshire at Hardwick Hall, who was painted there in extreme old age in 1679, lived within the household, eighteenth-century tutors, like dancing masters and other providers of manners and polish, usually did not. However, a small number of tutor portraits, including fig.9, testify to the enforced closeness of the tutor–pupil relationship on the often protracted Grand Tour. A rare and unpretentious glimpse of a tutor on his own is provided in John Downman's *Mr Gretton of Trinity College, Cambridge* (1778). At least three portraits from around 1750, notably Reynolds's *Lord Rockingham and Edmund Burke* (*c*.1765–6), portray secretaries with their employers in a format derived from Van Dyck's famous double portrait of *Thomas Wentworth, 1st Earl of Strafford with Sir Philip Mainwaring* (fig.4).

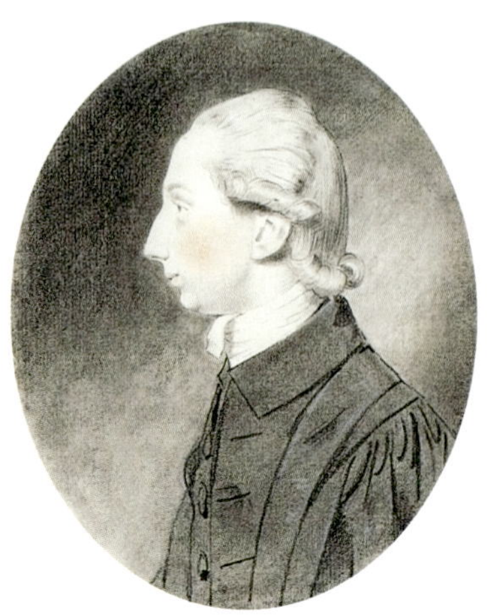

Cat.14 **Study for a Portrait of Mr Gretton of Trinity College, Cambridge, Tutor to Governor Holdsworth**
John Downman, 1778

By the eighteenth century, aristocratic families tended to employ tutors rather than sending their sons to boarding school. This sensitive study of a tutor in charcoal, with the flesh tones highlighted in red chalk, was made in Cambridge where Gretton was probably a fellow. Downman also drew the stewards to the Duke of Northumberland and the Earl of Darlington.

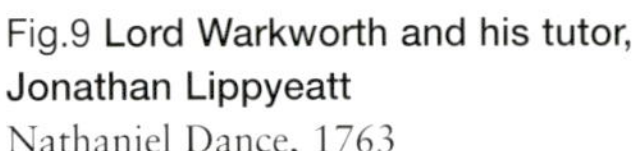

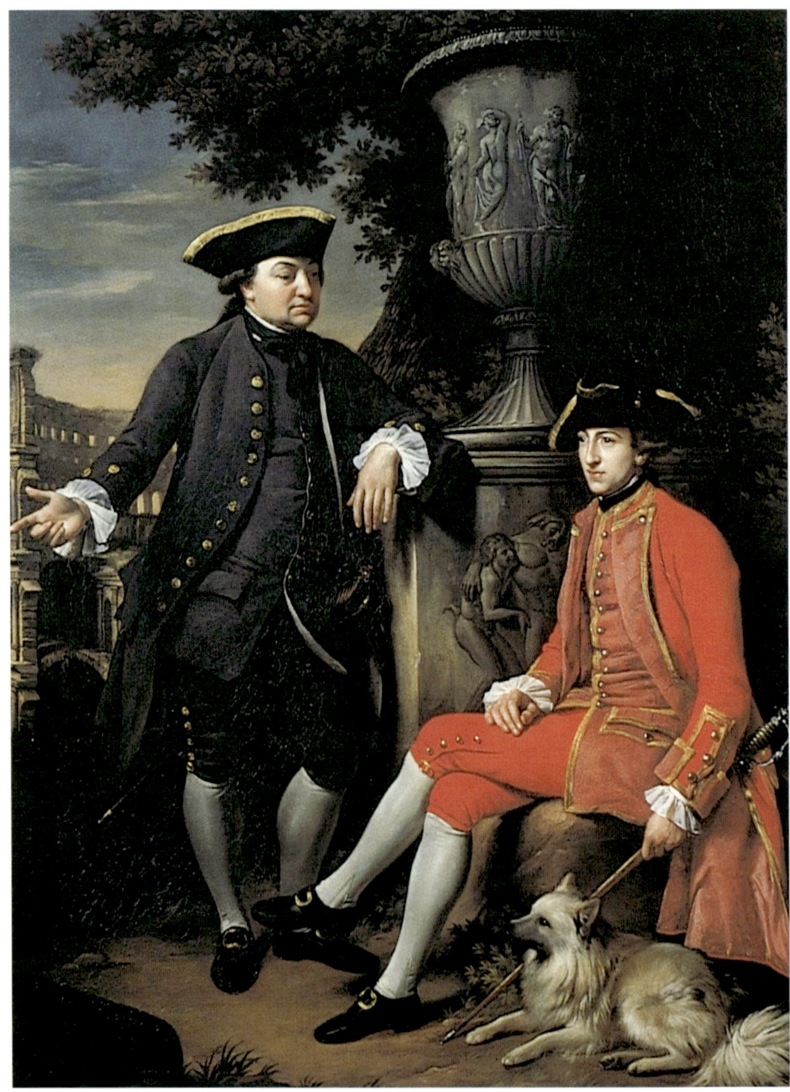

Fig.9 **Lord Warkworth and his tutor, Jonathan Lippyeatt**
Nathaniel Dance, 1763

Lord Warkworth made the Grand Tour from 1761 to 1763, accompanied by the seasoned tutor Jonathan Lippyeatt. This conversation piece depicts them in Rome in front of the Borghese vase, with Lippyeatt pointing out the Colosseum beyond. Surviving correspondence shows that he had to refer all key decisions about the tour to Lord Warkworth's father, the 1st Duke of Northumberland.

Female servants

The lady's maid was the principal maid in the house, and at the same high level in the hierarchy as the valet. She was responsible for dressing her mistress, for her hair and for her wardrobe. Her education 'above ordinary rank', tended to isolate her from other servants, including the housekeeper.[6] Although the lady's maid is the staple ingredient of genre painting, which often focused on the triangular relationship between master, mistress and maid, no portraits of this servant on her own, other than in the set at Knole, are known. It remains puzzling that the more lowly ranked housemaid (cat.27) should have been treated as a subject on her own, while the lady's maid appears only in a subservient role, for example in an early engraving of *An English Lady's Bedchamber* (*c.*1640) in the Pepys Library at Magdalene College, Cambridge.

A woman of 'age and experience'[7] the housekeeper was in charge of all other female domestics and in many smaller households directed most of the male servants as well. Her keys, visible in a portrait of *Mrs Ellis* at Norton Conyers in Yorkshire (1780), were symbolic of her control over the various household departments. The housekeeper's position of great responsibility and trust must account for the fact that there are more portraits of eighteenth- and early nineteenth-century housekeepers than of any other servant (cats 16, 26, 106), except those involved in field sports. Only at Bramham (cat.26) is a housekeeper shown in her working en-vironment; most portraits stress her status instead by showing her in the decorous, high-necked gowns which marked her out from the maids under her control. One portrait – of Mrs Garnett, long-time housekeeper at Kedleston (cat.16) painted in old age by Thomas Barber (*c.*1800) –

BELOW LEFT **Cat.15 The Experienced English Housekeeper**
Elizabeth Raffald, 1784

Elizabeth Whitaker was the housekeeper at Arley Hall, Cheshire, from 1760 to 1763, when she married the head gardener John Raffald. This cookery book, dedicated to her former employer, Lady Elizabeth Warburton, was first published in 1769. It contained over 800 recipes and became a bestseller.

BELOW RIGHT **Cat.16 Mrs Garnett**
Thomas Barber, *c.*1800

Housekeeper at Kedleston for over forty years, Mrs Garnett is shown in Robert Adam's Marble Hall with a catalogue of the collection ready to hand to visitors. She impressed Dr Johnson and others with her abilities as guide, one tourist writing in 1793: 'Of all the Housekeeper[s] I ever met with at a Noblemans Houses this was the most obliging and intelligent … she seem'd to take a delight in her business.'

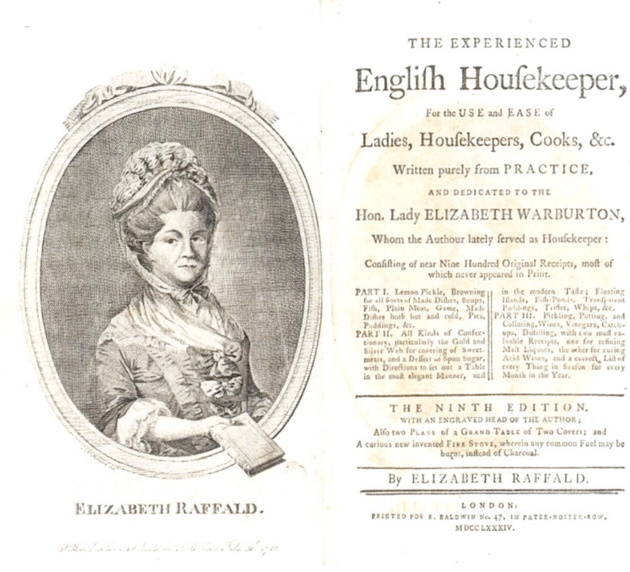
ELIZABETH RAFFALD.

THE EXPERIENCED

English Houſekeeper,

For the USE and EASE of

Ladies, Houſekeepers, Cooks, &c.

Written purely from PRACTICE,

AND DEDICATED TO THE

Hon. Lady ELIZABETH WARBURTON,

Whom the Authour lately ſerved as Houſekeeper:

Conſiſting of near Nine Hundred Original Receipts, moſt of which never appeared in Print.

PART I. Lemon Pickle, Browning for all Sorts of Made Diſhes, Soups, Fiſh, Plain Meat, Game, Made Diſhes both hot and cold, Pies, Puddings, &c.

PART II. All Kinds of Confectionary, particularly the Gold and Silver Web for covering of Sweetmeats, and a Deſſert of Spun Sugar, with Directions to ſet out a Table in the moſt elegant Manner, and in the modern Taſte; Floating Iſlands, Fiſh-Ponds, Tranſparent Puddings, Trifles, Whips, &c.

PART III. Pickling, Potting, and Collaring, Wines, Vinegars, Catchups, Diſtilling, with two moſt valuable Receipts, one for refining Malt Liquors, the other for curing Acid Wines, and a correct Liſt of every Thing in Seaſon for every Month in the Year.

THE NINTH EDITION.

WITH AN ENGRAVED HEAD OF THE AUTHOR;

Alſo two PLANS of a GRAND TABLE of Two Covers; and A curious new invented FIRE STOVE, wherein any common Fuel may be burnt, inſtead of Charcoal.

By ELIZABETH RAFFALD.

LONDON:

PRINTED FOR R. BALDWIN No. 47, IN PATER-NOSTER-ROW.

MDCCLXXXIV.

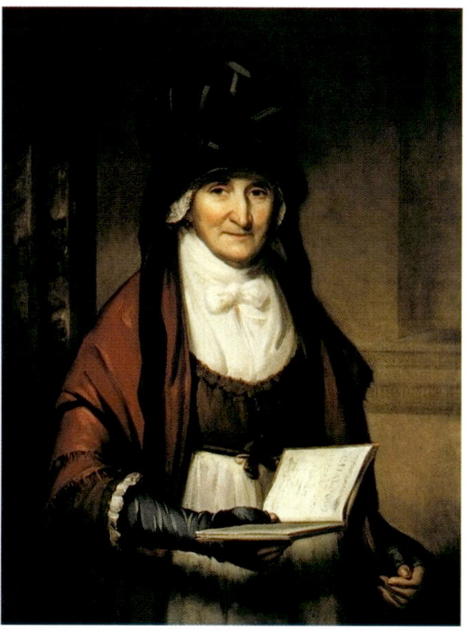

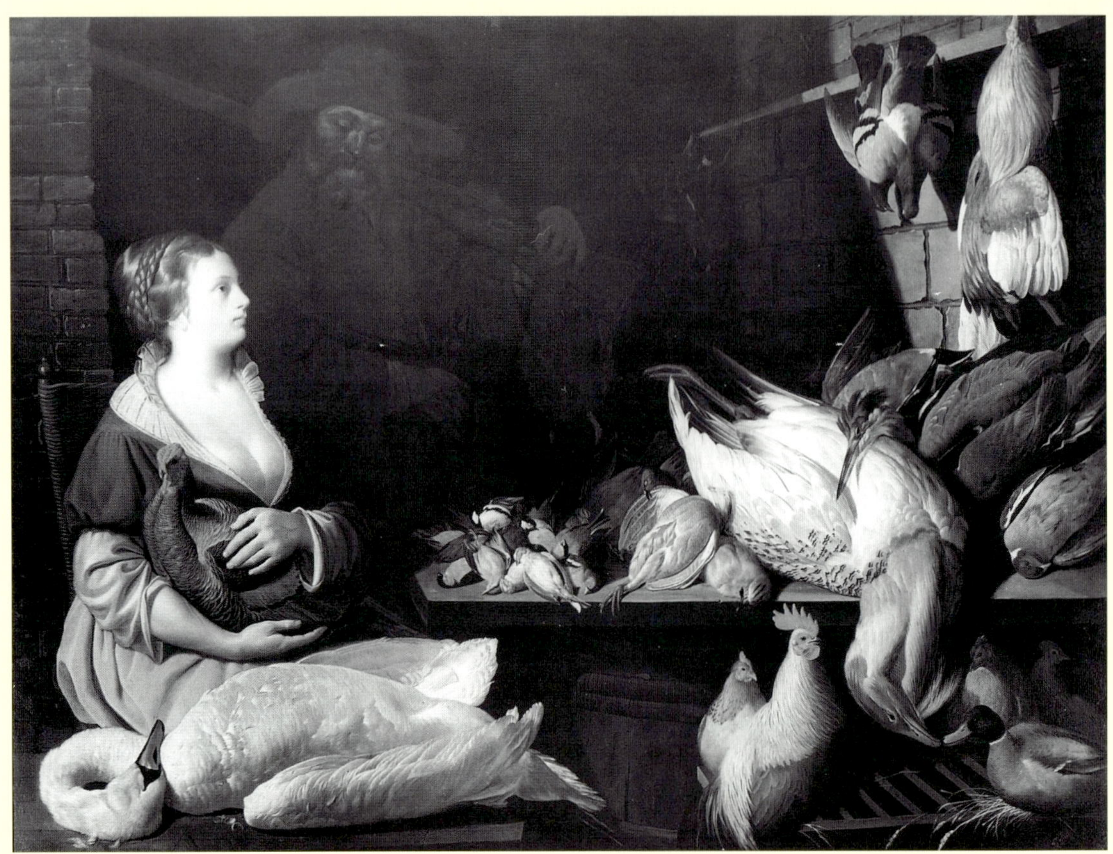

Fig.10 Cookmaid with Dead Birds
Sir Nathaniel Bacon

Bacon's scene is set in a kitchen or a game larder. There is a note of sexual innuendo in the girl's holding of the dead fowl, while a male servant with a shotgun who has delivered the game hovers behind her. A later commentator said of this painting in 1731 that Bacon was 'no limner, but took a fancy to the Cook-maid of the House'. Although this is surely apocryphal, Bacon presumably used a live model.

presents her in another crucial and more public role, showing paintings and furniture to visitors at a time when country-house visiting was already established. Some housekeepers, notably Margaret Lee, painted by Francis Cotes in 1764, owe their translation to canvas to the fact that they combined the role of housekeeper with that of mistress of the household.

The female cook came directly below the housekeeper in the hierarchy. Her duties were the same as those of her male counterparts, although she was held in lower esteem and no portraits survive apart from Sir Nathaniel Bacon's three early and magnificent cookmaids. However, the comfortably large cook makes a frequent appearance in caricature.

Like the tutor, the eighteenth-century governess was not strictly speaking a servant. In an age which placed a new emphasis on childcare and eduction within the home, she appears to have been treated more favourably

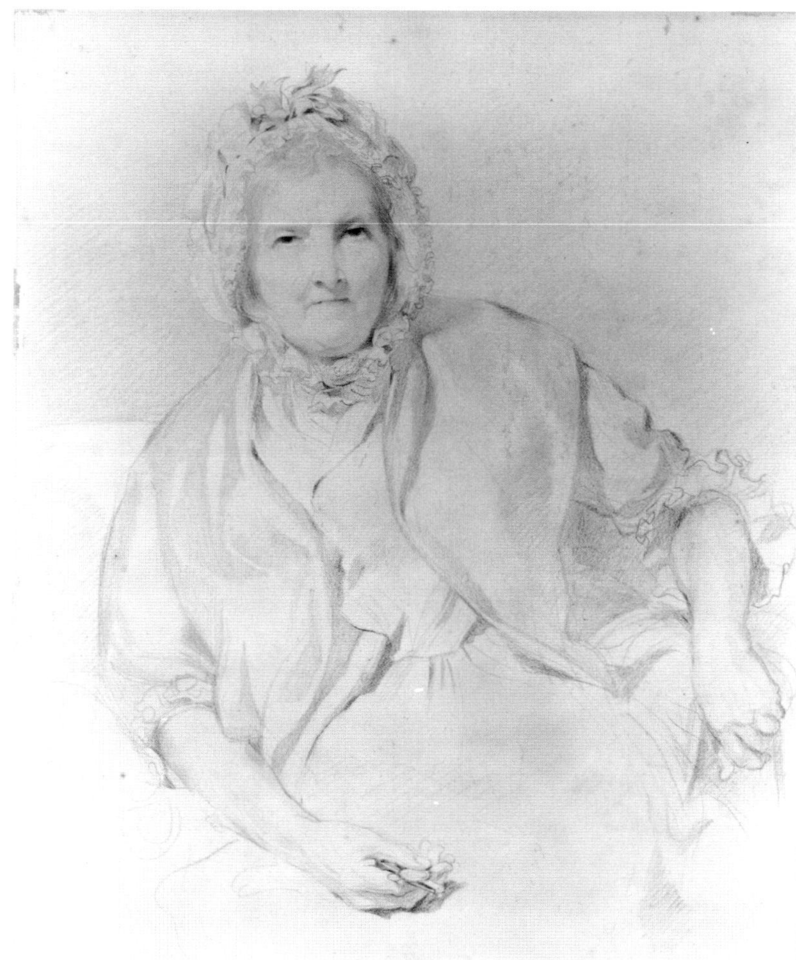

Cat.17 Isabel Smith, called Munia, Nurse to the Angerstein Family
Sir Thomas Lawrence, *c.*1800

Lawrence's sympathetic portrayal of this elderly nursemaid was probably an informal off-shoot of one of his portraits of her employers, the merchant John Julius Angerstein and his family. Lawrence drew it at Woodlands, the Angerstein's family villa at Blackheath. Angerstein was known for his philanthropy and his art collection later formed the nucleus of the National Gallery.

than her nineteenth-century successors (pp.178–79), but no pictures of her survive beyond a conversation piece of a governess reading to her pupils by Hugh Douglas Hamilton of Dunham Massey, Cheshire.

The nurse, only much later known as nanny, occupied a position outside the hierarchy of housekeeper, cook and maids, under the mistress of the house; the nursery wing is the architectural reflection of this separation. At the beginning of the century, upper-class parents saw their children only infrequently, and the nurse was largely responsible for their upbringing. However, from around 1750 it became increasingly common for 'even women of quality [to] nurse their children and to devote time to their education and welfare'.[8] The very close relationships that often developed between nurses and the families they worked for accounts for a number of small-scale, intimate studies of these employees (cats 17, 18). Nannies often remained as part of the household after retirement.

Under the housekeeper in larger households were a number of maids, who represented the utilitarian part of the household invisible to visitors.

These servants were only rarely portrayed in paint, although one of the greatest British servant portraits is of a housemaid (cat.24), and it is intriguing that the only other three portraits of maids that are known from the 'long' eighteenth century are also of this type of employee. There were also dairy-maids, whose association with rural pursuits accounts for their inclusion in genre scenes by Mercier and others; laundry-maids, who washed and ironed; and scullery-maids, who represented the bottom of this hierarchy. In more modest households some of these roles were combined – *Heads of Six of Hogarth's Servants* (cat.54) includes either two or three maidservants – while in the houses of tradesmen and shopkeepers, the maid-of-all-work had to shoulder all of these roles single-handedly, as well as acting as cook. Only very rarely is there any portrayal of the poorest servants. However, a Hogarth drawing for the *The Harlot's Progress* (fig.21) shows the harlot living in poverty attended by the lowest kind of serving maid, a 'bunter'.

The origins of servant portraiture

The earliest servant portraits in Britain emerged in the early seventeenth century from among the ranks of those musicians and entertainers who were close personal servants of the Crown and of the aristocracy (cats 2, 3, 4). However, around 1620–25, the talented amateur Sir Nathaniel Bacon (1585–1627) produced some very different pictures representing servants. These were three enormous paintings of cookmaids with dead birds (fig.10), game and garden produce, which probably formed part of the series of 'ten great peeces in wainscote of fish and fowl' listed at Bacon's house at Culford Hall, Suffolk in 1659;[9] two survive at Gorhambury in Hertfordshire while another is in the Tate. By the early seventeenth century, scenes showing low-life figures beside succulent displays of produce or slaughtered game had become highly popular in the Low Countries in the work of Rubens and Frans Snijders, and Bacon's paintings must have been inspired by his visits to the Netherlands.

These remarkable paintings had no sequel in Britain. Instead, the earliest servant portraits emerged from the tradition of animal painting; once again the inspiration came from the Low Countries. A mid-seventeenth-century English School painting at Lyme Park, Cheshire, of a *Keeper Gralloching a Buck* shows the beginnings of individualised portraiture developing from what is still essentially a static and naïve rendering of contemporary Flemish hunting pictures by Snijders or Jan Fyt. Probably not long afterwards, Francis Barlow (*c*.1626–1704) painted one of the earliest servant portraits to survive, a *Huntsman, Coachman and Keeper* in which the iconography is already remarkably assured; the three servants are identified emblematically – by hound, whip and dead fox – in what would become the standard approach to portraying servants in the next century. The frieze-like effect formed by the hounds across the lower half of the painting confirms the link between animal painting and servant portraiture. Barlow had, however, trained as a portraitist, and his sensitive delineation of the three servants shows a spontaneity of approach entirely different from contemporary Baroque portraiture. The themes of sporting art would be taken up in the eighteenth century, as would the dismissive attitude which suggested that sporting pictures were only tolerable because they depended on 'Princes and Noblemen's Fancies'; much the same view may have prevailed towards servant portraiture.

It was a very different type of servant portrait, pioneered in the 1680s by John Riley, characterised by an honesty and directness of approach to the sitter, that would provide the model for most later servant portraits. Riley's *Bridget Holmes* (cat.27) is typical of a number of portraits of elderly sitters whose age is crucial to their representation; it is not glossed over as in fashionable portraiture. The ethos of Riley's servant portraiture is reflected in the work of William Sonmans (fig.16) and in the informal sketches of Charles Beale II (cats 52, 53). All these portraits reflect the new spirit of scientific enquiry represented by the founding of the Royal Society.

Servant portraiture, 1700–1825

A number of key servant images date from the first twenty years of the eighteenth century. Several of these, notably the British School *Pot-Boy* in Bristol, *c.*1720, the two pendant portraits at Dudmaston, Shropshire (cat.19), and the portraits of the Scottish butlers of the Wemyss family by de Medina and Aikman are renditions of the 'hospitality portrait' which had developed in the late seventeenth century, while the Scottish clan portraits by Richard Waitt (cats 6, 7) also have a symbolic significance. Although fashionable portraitists such as Kneller (fig.25) and Richardson produced occasional servant portraits, and large numbers of servants are included in double portraits or conversation pieces of the first half of the century, only around 1750 did images of individual servants begin to be painted with some frequency. The second half of the century, and particularly the period from around 1780 to 1825, which includes the serial portraits at Knole, Erddig and Bramham, accounts for the vast majority of images of servanthood discussed in chapter 3.

Commissioning servant portraits

Who commissioned servant portraits, and for whom were they destined? Although most servant images in this period were commissioned by their employer to record faithful service, the instigator was not always the employer, and always to think of these portraits in terms of a deliberate commission can sometimes be misleading. Two important servant portraits by leading artists, painted in the second half of the century, offer an understanding of some of the other reasons for their production. Mary, Duchess of Montagu probably commissioned the portrait of her remarkable black valet

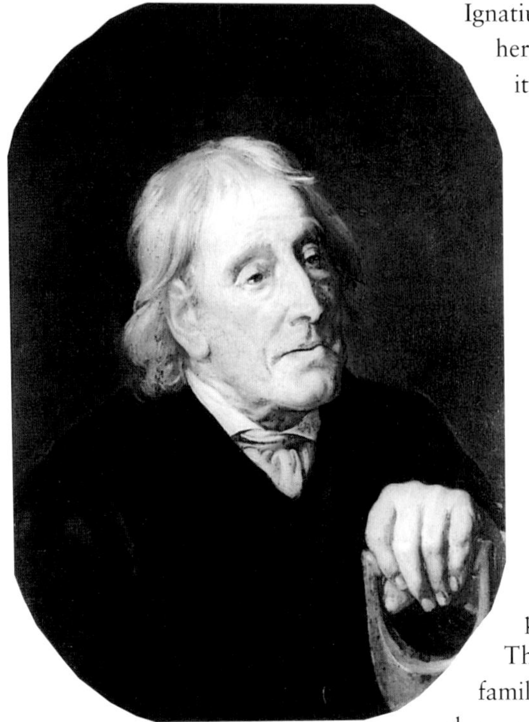

Fig.11 **Jonathan Jackman, Gardener at Wicken Park**
Johann Zoffany, 1780

Jackman had worked at Wicken Park for over sixty years when Zoffany visited the house to include Mrs Prowse, sister of the anti-slavery campaigner Granville Sharp, in his famous painting *The Sharp Family*. Because the portrait was unplanned, it had to be painted on 'an old Mahoganey Drawing Board'. Mrs Prowse did not let Jackman go to London to have the portrait finished in case the journey 'nocked him up'.

Ignatius Sancho (fig.28) from Gainsborough in 1768, at the time she herself sat to him. As the portrait belonged to Sancho himself, it seems reasonable to assume that the Duchess commissioned it as a present, in which case it is one of the very rare instances where a portrait of a servant was painted for a sitter's own benefit and enjoyment. Another is the portrait commissioned from Joseph Wright of Derby of *Old John, Head Waiter at the King's Head in Derby* (*c*.1780), which was then raffled, presumably to maintain him in retirement.

Johann Zoffany's portrait of *Jonathan Jackman* (fig.11) eighty-year-old gardener to Mrs Elizabeth Prowse of Wicken Park, Northamptonshire, represents a spur-of-the-moment decision, and was painted 'on the back' of a portrait of Jackman's employer. Zoffany had asked Mrs Prowse if he could paint her gardener while he waited indoors due to bad weather. However, it is typical of a number of portraits where the impetus came from the artist himself.[10] A comparable explanation may lie behind the study made by Sir Thomas Lawrence of *Isabel Smith*, nurse to the Angerstein family, which was probably made while Lawrence was painting her charges, or another member of the family. We know that Julius Caesar Ibbetson went further, specifically setting out to record 'some singular or worthy characters, old servants or oddities which are worth transmitting to canvas and so on to posterity'.[11] His portrait of the elderly manservant *Jenkin Dinsdale* (1812) can be viewed in this light.

Many more portraits were an off-shoot of commissions for sporting art, while other servant portraits were intended to form part of decorative schemes. Although no examples of servant portraits actually commissioned by a member of the below-stairs household exist, the role of the steward in such commissions may prove a fruitful topic for future research. Similarly, while the attribution of three paintings at Bramham to 'Lascelles the footman painter' is merely traditional, it remains possible that some of the more amateurish portraits were 'below-stairs' productions in which employers played no part.

An analysis of servant portraits by category of employment confirms that the principal staff to be represented in paint during the 'long' eighteenth century were the senior holders of household offices – principally stewards and housekeepers, and to a lesser extent butlers – although at Erddig the only indoor servant included is a long-serving former maid, not the housekeeper. However, issues of gender played a major role in a century when most portraits were commissioned by the male head of the household. Closeness to the master and his daily routine, especially as the companion of his leisure hours, was crucial in determining representation. So that while the coachman or gamekeeper appear frequently in paint, almost no portraits of valets survive. Lower servants were selected because of their strong or eccentric characters, their longevity and long service; those in livery were only rarely portrayed and servant portraits usually represent the sitter in a domestic role, not on display.

The reasons why certain men and women were chosen in preference to their fellows may often seem reasonably clear. But what prompted their employers to consider recording them at all, with its attendant trouble and expense, given that portraiture was normally reserved for the upper classes or for the distinguished? One answer may be that, in an age in which most servants moved jobs every few years and did not stay long enough to inspire affection in their employers, the virtues of old and faithful servants stood out against the general pattern of casual employment. Commemorated on the walls of the servants' hall, steward's or housekeeper's room, these servants could be held up as exemplars to less diligent employees.

Artists

Which artists were commissioned by employers to paint their servants? A number of leading fashionable eighteenth-century portraitists painted servants, including Hogarth, Reynolds, Gainsborough, Zoffany, George Romney, Tilly Kettle, John Russell, Hugh Douglas Hamilton, James Northcote, George Stubbs, and in Scotland, Sir John de Medina and William Aikman. However, these portraits were sometimes produced almost by chance, often in conjunction with existing commissions for employers. Given that most servants, with the exception of personal attendants, were not mobile, their portraits were painted not by fashionable metropolitan artists but by provincial hands. Often, employers selected leading regional painters, and some, notably Thomas Barber in Nottingham, Thomas Beach in the south-west and Richard Waitt in the Scottish Highlands, seem to have made a minor specialism of painting servant portraits.

Sporting artists such as George Stubbs at Wentworth Woodhouse, or George Garrard and John Widdas of Hull at Bramham became involved in servant portraiture through their employer's wish to record their prized horses and dogs; although many of their compositions show servants as subsidiary figures in sporting compositions, all three men also painted single images of servants.

Many servant portraits were painted at differing levels of technical competence by provincial painters, including George Alsop at Dudmaston, William Jones at Erddig, the Cheshire portraitist John Slack, who in 1750 painted the centenarian keeper at Lyme Park, John Ainslie in the Scottish Lowlands or Francis Lindo, who painted the Duchess of Northumberland's piper in 1756. Other artists, notably John Walters at Erddig, were artisans, journeymen or itinerant artists of whom almost nothing is known. Many more servant portraits are the work of unknown provincial painters, while a minority are in the naïve tradition.

Although the range of artists who produced servant portraits is so varied that conclusions are difficult to draw, one of the most interesting questions concerns whether they approached portraiture in a different way when representing servants, either enjoying more freedom than when portraying wealthy clients, or instead diminishing or even patronising sitters drawn from a lower social class than their own. How far do servant images simply echo fashionable or even official portraiture, or did a specific style of presentation and iconography develop? Although portraits such as George Stubbs's *Thomas Smith the Banksman* (before 1768) or Hogarth's *Servants* confirm that leading artists relished the possibilities of portraying sitters without flattery, showing them with both sympathy and respect, less competent practitioners were sometimes perplexed by the task handed to them, and often found it easier to fall back on imitations or even parodies of aristocratic or fashionable portraits. Portraits of sporting servants often do not differ markedly in composition from those of the employer class, although artists such as Thomas Gooch in *John Booth* (*c*.1798) managed to convey the dignity of labour within this format. However, in the earliest two paintings at Erddig, John Walters produced a mock-Baroque portrait complete with columns, and another with a fictitious coat of arms; only later did he offer more considered interpretations of sitters in their own environment. The portraits in the second Erddig series, however, are among the most successful of all servant portraits.

The Erddig portraits, together with those at Bramham, are unusual in their inclusion of settings specifically connected to the sitter. In most servant portraits, the only iconography which seems to have evolved is the very obvious device of displaying the tools of the subject's trade. Only very rarely are indoor servants shown wearing livery (cat.123), although this is probably only a reflection of the absence of lower indoor servants as sitters. However, hunt and other estate servants usually sport the family livery. While some employers seem to have preferred their servants to be portrayed in their 'best' clothes (cats 16, 18, 103), portraits of men in particular often show them in working dress, while Bridget Holmes wears plain maid's attire.

Format, iconography and setting

Servant portraits throughout the seventeenth and the 'long' eighteenth centuries were produced in widely differing formats and in a variety of media. Large numbers of oil paintings survive, from full-lengths and substantial but not life-sized portraits, to small bust-length ovals or roundels. Servants were also recorded more privately in pastel, drawings and watercolour, but it is hardly surprising to find that they were not usually painted in miniature – a format dictated by more intimate relationships than those existing between employers and servants – the exception being the relationship between a nurse and her former charge (cat.18). The only other miniature traced to date

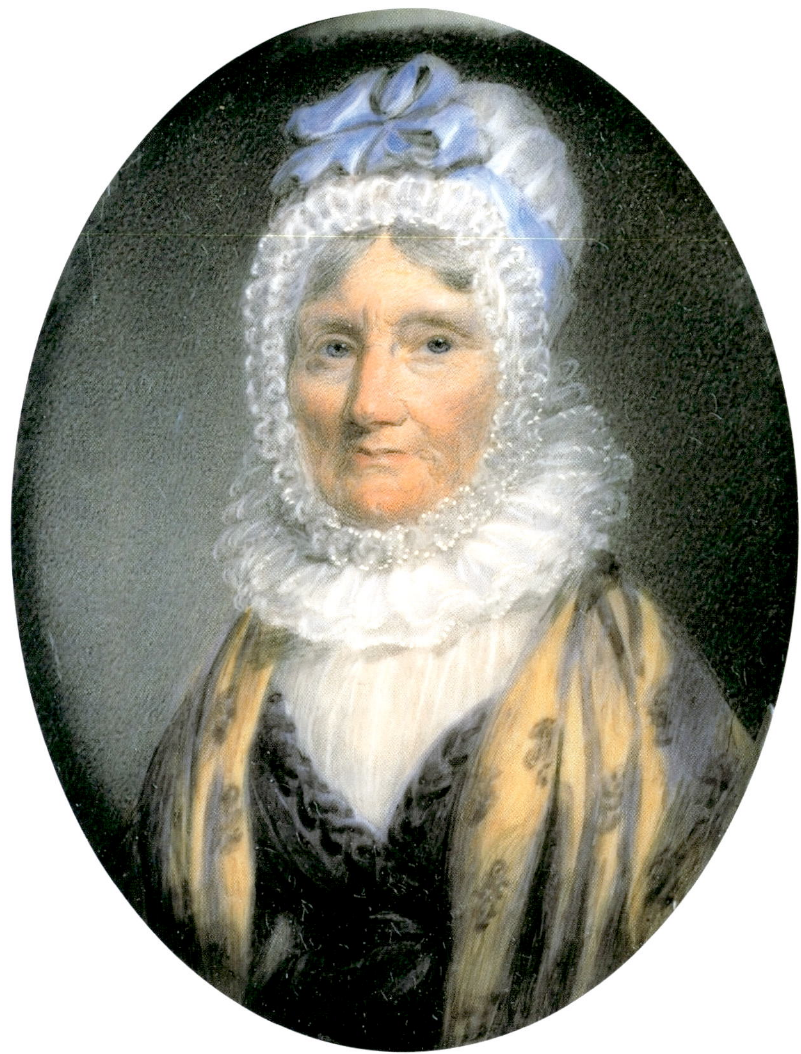

Cat.18 **Catherine Hughes, Nanny to the Williams Family of Bodelwyddan**
George Hargreaves, 1824(?)

This rare miniature of a servant was commissioned as a keepsake by one of her former charges, Mary Elizabeth Lucy (1803–89), future mistress of Charlecote, who noted on the back that it represented 'The dear old nurse at Bodleywithan. I had this taken of her when I married'. The commission illustrates the close relationships that often developed between children and the nurses responsible for their upbringing.

is by Ozias Humphrey of *William Gardener* (d.1793), groom-porter to the Dorset family at St James's (1790) who also appears as 'Superintendent' in the roundels at Knole.[12] Although described as an 'old and faithful servant to the Dorset family', Gardener was a relic of the era of gentlemen-servants, and it is as such that he appears in both portraits.[13]

Where did servant portraits hang? Although evidence is scant, a number of interesting pointers emerge. Some clearly hung upstairs or at least with other family portraits. Although *Bridget Holmes* is first recorded in the reign of Queen Anne in store at Windsor, it was moved soon afterwards to a position of some prominence over the chimney in the Eating Room of her husband, Prince George of Denmark. Lord Rockingham kept his portrait of the banksman *Thomas Smith* by Stubbs in the antechamber to his bedroom at Wentworth Woodhouse, in the same room as Van Dyck's great portrait of *Thomas Wentworth, 1st Earl of Strafford with Sir Philip*

Mainwaring (fig.4). A butler to the Wemyss family in Scotland, painted by Sir John de Medina in 1702, was incorporated as an overdoor in early eighteenth-century panelling in a principal bedroom, and has presumably occupied a position of some prominence from soon after it was painted. The portrait at Houghton of *Fulke Harold* (cat.10) hung in 1744 in the 'below-stairs' breakfast parlour, together with family portraits, but he was probably a landscape gardener and is presented very much as a 'gentleman'.

'Hospitality' portraits such as the late seventeenth-century butler at Eton College, or the full-length *Pot-Boy* of *c.*1720 at Bristol, were intended to welcome the visitor to the more important public spaces of the house. Entrance halls may have been considered particularly appropriate for such 'welcome' figures, or for portraits intended to display the estate's outdoor sporting life. Perhaps the most prominent hanging of servant portraits occurred in Scotland, where Richard Waitt's two spectacular portraits of the chief of Clan Grant's Piper and Champion (cat.6) hung as part of the anatomy of a clan in the Hall of Castle Grant, together with the clan armoury.

Many more portraits, however, must have hung downstairs. The series of portraits by John Ainslie, painted *c.*1817, hung in the steward's room at Dalkeith House. At Bramham, George Garrard's rendering of the interior of the steward's room in his portrait of *John Pollock* suggests that these small but relatively comfortable interiors, complete with paintings in gilt frames on the walls, may well have accommodated other smaller-scale servant portraits. Another obvious destination for servant portraits, as at Erddig, was the main communal space below stairs, the servants' hall (fig.12). Unfortunately, little can be gleaned from the position today of servant portraits on the back stairs, corridors or below-stairs rooms of country houses. Such hanging must reflect later arrangements of the nineteenth and twentieth centuries, when the employees concerned were long forgotten.

The servant as attendant

Although this book is concerned primarily with portraits where the servant occupies centre stage, there are many more examples where he or she is depicted with an employer, occupying a supporting role as attendant, in genres as diverse as fashionable portraiture, the conversation piece, sporting art and views of country seats. Surely the two most enduring of these conventions were the vogue for portraying black pages with their masters or mistresses, introduced into British portraiture in the 1630s by Van Dyck, and paintings of racehorses and hunters with their grooms.

The rise from around 1720 of a new art form, the small-scale, informal 'conversation piece' to satisfy the demand of the rising middle-class to be represented in portraiture, has been much discussed. Given that showing speech itself on canvas was impossible, artists depicted instead 'the relationships between people, the objects they kept around them, their furniture, and the drama of the resulting interplay'.[14] From near the beginning of its vogue, servants were included in this interplay with some regularity by artists such as Joseph Van Aken, Marcellus Laroon, William Hogarth, Charles Philips and especially Gawen Hamilton. In Van Aken's *An English Family at Tea* (*c.*1720), a maidservant stands centre stage, pouring water into the pot. As a sociable activity that was entirely consistent with virtue,[15] tea-drinking became a popular subject in conversation and the principal role of servants in such paintings is to dispense this valuable commodity, acting as agent of their employers' hospitality. Almost certainly, their inclusion owes even more to the perception of servants themselves as fashionable commodities, another symbol of their employers' status.

In Robert West's *Thomas Smith and His Family* (fig.26), a turbaned black page, although also engaged in tea-making, occupies a more subordinate role on the periphery of the canvas, a placing which is repeated in most early conversations including servants. With *The Porten Family* (*c.*1736) by Gawen Hamilton, the manservant is distinguished from the rest of the figures by his profile stance and uncovered head, which floats oddly in the background above the row of heads of his employers. Similarly, in Hogarth's *The Wollaston Family* the two servants are merely sketched in, and therefore differ tonally from the rest of the painting. As David Solkin points out, the new class of the 'polite', although more inclusive than the old aristocracy, unquestionably excluded servants;[16] if many of these paintings were commissioned by middle-class sitters, the more informal relationships that often resulted between employer and employee in smaller households are not reflected in conversation-piece portraiture.

Although servants continued to be included in conversations until 1750–55 in the paintings of William Hogarth, Arthur Devis, Francis Hayman and others, the concentration of servant images in earlier conversations of the 1720s to 1740s is explained by the location of these paintings in a sphere which straddles the public and private.[17] The subsequent history of the conversation piece would be dominated by portrayals of the nuclear family, which must account for the exclusion of servants from most later portraits. When servants are included in conversations in the second half of the century, above all in the work of Johann Zoffany, they are shown with affection and as part of a closely knit family group, as is the black page in *The Family of Sir William Young* or the elderly nurse in *The Colmore Family*. Zoffany's almost countless representations of black servants in his Indian conversation pieces show the same involvement of servants in the subject of the conversation.

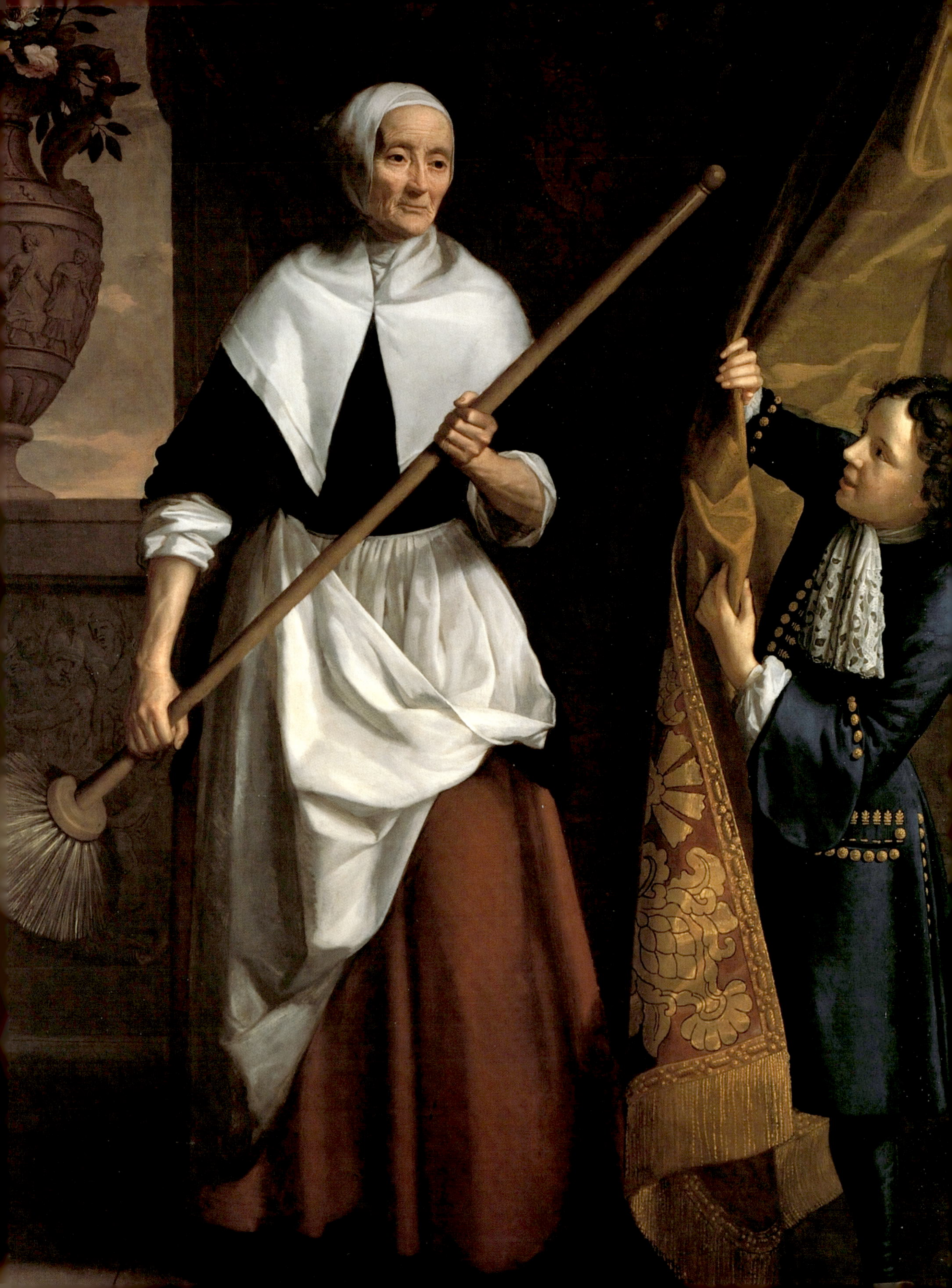

3 LOYAL SERVANTS

Anne French and Giles Waterfield

THE CENTRAL MOTIVATION for the production of servant portraits is loyalty. This is an old concept of loyalty, derived from the medieval ideal of lord and vassal. When the vassal pledged allegiance to his lord, the two individuals embarked on a relationship that embraced contractual issues such as military service, tenancy and finance, and most importantly, perhaps, a sense of mutual trust and obligation. It was expected that these bonds would be equally strong on either side: the vassal or servant served his lord, notably through military service, and in return the master protected his servant, looked after his interests and regarded him as a member of his extended family. Such relationships formed the basis for the medieval household, for many rural households in the seventeenth and eighteenth centuries, and for the long-lasting system of apprenticeship. They also inspired numerous portraits of the type discussed in this book.

In the nineteenth century, under the pressures of urbanisation and commercialisation, social relations became more impersonal as increasingly strong barriers grew up between home and workplace. Many of the vertical bonds that had transcended social divisions and brought communities together began to dissolve. Within our field the servant portrait becomes a less usual phenomenon and imaginary depictions of servants often (as in the pages of *Punch*) acquire a sharp element of satire and even antagonism. In these circumstances, rural communities of all kinds, and particularly the landed estate (whether large or small), were enclaves where older forms of social relations persisted.

The servant portrait, and especially groups of portraits associated with particular families, is one of the most potent symbols of the idealised 'old society'. These images make an eloquent case for the servants' attachment to their master and for the reciprocal warmth felt by employers towards their staff. These people, the images suggest, are more than employees: they are, in a positive sense, members of the master's 'family'.

OPPOSITE Detail of cat.27 **Bridget Holmes**
John Riley, 1686

This chapter looks at several unified series of servant portraits, as well as at some individual works. They range from the early eighteenth century (the Clan Grant images of 1714–26) to the present, and include paintings, drawings and photographs. Though the series portraits are not numerous (unless one includes photographs), their history is central to this publication. They were commissioned by a range of patrons, from dukes with huge incomes (like the Dukes of Buccleuch or Dorset) to untitled gentry families like the Yorkes of Erddig. They were all based on rural households, usually (though not always) at some distance from a large city. The choice of sitters differs considerably from one household to another: though sometimes a wide variety of individuals is included, often the concentration is on individuals noted for length of service. Some of the sets are executed by professional artists such as John Ainslie, George Garrard, Richard Foster and Andrew Festing, while others are by artisans and itinerant painters' hands and by amateurs. While the 'old society' began to break down in the late eighteenth and the nineteenth centuries, the determined ideological continuity of the rural landed classes and of the country-house idyll meant that works in this category continue to be produced, as paintings and photographs, up to the present.

Serial portraits

Of these images of faithful service, the most remarkable are the serial portraits at Erddig, Knole, Bramham Park and Drumlanrig (formerly at Dalkeith House). The very early set of portraits of his clan servants commissioned by Alexander Grant between 1714 and 1726 predates any of these, but are discussed in the context of the survival of medieval households into the eighteenth century (see chapter 1). Two sets of drawings survive from the early nineteenth century (see chapter 6). A later example of the vogue is provided by the set of portraits of his estate staff in Briantspuddle Village Hall, Dorset, commissioned by Sir Ernest Debenham between 1914 and 1919. Recently, the tradition has been revived in portraits of the staff of the Brudenell family at Deene Park by Richard Foster, *c.*1970 (cat.96), and in a set of portraits which is still ongoing, commissioned by the Earl of Leicester of his staff at Holkham from Andrew Festing (cat.98). If serial portraits represent a distinct phenomenon, they differ markedly from each other in scale and purpose as this account will reveal.

Dudmaston

The portraits of servants at Dudmaston (cats 13, 19) are amongst the earliest British servant images. Their importance as a group, and perhaps also as part of a regional pattern of servant portraiture in Shropshire and the Welsh borders, is reinforced by the circumstances of their commission. They were probably painted for Sir John Wolryche (1691–1723), who spent the eleven years from his majority until his death plundering the family estate to pay for his passion for horse racing, hunting, cock fighting and gambling. While Sir John may seem an unlikely patron to have commissioned 'loyalty' portraits, his passion for field sports clearly brought him into close contact with his outdoor staff. The fact that two other spendthrift sportsmen commissioned servant portraits at a comparable date (cats 35, 36, 44), suggests that modern preconceptions as to the type of employer likely to commission such records can be misplaced.

The sitter in cat.13 (see chapter 2) may be Sir John's favourite servant, the huntsman and keeper George Griffith, who also appears, wearing the distinctive blue and red family livery, in the contemporary painting of *The Wolryche Hunt* which dominates the Entrance Hall and hangs adjacent to all three servant portraits. Like the triple portrait by Francis Barlow (see p.48), this unaffected portrayal of a family retainer by a provincial artist working in the tradition of Riley and Richardson is intended not simply as an individual portrait, but as a statement about the importance

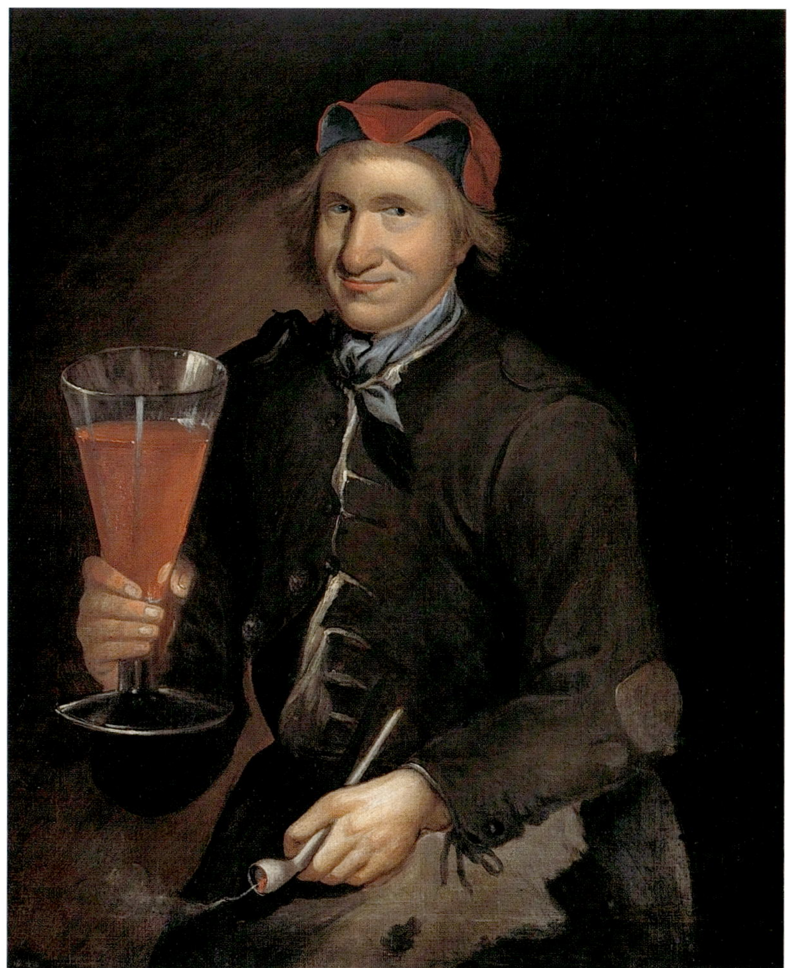

Cat.19 **The Wolryche Fool as an Older Man**
George Alsop, mid-eighteenth century

Despite his distinctive blue and red cap in the Wolryche colours, the sitter's patched coat and apron suggest that he is probably a 'below-stairs' servant. Many early servant portraits show lower servants wearing similar torn or patched clothing. Although this portrait is attributed to local artist George Alsop, who in 1719 signed the 'pendant' pot-boy, the handling in this second unsigned portrait is quite different.

at Dudmaston of sporting life. The two other servant portraits at Dudmaston are framed as pendants and were traditionally identified as the Wolryche Fool as a boy, and again as an older man (cat.19). However, there is no facial similarity between them and it now seems likely that they represent two different menial servants of the household. Prominent in both paintings is a massive glass goblet filled with ale, which remarkably survives (cat.125). The presence of a hospitality cup lends added significance to the positioning of these two 'welcome' portraits in the Entrance Hall.

Erddig – servants as friends

Far from representing an anomaly, as was once thought, the Erddig servant portraits can now be placed within the context of this distinctive tradition for portraying servants. Nevertheless, this is a unique recording by successive generations of the Yorkes, first on canvas and later in photographs, of their long-serving staff from the 1790s up to the early twentieth century. The paintings in the Servants' Hall there are rightly cited as the outstanding examples of this genre.

The earliest servant portraits at Erddig were commissioned in 1791–6 by Philip Yorke I (1743–1804), the most charismatic and talented of the Yorkes, from local Denbigh artist John Walters who was probably an artisan in practice, not a portraitist.[1] What prompted this fascinating commission from a family not noted for its collecting activities, nor even for its portrayal of its own members, their horses and their dogs? As Merlin Waterson points out, the Yorkes had more portraits of their servants than of themselves. The series presumably had its origins in Philip Yorke I's own idiosyncratic personality, which included an 'unusual degree of devotion towards his family's seat and its contents'.[2] He may have known of other local examples of servant portraiture – within a short distance there were important examples at Hawarden, Edwinsford, Chirk Castle and Dudmaston, although most of these date from earlier in the century, and seem unlikely to have been a direct source of inspiration.

Only one of the sitters chosen is a woman and a (former) indoor servant; Jane Ebrell was 'spider-brusher' (housemaid) to John Meller, Philip Yorke I's great-uncle and founder of the family dynasty at Erddig. Later, she married Simon Yorke I's coachman, and is shown here in 1793 at the age of eighty-seven, in a classic example of a portrait inspired by longevity. Two members of the outdoor staff, *Jack Henshaw*, 'best of beaters' (1791), and *Edward Prince* (cat.20), estate carpenter (1792), are accompanied by the kitchen porter *Jack Nicholas* (1791), whose duties were largely outdoors provisioning the kitchens from the Erddig gardens, and whose lowly position in the hierarchy did not disqualify him from representation.[3] The set is completed by portraits of two other men who, although not Erddig employees, were key contributors to the household: the blacksmith *William Williams*, who appears to have worked for the estate on contract

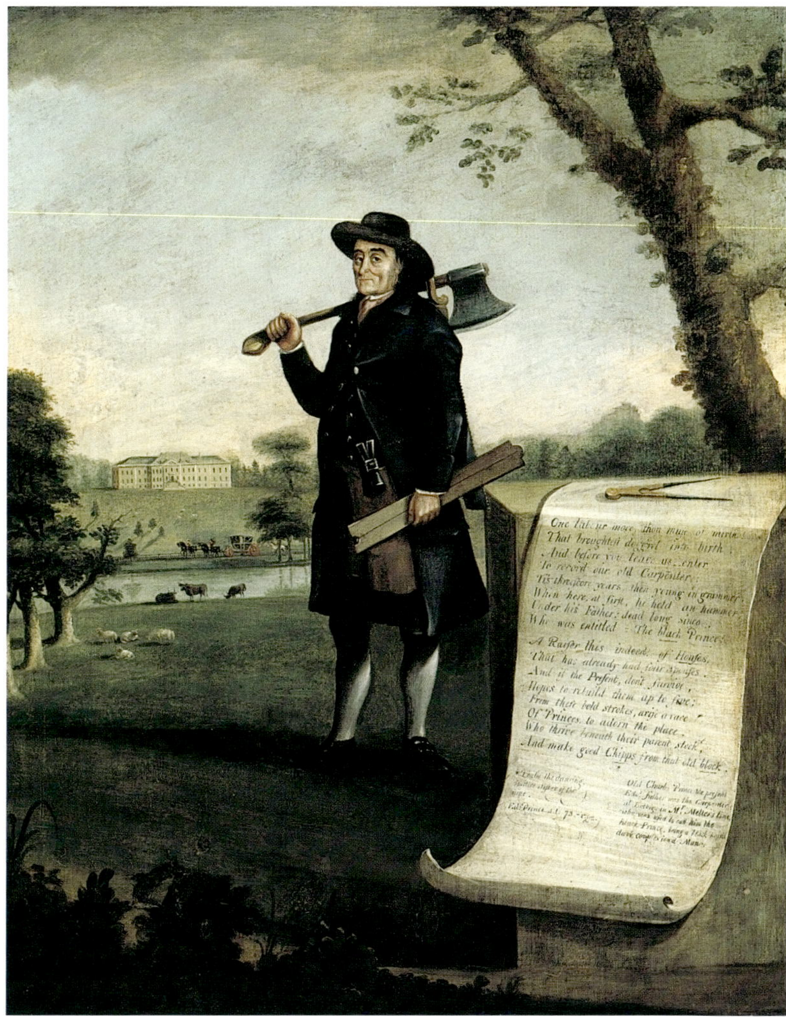

Cat.20 **Edward Prince, Carpenter**
John Walters, 1792

According to his employer Philip Yorke, Edward Prince, seventy-three in this portrait, had worked at Erddig for sixty years. His father had been head carpenter before him and Yorke's poem, inscribed on the scroll, makes a punning reference to the Prince 'dynasty' at Erddig. With four wives, the carpenter had produced 'a race of Princes, to adorn the place', who made 'good Chipps from that old block'.

rather than on a weekly wage, and the Wrexham butcher and publican *Tom Jones*, whose inclusion illustrates the symbiotic relationship between estates and their suppliers found also in George Eliot's *Middlemarch* (1871–2).

If Philip Yorke had seen other nearby servant portraits, his own commission went far beyond existing examples. The fascination of these portraits lies in the way in which John Walters, surely on Yorke's instructions, attempted to develop an iconography suited to these sitters from below stairs. The most striking device employed is the inclusion in all of the portraits, except the earliest two, of accompanying scrolls to incorporate Philip Yorke's *Crude Ditties*, those light-hearted rhyming couplets (cat.104) on his servants' personalities and their relationship to Erddig. Full of puns, apostrophes to the classical gods, bathos and absurd metaphors that run in parallel with the Yorkes' visual recording of their servants, these verses were to develop into a similarly long-lasting family tradition.

But Walters also grapples with different artistic traditions in what is one of the first thoroughgoing attempts in Britain to portray servants in their own milieu. In *Jack Nicholas*, one of the earliest portraits, he produced a somewhat naïve, jocular parody of a Baroque portrait: the kitchen-man, basket with two live ducks in hand and an avenue of trees behind him, takes snuff in front of a Baroque column and pedestal. Similarly, *Jack Henshaw* (1791) shows an awareness of French or Italian eighteenth-century portraits of sportsmen, and of recent portraits by Gainsborough; the fictitious coat of arms with the motto '*Henshaw de Henshaw*' confirms that the facetious nature of the inscription is carried over into the portrait itself.

The later portraits, particularly those from 1793, are more informal, showing the sitters quietly going about their business or sitting at home. Merlin Waterson relates this significant feature of the portraits to the gentry's move away from parading servants as a symbol of wealth.[4] This quality can perhaps best be seen in the portraits of Jane Ebrell seated dourly in front of her half-timbered cottage with mop and broom, or William Williams standing outside his forge, while *Edward Prince* (cat.20) is a successful adaptation of the country-house portrait, with its framing trees and pastoral motifs adapted from classical landscapes to the servant portrait. The self-respect with which Prince holds his axe over his shoulder conveys the dignity of labour, with no hint of the jocular tone of Philip Yorke I's accompanying verses. A crudely painted portrait of a black boy (post-1750) which also hangs in the Servants' Hall was perhaps deliberately acquired by Philip Yorke to represent the black servant who earlier 'blew the horn for John Meller'; the Erddig inscription claiming him as Meller's servant is painted over another identfying him as a certain John Manby.

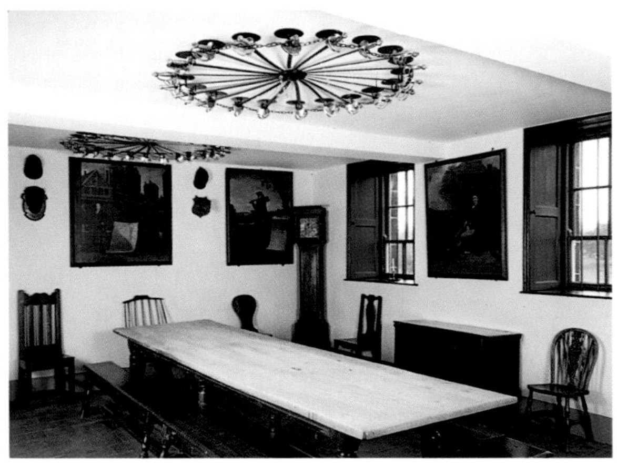

Fig.12 **The Servants' Hall at Erddig, Wrexham**

Many servant portraits must have hung in the servants' hall below stairs. Only at Erddig, however, does a set of servant portraits fill the wall space of this communal room. This room had been used as a servants' hall since 1720. Unlike so many houses, the servants' quarters here were never isolated from the rest of the house.

Further portraits at Erddig

In 1830 three further servant portraits were painted at Erddig by the Welsh artist William Jones (active 1808–30). Although hailing, like Walters, from an artisan background, Jones had trained at the Royal Academy Schools and these portraits are of a much higher quality than their predecessors. As Alastair Laing notes, this lapse of almost forty years before Simon Yorke II (1771–1834) followed in his father's footsteps, requires explanation. Given that he seems to have adopted a preservationist approach to his family's collections, it was in character for him to have commissioned these portraits as a continuation of the earlier series, probably to complete the decoration of the Servants' Hall, instead of taking a positive decision to commemorate his staff as his father had done. With these additions, there is no space in the room for further portraits. Today the series still hangs in the Servants' Hall on the lower ground floor at Erddig, and there seems little doubt that it was intended to hang here from its inception; these reduced-scale full-lengths seem expressly designed for the height of the room (fig.12).

What were the priorities in this second series? Like his father, Simon Yorke chose to represent the male staff with whom he came into daily contact, although he may also have wished to harmonise these paintings with their predecessors by focusing on sitters in the same or comparable offices. The sitters were the carpenter *Thomas Rogers* (cat.21), who was Edward Prince's successor in this office; the gardener *Thomas Pritchard*, who doubled as a beater, and the woodman *Edward Barnes*. Rogers, painted in his carpenter's shop when he was only forty-eight, is a prime exemplar of the loyal servant; he worked until 1871, retiring at the age of ninety after an astonishing seventy-three years of service. The other two sitters were both elderly, sharing a liking for fishing and alcohol and possessed of those colourful personalities that appealed so strongly to the Yorkes.

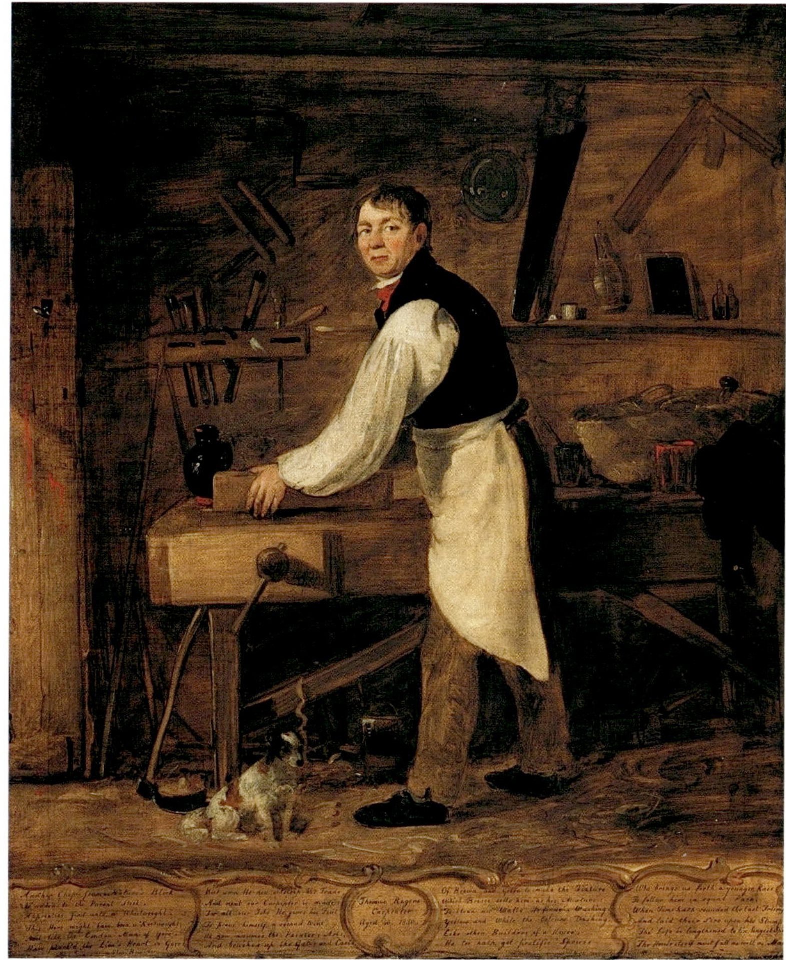

Cat.21 **Thomas Rogers, Estate Carpenter**
William Jones, 1830

This portrait of Thomas Rogers in his carpenter's shop represents a significant departure from the pastoral setting of the earlier Erddig portraits. It is, instead, a confident portrayal of a working man, interrupted only momentarily at his duties. William Jones's depiction is so accurate that Rogers's tools can be identified in racks on the walls. Remarkably, some of these, stamped with Rogers's initials, survive.

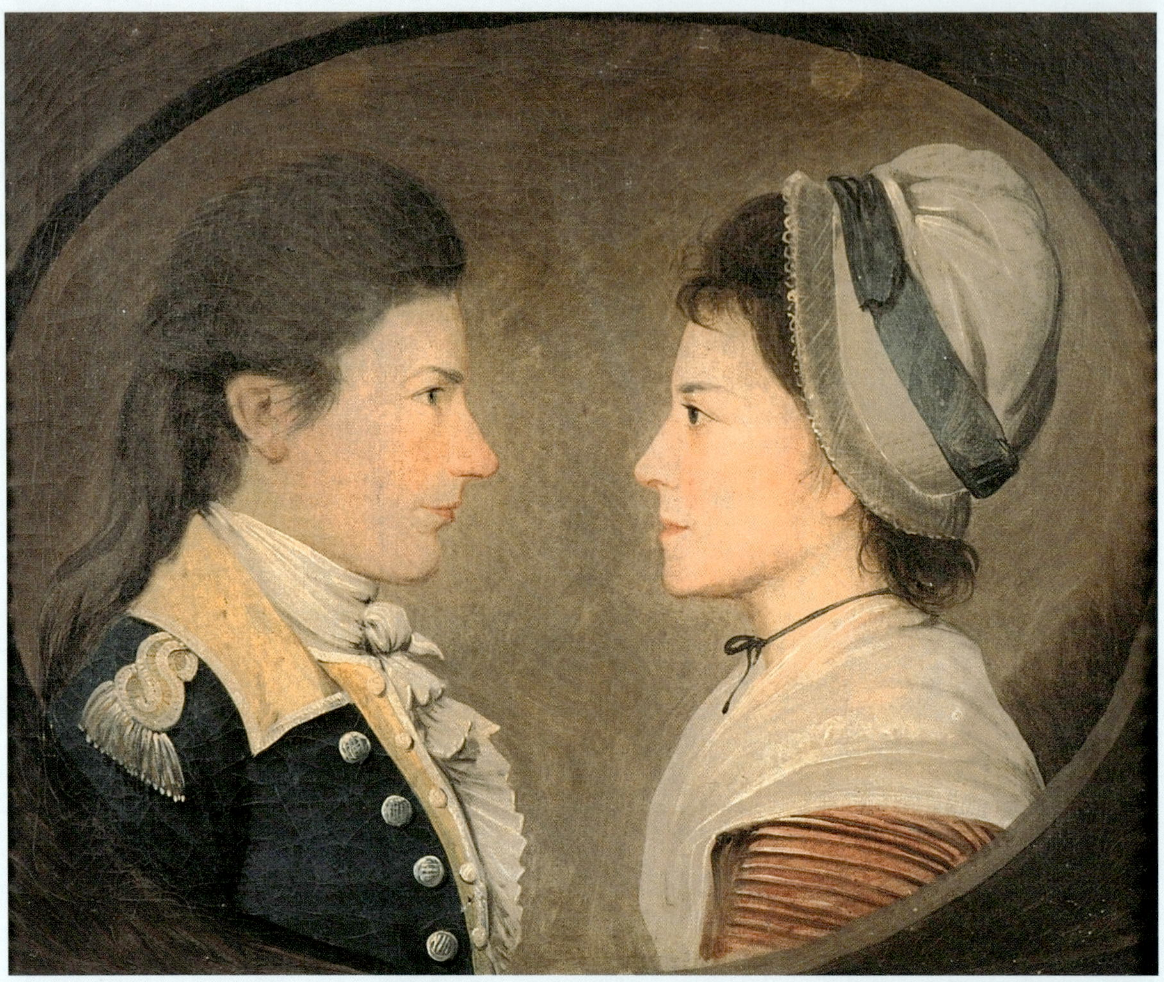

Cat.22 **Two Servants (Daniel Taylor and Elinor Low)**
Arnold Almond, 1783

KNOLE

In 1790 the cantankerous Dr Trusler, in his *London Advisor and Guide*, stressed that caution needed to be shown when developing 'attachments' to servants. Country persons of simple tastes and manners were recommended in order to avoid the problems associated with employing persons who had aspirations to ape the status of their employers. Trusler was, by his own admission, stimulated in his contempt of servants by an embarrassing incident; when visiting a nobleman he mistakenly introduced himself to a finely dressed servant believing him to be his master. Remarks on the capacity of servants to assume fine dress and coiffures were central to the moral and critical discourse on the serving classes in the eighteenth century. Typically, such complaints were accompanied by commentaries on the means by which such menials were able to afford luxuries; laments on the decline of 'subordination', indulgence of masters, profiteering and pilfering amongst servants.

The remarkable series of miniature portraits of the servants of the Duke of Dorset, painted by Arnold Almond in 1783, provide clear evidence of the capacity of eighteenth-century servants in the great English households to assume a fashionable appearance. Most of these portraits of domestics might well, had there not been a clear provenance, have been mistaken for images of the gentry. Even the labourers and outdoor servants have a distinct air of respectability. The surviving twenty-one images constitute the single most valuable visual record of the English servant classes in that century. The loss of over half of the series – there were originally some forty-six paintings – is a tragedy. We are missing, for instance, the portrait of the housekeeper Mary Tartier, second only to the steward in status and pay. Almond's images are refreshingly free of the exaggerated characterisation sometimes encountered in the other great Anglo-Welsh series, the servant portraits at Erddig. His portraits assume their peculiar dignity partially on account of the fact that each servant was not shown with the instruments of their occupation – a record of their roles in the household was provided in the form of a key. We see the person first and can enquire into their particular function later.

The reason why these portraits were made can only be the subject of informed conjecture. As a group they represent the establishment run by William Gardener, the Duke's 'superintendent'. His portrait appears at the head of the list, which functioned as the original manuscript key to the series. Gardener, who entered service in 1735 and had been steward since at least 1765, was a well-educated and accomplished man; his social standing was such that he customarily assumed the title 'esquire'. As inventories show, he had a set of well-appointed rooms at Knole and it may be that these portraits began life as exhibits in his apartments, passing later into the main family collection. We know from accounts that the Duke, under the administration of Gardener, instigated a policy of annually rewarding good service with a gratuity. The tribute of a portrait may be associated with this policy.

In the early 1780s, when the portraits were made, Gardener had an extra function at Knole: he ran the practical affairs of the Duke's mistress, Madame Baccelli. On behalf of the Duke he paid her servants – the portraits of five of these being in the surviving group – and answered her extraordinary tobacco and laundry bills. In the late 1770s and early 1780s the Duke devoted some of his money and energies, and much of his passion, to the relationship with Baccelli, who was, by all accounts, a remarkably sexy theatrical personality. By 1778 Knole was adorned with numerous competing painted portraits of this vivacious woman, and in the mid-1780s these were joined by a more languid image, a hardly decent reclining nude portrait by the sculptor John Baptiste Locatelli. This was made at approximately the same time as Almond's portraits.

The Duke cut an extravagant figure; fashionably dressed and multilingual, his Grand Tour tastes were complemented by a cosmopolitan disregard for conventional sexual morals. In the 1770s and early 1780s, he devoted himself to leisure, avoiding public office; sport, in particular cricket, was his passion. Three cricketers whom he kept as servants at Knole featured in Almond's original group of portraits: John Bowra, described as a shepherd, was employed in catching practice while Fish and Stevens (alias 'Lumpy', who was one of the most famous bowlers of the day) were probably employed to hone the batting skills of the Duke, who opened for the great Hambledon Cricket Club.

Taken together, the portraits convey an impression of a household in pursuit of both cosmopolitan and distinctly English pleasures. A number of foreign servants provided for a life much devoted, if household bills are to be believed, to exotic and Continental culinary tastes. By the testimony of Almond's images, some of the servants seem to have assumed a touch of that erotic glamour evinced by Baccelli. Her attendants Daniel Taylor and Elinor Low are presented as a fashionable couple looking into each other's eyes (cat.22). There is a strong suggestion of a sexual relationship formed outside the realm of marriage, a 'low-life' equivalent to that of their master and mistress. A compilation of over-dressed, possibly licentious, urbane, foreign characters, these servants constitute the inverse to the household of simple and obedient drones which the moralistic Dr Trusler was to recommend in 1790.

MATTHEW CRASKE

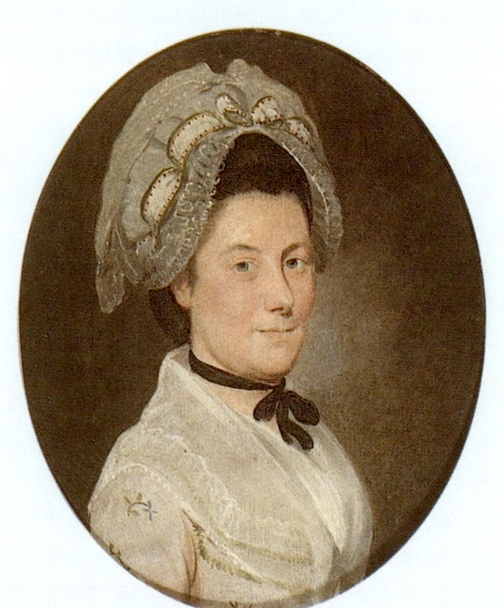

Cat.23 **Mary Hayes, Housemaid**
Arnold Almond, 1783

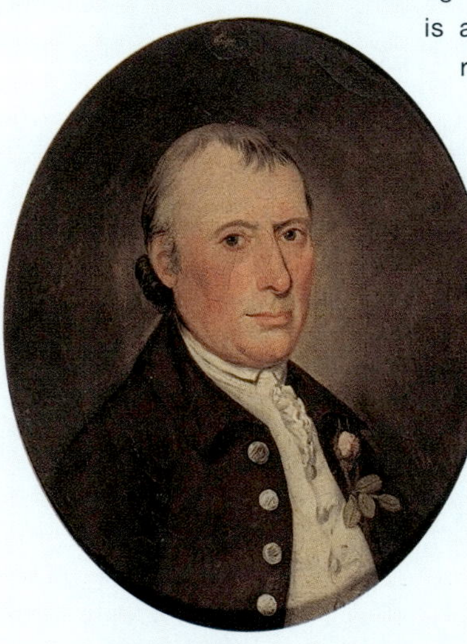

Cat.24 **John Holt, Gardener (?)**
Arnold Almond, 1783

The view we receive of the Yorkes' relations with their servants from these portraits and their accompanying verses is one-sided from the employers' perspective. Only by combining this with surviving documents which confirm their true concern for their staff, can one conclude, in Waterson's words, that Erddig was probably 'genuinely one community' throughout the period when these remarkable images of servanthood were produced.

Bramham Park

Several members of the Lane Fox family of Bramham Park in Yorkshire were Masters of the Bramham Moor Hunt, and Bramham shared with Lyme Park and Bowhill a tradition of recording its sporting servants over several generations. Among the distinguished artists who worked for the family were George Stubbs and J.L. Agasse (1767–1849), while the Lane Foxes were still recording a long-serving huntsman in 1902. However, the set of seven servant portraits painted at Bramham *c.*1822 by another leading sporting artist, George Garrard (1760–1826), stands out from these other commissions.[5] Although the sitters chosen in these intimate, small-scale full-lengths are mostly estate staff (the coachman *William Fox*, the gatekeeper *William Wright*, the head gardener *Mr Chambers*, another gardener (cat.25) and a cheerful carter who presumably owes his inclusion to his close association with the below-stairs household), two key indoor servants are also included: the housekeeper *Mrs Brown* (cat.26) and the steward *John Pollock*. This set comes closer than any other to providing an anatomy of a whole household, clearly defining each servant's role and place within it, and offering a subtle grasp of the nuances of servant hierarchy. While the portraits at Knole (cats 22, 23, 24) cover more household offices, they are only bust-length, and do not feature the sitter's environment. Five of these portraits were recently purchased for the collection at Temple Newsam, together with a sixth portrait of an elderly retired domestic smoking a pipe by the Yorkshire artist John Widdas of Hull, apparently painted later to match Garrard's format.

Both Garrard and John Widdas spent extended periods at Bramham in the early 1820s, painting (and occasionally sculpting) the Lane Fox family. It seems likely that the Garrard servant portraits are the impromptu offshoot of these other commissions, which would have been

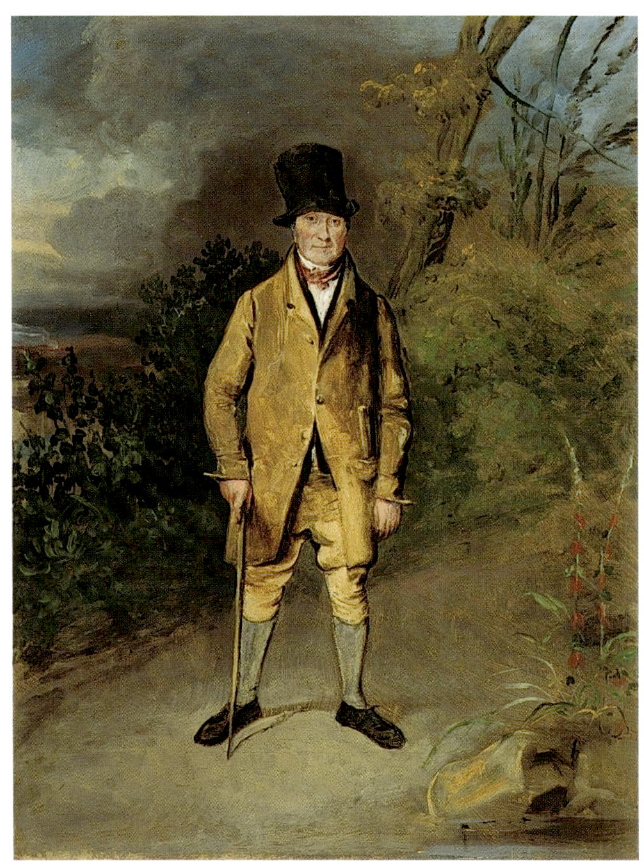

Cat.25 **A Gardener at Bramham Park, Yorkshire**
George Garrard, *c.*1822

Garrard included two gardeners in his Bramham series: a head gardener and the assistant shown here. Whereas the head gardener stands on the terrace wearing a tail coat and breeches, his subordinate wears a loose working coat and stands in a less formal part of the garden. Both men, however, sport the distinctive top hat associated with their profession.

considered his principal employment there. It is just possible the impetus came from Garrard himself and that the set commemorates his friendship with the servants who must have looked after him during his visit. However, it is much more probable that these seven portraits were commissioned from Garrard by the young George Lane Fox (1793–1848) himself. James Lomax has suggested that they are a 'testimony to the good relations which must have existed on either side of the green baize door at this time'. However, Fox was a gambler, not a benevolent employer in the Erddig mould, like his eponymous son; a closer parallel here seems to be with Dudmaston (see pp. 58–60), where the tenure of another extravagant young sportsman also caused servant portraiture to flourish.

Three further portraits from Bramham probably post-date the disastrous fire of 1828 and hence represent another addition to Garrard's original set. The sitters were the Bramham keeper Sammy Pickard, an earth-stopper David Woodall and a footman carrying a set of silver serving dishes on a tray. These paintings, clearly by a different hand, are ascribed by family tradition to 'Lascelles the Footman Painter', presumably the sitter in this latter portrait. Given that the Bramham estates adjoin Harewood, seat of the Lascelles family, it has been suggested that the putative artist was an illegitimate scion of this family. If this were true, these would represent the only known examples of servants portrayed by one of their fellows.

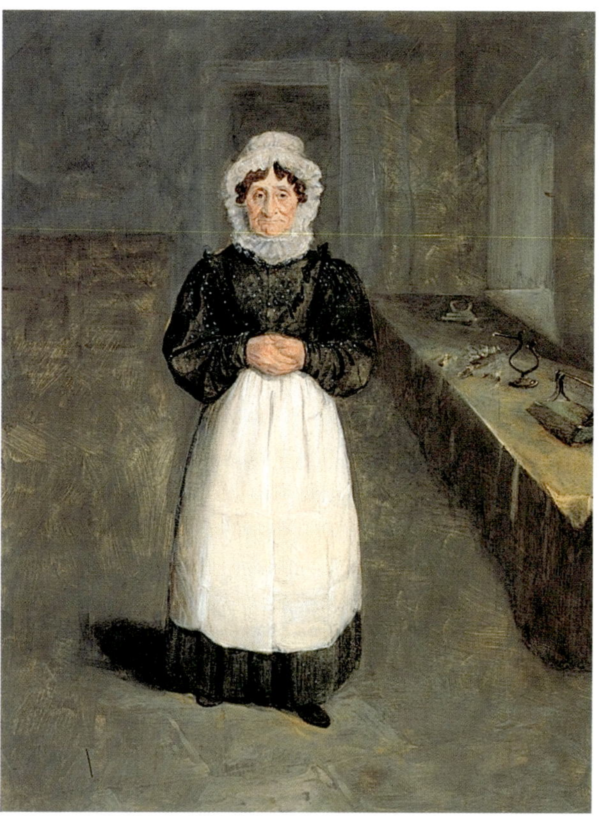

Cat.26 **Mrs Brown, the Housekeeper at Bramham Park, Yorkshire**
George Garrard, 1822

Mrs Brown is shown, presumably on a tour of inspection, in the Dry Laundry at Bramham containing a mangle and flat irons on the bench along the wall. Garrard's portrayal of the elderly housekeeper is unflinching. Her severe, high-necked gown with an apron and deliberately out-of-date cap, reflect her dignity, discretion and distance from the junior members of staff.

The individual image

Images recording faithful, long-serving individual family employees were painted in the same period as the serial portraits discussed above. Length of service and longevity were important factors, along with the sitter's role within the household. However, the reason for commissioning portraits of individual servants often focused not just on their role, but on qualities which set them apart from their fellows, while occasionally one servant could be taken as an exemplar for the whole below stairs community. Failings such as excessive drinking seem occasionally to have been as important as devoted service in determining representation. Only two examples of individual servant portraiture – reflecting the indoor/outdoor dichotomy – can be included here: John Riley's very early 'Necessary Woman' *Bridget Holmes* and James Northcote's portrait of keeper *Robert Shaw*, apparently the only servant to be recorded in triplicate.

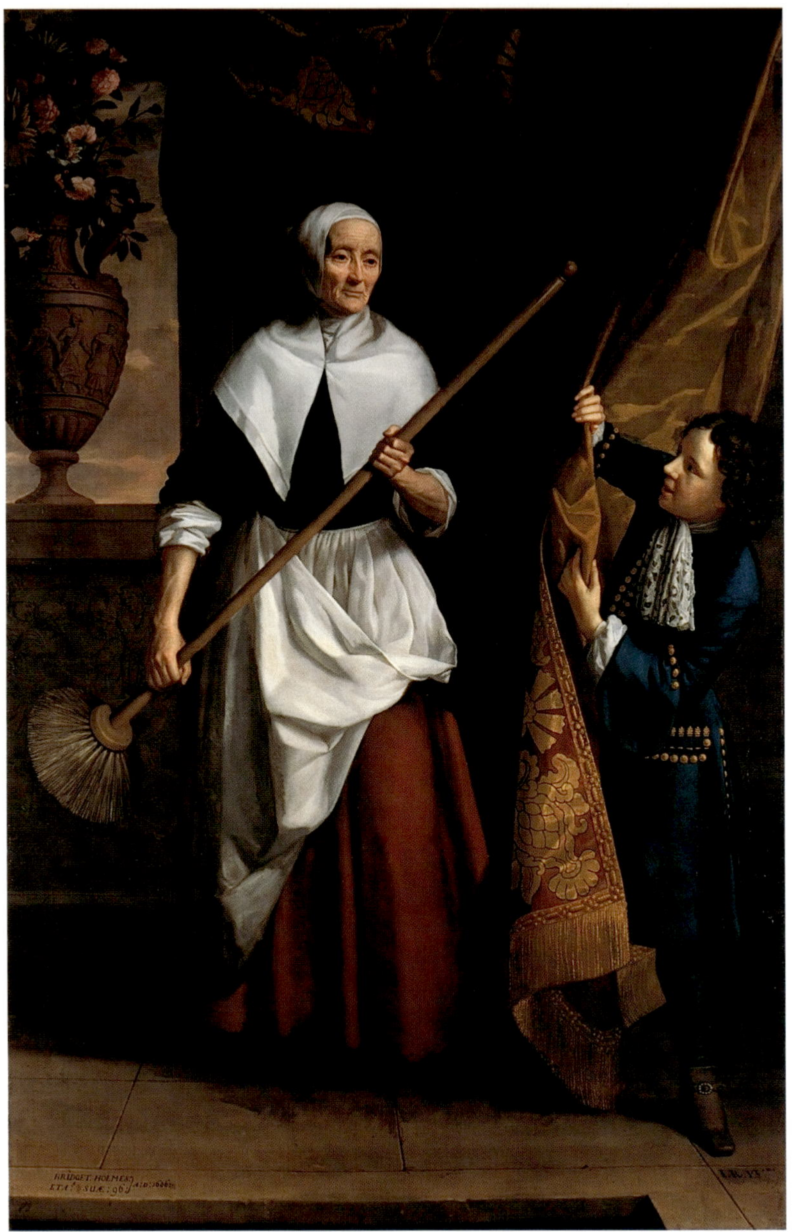

Cat.27 **Bridget Holmes**
John Riley, 1686

In this parody of fashionable portraiture, Bridget Holmes wields her mop playfully against a mischievous page who peeps out at her from behind a curtain. This may be the Page of the Backstairs, Tobias Rustat. In contrast to the housemaid, he is smartly dressed in contemporary fashion. The device of showing a secondary figure hiding from the protagonist is common in Dutch seventeenth-century genre painting.

A parody of a Baroque portrait

Bridget Holmes is one of the most remarkable portraits of the seventeenth century. Painted in 1686 by John Riley (1646–91), it represents a ninety-six-year-old 'Necessary Woman', whose task it was to dispose of the contents of chamberpots. Her career as one of the lower servants in the royal household began in the reign of Charles I and ended only under William and Mary. Bridget Holmes died in the year of her centenary, four years after this portrait was painted. With its prominent inscription

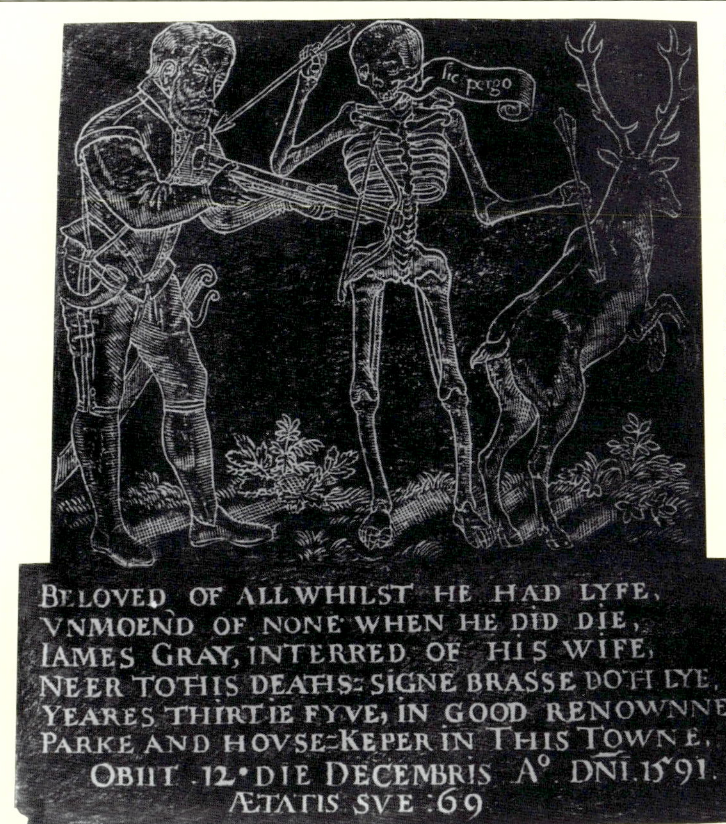

Fig.13 **Brass Rubbing at Hunsdon Church, Hertfordshire, commemorating the 'Parke and Hovse [horse] Keper' James Gray**
Unknown artist, 1591

This remarkably early example of the close rapport and loyalty between landowner and huntsman that later produced so many servant pictures is the only known record of a servant in a memorial brass. Gray is shown in the course of his duties, pointing a crossbow at a stag, but is himself about to be pierced with an arrow by Death, who, as on many tombs of the period, is shown as a skeleton.

giving her age, this might appear to be a paradigm of the portrait of the long-lived and long-serving employee.[6] The sitter's longevity in an age which revelled in recording nature in its more extreme manifestations was at least as important a factor as her loyalty in prompting this commission. She must also have stood out as one of a minority of women employed in a royal household which had recently undergone extensive retrenchments.

Given the portrait's date and known presence in the royal collection as early as the reign of Queen Anne (when it hung in a prominent position in Prince Georges's Eating Room), *Bridget Holmes* was presumably a direct commission from James II during his brief reign from 1685 to 1688. Indeed, the king commissioned a second portrait from Riley of a much more senior servant, *Katherine Elliott*, who as nurse to James himself and Dresser and Woman of the Bedchamber successively to his two wives, would have occupied a much closer relationship to the royal family. Far from being a straightforward portrait of a faithful aged retainer, *Bridget Holmes* is an exercise in the mock-heroic; the sitter is shown full-length in a portrait that deploys the full panoply of fashionable Baroque portraiture and pokes fun at all such pretensions. The grandiose setting of cascading damask curtain, column and vase complete with a classical frieze is belied by the

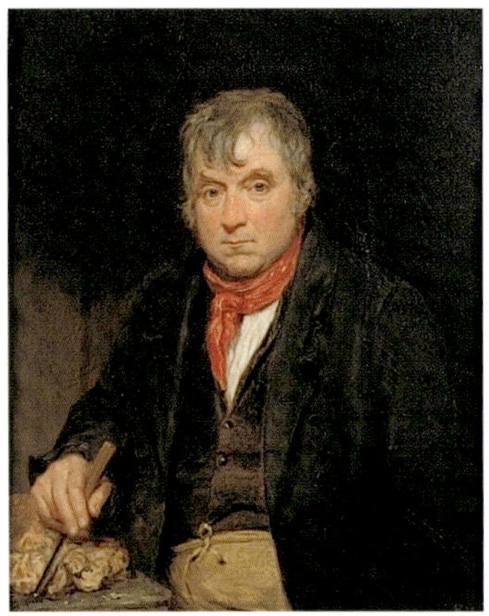

Cat.28 **Jonathan Ritson, Wood-carver**
George Clint, *c.*1830

Ritson (*c.*1780–1846), a talented woodcarver, worked firstly at Arundel Castle and then for Lord Egremont at Petworth. This painting was commissioned by Egremont, with one of Grinling Gibbons, for the Carved Room at Petworth where Ritson supplemented Gibbons's carving. The picture exemplifies the landowner's celebration of a brilliantly gifted employee.

appearance of the aged servant, dressed in a very plain, old-fashioned gown, a prominent 'neckerchief', and the coif and apron that had been standard maid's wear for generations. However, her quiet dignity and unidealised features confirm that although Riley was noted for his unadorned likenesses and may therefore have enjoyed poking fun at the Baroque excesses of his chief rivals in portraiture, the humour was not at her expense.

Robert Shaw, Keeper of the Forest of Bowland

An astonishing record in paint of faithful service is provided by three paintings by James Northcote (1746–1831) of the keeper *Robert Shaw*, who appears in an exceptional half-length portrait (cat.29), a small oil study and an ambitious sporting painting in imitation of Frans Snijders entitled *Buck Hunting in the Forest of Bowland*. When this was exhibited at the Royal Academy in 1806, Shaw was described as the 'late keeper, represented at the age of 84'.[7] Clearly, Shaw was a much-loved servant; however, his place in the collection at Browsholme Hall almost certainly owed more to

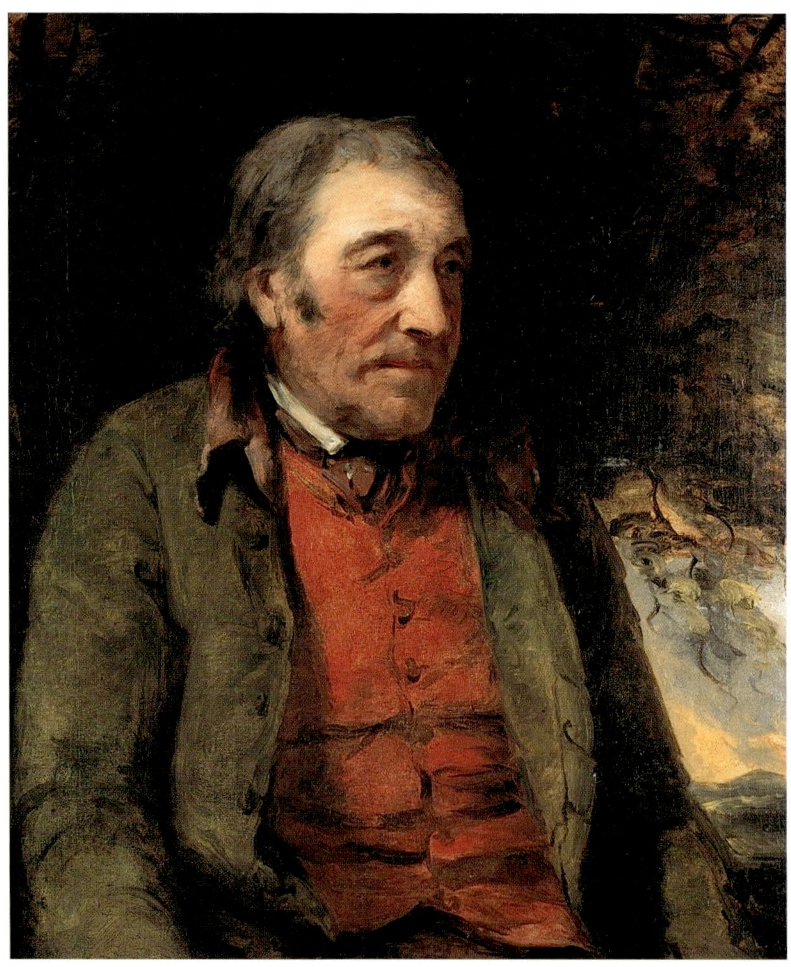

Cat.29 **Robert Shaw, Keeper of the Forest of Bowland**
James Northcote, *c.*1806

Wearing distinctive livery comprising a crimson waistcoat and green coat with a maroon collar, Shaw appears against a backdrop of trees and the Lancashire hills in a composition strongly influenced by Sir Joshua Reynolds, whose pupil Northcote was. Given that an oil sketch close to this finished composition is in full-length format, this may orginally have been intended as a larger-scale portrait.

his long tenure as Keeper of the Forest of Bowland, west of Browsholme, Lancashire, seat in the early nineteenth century of Shaw's employer, Thomas Lister Parker. The Parkers held the office of Bowbearer with jurisdiction over the Forest under the Forester, the Duke of Buccleuch. Together with its pendant, Northcote's double portrait of Parker's friends *The Rev. Dixon Hoste and William Assheton Out Rough Shooting With Their Dogs*, the portrait *Robert Shaw* dominated the Dining Room at Browsholme, demonstrating the principal features of sporting life in this hunting preserve – grouse shooting and deer stalking.

A colourful Regency figure and friend of the Prince Regent, Parker's profligacy bankrupted the family estates and soon dried up the flow of fancy and sporting pictures and portraits he commissioned from Northcote between 1801 and 1809. It seems likely that Northcote's two portraits of Shaw were an offshoot either of *Buck Hunting* itself or of another of these commissions; neither is recorded in Northcote's account book.[8]

The Buccleuch servants

In the early nineteenth century a particularly important group of servant portraits was commissioned by one of the wealthiest and most aristocratic families in Britain. A senior branch of the Scott family became Dukes of Buccleuch in 1663, later adding (through marriage) the dukedom of Queensberry. In Scotland they owned (and still own) great houses at Dalkeith Palace, close to Edinburgh, which was their principal residence in the eighteenth and nineteenth centuries, at Bowhill in the Scottish borders, and further west at Drumlanrig Castle in Dumfriesshire. The 3rd Duke of Buccleuch, known as Duke Henry, who held the title from 1751 to 1812, was famously painted as a young man by Gainsborough in the guise of a 'man of feeling'. The portrait was not deceptive, since he was widely admired for his goodness and his generosity to the poor. He was a close friend and frequent correspondent of his kinsman, the writer Sir Walter Scott, whose baronial house Abbotsford in the Scottish Borders is close to the Buccleuch seat of Bowhill. Walter Scott was also a friend of the 4th Duke, another man of strong character and high intelligence, who died young in 1819; Scott took a paternal interest in the 4th Duke's successor, 'little Duke Walter'.[9]

Walter Scott may well have contributed to the Buccleuchs' interest in commemorating people who worked for them. This was an interest of

Cat.30 **Peter Mathieson, Coachman to Sir Walter Scott with Donald the Pony**
G.D., 1851

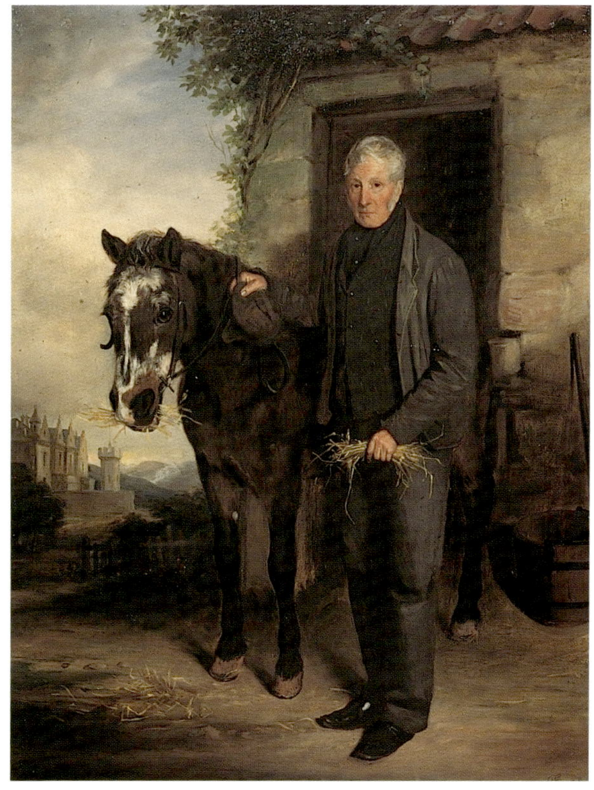

Cat.31 **Thomas Hudson, Keeper at Bowhill**
William Douglas, 1810

This vivacious little portrait by a Scottish artist who specialised in miniatures shows the favourite gamekeeper of the 4th Duke of Buccleuch at Bowhill in the Scottish borders. Hudson was also a poet, whose work was commended by Walter Scott. The Buccleuchs commemorated their gamekeepers and huntsmen for over two centuries.

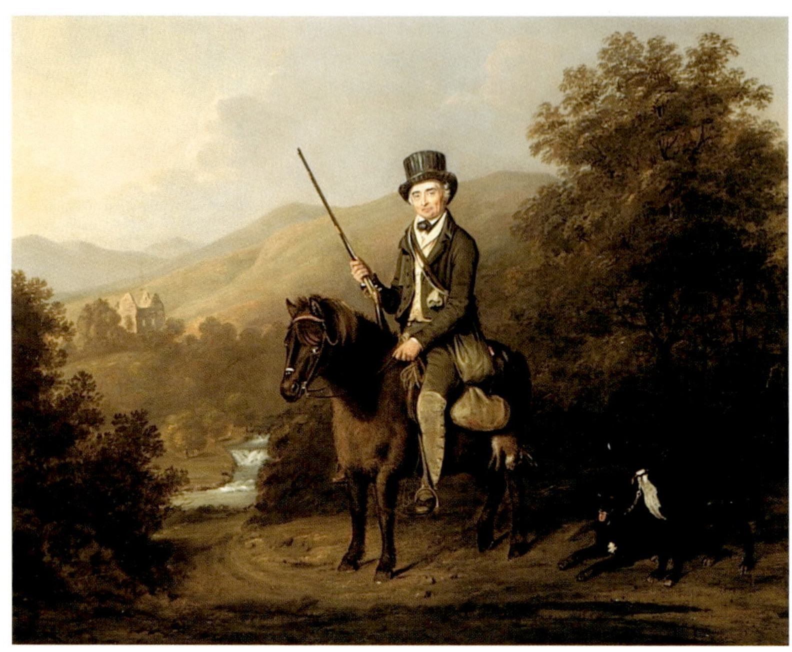

Scott himself: he enjoyed very close and friendly relations with his staff, notably his gamekeeper Tom Purdie, whose portrait he commissioned from C.R. Leslie. The tradition was continued after his death, when in 1851 portraits of Peter Mathieson, Scott's coachman (cat.30), and John Swanston, his gamekeeper, were commissioned by Scott's son-in-law and biographer J.G. Lockhart, and hung in the Ante-Room to the Armoury at Abbotsford as part of the creation of a shrine to Scott's memory within the house. Scott's interest in Scotland's rural traditions and his belief in country people as representatives of the best values of the old Scotland must have influenced the attitudes of these dukes to their households.

From the late eighteenth century onwards, successive Dukes of Buccleuch, commissioned several images of members of their households, especially those at Dalkeith House and Bowhill. Their patronage was highly individual in character, not least in the choice of sitters. From Duke Henry's time until well into the twentieth century, the family systematically developed an existing fashion by commissioning a series of portraits of their keepers and huntsmen. An extended set of such images hangs today (as they have since at least the nineteenth century) in the entrance hall at Bowhill, in the room traditionally given to representatives of life out of doors. Bowhill was particularly suitable as the home of this set since it is only a few miles from the kennels of the Duke of Buccleuch's Hunt at Saint Boswells. The most imposing image is a portrait of *William Williamson*, huntsman from 1816 to 1862: his length and excellence of service is celebrated by the fact that it was painted by Sir Francis Grant, and that it hangs in the most prominent position, over the fireplace, where it is flanked by two of Williamson's successors in the post (both of whom served for around forty years). Less ambitious is the small and intimately humorous image of *Thomas Hudson, Keeper at Bowhill*, painted in 1810 by William Douglas (cat.31). A draconian preserver of the family's property,[10] Hudson was a favourite of the 4th Duke and an amateur poet in whose work Walter Scott found 'a wild poetical turn'.[11]

The most united set of Buccleuch images is the series painted between 1817 and 1820, by the somewhat obscure Edinburgh artist John Ainslie. Here the family chose a type of sitter hardly found elsewhere, and certainly not as a series: the professional advisers to the family. The portraits must have been intended as a set: they use a standard half-length format with the sitters all wearing sober dress and dour expressions, and are uniformly framed. The subjects are Major Walter Scott (who may have been an illegitimate member of the family), Bailie William Tait of Pirn, who was Chamberlain (estate manager) of the Dalkeith Estate, Dr Graham of Dalkeith (the family physician) and a certain Signor Guistinelli, reputedly aged 103, though his position is not known. These men were closely tied to the family on whom their positions primarily depended: Graham, for example, was the medical adviser to the 4th Duke during his decline into ill health (Walter Scott considered him insufficiently decisive) and the Duke was godfather to his son. By the beginning of the twentieth century, these works hung together in the House Steward's Room at Dalkeith House.[12]

Perhaps the most memorable work in this series is another portrait by John Ainslie.[13] Also painted in 1817, it shows one of the uppermost of upper servants. This is Joseph Florance, the celebrated French chef to three Dukes of Buccleuch. French chefs were employed only by the grandest of the aristocracy and plutocracy: in 1837 a male French chef might expect to be paid between £150 and £200, compared to a house steward (one of the most senior members of a household) on £75 and a housekeeper on £40. Within this distinguished group, Florance was, according to Scott, 'of high distinction in his profession'.[14] The two men enjoyed a friendly relationship: when Scott visited Drumlanrig after writing *Guy Mannering*, the chef created a dish called *Potage à la Meg Merrilies de Derncleugh* based on one described by Scott in the novel: it consisted 'of game and poultry of all kinds, stewed with vegetables into a soup, which rivals in savour and richness the gallant messes of Camachos's wedding ...'[15] In his notes to later editions of the novel, Scott acknowledged this culinary tribute.

The image of Florance is one of the most memorable of servant portraits, and a tribute to high professionalism (cat.32). Shown in bold outline, he wears a brown fur hat above his chef's white coat and, in the cord round his waist, a cooking knife for gutting the animals (possibly a playful reference to the sword worn by an aristocratic sitter). He points dramatically to the menu for a dinner which lists numerous dishes, some named after the family, including '*Croquettes à la Montagu*'. On the kitchen table in front

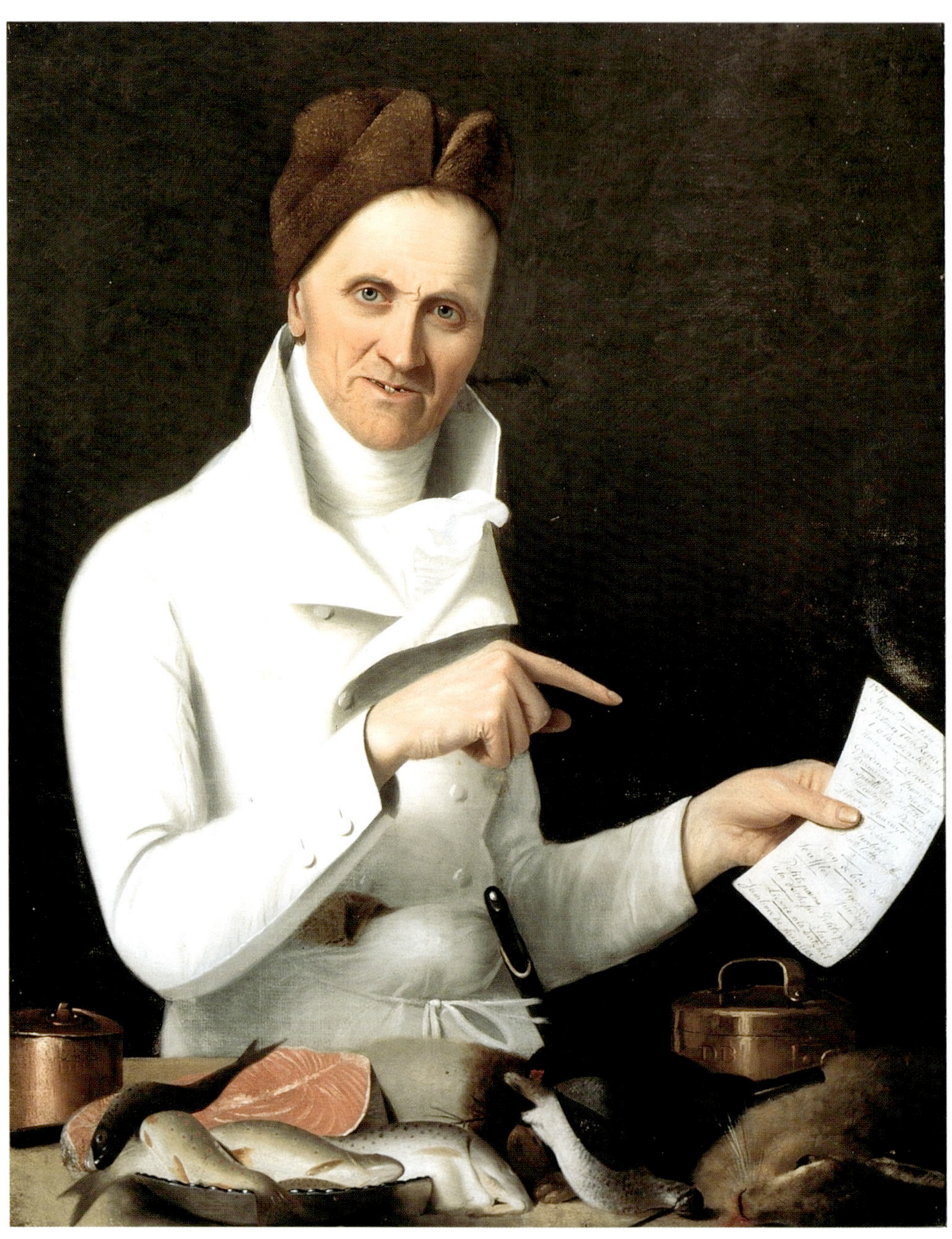

Cat.32 **Joseph Florance**
John Ainslie, 1817

of him lie, as though in a seventeenth-century Dutch still-life, the snipe, hare, mallard and turbot needed for these dishes, besides a saucepan and casserole monogrammed DB (for Duke of Buccleuch). Florance was more than a chef, he was a friend. When the 4th Duke travelled to Lisbon during his last illness to try to recover his health, Florance accompanied him. In 1827, having served three generations of the family, he held a position of sufficient confidence to be able to write a long letter to the 5th Duke,

'My Lord, According to your Grace's desire and my fervent wish that the establishment of your house when it takes place should be so arranged that you can do it yourself without much trouble.

It must be gratifying to a Nobleman to know how he stands with the world, with his income, and with his expences. To facilitate this, the greatest regularity must be established and your Grace must set the example of enforcing your commands, your Orders will always be given with moderation and reflection …

My plan is simple & will be gratifying to all honest men. The expenses of your household must be laid before your Grace once a week without the exception of a farthing. For the day I should recommend tuesday, on monday the steward will gather the bills, and your secretary will arrange them so that you may see the whole at one view. By the same means if there are errors, irregularities or false dealing, all will be discovered … You ought to see and know every thing, not alone in your cabinet, but at your table servants are much more inclined to listen to what is passing than to attend to their duty. If they are not attentive, not clean, or not in proper time at their post your Grace may be assured that the Master's eye is better than much gold.

All will depend upon yourself to make your Household a happy one, if you have a bad servant part with him, a diseased sheep spoils a whole flock … Your servants should be men of ability, particularly your Cook, he ought to have a perfect knowledge of his Profession, a real good Cook is always the cheapest …

I should strongly advise that the master Cook should wait at table when there is company, an epicure wishes to know of what the dishes are composed of …

I regret that I am so old, but still it would be the happiest day of my life if I could be useful to the son of my late Master's father, and Grandfather, and my benefactors …

Your attached and faithful servant
J. Florance, Grove July 22nd 1827

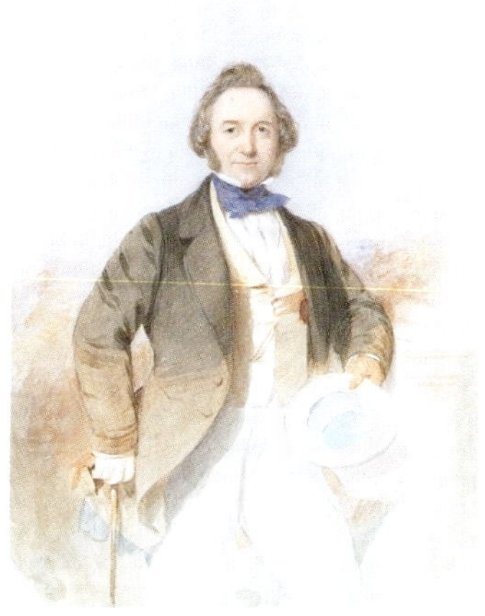

Cat.33 **Joseph Paxton**
Octavius Oakley, *c.*1850

From being gardener to the Duke of Devonshire, Paxton became designer of the Crystal Palace and of country houses for the Rothschilds. Paxton is a prime example of the occasional flexibility of the class system in the case of notable ability, and of the help sometimes offered to servants by employers.

who was about to celebrate his coming of age, advising him on the management of his household (cat.133). Florance may be compared with Sir Joseph Paxton (1803–65), head gardener to and close friend of the 6th Duke of Devonshire, who rose by his abilities not only to achieve a high position of trust within a ducal household but to become an internationally celebrated engineer and architect. Paxton acquired a landed estate and was elected to Parliament.

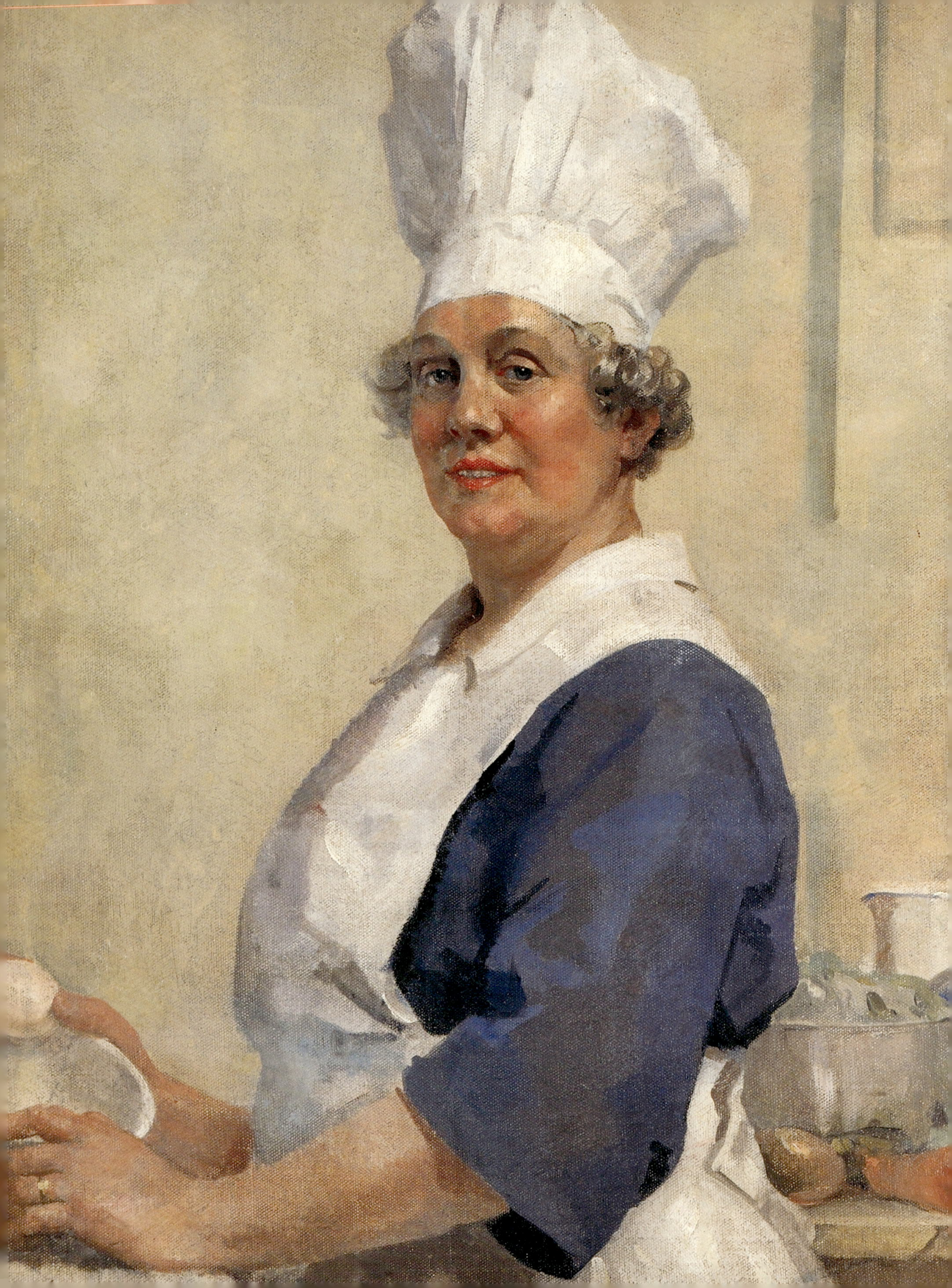

4 SERVANTS IN INSTITUTIONS

Giles Waterfield

IN THE SEVENTEENTH AND eighteenth centuries, the control and administration of public affairs moved gradually away from the Court (and on a local level, from great households) to a variety of public and semi-public bodies. At the same time, numerous new types of institution emerged, providing for the needs of a society based on commerce rather than agriculture, and an increasing urban population. As these novel institutions developed, they shared many of the characteristics of the large private household: notably in the organisation of their staff and in attitudes to employees. Behind the impressive façades of banks, colleges, clubs and museums existed little communities that were not dissimilar to private households, and it is not surprising that many of these 'public' bodies sought to commemorate those who worked for them. And as private establishments have contracted or disappeared in the twentieth century, some of the institutions considered in this section have survived, with structures similar to those that they had three or four hundred years ago.

From medieval times, institutions of various types employed people who carried out functions closely related to those of the private domestic servant – indeed the term 'servant' was often used into the eighteenth century to mean any person employed by an institution, rather than just a domestic servant. This applied to monasteries and convents, and to colleges which for many years had monastic (though not necessarily abstemious) constitutions. The standards of loyalty expected in private households, and the practice of commemorative portraiture, existed also in institutions. On the other hand, the nature of the loyalty convention and of the associated portraiture show interesting variations, with the servant sometimes elevated to the status of a symbol for their institution.

The institutions which deserve study in this context are generally private associations or collegiate bodies rather than publicly funded state organisations. The majority were for many years all-male institutions,

OPPOSITE Detail of cat.36 **The Arts Club's Woman Chef**
Francis Edward Hodge, 1935

with women playing almost no part until the late nineteenth century (at the earliest). Among the bodies that occasionally commemorated their junior staff were old-established academic institutions such as Oxford and Cambridge colleges, and the old 'public schools', including Eton and Winchester colleges, generally founded in the late medieval period on the same principles as universities' colleges. The seventeenth century saw the emergence of new types of institution, such as a national bank and cultural organisations, with the foundation of the Ashmolean Museum in 1683, followed by the British Museum in 1753 and the Royal Academy of Arts in 1768. Here again, junior members of the establishment were found worthy of record.

Over the same period, the focus of entertainment and informal power-broking for fashionable society gradually moved away from the Court to commercial or private meeting-places. These included (for men) the coffee houses which emerged in London from the Restoration onwards, and (for both sexes) places of entertainment such as the ultra-fashionable Almack's Club in London (founded in the early 1760s by William Almack, who, significantly, had been valet to a duke). Their successors, the gentlemen's clubs of London, Edinburgh and other cities began as gaming houses but in the early nineteenth century came to offer comfortable alternatives to domesticity for a controlled membership. Here again, the domestic staff were and are painted or photographed. Even inns, restaurants and hotels occasionally adopted the practice, a reminder that servant portraiture should be seen in a broader context. In 1760 Joseph Wright of Derby (1734–97) was commissioned to paint 'Old John', head waiter at the King's Head, a coaching inn in Derby: the picture was to be raffled, presumably for the sitter's benefit.[1] In a different vein, which anticipates nineteenth- and twentieth-century images of club servants, portraits of two waiters at Ye Olde Cheshire Cheese, a chop house in the Strand in London, were painted during the 1820s. One of these, by the Strand artist Thomas Charles Wageman (1787–1863), shows William Simpson, in whose honour the picture was executed, standing confidently, as though pausing from his duties, in one of the dining-rooms.[2] The pose, and the relationship between the sitter and the setting which defines his identity, are close to the contemporary depictions of servants at Erddig and Bramham Park (see chapter 3).

Fig.14 **William Simpson, a Waiter at Ye Olde Cheshire Cheese**
Thomas Charles Wageman, 1829

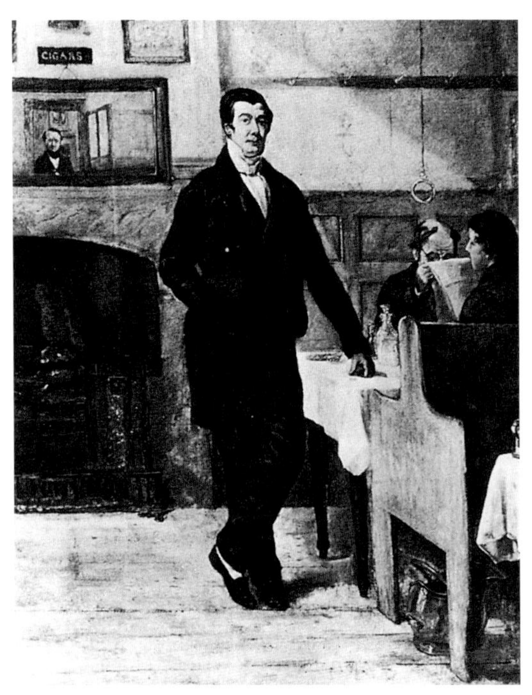

For many of the bodies that emerged in the seventeenth and eighteenth centuries and were concerned with public administration, or naval and military affairs, as well as for older educational centres, a sense of identity was stimulated by the creation of images of their most important members. These might be generals and admirals, heads of colleges, Governors of the Bank of England or officers of clubs. This approach parallels the accumulation of a corpus of portraits of the members of a landed family. As one might expect, subordinate employees were less often featured, but frequently the people employed in domestic or quasi-domestic posts as housekeepers, cooks, porters, parlour messengers or bullion porters, stayed in their posts for extended periods and impressed their characters on the institution (in a way which was less true of the domestic household). Quite often, they were recorded in images. The criteria which apply to the domestic servant re-emerge: length of service, longevity, a close working relationship with their seniors, and in some cases their strong individuality.

College servants

Probably the largest group of portraits of this type belong to the old colleges. In comparison with the practice of private employers, the number of servants depicted by these colleges is proportionately quite large, especially in the later period. In the seventeenth century (when the first such images emerge), all the colleges employed a number of 'common servants'. The term distinguished them from the servitors (at Oxford University) and sizars (at Cambridge), poor scholars who earned their fees and maintenance by providing domestic service for richer members of the institution (and who seem never to have been depicted in that role).

The employment of non-academic servants was often laid down in college statutes which stipulated the appointment of a manciple (equivalent to a steward) and a butler (junior to the manciple, and in charge of the buttery), as well as a barber and laundress. This was a regular pattern in the sixteenth and seventeenth centuries, though the number of such employees was often small. In the 1690s each college might have around fourteen such servants, though it might be as few as four, assisted by outside casual staff as well as choristers (who in the Middle Ages were expected to make the college fellows' beds).[3] As members of college foundations with positions ordained by the statutes, the 'common servants' received substantial privileges and enjoyed a higher status than equivalents in private households. They were closer in status to college fellows (who were also paid employees) than domestic servants were to private individuals.

Actual or allegorical servants helped to define a college's character. As we have seen, the symbolic importance of a servant is proclaimed by the image of *The Trusty Servant* at Winchester College (cat.1). One of the earliest portraits of an actual employee is John Riley's *The Scullion at Christ Church*, Oxford (cat.34), of the 1680s. This is a remarkable document of the college's attachment to a junior member of staff (whose name is not recorded). He is shown in unidealised dress (a patched coat, with mittens on his hands, possibly to protect them while he polished silver),[4] and yet in no way derided. He holds a piece of plate as though it were a badge of office. His close association with the college – indeed perhaps his

Cat.34 The Scullion at Christ Church
John Riley, *c.*1680s

The scullion was a menial member of staff, but scullions of remarkable character or length of service were sometimes painted. Christ Church, Oxford (in the background), was the centre of Protestant opposition to the Catholic King James II, and this man is traditionally identified as a symbol of the College's resistance to tyranny.

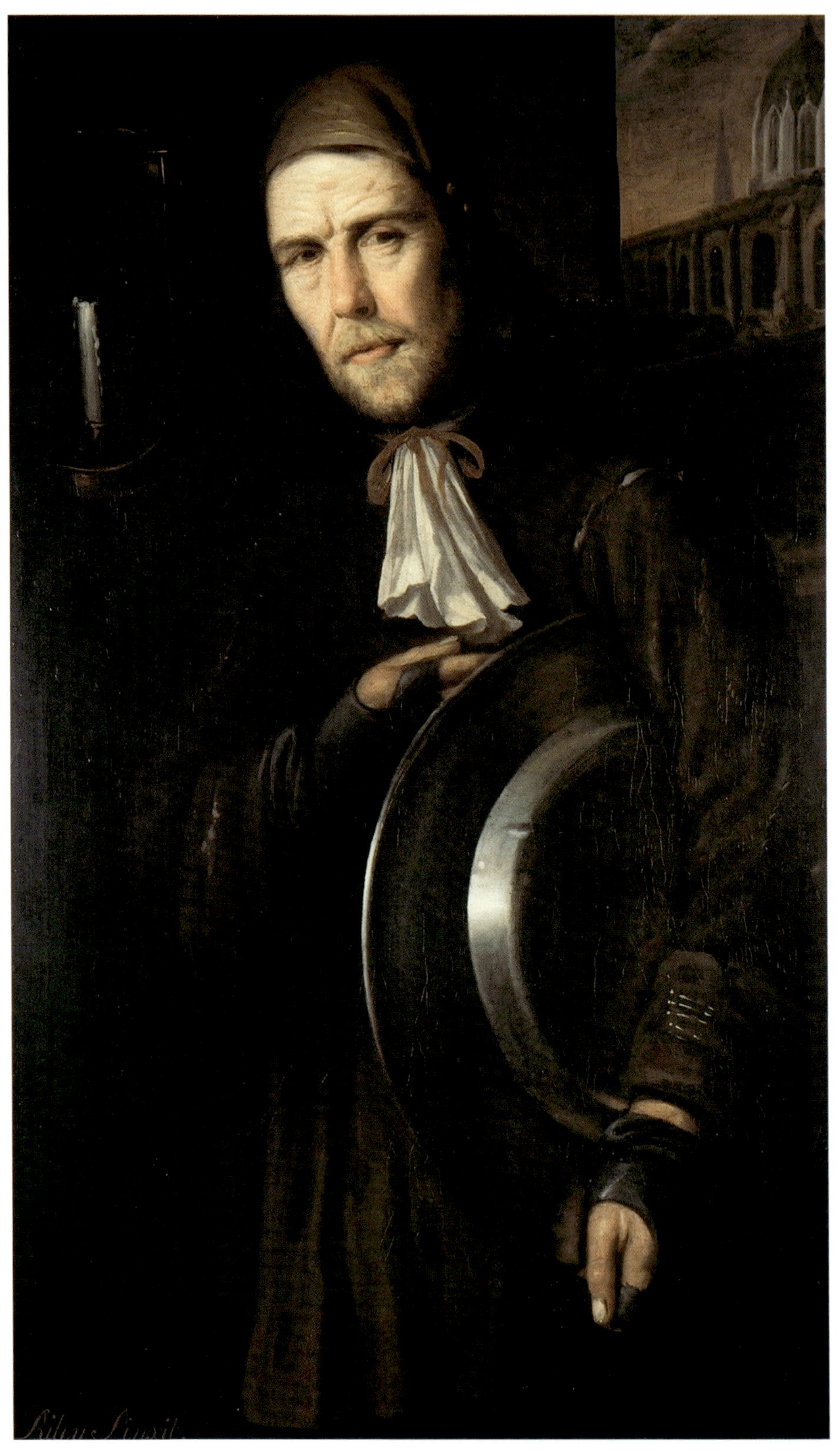

status as its representative – is conveyed by the depiction of its sixteenth-century entrance block crowned by Tom Tower, very recently completed by Christopher Wren. There may be a particular significance to this image, painted at a time of political and religious disturbance. During his short reign from 1685 to 1688, James II attempted to impose a Catholic regime on the strongly Protestant University of Oxford, and appointed a Roman Catholic Dean to Christ Church in 1686. Christ Church was not only the largest and richest Oxford college at the time, but one of the centres of opposition to the royal tyranny. The loyal scullion, who was reputed to sing 'Satirical and Political Ballads against the party of James II', at a time when it was not safe to do so, may have been intended to stand as a symbol of the College's virtues and adherence to the Protestant faith. Such an approach would develop, in a portrait of a known individual of ironically humble status, the emblematic theme of the faithful servant, the 'common man' as embodiment of truth.[5] A comparable though less highly charged image, painted at the same period, is the anonymous portrait of Edward Wise, College Butler at Eton, who died in 1684. Here the butler (a statutory member of the establishment, wearing livery) personifies the college by representing the hospitality of this old-established royal foundation. He holds a 'Strangers' Cup' and a piece of bread offered on a knife, the two traditionally symbolising the welcome offered to an arriving guest and, by extension, to the world in general.[6]

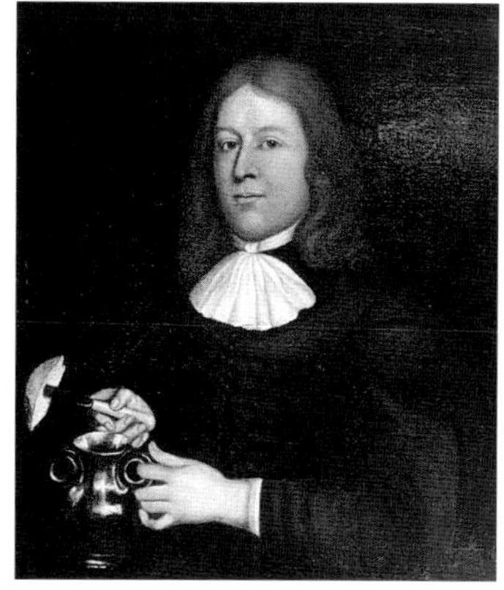

Fig.15 **Edward Wise, College Butler at Eton College**
British School, *c.*1680

This painting is probably a portrait of Wise although the Strangers' Cup dates from after his death. The probate inventory of his possessions suggests that he was fairly wealthy. He owned a number of pictures of which this may have been one.

Length of service has always been one of the most important reasons for commissioning portraits of college employees. This rule appears to have applied to a rare early portrait of a woman. Women were not employed as college servants in the seventeenth century, and in theory were not allowed to enter colleges: only laundresses avoided this rule as long as they were of such 'age, condition, and reputation' as to arouse no suspicion. In 1691 the painter William Sonmans (d.1708), who worked regularly in Oxford and had recently executed portraits of King William III for Wadham College, depicted a certain Alice George.[7] Reputed to be the college laundress, she was celebrated for her enormous age: in 1681, when she was described by the philosopher John Locke, she was said to be 108 years old. At a time when the university was inspired by a spirit of scientific enquiry, her age was a matter of much interest at Oxford on medical grounds, and Locke analysed her appearance, health and diet.[8] The image has something of the character of the specimens collected in seventeenth-century cabinets of curiosities, in which aberrations of nature provided material for scientific analysis. Such a detached approach to recording an ancient person, or another human example of nature's aberrations, was to be a characteristic of what one might term 'vernacular portraiture' well into the nineteenth century.

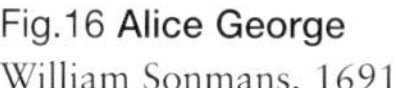

Fig.16 **Alice George**
William Sonmans, 1691

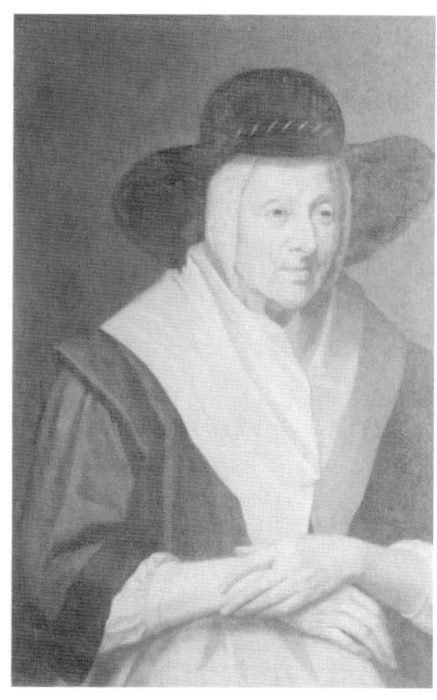

During the eighteenth century, many colleges both at Oxford and at Cambridge became somewhat indolent. The number of undergraduates fell considerably, and many fellows were more interested in obtaining

Cat.35 Thomas Hodges, College Servant
L.L., 1768

Hodges was servant to the Chaplains' Room, at New College, Oxford, which housed ten chaplains, often noted for their fondness for good living rather than their piety. Hodges' dress suggests that it was handed down to him by someone he worked for. Servants in colleges enjoyed considerable status, in contrast to those in private establishments.

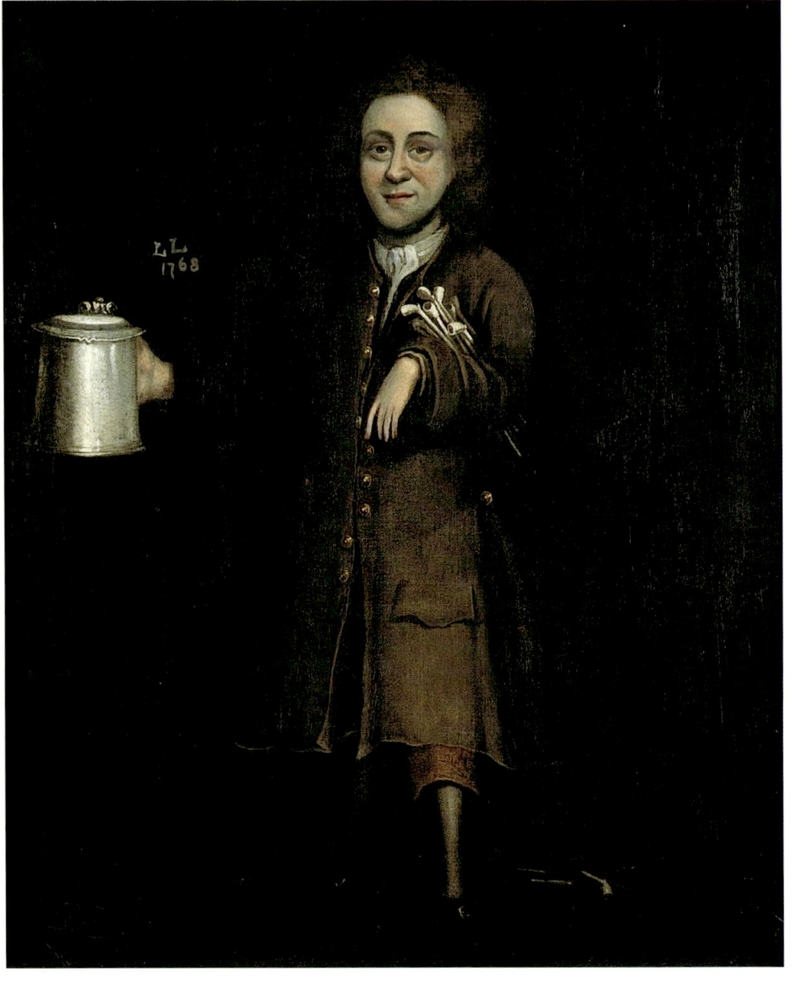

clerical livings than in the life of their colleges. Portraits of employees become rare. One example, which gives a new twist to the tradition of the emblematic servant, is a naïve depiction of Thomas Hodges, servant to the Chaplains' Room at New College, Oxford. The work is signed 'L.L' (not identifiable initials) and dated 1768.[9] Painted in the tradition of the Eton butler, the image has an individual and vulnerable quality, with an element of jaunty humour. Hodges, whose left side is disabled, wears slightly old-fashioned dress which is too large for him (and was no doubt handed on by one of his employers). He was a member of a dynasty of college servants whose grandfather (or conceivably father) was a porter at the same college. This body was wealthy and well-staffed in the eighteenth century, as suggested by its statutory employment of ten chaplains with a common room of their own. An ironic statement may be implied in the picture by the chaplains' servant holding, like attributes, a tankard and a bundle of clay pipes. The chaplains at New College were particularly lax and fond of drink:

in the 1760s the subwarden, the famous Parson James Woodforde, encountered problems with clergy who failed to take prayers in chapel as their duties required. The painting may offer a comment on their negligence.[10]

As the system of servitors and sizars died out at the beginning of the nineteenth century, the richer colleges, in particular, recruited more domestic servants to deal both with the growing number of fellows and undergraduates and to provide the high standards of domestic service – in terms of staff, rather than physical comfort – expected by well-born junior members. As a recent study of scouts at Oxford University illustrates,[11] many of the people – largely men – employed in these positions until after the Second World War spent their entire careers working for their colleges (more frequently than their equivalents in private households). They often assumed an almost pastoral role for the undergraduates, particularly necessary when dons ignored such involvement. In some cases – such as Richard Gunstone, Junior Common Room Steward at Magdalen College, Oxford, from 1880 to 1914 – they became celebrated figures, Gunstone being commemorated in Compton Mackenzie's novel *Sinister Street* (1913–14).

A number of these college servants have been painted or photographed since the second half of the nineteenth century. Perhaps the most interesting group is a set of ten portraits held by Trinity College, Oxford, all long-serving members of the college staff, many of whom worked there for fifty or sixty years. The portraits, which date from 1927 to 1996, were commissioned by the college from well-known artists such as Muirhead Bone (1876–1953) and John Ward (b.1917), reflecting the value attached to the commissions. The sitters are generally shown in their working roles or at least wearing appropriate professional dress. Generally, we know little about the sitters' views of these images, so it is interesting to know that at Trinity the portraits were not necessarily relished by their subjects. Richard Cadman, a scout who worked for the college for sixty-seven years and was drawn by John Ward shortly before retirement, found the drawing 'demeaning'.[12] The women's colleges that were founded from the late nineteenth century onwards also celebrated their new identity by commissioning group portraits. At Girton College, Cambridge, which moved to its present site in 1873, the staff considered necessary even in what was a relatively small and impecunious college are shown in a photograph of 1907. The arrangement of figures echoes contemporary group portraits of school pupils and country-house servants.

A similar attitude to staff is evident in clubs in London and other major cities, where the pattern of service with a hierarchy and, at least in the nineteenth century, the expectation that many members of staff would live in, also resembled that of the private house.[13] Again, length of service has been the prime reason for club members

Fig.17 **Richard Cadman**
John Ward, 1964

Trinity College, Oxford, has actively commissioned portraits of staff members, some of whom served the college for remarkably long periods. Cadman worked at Trinity from 1901 to 1968, concluding his service as Head Scout, and was painted by Ward in his pantry at the age of ninety.

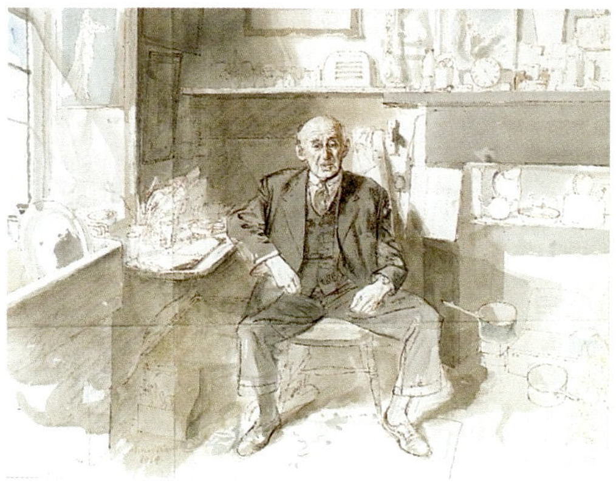

Fig.18 **College Staff at Girton College, Cambridge**
Unknown photographer, 1907

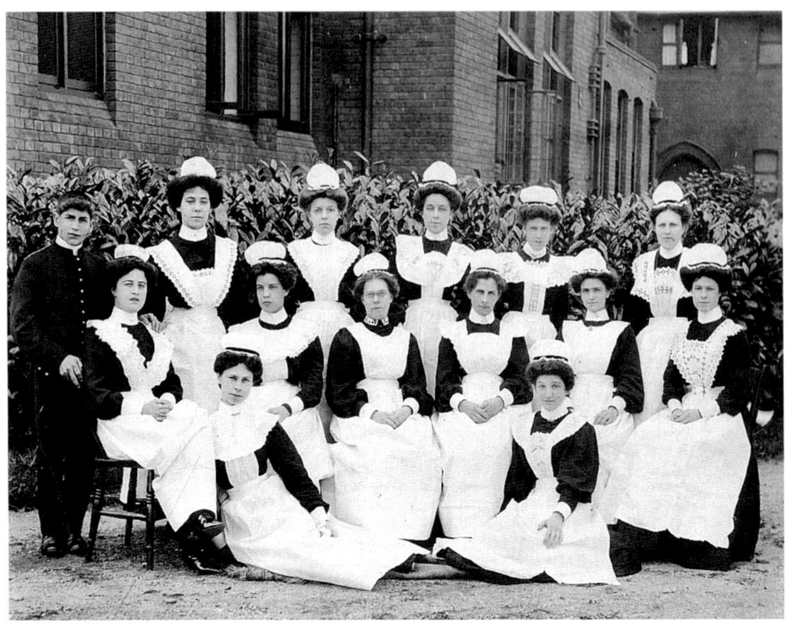

commissioning paintings, drawings or photographs of staff. One of the most striking examples is a portrait at the Arts Club in London (one of several portraits of staff in the club's possession). It shows Alice Draper, Club Chef from *c.*1933 to 1940 and famous for her soups and sweets (cat.36). She was an early example in the world of the traditional London club of a woman occupying so important a post (though the Arts Club was historically less traditional than many clubs in its attitude to women guests and staff). The artist was Francis Hodge, a member of the club and a specialist in landscape and figure painting with a penchant for portraits of soldiers and bishops. His image of George VI was much admired.[14] The Arts Club painting conveys a vibrant and positive approach to the image of the employee, anticipating the self-confidence shown in the photographs of chefs collected by the National Portrait Gallery in the 1990s. Surrounded by instruments of office and bursting with vitality, the sitter gazes cheerfully at the viewer.

Photographs, and extended descriptions of 'characters' among the staff, appear in several institutional histories of clubs, affectionately recording long-serving members of these small communities and particularly hall porters and wine waiters, who had the most frequent contact with members.[15] Just occasionally, as in the photograph of a barman published in a history of Boodle's Club in London in 1962 (cat.37), the image reflects the fact that even the most loyal servant may suffer fatigue.

Institutional servants

Emergent public or semi-public bodies such as the Bank of England (founded in 1694) tended to have a collegiate atmosphere. As in colleges, members of staff often spent their whole careers at the Bank, where there were

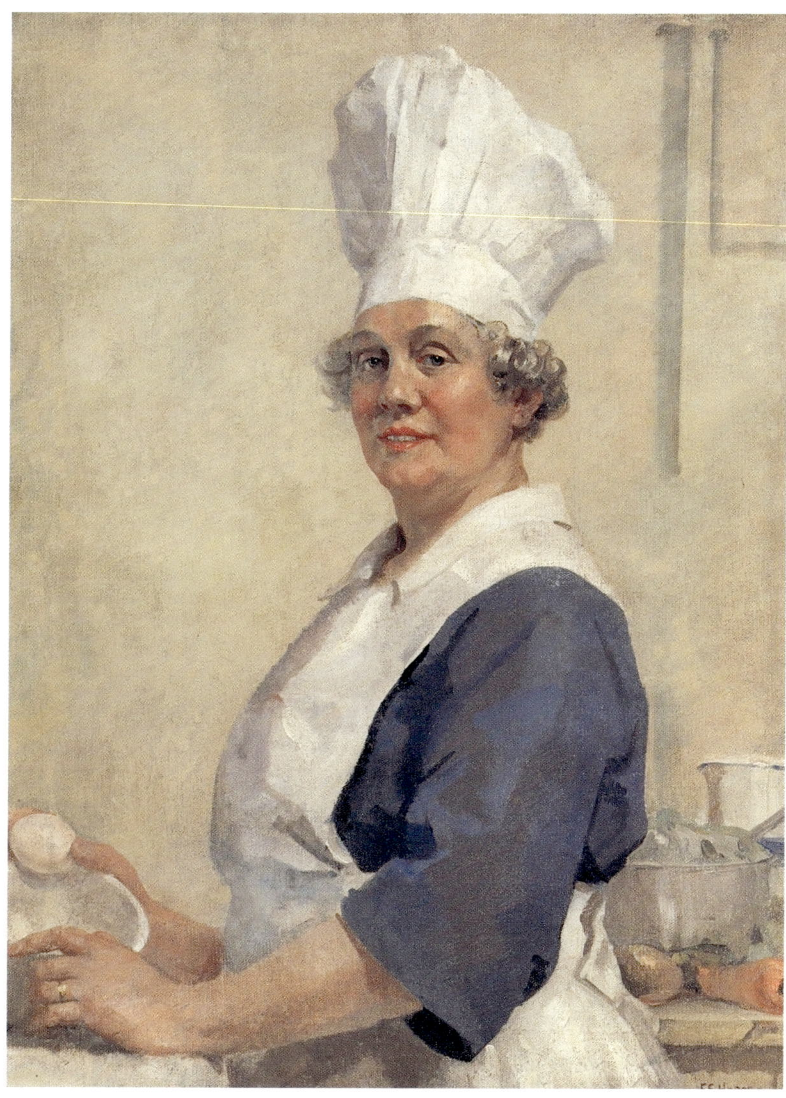

Cat.36 **The Arts Club's Woman Chef**
Francis Edwin Hodge, 1935

always employees in residence. The family-like atmosphere must have been comparable to a great household, with many of the responsibilities of the staff being analogous. The Bank has commemorated its employees since the eighteenth century, though it only began to commission portraits of its governors and directors around 1900. A notable (though small-scale) example of its patronage is an anonymous etching of the 1760s showing William Banning, who served as Gate Porter from 1763 to 1777. As was often the case, his wife Elizabeth worked in the Bank as housekeeper.

Banning was an important figure at the Bank, the man who stood at the entrance to assist desirable visitors and repel the undesirable. He is depicted wearing the robe (which was scarlet) and the bicorn hat, his livery on days when the Bank's Court was meeting, and he holds a silver-topped

Cat.37 **Will They Never Go Home?**
Roger Fulford, 1962

Like other club histories, Roger Fulford's book *Boodle's 1762–1962* celebrates 'loyalty and long-service' among institutional servants. Descriptive captions and photographs of staff at work pay tribute to 'the splendid tradition of service in the Club', although this image of a barman hints at the burden this can be on staff.

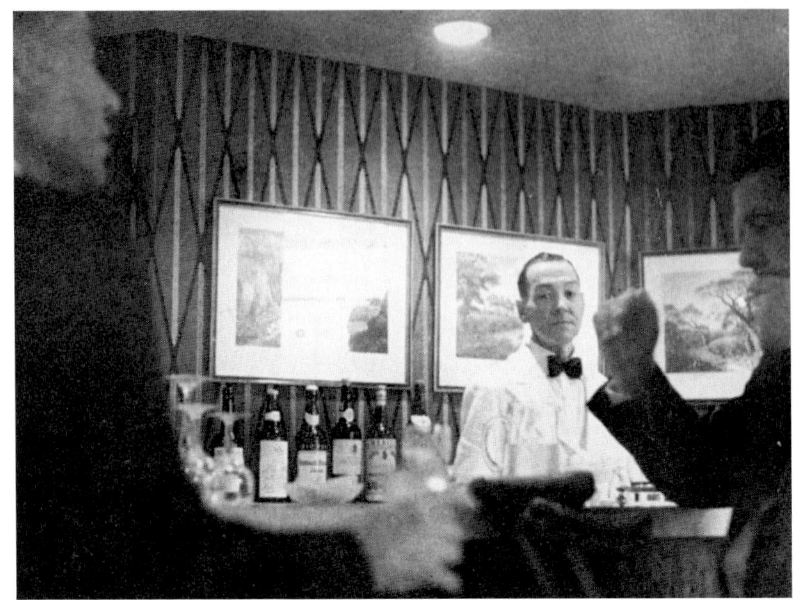

Cat.38 **William Banning, Head Gate Porter at the Bank of England 1763–77**
Unknown artist, *c.*1760

The Bank of England has a long tradition of portraying its employees. William Banning, gate porter from 1763 to 1777, attired in his finest livery of scarlet robe and bicorn hat, embodies the dignity of the Bank.

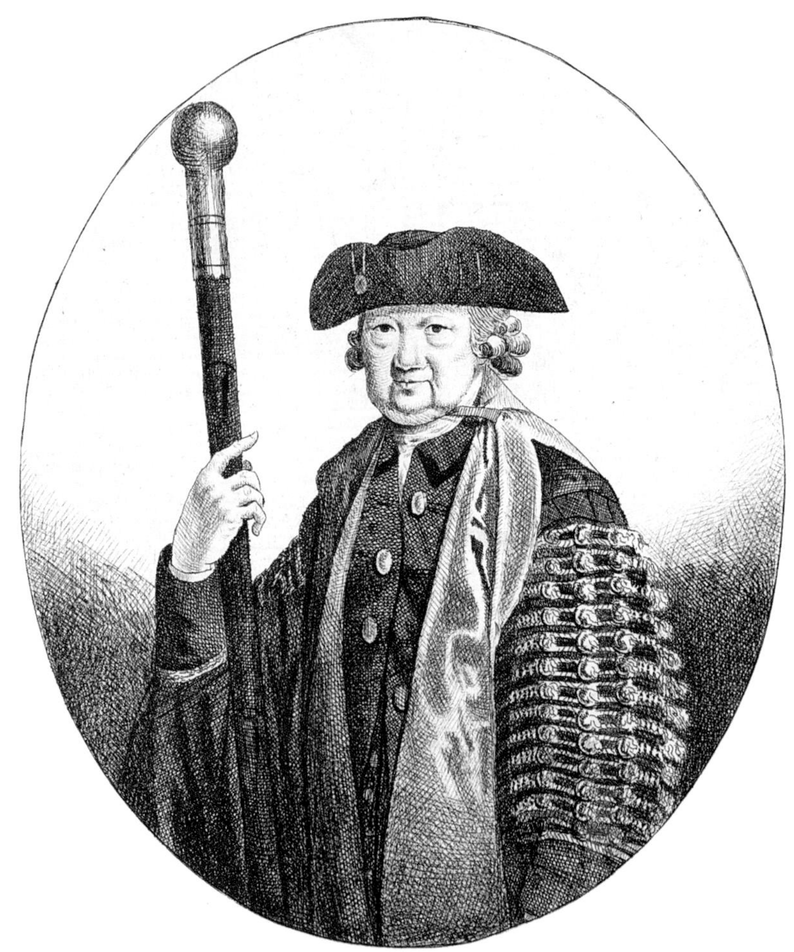

bamboo cane, a symbol of his office. The etching is now reproduced on the £50 note. Banning's image may be compared with seventeenth- and eighteenth-century depictions of porters at great houses such as Longleat, Wiltshire,[16] and Belton House, Lincolnshire. In the picture of Belton, *c.*1720, the porter is the most prominent figure in the composition, standing four-square in front of the house, which cannot be entered without his approval. A variation on the theme of porter emerges in a pastel of an official porter at the Royal Academy (possibly John Withers, who was senior porter there) executed in 1792 by John Russell, himself a Royal Academician (cat.39). In this dramatic depiction, the porter is posed in the entrance hall at Somerset House as the crowd of visitors struggles to gain admission to the annual Summer Exhibition. He holds an admission card and an exhibition catalogue. Like other porters, he both greets and admonishes the arriving visitor, excluding those who are not suitably equipped; like them, he embodies the character of the institution he represents.[17]

A similar spirit emerged in the early days of the British Museum, founded in 1753. Here too a quasi-collegiate system of residence applied, with the Principal Librarian, the various keepers (academic officers) and the domestic staff almost all living in from the earliest days. The establishment set up on the museum's foundation allowed, on the domestic side, for a

Fig.19 **View of the South Front of Belton House, Lincolnshire**
Unknown artist, *c.*1720

Belton House was built in the late seventeenth century for Sir John Brownlow. This view shows the south front of the house, protected by a wrought-iron screen and by the porter, embodiment of the house's dignity. His staff survives at the house.

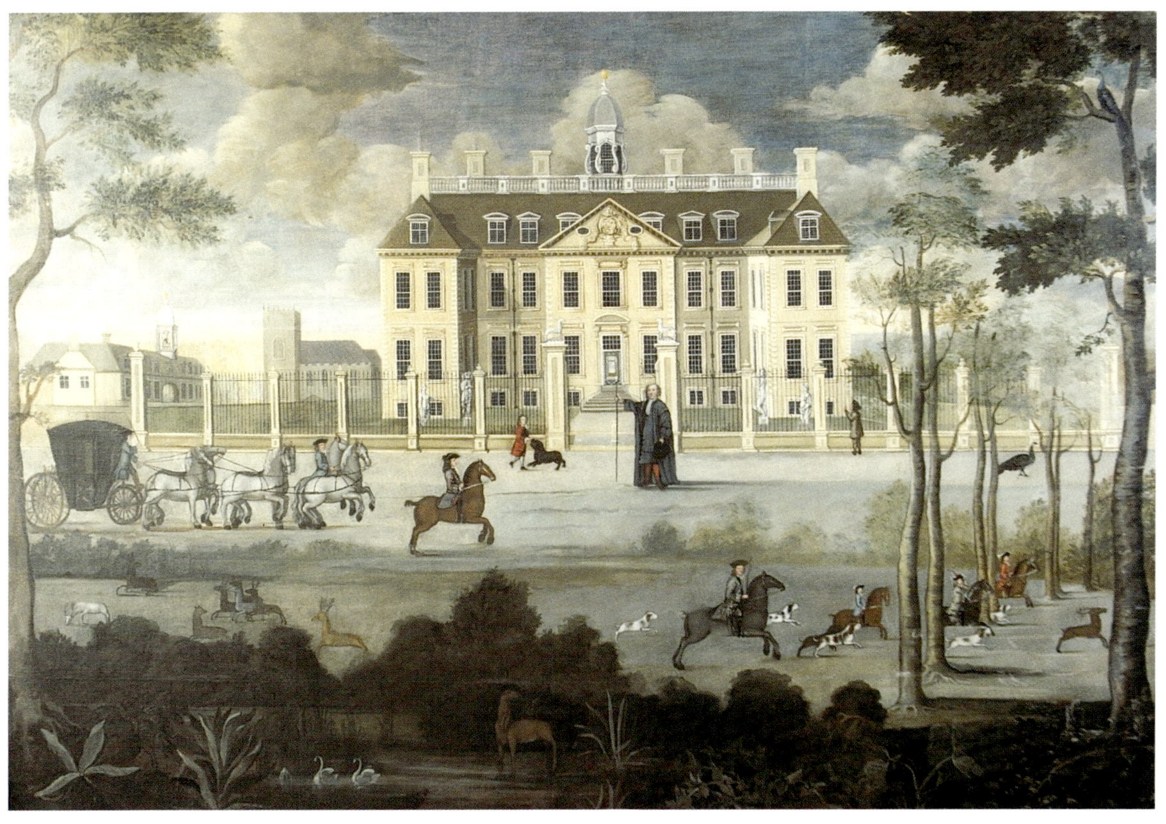

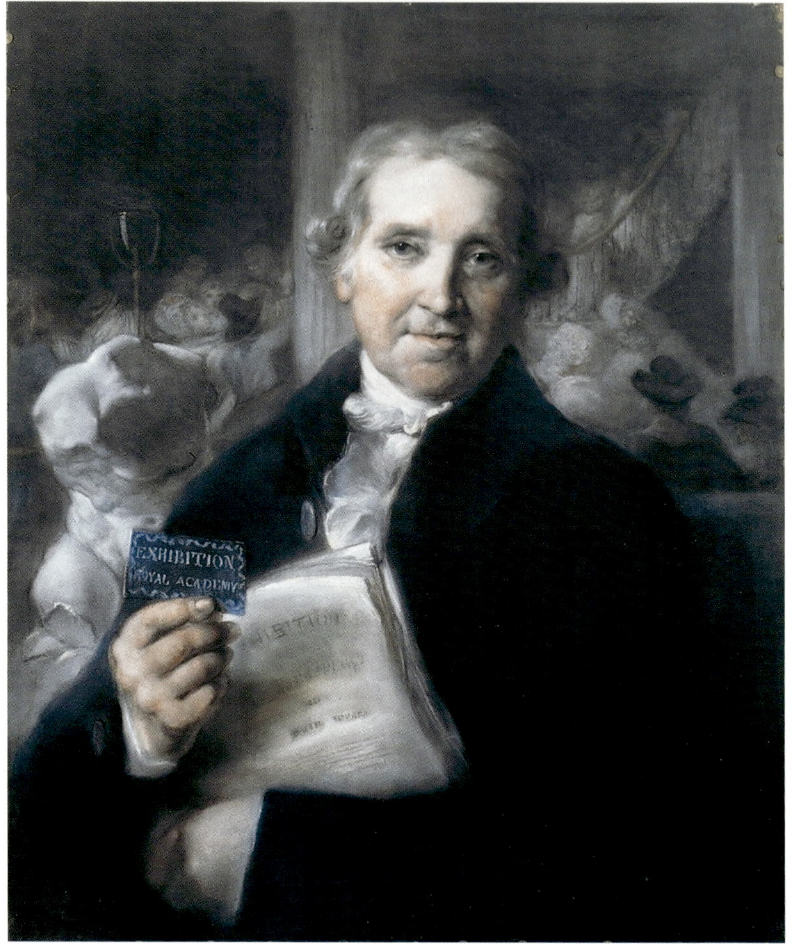

Cat.39 **One of the Porters of the Royal Academy (John Withers?)**
John Russell, *c.*1792

This dramatic image shows one of the senior porters at the Royal Academy on duty in the entrance hall, holding an admission card and exhibition catalogue. The artist, a Royal Academician, won much acclaim for his portraits, particularly in pastel, and depicted members of the royal family and the aristocracy.

messenger, a porter, two watchmen, a gardener, a principal housemaid and three other housemaids. In many cases relations of existing staff members were appointed, creating 'dynasties of servants'.[18] The British Museum has a portrait of an early nineteenth-century porter, William Scivier, characteristically shown holding open the door to the (old) museum building, and of Mary Bygrave, head housemaid, and a remarkably long-serving member of staff (cat.106). She entered the establishment in 1780 at the age of ten 'to assist her aunt', who had been housekeeper to Sir Hans Sloane, and became the first head housemaid at the Museum. She lived with her husband, an attendant at the Museum, in the east wing of the old building. She is depicted in plain but rich clothing which reflects her status as an upper servant in a great institution but she was less severe than she might appear, being still in old age susceptible to flattery about her looks from young men. The anonymous drawing was done in 1844, shortly before her death while still in service in 1846: she provided a remarkable link to Sir Hans Sloane, whose collections formed the basis of the museum and who died in 1753.[19]

In this story, one major organisation does not appear to have followed the usual pattern: the armed services. While they obtained portraits of their most distinguished generals and of their colonels-in-chief, even the oldest-established regiments of the British Army such as the Guards Regiments have seldom possessed depictions of soldier servants or of staff attached to regimental messes. There may be a number of reasons: the positions held by such servants tended to be transitory and they were often privately employed by officers, while the nature of military service precluded extended employment. In addition, the hierarchical nature of the Army made it unlikely that a regiment would wish to be represented by a private soldier, still less a soldier-servant.[20] Two exceptions from the Second World War, both done for the soldier-artist's personal pleasure, prove the rule. In 1939–40 Edward Ardizzone drew a humorous sketch of a pompous padre in a French bedroom, having his boots pulled off by a tiny batman,[21] while in 1941 Rex Whistler produced a fine example of such an image. Whistler, who had made a reputation for his decorative schemes

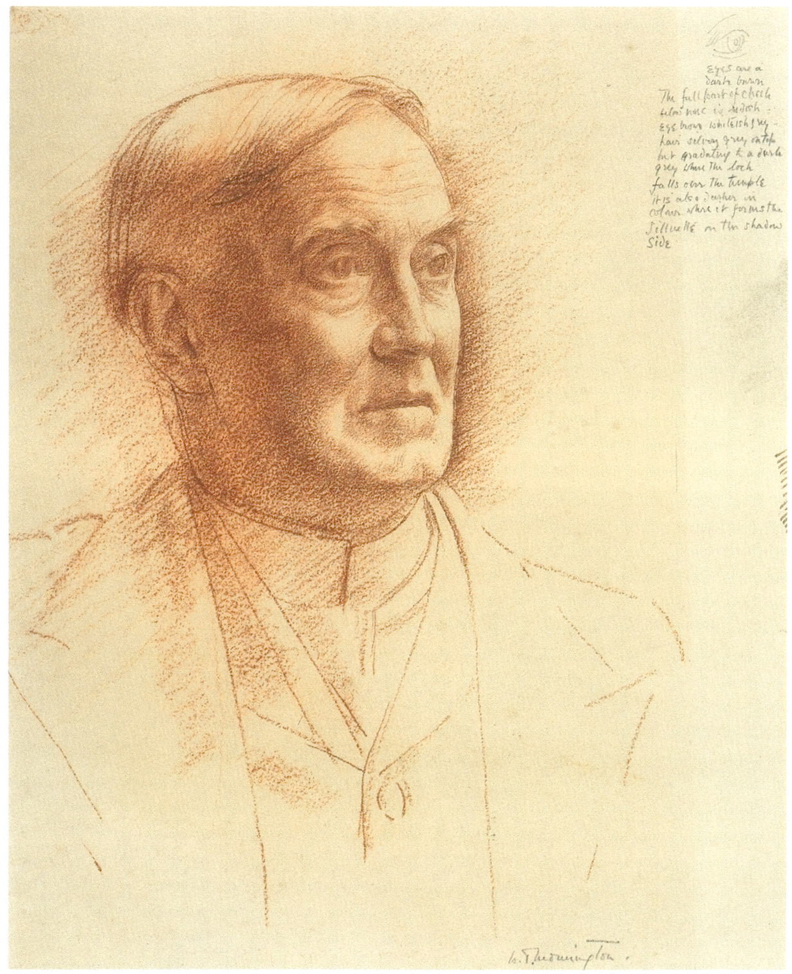

Cat.40 Samuel Barnetson, Parlour Messenger
Thomas Monnington, 1937

As part of the decoration of the Bank of England in 1937, Monnington was asked to paint *The Doorkeeper Receiving a Message in the Entrance to the Parlour*. The picture included portraits of three highly respected senior staff. This sensitive work is the sketch for Barnetson, First Parlour Messenger (one of the top service jobs).

at various country houses and for his lively sense of visual humour, had entered the Welsh Guards as a volunteer in 1940. In the Army he engaged in various artistic activities, creating a decorative interior for the Officers' Mess (as a tent with striped poles, hung with satirical portraits of the officers) when the mess was accommodated in a hut at Codford in Wiltshire, and executing several portraits. In 1941 he was posted to Sandown Park, the race track in Surrey. Whistler believed that his talent was expanding in these unusual circumstances, and some of his images are in a more serious vein.[22] Needing models, he painted Sergeant J.W. Isaacs, Master Cook of the regiment and therefore a senior non-commissioned soldier as well as a well-known 'character'. Wearing his chef's outfit and a regimental cap, Isaacs is placed in an unusual pose, close to the viewer (with only a sketchy

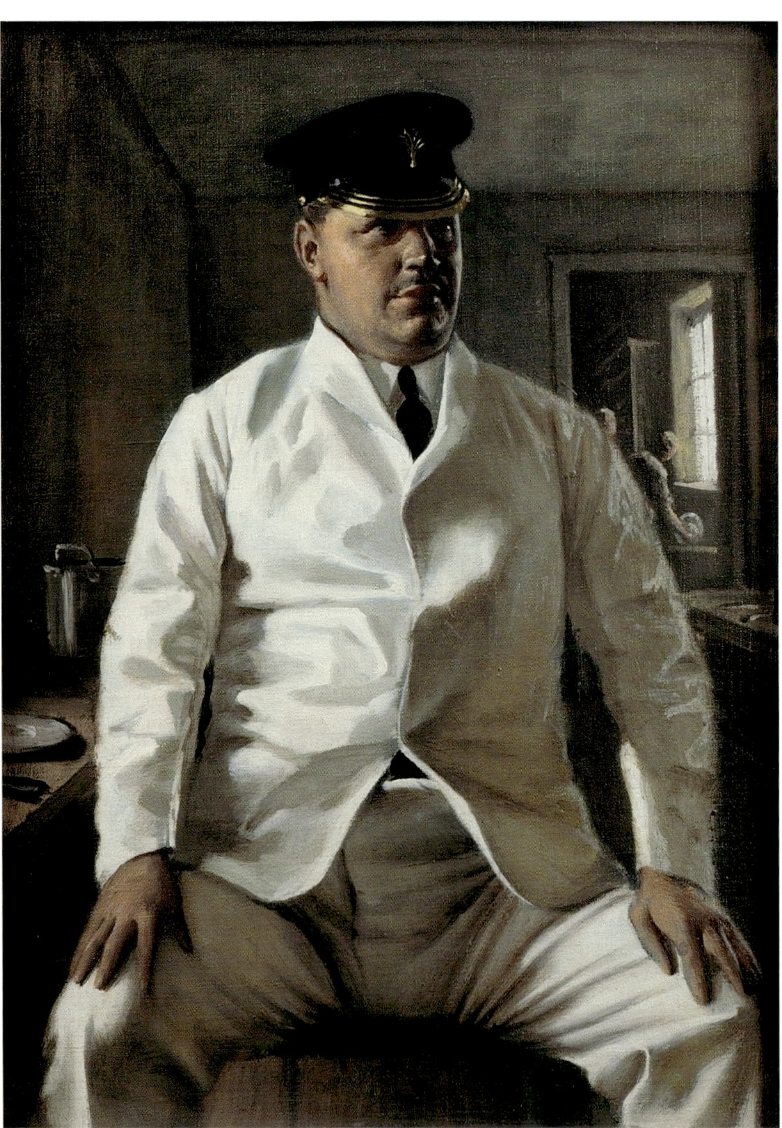

Cat.41 **The Master Cook, 1st Battalion Welsh Guards Sergeant J.W. Isaacs**
Rex Whistler, 1940

Portraits of military or naval servants are rare, though many such individuals existed. During a quiet period of service early in the Second World War, Whistler painted Sergeant Isaacs, Master Cook of the Welsh Guards, depicting him with all the gravitas his important position conferred.

indication of the kitchen and support staff in the background), with his legs wide apart, and dominating the composition.[23]

The Royal Navy seems equally to have had little interest in images of sailor servants. Only in the case of a man who worked for the most famous of British sailors did the cult of the master stimulate interest in his attendant and ultimately a portrait. This man is Tom Allen, 'body servant' to Admiral Nelson from 1795 until just before the Battle of Trafalgar. Though originally a seaman who came from the same Norfolk village as his master, Allen was privately employed by Nelson, whom he also accompanied on land. Accounts of Allen's rough and ready character, his frankness and courage, his forwardness to tell his master in public when he had drunk enough and his unique ability to persuade him to rest before battle, became part of the Nelson myth, perpetuated in a succession of eulogistic biographies, first issued soon after Trafalgar and continuing long after the hero's death. 'Many a time did he coax his master away from the wet deck and raging storm, and care for him only as a soul of the utmost affection and fidelity could have done. Rough and unpolished, but a diamond withal,' writes Hilda Gamlin of Allen in 1899,[24] a typical offering when the Nelson myth was as strong as ever. However memorable Allen may have been, he did not qualify for a portrait in his own right. In the 1830s, the Scottish painter John Burnet embarked on an ambitious composition called *Greenwich Pensioners Commemorating the Anniversary of the Battle of Trafalgar*, which was intended to be a pendant to David Wilkie's much earlier and hugely successful *Chelsea Pensioners Reading the Waterloo Despatch*, of 1822. After several years of persuasion, Burnet induced the Duke of Wellington, who owned the Wilkie, to buy his painting. One of the principal figures in the composition was Tom Allen, who had suffered considerable hardship after Nelson's death and at the end of his life was a pensioner at the Greenwich Hospital.[25] In this instance it was the commercial instincts of an opportunistic artist that earned the sitter his portrait.

This survey has outlined some of the ways in which institutional portraits differ from the other types of images discussed in this book. This is a particularly active branch of the tradition, since many of the institutions cited here continue to flourish in a way that hardly applies to private households. They suggest to the modern observer that the character of the most powerful and venerable institutions can still be shaped by the individuals who work there, and traditions of mutual loyalty and respect can survive even in the era of the bottom line.

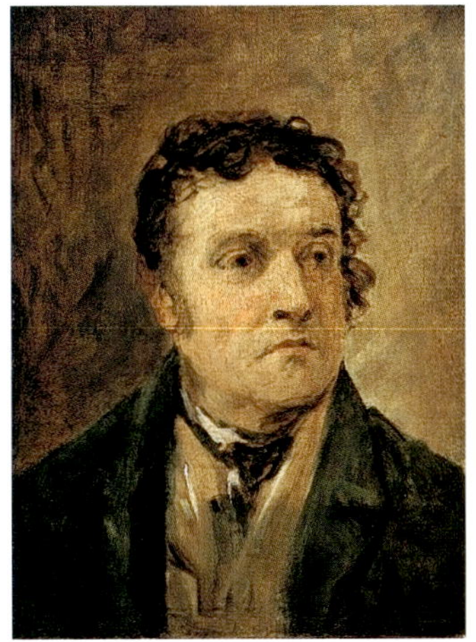

Cat.42 **Thomas Allen, a Greenwich Pensioner and Servant to Lord Nelson**
John Burnet, *c.*1832

Though many naval officers had personal servants, they are almost never recorded. This rare exception shows one of the most famous naval servants. 'Body servant' to Horatio Nelson from 1795 to around 1805, Allen was renowned for his loyalty and his rough-tongued willingness to tell his master how to behave.

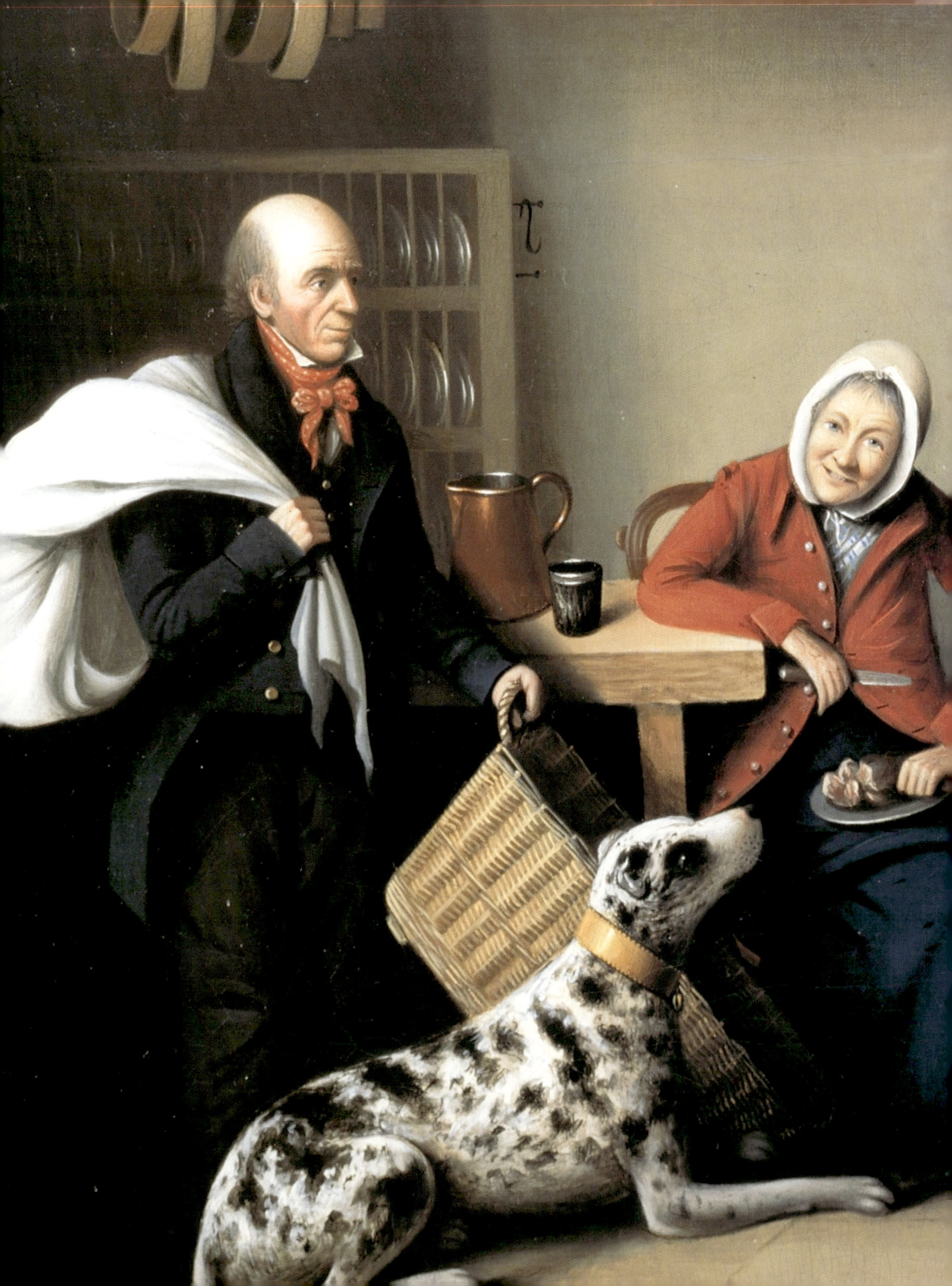

5 LIFE IN SERVICE

Giles Waterfield

WHAT WAS LIFE IN SERVICE like for those who experienced it? The evidence from professional writers is sparse, as one might expect. Until the nineteenth century, those who dealt with the subject were faced by negative prejudice: when Jonathan Swift's satirical *Directions to Servants* was published posthumously in 1745 (cat.107), academic critics were dismayed that he should address such a subject, even humorously. One critic wrote in 1758 (in a passage typical of the views of the privileged): 'A man of Swift's exalted genius ought constantly to have soared into higher regions. He ought to have looked upon persons of inferior abilities as children, whom nature had appointed him to instruct, encourage, and improve.'[1] Equally, in contrast to the quantity of servant portraits, few painters addressed the subject of servants at work, unless as attendants or as guardians of horses and dogs. When life in service was depicted, it often provided the context for a moralising narrative or an appealing genre subject, such as Henry R. Morland's paintings of maids. Only in the late nineteenth and early twentieth centuries did painters begin, quite frequently, to depict servants at work.

All the same, from the millions of people who have worked in this capacity, a few voices do survive. In the seventeenth century, when most people working as servants were likely to be illiterate, they are rare. The most telling accounts of servant life are extracted from a variety of surviving legal documents, as has been done by Peter Earle and Lawrence Stone.[2] These stories often contain brief autobiographies and give some impression of how it felt to be a servant. In the eighteenth century, more personal accounts by servants begin to emerge, as in the lively verse of the young literary footman Robert Dodsley (cat.110) and the memoirs of John Macdonald,[3] the intelligent and dashing footman who served a succession of masters and mistresses in mid-eighteenth-century London, Edinburgh and Dublin, as well as far overseas.

OPPOSITE Detail of cat.48 **Fish Nell, John Sutherland, Laundryman and 'Dummy' King (Servants at Dalkeith House)**
Attributed to John Ainslie, 1832

In the Victorian period, first-hand accounts of the lives of servants become less unusual: whether it is H.G. Wells in his novel *Tono-Bungay* (1909) evoking the sleepy life of Bladesover House (actually Uppark in Sussex), where his mother worked as housekeeper during his childhood, or Hannah Cullwick writing her diary of life as maid-of-all-work and occasional cook in mid-Victorian London, or the memoirs published by John Burnet in *Useful Toil*.[4] A new type of book begins to appear in the late nineteenth century: the first-hand memoir of life in service. One of the earliest of these is John Wilkins's *The Autobiography of an English Gamekeeper*,[5] published in 1892 by editors (their contribution was to write down Wilkins's spoken reminiscences) who reckoned that the author was 'the first of his profession to publish genuine reminiscences'.[6] Wilkins offers a vivid account of the often dangerous experience of looking after game and battling with poachers.

In the twentieth century the servant's (or ex-servant's) memoir becomes increasingly popular, and a change of mood is apparent, no doubt reflecting the taste of the public. This new style emerges in the 1920s – at a time

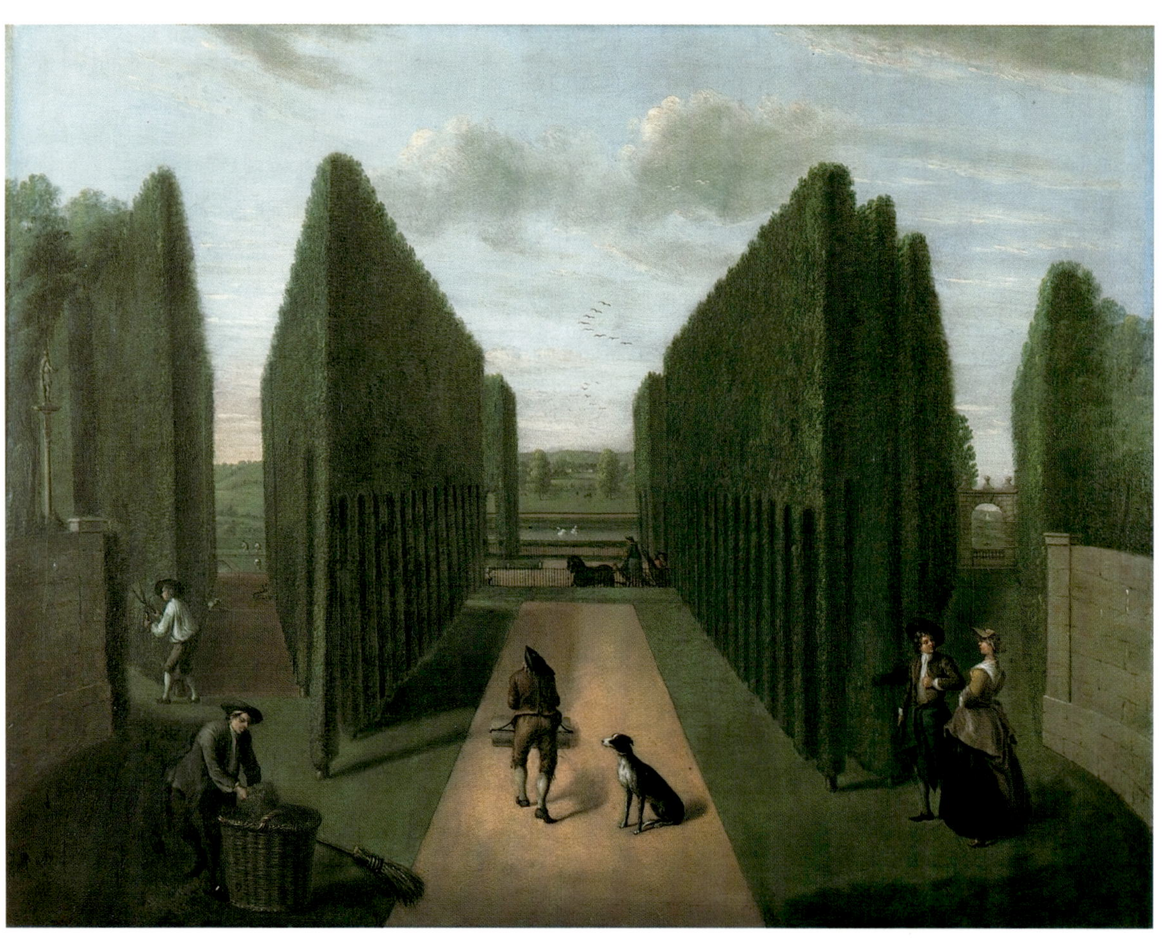

Cat.43 **The Allees and Arcades behind the House**
Balthasar Nebot, 1738

After a transformation that introduced architectural features by James Gibbs, the gardens of Hartwell House, Buckinghamshire, were painted for their owner in eight views by Nebot. They provide a detailed depiction of garden labourers in their working environment. This painting's portrayal of clipping hedges, rolling a gravel walk and scything shows how the practical upkeep of estates depended on a wide array of workers, mostly unskilled labourers engaged on a seasonal basis, and sometimes paid for out of the gardener's salary.

when the traditional values of landed society were obviously breaking down – with such works as Eric Horne's *What the Butler Winked At* (1923), which was sufficiently popular to earn a sequel. Twentieth-century memories are sometimes loyal and nostalgic, but are also often remarkably bitter in their denunciations of the arrogance, meanness and coldness of the gentry. As Horne remarked, 'The gentry ... hold all the trump cards, and always win if a servant is the opponent. Do they ever ask themselves this question, "Where did I come from? And why? Where am I going to, and when?" '[7] Recently this chronicle has been supplemented by oral history projects at the University of Essex and the National Sound Archive at the British Library, which have collected numerous recollections of people working in domestic service.

Many of the most evocative historic descriptions of life in households, large or small, and of relations between employers and staff, have derived from the diaries and letters of employers, including figures such as Samuel Pepys and the eighteenth-century Parson Woodforde (who appears to have fulfilled the expectation that clergymen would treat their servants kindly). In the nineteenth century, Jane Carlyle's letters[8] give a vivid impression of life in a small household where only one maid was kept. In terms of the work that servants were expected to carry out, numerous manuals from the early nineteenth century on shed light on the nature of their duties. In the later nineteenth century the views of servants held by their employers are repeatedly recorded in the memoirs of the gentry.

What general impressions emerge from this material? Firstly, the transitory nature of domestic service from the seventeenth century (and probably earlier) until the twentieth. Servants came and went at a great rate; in the late seventeenth and early eighteenth centuries, 'most men had left service before they were forty. This was partly because employers did not want middle-aged footmen or valets, but also because servants themselves tended to see the work as part of the life-cycle rather than a career for life.'[9] The testimony of Richard Morris, aged thirty-two (*c.*1700), suggests how a young man earned his living as a servant to the nobility and the well connected:[10]

> I was bred a seedsman, but now followe noe calling or profession but that of goeing into service ... About eight or nine yeares since I was butler to the Lord Jersey with whome I lived about a yeare and voluntarily left his service because the steward claimed part of the card money. Then I went to Sir Godfrey Kneller in Great Queen Street with whome I lived eight months as his valet de chambre and voluntarily quitted the same because I gott little perquisites.

After working as a butler in Bond Street, he moved to Lord Mohun and was promoted to be 'his gentleman', before being dismissed after nine months for 'disobligeing the steward'. His next employer was Lieutenant General

JOHN MACDONALD FINDS A NEW JOB

'When I had been a week in London, I met the Irish Chairman that carried Mr Hamilton and Major Joass when in London. I said to him: "Do you hear of any place for me?" "By G—d, Johnny, I do; go to Major Libbelier; he lodges at a hair-dresser's in Lower Grosvenor Street; go to him, Johnny, early to-morrow morning." I went – the maid told him I was below. "Call him up." "Well, sir, what are your commands?" "Were you ever in Ireland?" "Look to my recommendations." He read them, and said; "I know Colonel Skeene, and Major Joass in particular. Then you have been through Ireland?" "I have, sir." "Very well, I'll give you fourteen shillings a week; and if I go to Ireland, I'll give you sixpence more a day on the road." I dressed him and he was pleased.'

John Macdonald,
Memoirs of an Eighteenth-Century Footman

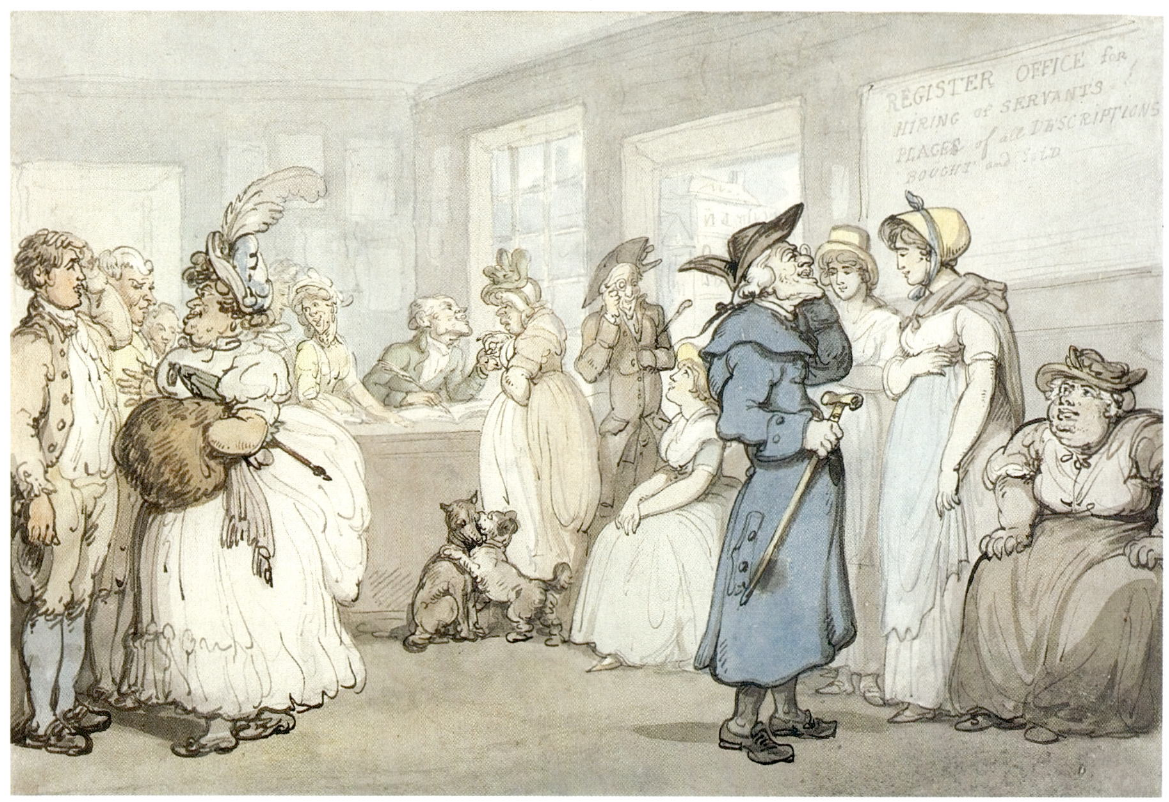

Cat.44 **Register Office for the Hiring of Servants**
Thomas Rowlandson, *c.*1800–05

Register offices were private employment agencies, first established by Henry Fielding in 1749. They collected fees for listing vacancies and servants' qualifications in order to bring together Londoners who offered and sought employment. Rowlandson's depiction of the register office reflects its unsavoury contemporary reputation. Two elderly men abuse the employer's right to inspect applicants by unashamedly quizzing pretty servant girls, while a fat matron ogles a young man. In the background the financial transactions are satirised by two cavorting dogs.

Churchill – Morris was sent away after a year – followed by the Duke of Buckingham as 'Groome of the Chamber'. After six months he 'left the same because my Lord Duke struck me', moved to John Dormer (dismissed 'at the instigation of his wife as I verily beleive'), then Charles Caesar ('turned out of such service but for what I knowe not') and finally the Earl of Northampton. Morris held nine positions in eight or nine years, experiencing little difficulty in finding new jobs in spite of dismissals, or in meeting the requirements of a variety of senior posts.

Servants appear, all through our period, to have been taken on and dismissed at great speed, often being asked to begin their duties the day they had first met a prospective employer. While the situation was more stable in large rural households, even there servants moved regularly: at Petworth House in the nineteenth century the junior servants often stayed only a year or two before moving on in search of novelty or promotion. As Eric Horne put it while a boy in his teens, 'After about two years I thought it time I should make a move, and be getting on, as I was worthier a better place.'[11] Only those who had reached the position of a senior servant in a large household, or were particularly attached to a family, assumed the role of loyal retainer.

Privacy was a problem for both sides, and it is clear from the ruminations of Swift and from servants' reminiscences that the affairs of their employers were a source of fascination to them. In the seventeenth and eighteenth centuries, families lived at close quarters with their staff, enjoying little privacy even in the bedroom. Many of the architectural and social barriers set up in the Victorian period were aimed at creating as much independence as possible for the family and their guests.

Life in the servants' hall mirrored life above stairs, with the precedence practised by the aristocracy imitated by their employees. While it was acceptable for the servants' hall to mimic the order of precedence of high society, an activity which did worry the privileged was the tendency of servants to ape their betters, to wear fine clothes, and to imitate the manners and language of the well-born. When such signs of status were taken over by those who were not entitled to them, how could the upper classes make their superiority apparent? Language and dress had to be carefully regulated.

The servant problem

The 'servant problem', as it was known, is an old one. It seems to have attracted particular attention at certain periods, as in the early eighteenth century when several writers commented at length on the iniquities of servants, and in the late Victorian era. In 1724 the novelist, travel writer and pamphleteer Daniel Defoe published *The Great Law of Subordination Consider'd; or the Insolence and Unsufferable Behaviour of Servants in England, Duly Enquir'd Into*. This curious volume, more a collection of diatribes and revealing anecdotes than a sustained thesis, addresses the wrongdoings of servants, a category which Defoe interprets broadly to include working employees of all sorts as well as apprentices and 'menial servants'.[12] It criticises their insolence, arrogance, dishonesty (maids who have erred sexually in London travelling to the countryside so that they can return to the capital as fresh country girls), greed and impropriety (notably their taste for expensive

The GREAT LAW
OF
Subordination conſider'd;
OR, THE
Inſolence and Unſufferable Behaviour of SERVANTS in *England* duly enquir'd into.
ILLUSTRATED
With a great Variety of *Examples*, *Hiſtorical Caſes*, and *Remarkable Stories* of the Behaviour of ſome particular SERVANTS, ſuited to all the ſeveral ARGUMENTS made uſe of, as they go on.

In Ten Familiar Letters.

Together with a
CONCLUSION, being an earneſt and moving Remonſtrance to the Houſe-keepers and Heads of Families in *Great-Britain*, preſſing them not to ceaſe uſing their utmoſt Intereſt (eſpecially at this Juncture) to obtain ſufficient Laws for the effectual Regulation of the MANNERS and BEHAVIOUR of their SERVANTS.
AS ALSO
A PROPOSAL, containing ſuch Heads or Conſtitutions, as wou'd effectually anſwer this great End, and bring SERVANTS of every Claſs to a juſt (and yet not a grievous) Regulation.

LONDON:
Sold by *S. Harding*, at the *Poſt-Houſe*, in *St. Martin's-Lane*; *W. Lewis*, in *Covent-Garden*; *T. Worrall*, at the *Judge's-Head*, againſt *St. Dunſtan's-Church*, *Fleet-ſtreet*; *A. Bettesworth*, in *Pater-Noſter-Row*; *W. Meadows*, in *Cornhill*; and *T. Edlin*, at the *Prince's-Arms*, againſt *Exeter-Exchange*, in the *Strand*, 1724.

Price Three Shillings Sixpence.

Cat.45 **The Great Law of Subordination Consider'd**
Daniel Defoe, 1724

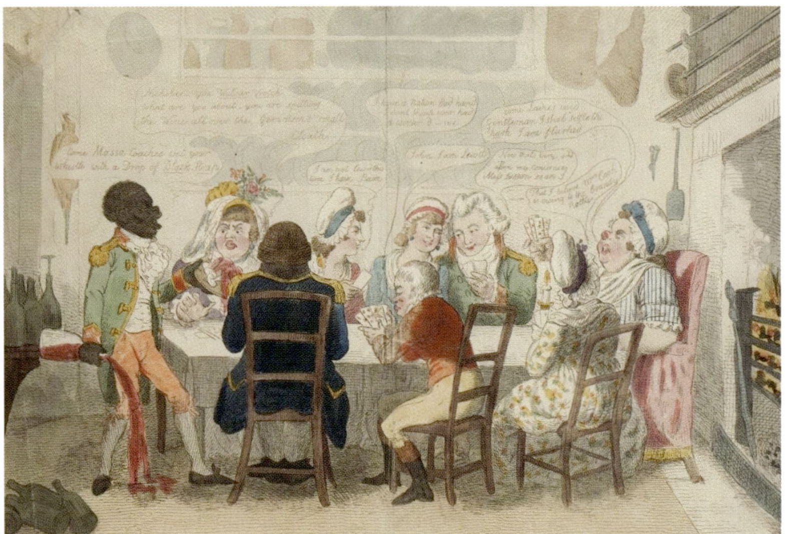

Cat.46 **Loo in the Kitchin or High Life Below Stairs**
Woodward after I.R. Cruikshank, 1799

clothing beyond their station which make it impossible to tell master or mistress from servant). Defoe repeatedy stresses the lack of discipline within society which allows servants to err from the conduct which is proper to them, an error which can lead to fatal consequences.

In his unfinished and fragmentary satirical *Directions to Servants* (cat.107) Jonathan Swift (who had already in his *Journal to Stella* [1710–13] described his own unreliable and frequently drunk servant Patrick)[13] gives a vivid impression of how inefficient, corrupt, self-seeking, rude and insanitary domestic servants could be. The *Directions* offer, in the form of letters, instructions to 'the Butler, Cook, Footman, Coachman, Groom, House-steward and Land-steward, Porter, Dairy-maid, Chamber-maid, Nurse, Laundress, House-keeper, Tutoress, or Governess'[14] as to how they may reduce their work, avoid blame for breakages or illicit absence, extract money from tradesmen, steal food and drink from their master and mistress, eavesdrop and deceive.

What emerges from both Defoe's and Swift's essays on servants is not only their hostility to the 'lower orders' but their perception of the potential for widespread disorder in society. This is a recurring theme from medieval times until at least the late nineteenth century: the fear of the mob and the danger of the lower orders getting out of control. Servants, however they were defined, could overturn the social order in the same way,

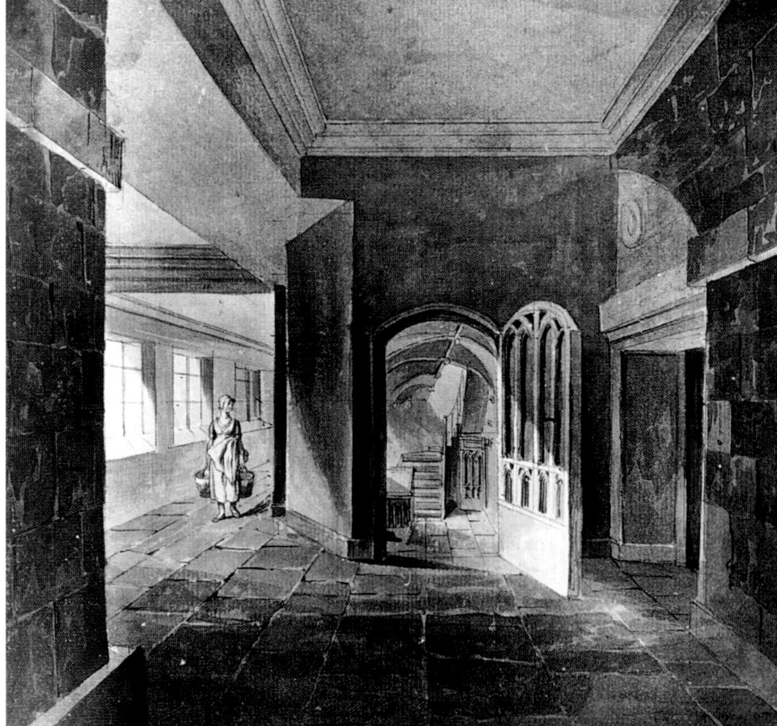

Cat.47 **The Passage to the Gothic Room at Stowe House**
J.C. Nattes, 1807

In one of a set of over one hundred views recording the house and grounds at Stowe, a maid carries buckets along a basement passage leading to the stairway of the new Gothic library designed in 1805 by Sir John Soane for the 1st Marquess of Buckingham. The existence of a draft frontispiece indicates that these drawings, executed in 1805–09, were intended for publication. Unlike two earlier sets of topographical engravings of Stowe published in the 1730s and 1750s, the views by Nattes record several service areas and provide glimpses of the under-servants labouring to maintain the house and gardens.

SWIFT'S DIRECTIONS TO SERVANTS

Directions to: 'All servants in general':
The general Place of Rendezvous for all Servants, both in Winter and Summer, is the Kitchen; there the grand Affairs of the Family ought to be consulted; whether they concern the Stable, the Dairy, the Pantry, the Laundry, the Cellar, the Nursery, the Dining-room, or my Lady's Chamber. There, as in your own proper Element, you can laugh, and squall, and romp, in full Security.

When you are chidden for a Fault, as you go out of the Room, and down Stairs, mutter loud enough to be plainly heard; this will make him (the master) believe you are innocent.

To the Butler: 'When you are to get Water on for Tea after Dinner. . . pour it into the Tea-kettle, from the Pot where Cabbage or Fish have been boiling, which will make it much wholsomer, by curing the acid corroding Quality of the Tea.

Cat.48 **Fish Nell, John Sutherland, Laundryman and 'Dummy' King (Servants at Dalkeith House)**
Attributed to John Ainslie, 1832

Three long-standing servants are shown at Dalkeith House. King carried the letters to and from the house, always accompanied by his notoriously fierce dog. This unusual group portrait, in the Dutch seventeenth-century manner, shows the servants surrounded by their working equipment, illustrating the self-sufficient character of a great house.

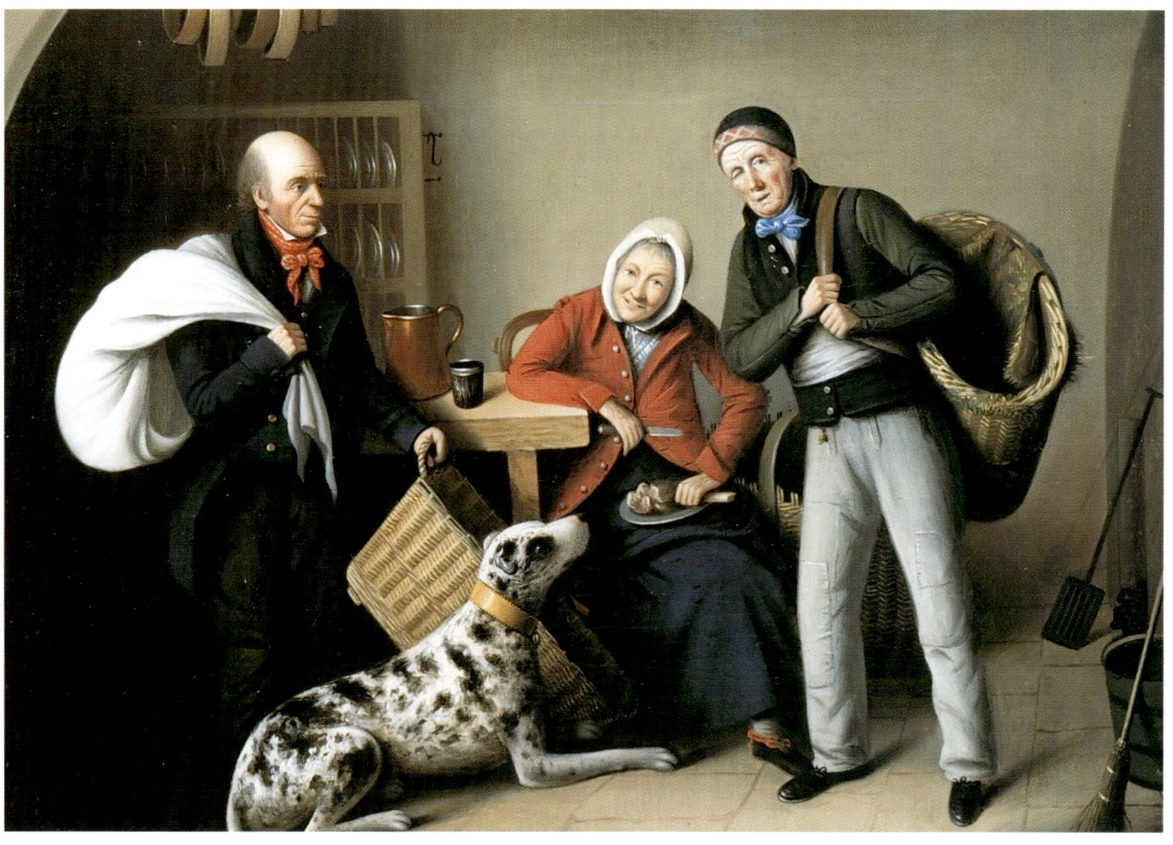

whether domestically (as in Swift's hard-edged cruel fantasy) or in Defoe's more wide-ranging interpretation of the iniquities of the lower orders. The subject aroused appalled fascination, rather as a prison riot might today.

The numerous manuals for servants and their employers indicate how hard servants were expected to work. Again, there was a good deal of variety of approach. Some servants, particularly footmen, were intended to function as symbols of extreme wealth, as Thorstein Veblen suggested in his definition of 'Conspicuous Leisure'. In the eighteenth century and still at the end of the nineteenth, 'their sole office is fatuously to wait upon the person of their owner, and so to put in evidence his ability unproductively to consume a large amount of service.'[15] In the case of footmen, they spent a great deal of time idly in the front hall of their employer's house. Their livery expressed their status: it was magnificent and it was deliberately archaic (based on court dress of the early eighteenth century). It suggested ancient grandeur, and its highly expensive ornamentation indicated that its wearers engaged only in ceremonial activities.[16]

For women servants life was often more difficult than it was for men. It was not only in small houses with only a solitary servant that hours were long and harsh. By the nineteenth century it was expected that servants would work, effectively, almost all their waking hours, with their very limited free time painfully negotiated with their mistress. They were encouraged, instead, to enjoy the pleasure of work. The numerous manuals for servants produced in the nineteenth century show that high standards of professionalism were emerging, stimulated by a growing awareness of the importance of hygiene, as well as the need to maintain large quantities of furniture and adornments and to provide increasingly elaborate meals. The performance of domestic service became, in the views of manual

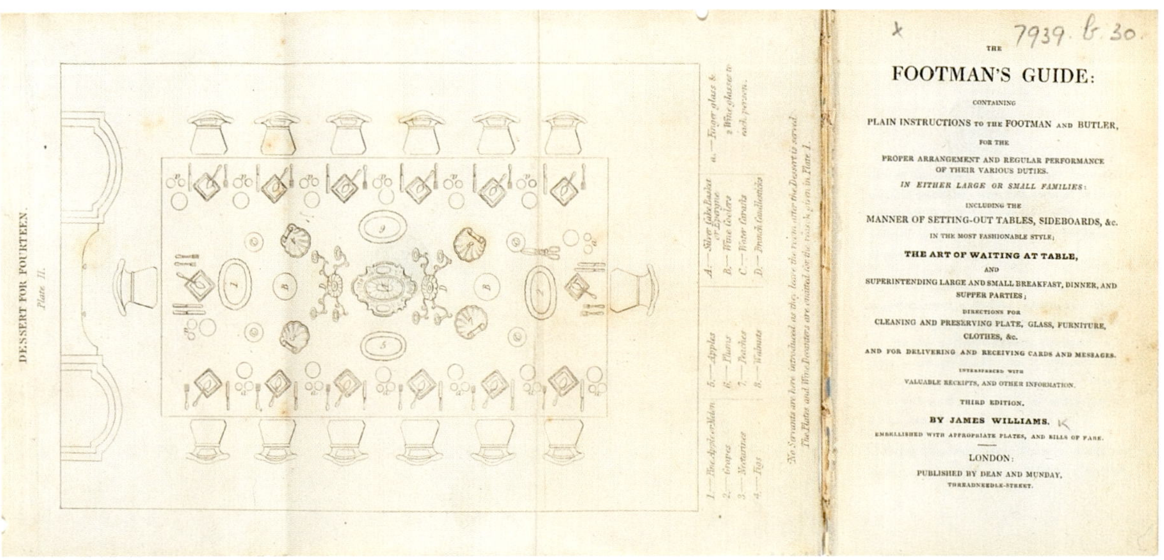

THE
FOOTMAN'S GUIDE:
CONTAINING
PLAIN INSTRUCTIONS TO THE FOOTMAN AND BUTLER,
FOR THE
PROPER ARRANGEMENT AND REGULAR PERFORMANCE
OF THEIR VARIOUS DUTIES.
IN EITHER LARGE OR SMALL FAMILIES:
INCLUDING THE
MANNER OF SETTING-OUT TABLES, SIDEBOARDS, &c.
IN THE MOST FASHIONABLE STYLE;
THE ART OF WAITING AT TABLE,
AND
SUPERINTENDING LARGE AND SMALL BREAKFAST, DINNER, AND
SUPPER PARTIES;
DIRECTIONS FOR
CLEANING AND PRESERVING PLATE, GLASS, FURNITURE,
CLOTHES, &c.
AND FOR DELIVERING AND RECEIVING CARDS AND MESSAGES.
INTERSPERSED WITH
VALUABLE RECEIPTS, AND OTHER INFORMATION.
THIRD EDITION.
BY JAMES WILLIAMS.
EMBELLISHED WITH APPROPRIATE PLATES, AND BILLS OF FARE.
LONDON:
PUBLISHED BY DEAN AND MUNDAY,
THREADNEEDLE-STREET.

Cat.49 **The Footman's Guide**
James Williams, 1840

SAMUEL AND SARAH ADAMS GIVE INSTRUCTIONS TO A NEW SERVANT:

The supreme Lord of the universe has, in his wisdom, rendered the various conditions of mankind necessary to our individual happiness: some are rich, others poor – some are masters, and others servants.
Subordination, indeed, attaches to your rank in life, but not disgrace . . .
The grand foundation of your good character must be Industry, fidelity to your employers, and an inviolable attachment to truth, both in words and deeds.

From *The Complete Servant* (1825)

writers, an intrinsically worthy goal, as Samuel and Sarah Adams made clear in their publication of 1825, *The Complete Servant*. In contrast with the laxity of the eighteenth-century situation, devotion to duty and the search for professionalism were set up, at least by employers and upper servants, as ideal targets for the Victorian servant.

By the middle of the nineteenth century most larger households had evolved into highly professional organisations. The working of these households is seldom illustrated, other than satirically (as in *Punch*, cat.91) or by the Yorkshire artist Frederick Elwell. In *The Housekeeper's Room* (1911), he shows an elegant room in an imaginary house in which the housekeeper gives her instructions for the day to a footman and housemaid. She sits while they stand deferentially before her: the functioning of an almost military hierarchy is evident (cat.50). A similar sense of order is apparent in Elwell's *The Squire (or Family Prayers)* (1931; fig.20). This is another rare, imaginary depiction of an important event in the life of many households, large or small. The master of the household sits at a table from which breakfast has not yet been cleared away, with his daughter to his left. The maids are lined up on benches to one side of the room, with the menservants grouped against a separate wall. Family prayers (which developed in the medieval period) were a crucial statement of a household's cohesion, and

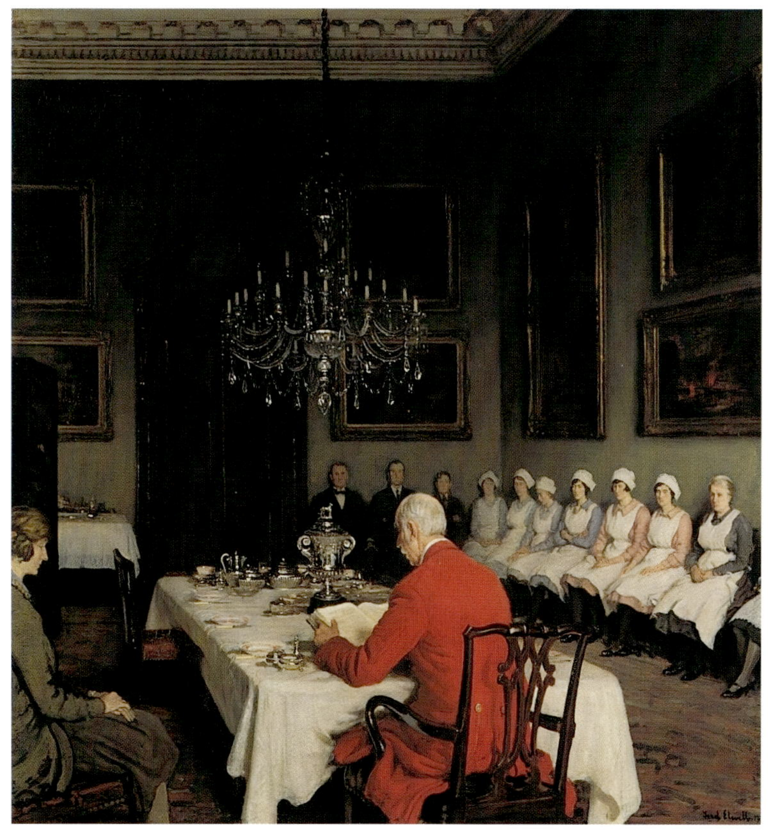

Fig.20 **The Squire (or Family Prayers)**
Frederick Elwell, 1931

Elwell combined a number of models in this fictitious rendering of the interior of a country house in Yorkshire, showing the only moment in the day when family and staff came together. For the household that did not have its own chapel, the dining room was the usual venue for this event.

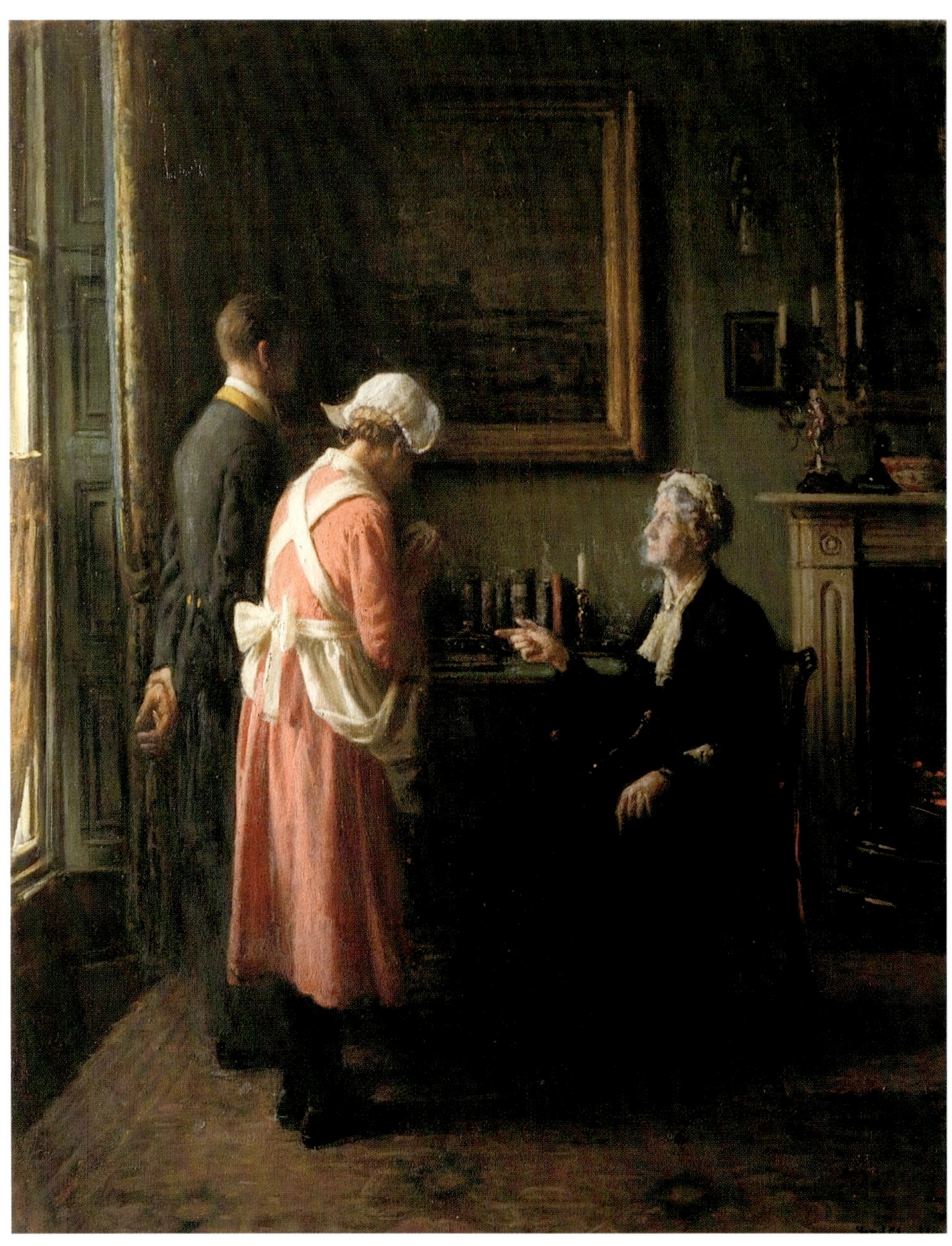

Cat.50 **The Housekeeper's Room (Morning Orders)**
Frederick Elwell, 1911

of the employers' supervision, at least in theory, of their servants' moral lives. This was the only occasion when family and servants would assemble in one room, though as one disgruntled ex-servant remarked, it was hard to believe that these five minutes were more than 'a waste of time'.[17] Prayers symbolised the rule of order, the adherence of the servants to the version of the Christian faith followed by their employers and the protective role of the employer.

Daily life for a servant was hardly comfortable, at least until the end of the nineteenth century, unless one was at the top of the system. In a large household one might expect to be fed rather well, though plainly, often on roast joints, but in houses where only one servant was kept the food would often be the family's left-overs. By and large the standard of living seems to have been equivalent to, or slightly higher than, what a servant could expect at home. Visual depictions of servants' bedrooms or the servants' hall seem to be almost non-existent: one must rely on sparse written evidence and on the dingy visual evidence offered today by empty bedrooms in the attics of country houses with tiny grates and views only of the roof.

At the same time, life was not entirely bleak. Life in service may have been regarded as a last resort in terms of employment, but it did offer some stability, and the remuneration was often not too low by contemporary standards. If one worked at the top of the profession, opportunities for entertainment certainly existed, organised by the staff for themselves or provided by employers. The servants' ball, which often took place around Christmas, was a recurring feature of country-house life from at least the seventeenth century until the early twentieth (Monica Dickens describes one such ball in the 1930s). Occasional depictions, and rather more descriptions of these events survive: the family and their friends would dance with the servants, with the master and mistress often opening the dance with the butler and housekeeper. They could be homely affairs, like the dance held at Newstead Abbey in the eighteenth century for which a rare depiction survives; or in a very wealthy house they might be splendid events.

Frederick Gorst describes the huge Twelfth Night parties held at Welbeck Abbey before the First World War. Some 1,200 guests, including all the staff, all the tenants on the estate and the local tradesmen and their wives were invited to a party for which a London orchestra and caterers, with 'a swarm of fifty waiters', were engaged. As Gorst remarked, 'It was quite a revelation to see all of the members of staff in ball dress ... as I looked around, I found that we had acquired a new kind of individuality and gaiety for the evening, and, stranger still, that we were seeing each other from a new aspect – as people, not as servants.'[18]

Cat.51 **William, 4th Lord Byron and Household at Newstead Abbey**
Peter Tillemans, 1726

This rare image depicts a servants' ball at the house of the Lords Byron in Nottinghamshire. The ball was probably held in the servants' hall. Many of the figures are identified, including William, 4th Lord Byron (1670–1736), seated at the table on the left, and Frances Lady Byron (his third wife), who is dancing. Three Byron sons are also present, two of them little boys in white dresses, and the third in his nurse's arms. Household members including the Chaplain (in black), are dancing, drinking and flirting.

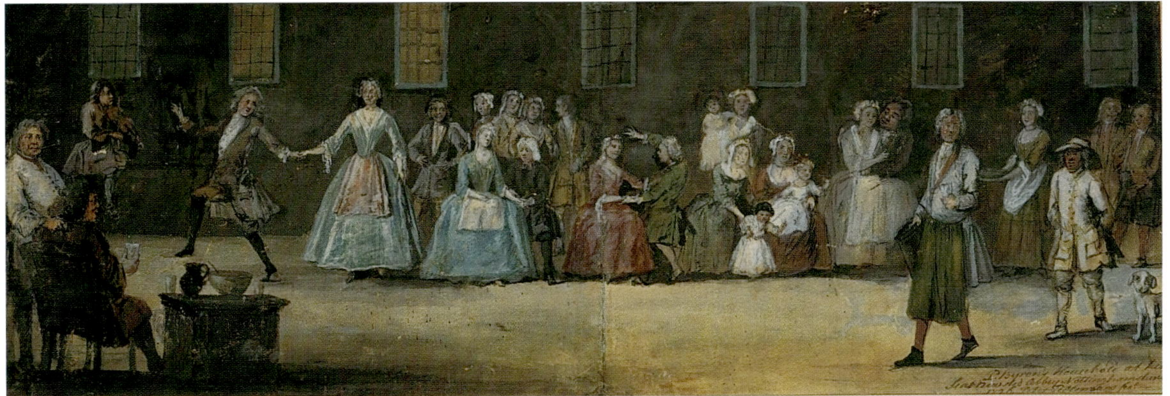

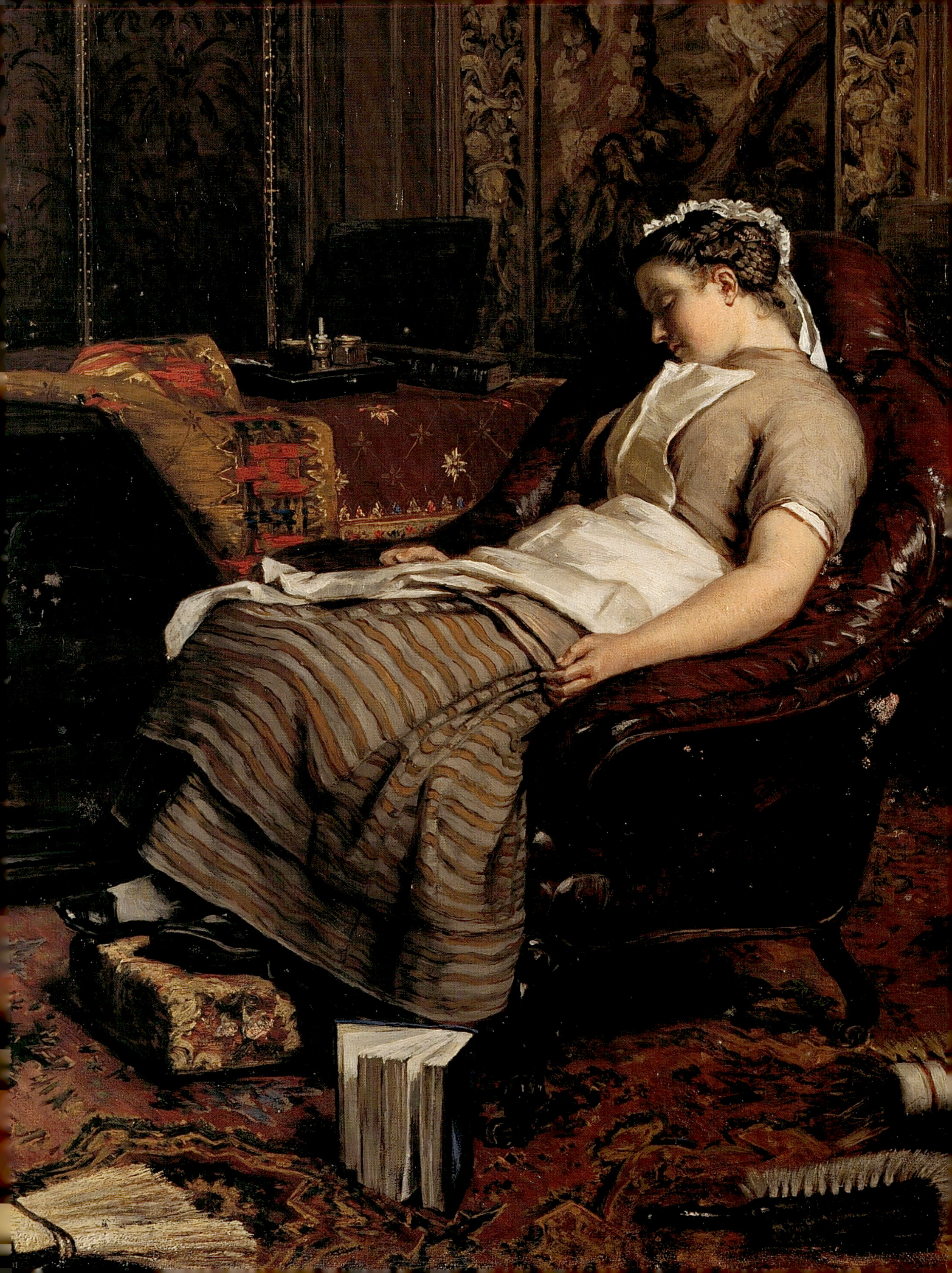

6 SERVANTS AS ARTISTS' MODELS

Anne French

IN THE LATE SEVENTEENTH and mid-eighteenth centuries, two very different artists – Charles Beale II and William Hogarth – produced records of their households in paint. These are not only of exceptional artistic importance – given that artists' households were much smaller and more informal than the great households of the day, and that relations with servants were correspondingly closer – they also act as a counterbalance to the type of servant usually represented in portraiture.

From 1779 to 1781 Charles Beale II (1660–1714 or 1726), son of the portrait painter Mary Beale (1632/3–1699), used the family's servants as models for an extensive series of red chalk drawings from life originally contained in three albums (cats. 84–5)[1]. These intimate, spontaneous studies have virtually no parallels in seventeenth-century art. Their origins, remarkable in the age of Lely when artists worked within the prescribed conventions of Baroque portraiture, can be found in the Beales' social background, in their household and studio organisation, and above all in the ideas and moral outlook current in their intellectual circle. Unlike most of those who made or commissioned servant portraits, Mary and her husband Charles Beale I (1631–1705) came from Puritan families of the Parliamentarian persuasion and were members of an intellectual circle in London which included leading clergymen, poets and members of the newly formed Royal Society.[2] In the cultivated milieu in which the Beales 'entertained courtiers and commoners together ... social barriers seem to have been relaxed'[3] and it seemed probable that this same informality extended to the Beales' treatment of their servants. Mary Beale's own *Discourse on Friendship*, written in 1666–7, provides clear evidence that she was aware of the potential for abuse in unequal relationships if those in more powerful positions imposed 'their owne opinions as Laws, esteeming themselves injured if not punctually obeyed'.[4] Charles Beale II's servant drawings surely reflect such convictions.

OPPOSITE Detail of cat.60 **Idleness**
Patrick Allan-Fraser, *c.*1871

Cat.52 Susan Gill, Maid to the Beale Family
Charles Beale II, 1680s

Beale's drawings of his family's maidservants are student exercises in life drawing, made when he was his mother's drapery painter. Mary Beale herself also made works for 'Studie and Improvement' in the early 1680s, and mother and son used many of the same models. This drawing is one of 88 sketches in Beale's '3rd Book' of 1680.

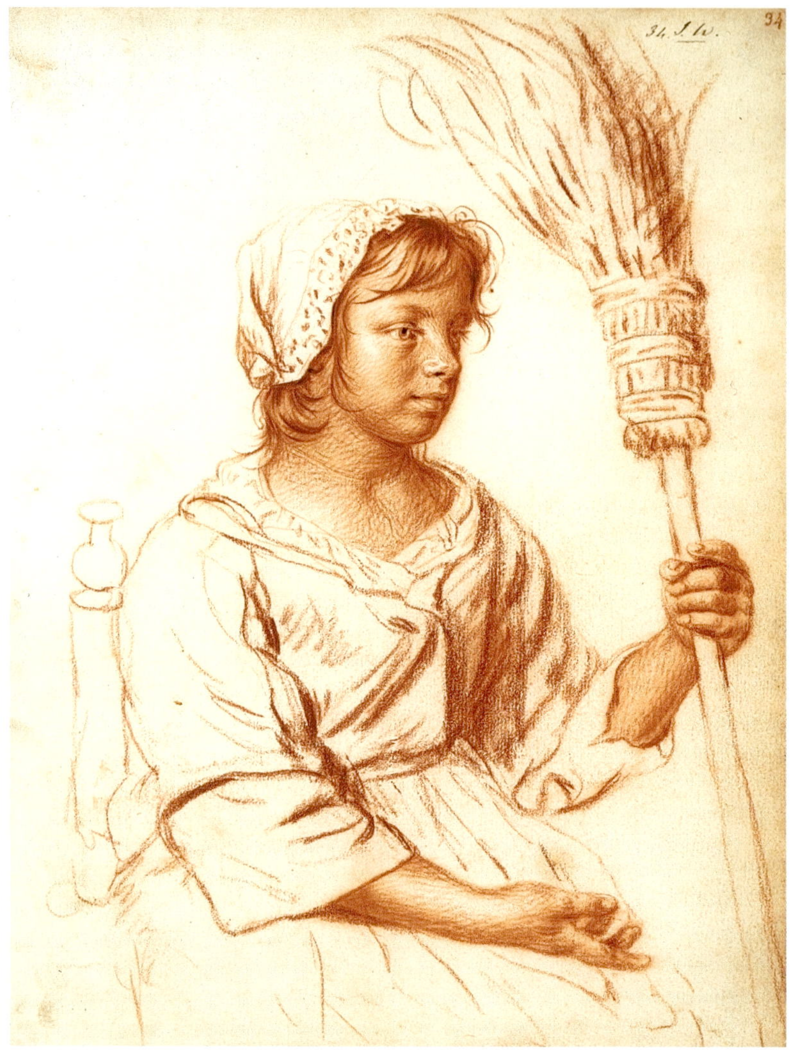

Mary Beale and her son seem to have looked to those with whom they came into daily contact in the years 1679–81 to fulfil an apparently insatiable appetite for models. Male models could be found in the studio itself, and Charles sketched the family's liveried porter, Tom, while a local tradesman, the family's colourman Carter, was a favourite sitter. For female models he turned principally to the family's maidservants. The only maidservant in Beale's '3rd Book' who can be confirmed as such by her activity – she holds a besom or broom – was formerly identified as Susan Gill, whose employment with the Beales is recorded in 1677. Other maidservants, many of whom were frequent sitters, included Su Jaxon (or Jackson), who is perhaps the model in cat.53 on the facing page, Mary Waller, 'Dowdy', 'Buttermilk', Anne Meeles, known as 'Mumping Nan', and the unidentified 'Mumping Kate'.

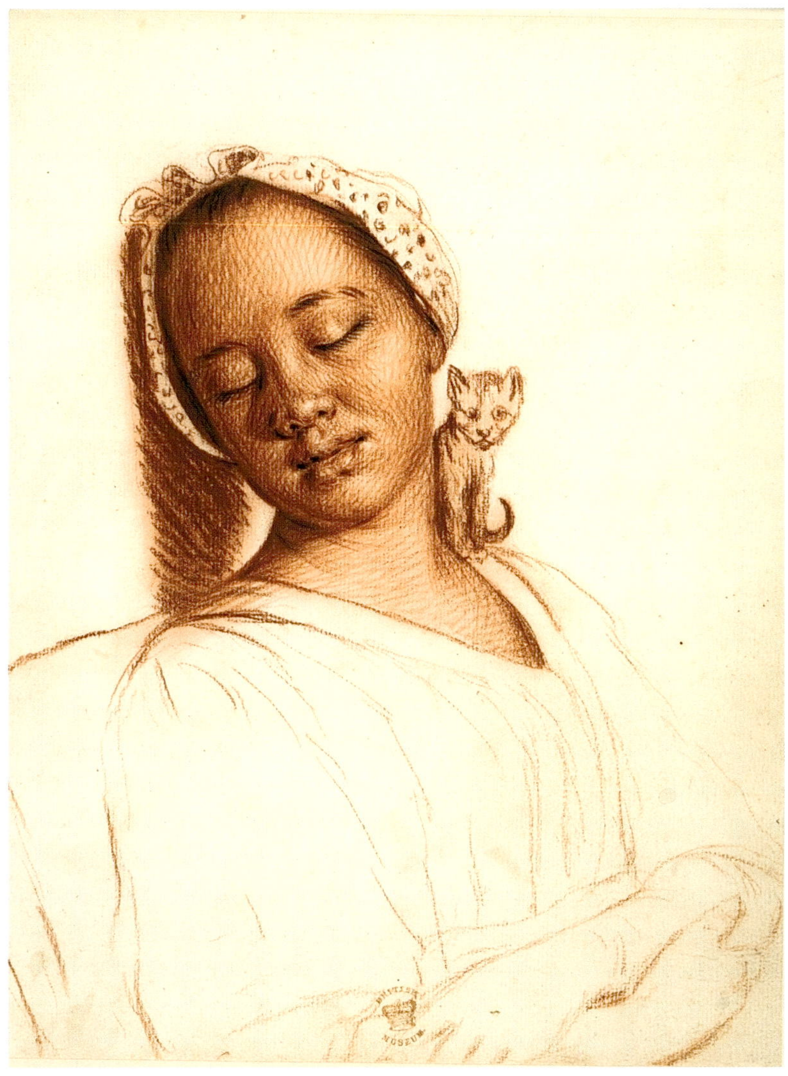

Cat.53 A Servant Girl Asleep
Charles Beale II, 1680

The Beales' maid Su Jaxon or (Jackson), perhaps the sitter in this portrait, was one of Charles Beale's most frequent models. The plain dress here is relieved only by the vertical pleats of the material, and by the lace-edged cap. Beale seized on this feature in his drawings of maidservants to provide visual relief.

Like those of his mother and John Riley (cat.27), Charles Beale's portraits seek to record a simple, truthful likeness, with no hint of flattery, and they find a clear parallel in the concerns of their friends in the newly established Royal Society who urged close observation as a basis for 'realism, accuracy and honesty'.[5] The poet Abraham Cowley, who was closely associated with the Society, recommended that the artist 'before his sight must place/the natural and living face';[6] and these very direct close-up studies conform not only to this recommendation but to the advice offered by another contemporary that the artist should observe not just 'scarres' and moales' but the 'glancing of the eyes, and the effect of laughter on the face'.[7] Models are shown at work, reading or pouring coffee, or in repose, relaxing in chairs or even asleep. Beale experiments with differing poses, facial types, expressions and lighting, using his distinctive medium of waxy-red chalk, strengthened in the eyes and lips with black lead and black chalk; the costume is treated in outline only. The cross-hatching in red chalk used for the faces is particularly expressive.

William Hogarth's servants

Unlike Beale, Hogarth chose to record his servants within the compass of a single canvas. Whereas Beale turned to his servants as models to aid his artistic training, Hogarth's portrait of his employees, painted in the later years of his life, is a much more reflective and profoundly moving analysis of the differing characters of members of his household, representing almost a summation of his career as a portraitist. Hogarth's *Servants* captures likenesses unaffected by fashion or considerations of status, and represents perhaps the single most important image of British servanthood.[8]

Very little is known of Hogarth's domestic life in a household which included his wife Jane, his sister Anne Hogarth, his mother-in-law Lady

Cat.54 **Heads of Six of Hogarth's Servants**
William Hogarth, *c.*1750–55

The placing of the six servants' heads against a plain buff background makes this more a spontaneous oil sketch than a finished portrait. Hogarth's choice of his servants as models enabled him to depict the 'seven ages of man' from youth to old age. The portrait demonstrated his ability to convey what Henry Fielding called 'the Affections of Men on canvas'.

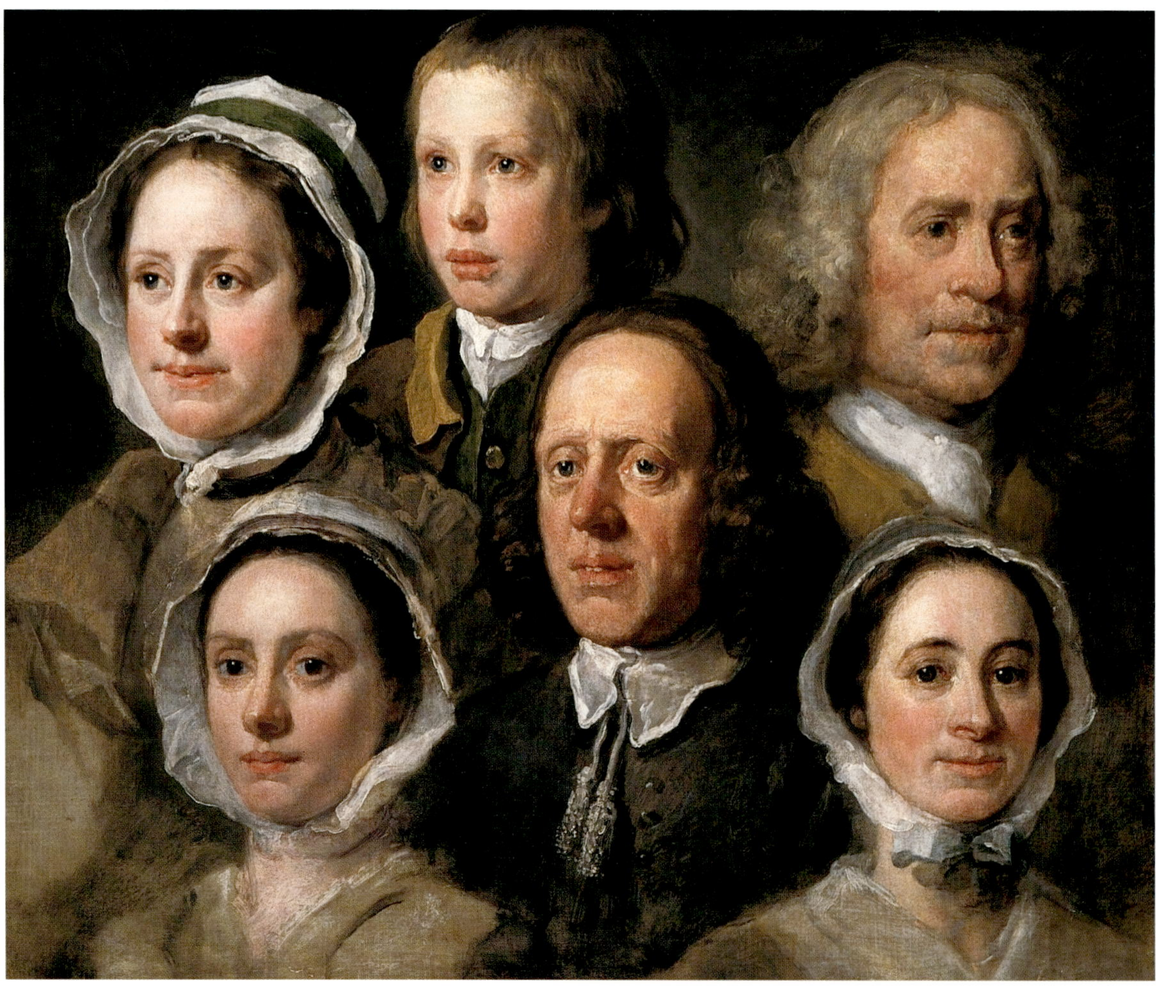

Thornhill and two young women, one of whom was Jane's cousin and companion Mary Lewis. To service this extended household, which moved between a London base in Leicester Fields and a country retreat at Chiswick, the Hogarths probably employed the complement of six servants seen here (a seventh head, however, is discernible in the lower left corner). Although this is often described as modest, it ranks with the number of servants employed by contemporary clergymen and less wealthy gentry. Only the elderly manservant can be identified with any conviction, as Ben Ives, but Jane Hogarth is recorded as having had a servant called Samuel and a housemaid called Mrs Chappel who worked at the Chiswick house and reached her centenary. Although the servants' positions within the household can only be guessed at, Ronald Paulson's suggestion that the sitters are a coachman, valet (or butler or footman?), housekeeper, boy, and two maids is convincing.

Hogarth's 'warm-hearted yet strict' treatment of his servants is noted by his early biographers, and some of his employees appear to have stayed with the family for many years. While it is dangerous to extrapolate his behaviour in the private sphere from that in the public, such attitudes are consistent with Hogarth's much more fully recorded artistic life, where his lifelong support for the St Martin's Lane Academy was based on his belief in a 'self-regulating community of equals, where superior and inferior among artists should be avoided'.[9] If Hogarth's *Servants* has affinities with other eighteenth-century 'loyal servant' portraits, it is essentially a 'friendship' portrait, comparable to those paintings of family and friends with which Hogarth surrounded himself in his later years – and hence a more personal testament to affection and trust than most such exemplars. The painting can also be seen as a private study, inspired by Hogarth's love of painting. However, there were probably other, more practical reasons for its production. The picture hung in Hogarth's studio, and may have acted as an advertisement for his exceptional skill at differentiating character, although it may predate by a few years his unsuccessful attempt to revitalise his career as a portraitist from around 1757.

The compelling power of Hogarth's image derives in large part from its sketch-like quality, what Lawrence Gowing has called a pointed defiance of all compositional devices. The accumulation of heads, unusual in portraiture, is reminiscent of the principle of accretion found in Old Master drawings and in Hogarth's own graphic work. The servants look out individually towards the viewer, entirely self-contained, each set of eyes retaining its own focal point, although the division of the six heads into three loose vertical pairings lends the painting an overall rhythm and unity.[10] The heads are placed together in a narrower confine of space than would have been acceptable in a commissioned portrait, which 'unconsciously expresses the sitters' inferior rank'. However, if his *Servants* 'signifies subordination, it signifies democracy even more';[11] painting his social 'inferiors' enabled him to analyse his sitters without flattery, but it is his emphasis on a shared humanity that marks out this image of servanthood from all others.

Two other eighteenth-century artists also painted or drew their own or their family's maidservants. If an early inscription on the mezzotint by John Faber Jr after Philippe Mercier's print *Molly, Girl with a Tea Tray* (fig.22) is to be believed, the sitter is his maid Hannah; however, this comes closer to his genre paintings of maidservants (pp.133–4) than to Hogarth. In the late 1780s, Paul Sandby made a series of intimate, domestic studies in watercolour centred around the young children of his son Thomas Paul Sandby and his wife Harriet, and their nursemaids. These share the informality of Beale's and Hogarth's treatment of their servants.

George Morland and his manservant Gibbs

Service in poverty is recorded only rarely in paint, with the exception of genre painting (fig.21). *The Artist in His Studio with His Man Gibbs* by George

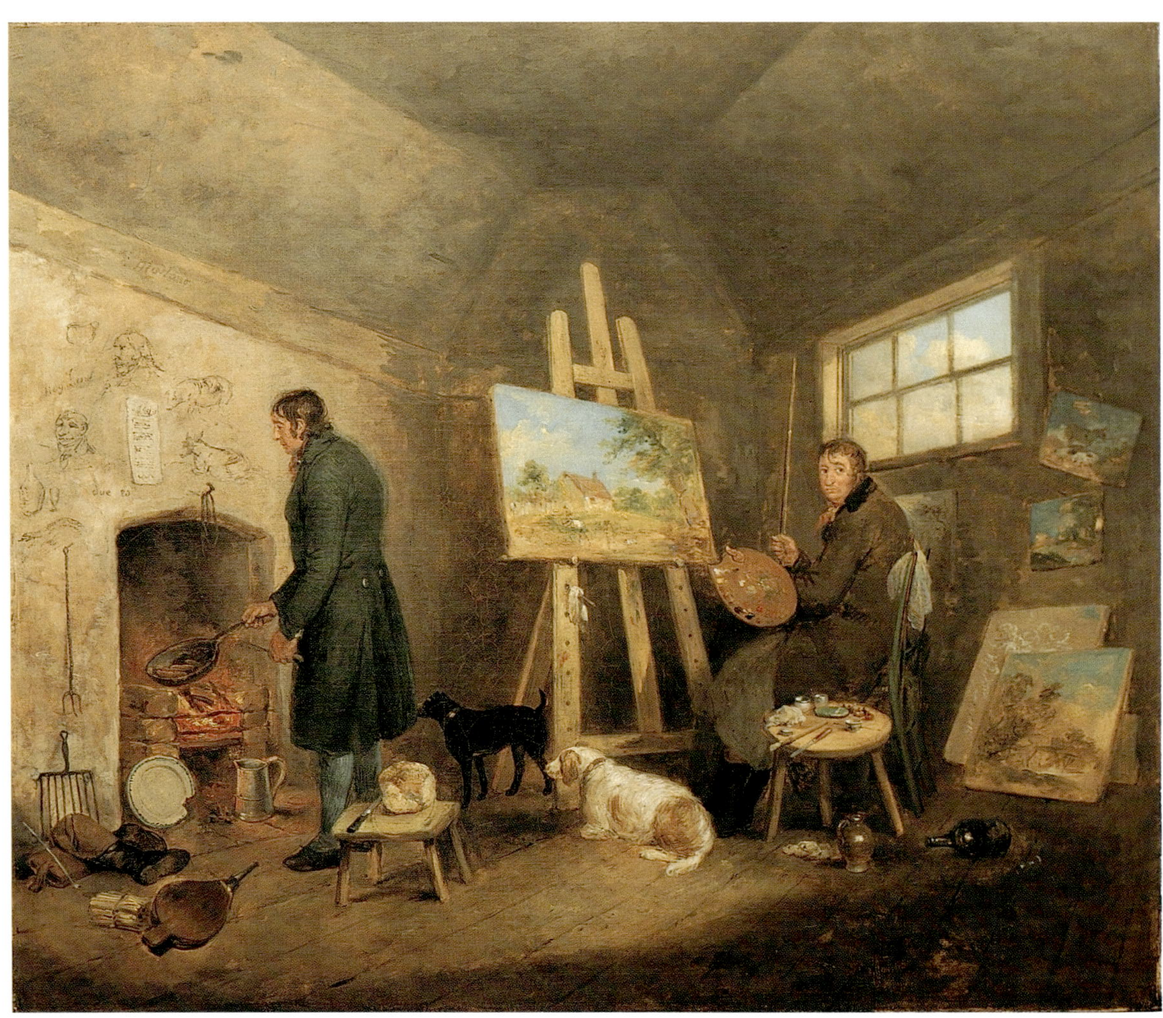

Cat.55 **The Artist in His Studio with His Man Gibbs**
George Morland, *c.*1802

Morland never gave up employing a manservant, even in the last impoverished years of his life, apparently regarding this as his link with respectability. He paid Gibbs one guinea per week, needing his assistance at the easel as, in declining health, he hastily completed canvases to satisfy creditors.

Morland (1763–1804) therefore constitutes a remarkable document in which a servant is shown sharing his master's virtual destitution. Morland was among the most talented British eighteenth-century artists. However, as Barrell points out, he 'isolated himself from the contemporary culture of the polite classes for whom he painted' preferring to 'spend his time with his social inferiors'.[12] His profligate lifestyle, which included an addiction to alcohol, meant that he was constantly in debt and frequently having to move to avoid creditors. In 1799 he was finally imprisoned, living within the rules of the King's Bench.

This self-portrait (cat.55) was probably painted soon after his release from debtors' prison in 1801, only a few years before his early death from alcoholism, and probably not long before he was obliged to give up painting owing to ill-health. Morland depicts himself and his manservant in the garret of lodgings in Paddington which had been rented by his wife while he was in prison. The artist is at his easel, with a pile of unfinished canvases stacked nearby, while Gibbs, described by one biographer as Morland's cook, fries sausages over the fire. The bare floor boards, in a room decorated only with the artist's animal sketches on the wall above the fireplace (which also appears to contain notification of an unpaid bill), disordered belongings and the meagre fare of bread and sausages illustrate the broken condition to which Morland has sunk, as, equally, does the artist's own appearance. The inclusion by Morland of Gibbs as his companion is far from accidental; his preference for working-class company is known to have embraced servants. Morland is said to have kept two grooms and a footman in his more successful days.[13] Gibbs was a replacement for Morland's former servant George Sympson, who had been obliged to leave during Morland's imprisonment.

Amateur artists and their servants

Drawing was a highly fashionable activity with the leisured classes in the eighteenth and early nineteenth centuries. Two extended, and very different records of servants in drawing or watercolour were produced by amateur artists in the period from 1815 to 1830.

The Dartmouth family's servant drawings

Principally in 1815 and 1820, the artist children of George, 3rd Earl of Dartmouth, Heneage (cats 56, 57), Anne, Charlotte, and Barbara Maria Legge, then in early adulthood, made twenty-three sketches of the servants at their Staffordshire house, Sandwell Hall.[14] The Legges were among a small number of often inter-related aristocratic families who were active as amateurs over more than one generation, and the mother of this large family, Frances, was the sister of Heneage Finch, 4th Earl of Aylesford, one of the most talented of eighteenth-century amateurs. The Dartmouths were pupils of William Mulready (1786–1863) who, like many professionals,

Cat.56 **James Richards**
Heneage Legge, 1815

James Richards is one of two kitchen-men protrayed by Heneage Legge in 1815. The group of servant drawings sketched by him and his sisters shows them experimenting with different poses and techniques under their drawing master Mulready. Heneage Legge's preferred method of draughtsmanship was for loose, dramatic effects in black chalk on blue paper.

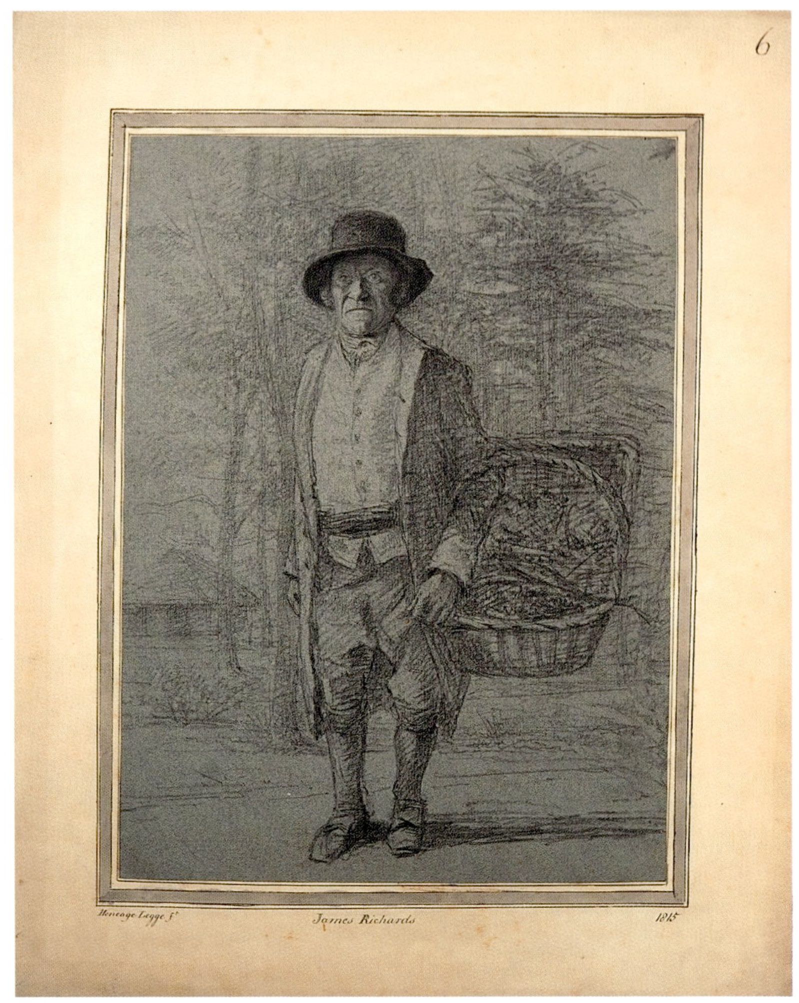

supplemented his income by teaching, and the ten servant drawings dating to 1815 can probably be seen as student exercises, in which several of the Legge siblings participated.

Although most of the sitters' names are recorded, it is only possible to identify a small number as definitely representing servants. *P. White*, drawn in 1820 by Lady Barbara Newdigate (*née* Legge) in fashionable garb, is surely the Sandwell housekeeper, while *Mary Arms* (1815), plucking a goose or duck, may be an elderly kitchen-maid. Rather more of the outdoor staff can be recognised, from *David Davies* with his spade, *William Meade*, whose whip or crop suggests that he is a coachman, huntsman, or keeper, to *Thomas Arms* and *James Richards* (cat.56), who, with their large wicker baskets comparable to that held by Jack Nicholas, the kitchen porter at Erddig, are surely kitchen-men.

Some of the sitters may have been tenants on the Sandwell estate, or retired servants, instead of being actually in service with the family, although

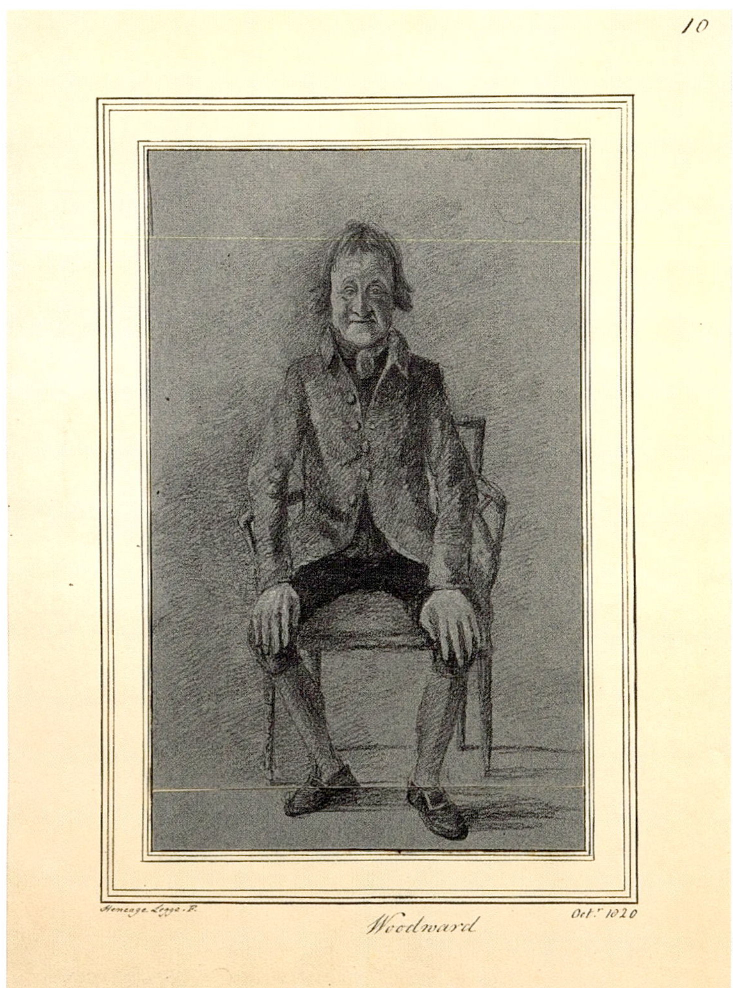

Cat.57 **Woodward**
Heneage Legge, 1820

Heneage Legge made three further studies of servants, experimenting with more complex poses and expressions. Woodward sits bolt upright in a chair, fixing the spectator with an alert, quizzical gaze. The family's interest in sketching their servants continued into later life; studies by three of Heneage's siblings date from the later 1820s to 1850.

the former would beg the question as to how they were so well known to the Legges that they became the subjects for their drawings. Mrs Mason, listed as a tenant in 1814–15 at the relatively high rent of £10 per annum, may be the dignified, well-dressed model who sat to Charlotte Legge in that year, while a Thomas Woodward was paying £2 3s in 1819–20 at the time '*Woodward*' (cat.57) sat for his portrait.[15] The drawing itself, however, showing Woodward seated on a Chinese Chippendale chair, wearing breeches, coat and buckled shoes, together with its familiar inscription, strongly implies that this is an indoor servant, perhaps a footman or butler.

The Hawksworth Fawkes Album

Like the Dartmouths, the Fawkes family of Farnley Hall in Yorkshire were gifted amateurs. Walter Fawkes, J.M.W. Turner's great patron and friend, was himself a talented draughtsman, and at least three of his children are known to have sketched, among them Walter's eldest surviving son

Cat.58 **A Cowper Brewer**
Francis Hawksworth Fawkes, *c.*1820s

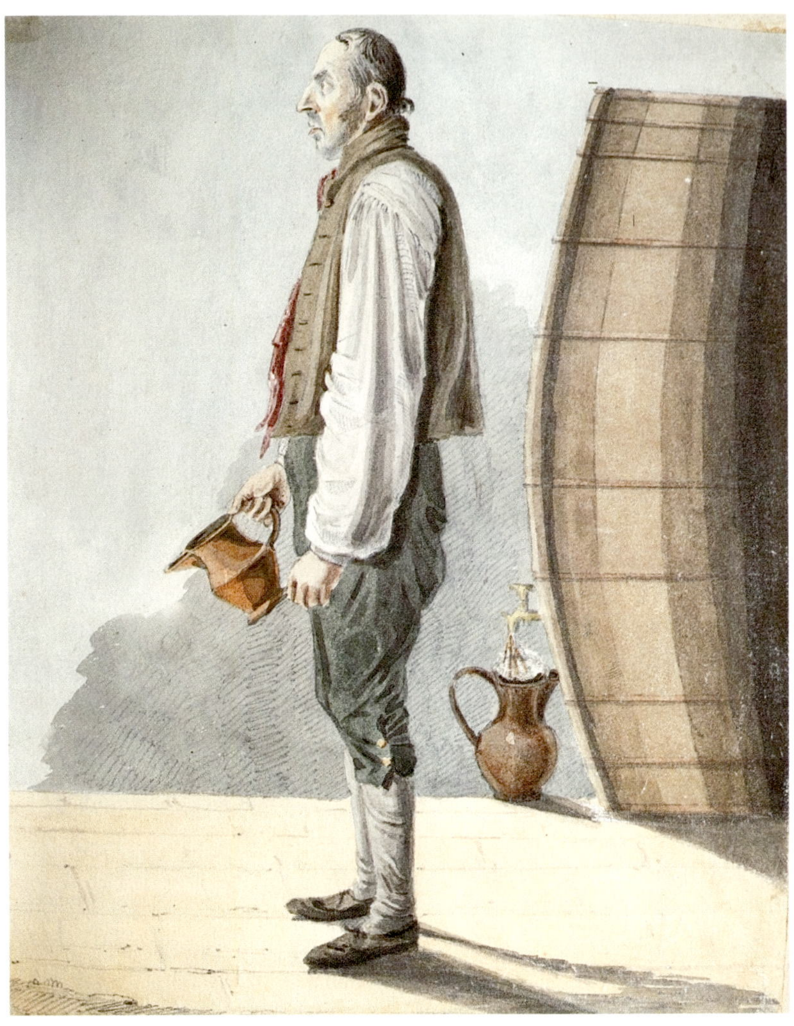

Francis Hawksworth (1797–1871), who compiled a watercolour album containing 126 affectionate, if often trenchant, caricatures of his relations, friends and neighbours among the Yorkshire gentry and clergy, and of seventeen of the family's servants (cat.58) in the 1820s. In 1802, the family employed fourteen male servants, so these drawings, all but one of which is of male employees, probably represent a considerable proportion of the complement of male staff. Unlike the Dartmouth drawings, these are not individual studies made under a drawing master for improvement, using models conveniently close to hand. Instead, they are contained within the context of an album which was almost certainly created for indoor amusement, and the servants' inclusion is therefore very much as part of an extended 'family'.

The predominantly male flavour of the album, which includes a number of sporting cartoons accompanied by inscriptions mercilessly poking fun at inept sportsmen, does much to account for the inclusion of

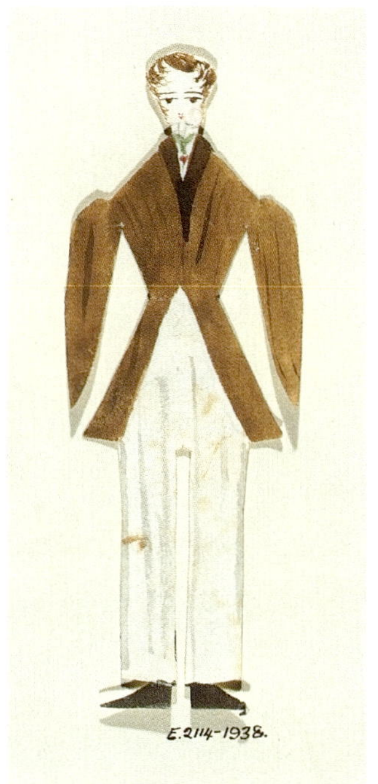

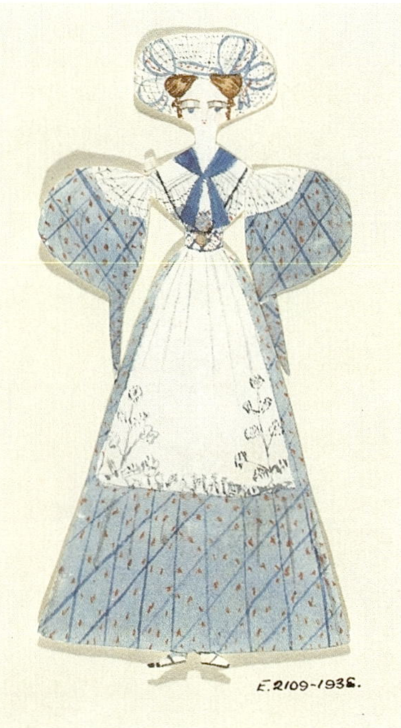

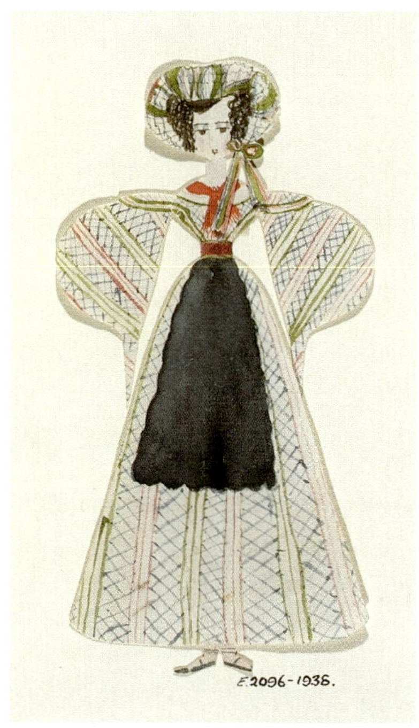

Cat.59 **Cut-outs: Family servant, Mr Swift, known as 'Horrible Dick'; Lady's Maid Miss Morpline; Family Embroiderer Miss Collins**
Susan and Marion Drummond, *c.*1830–32

These cut-outs of family servants in and out of livery were made by children of the Drummond family of Denton in Buckinghamshire. Cut-outs, then as now, offered an amusing occupation for young girls. Their skills at such activities could lead to elaborate designs such as the paper cut-outs made earlier by the blue-stocking Mary Delany and her circle.

no less than five keepers among the servant drawings, which represent an almost continuous series in the album from Nos 92 to 115. Shooting was a key element of life at Farnley. The other identifiable staff in the album are the coachman, gardener, cowper brewer, cowman, carpenter, kitchen-man and 'Old Maude', who carted coals. Only two indoor staff appear: a liveried footman John Lilford and maid Hannah Holmes, the only female servant recorded. Given that the humour is that of a man robustly satirising his male contemporaries, it is significant that the servant images are noticeably less biting in their satire than the other drawings, hovering on the borderline between a straightforward sketch and a caricature. Either Fawkes felt uncomfortable satirising those less fortunate than himself, or he reserved his sharpest satire for those he knew familiarly. The 'Mr George Fox' portrayed is presumably the Fawkes's neighbour George Lane Fox of Bramham, who also had portraits of his servants painted in the 1820s (see p.67).

The nineteenth century

In 1871, the wealthy elderly Scottish artist and art patron Patrick Allan-Fraser of Hospitalfield (1813–90) exhibited at the Royal Scottish Academy a genre painting, *Idleness* (cat.60), for which the model was one of his own maidservants. Instead of representing an idle servant – the painting was long known as *An Idle Housemaid* – the painting indicates that the maid has fallen asleep while dutifully trying to absorb a dull and long-winded improving book entitled *An Unpopular View of our Times* (1861), written by Allan-Fraser himself. Allan-Fraser's foray into servant portraiture was no

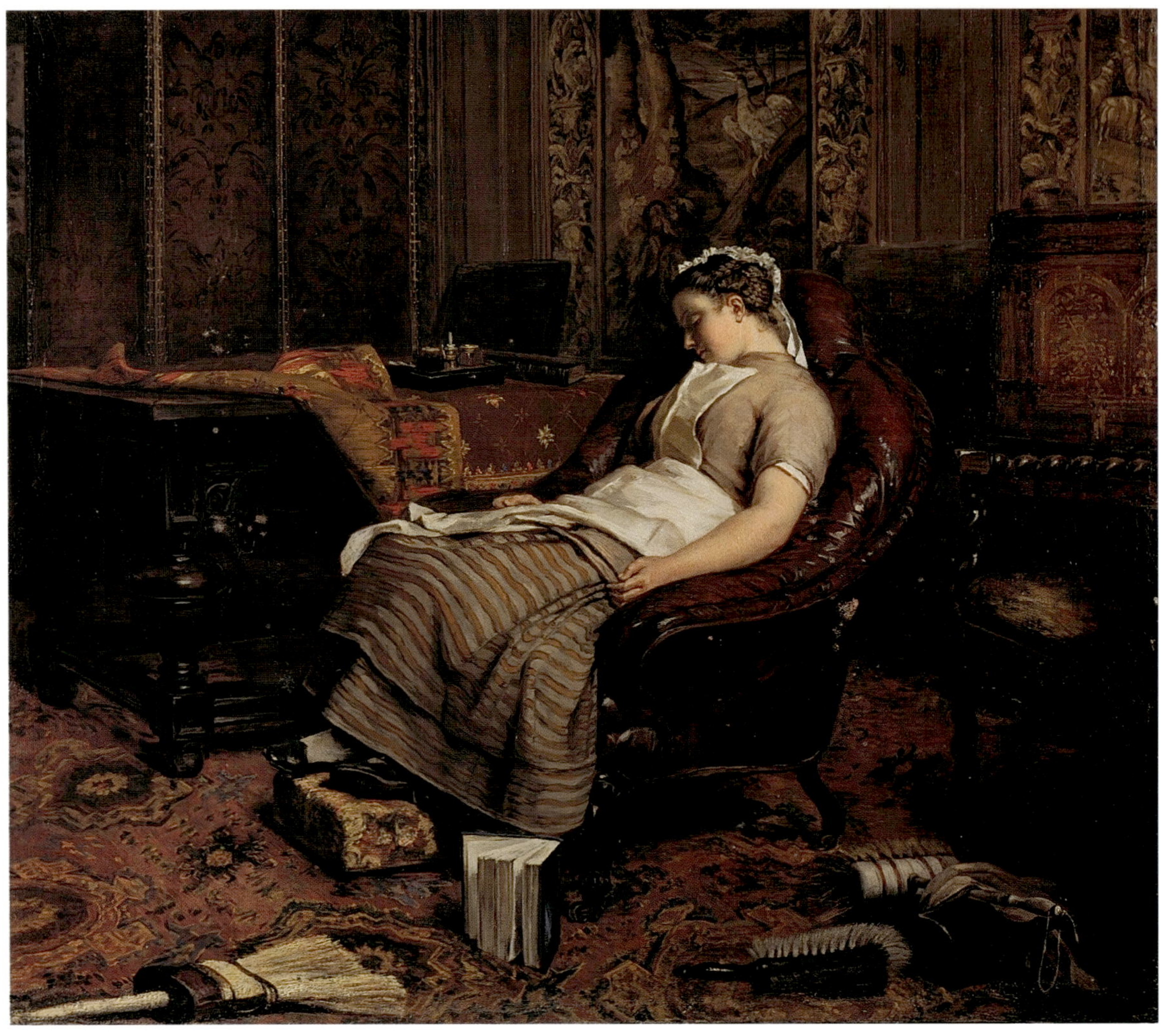

Cat.60 Idleness
Patrick Allan-Fraser, *c*.1871

Allan-Fraser's studio at Hospitalfield, in which he painted this housemaid, still survives. However, the tapestries and other contents shown here do not. Before his marriage, Allan-Fraser was a professional artist and a pupil of Robert Scott Lauder in Rome. In 1841, after his return to Scotland he exhibited with The Clique, a London sketching club which included W.P. Frith and Augustus Egg as members, both of whom also portrayed servants.

isolated event, but sprang from his social philosophy and philanthropic outlook. Like earlier patrons involved in servant portraiture, he and his wife Elizabeth were beneficent employers. Having restored Elizabeth's family estates to profitability, the Allan-Frasers' reconstruction of Hospitalfield – the original of Scott's Monkbarns in *The Antiquary* – saw them gradually moving away from the baronial style towards 'a closer association with the natural environment', encouraging local workmen to develop their talents. Among these was the coachman's nephew, David Maver, who carved the Drawing Room ceiling with a 'catalogue of the botanical life of the estate' in fruitwood.[16]

The twentieth century

The early twentieth century saw a revival in the practice of artists turning to their servants as models. Sometimes these sitters were maids. However, with the decline of live-in servants, and the departure of younger girls to work in factories or shops, the char became the archetypal servant of the new century, and these women provided artists with models full of character. So, too, did the landlady, who, although not strictly a servant, often waited on and fed her lodgers. One particular theme became predominant: the servant as an element in still-life painting, which derives from a revival of interest around 1900 in Dutch genre painting. Here servants appear as a by-product of the artist's depiction of the domestic interior, their inclusion dictated largely by aesthetic considerations.

Given their focus on painting subjects drawn from everyday life, including intimate interiors with 'women sewing – women taking tea – persons conversing in parlours',[17] and ventures into the land of the bedsit, Camden Town artists might have been expected to produce important portrayals of servants. Early examples include Harold Gilman's *In Sickert's House, Neuville* (*c.*1907)[18] and *The Kitchen* (*c.*1908; cat.61) painted shortly after his meeting with Sickert in 1907, the year in which both men became founder members of the Fitzroy Street Group. Both show maidservants as an element of what is effectively a still-life painting; *The Kitchen* probably represents the interior at 15 Westholme Green, Letchworth, Hertfordshire, where the Gilmans lived from 1908 to 1909. The subject of a figure viewed through an open door had already appeared in Sickert's *Woman Washing Her Hair* (1906), and in Duncan Grant's *The Kitchen* (1902).

If the subject of Gilman's *The Kitchen* is pure Camden Town, then the handling and muted tones reflect the tonal qualities of Whistler and the influence of Velásquez and of Dutch seventeenth-century genre scenes, where servants are routinely represented in domestic interiors. Vermeer was a rediscovery of this period, and *The Kitchen* undoubtedly exudes a 'Vermeer-like quietude'.[19] The sense of bleak isolation, evident in the way in which the maid's face and back are deliberately turned away from view, is perhaps a metaphor for the distance between servant and employer, while the open doorway offers the viewer a limited glimpse of her enclosed world.

Some years later, in 1916, Gilman painted several portraits of his landlady Mrs Mounter,[20] in rooms near Fitzroy Square, London, which he had rented following his separation from his first wife. Though not a servant, Mrs Mounter certainly looked after her lodger, and these

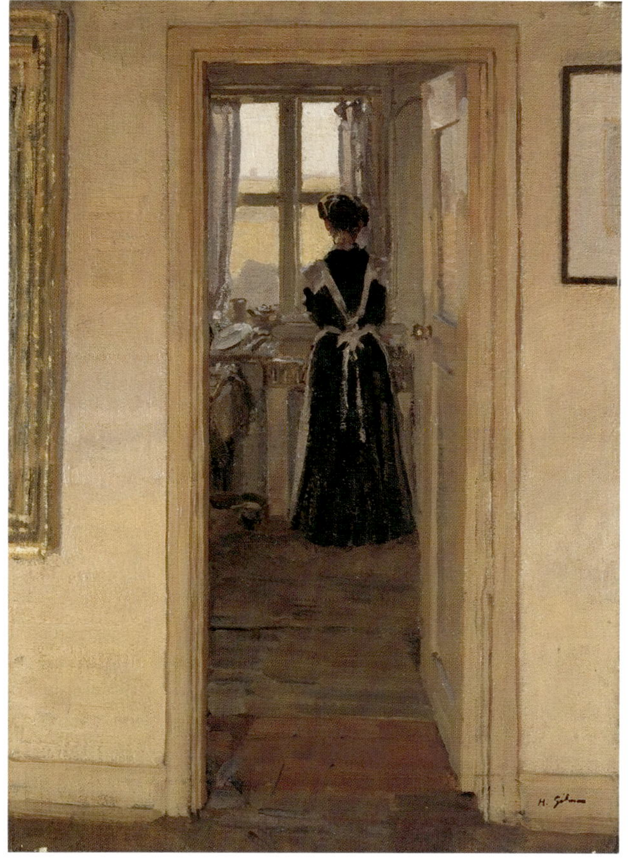

Cat.61 **The Kitchen**
Harold Gilman, *c.*1908

Among the artists who included servants as compositional elements in interiors were several members of the Camden Town and Bloomsbury groups including Gilman himself, Walter Sickert, Duncan Grant and Vanessa Bell. Even as late as the 1930s many artists could still afford to employ servants, and they formed a natural subject for inclusion when artists focused on their own living spaces.

powerful images offer a striking interpretation of an ordinary working woman within the constraints of what is, again, a still-life painting, this time modelled on Cézanne.

Walter Sickert (1860–1942) also used his servants as models. His odd-job man 'Hubby' and charlady Marie, appear together in a number of his interiors, notably *Ennui* (*c.*1914)[21] in which Sickert explored the despair and isolation created by boredom and a dislocated relationship. In the later *L'Armoire à Glace* (1924)[22] conceived in Dieppe two years earlier, the model was Marie Pepin, Sickert's maidservant since 1911. As the title makes clear, the model seated in the background takes second place to the wardrobe itself, which partially obscures her.

The Bloomsbury group's interest in copying natural appearances with 'disinterested vision' also led Duncan Grant and Vanessa Bell to select subjects close to their everyday lives, including their maids and charwomen. Like Beale's or Hogarth's before them, these relate to 'friendship' portraits of others in their circle. Vanessa Bell's contemplative *Interior with Housemaid* (1939),[23] which looks back to the Gilman 'still-life' mode, includes the figure of the 'angel of Charleston', Grace Higgens, who worked for them for nearly fifty years as maid, nanny, cook and housekeeper, and was the only non-family member to attend Bell's funeral. *Mrs Langford* (1930)[24] was Grant's charwoman at 8 Fitzroy Street and 'did' for many artists in the area during the 1930s; she was a source of local gossip and a 'real character' according to Grant, whose moving portrayal echoes Cézanne.

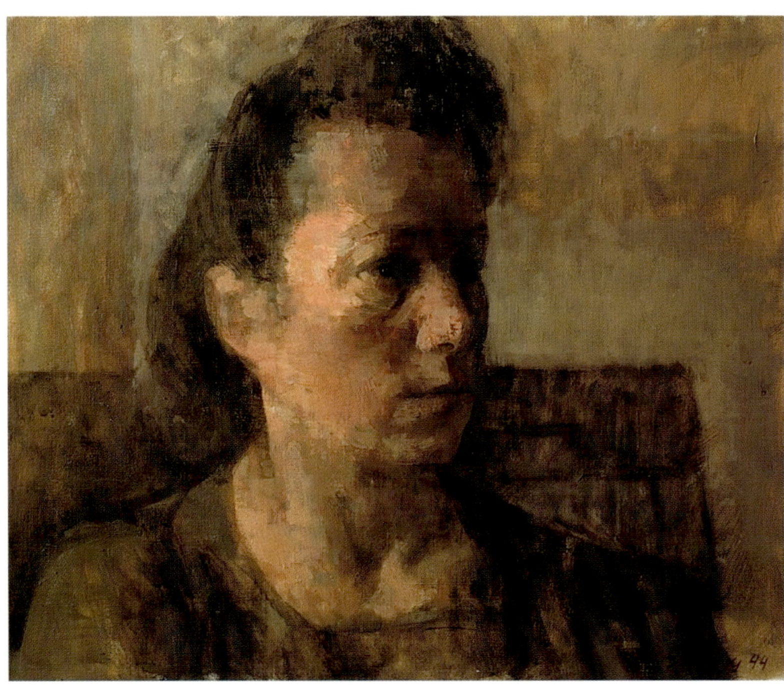

Cat.62 **Mrs Roberts**
Sir Lawrence Gowing, 1944

Gowing was studying Masaccio's *Tribute Money* at the time he painted Mrs Roberts. He recognised that the 'unidealised sympathy and the visual authenticity' evident here were inspired by this Renaissance painting. Unusually for a servant portrait, the sitter's reaction to her portrait survives: 'It's me, isn't it?' she told the *Daily Sketch* in 1945. 'Perhaps in another hundred years I will be hanging in a national museum'

In the 1920s another member of the Bloomsbury set, Dora Carrington (1893–1932), found at her home, Tidmarsh, all the subjects she needed: the mill itself, the garden and river, and her maid-of-all-work, Annie, whom she painted at least twice, against a backdrop of kitchen shelves (1921), and in a pinafore (*c*.1925). The earlier portrait, which Carrington sent for exhibition to the International in April 1921, represents a conscious exercise in the simplified and monumental forms of Renoir, an interest shared with Mark Gertler, in his own directly comparable *Servant Girl* (1923). As Gertler wrote to Carrington: 'I wonder which is the most Renoir-like, your girl or mine.'[25]

A direct descendant in spirit of Gilman's *Mrs Mounter* is the sensitive study of his 'gaunt and gracious'[26] cleaning lady *Mrs Roberts* (cat.62) by Sir Lawrence Gowing (1918–91). A member of the Euston Road School, which sought to recall contemporary art to the observation of ordinary life, including the study of the working classes, Gowing's portrait of Ellen Roberts, painted at the Gowings' home in Paultons Square, Chelsea, in 1944, exemplifies his comment that 'I privately thought of the subdued but respectful manner in which I painted as in some way identifying with people deprived of the fruits of their labour ...'[27] 'One's whole aim is to integrate virtues, vices, boredom, passion until they hang together inseparably, the visible evidence of a person to be taken as a whole.'[28] If respect for those in a socially inferior position is implicit in the earlier portraits of their servants by Beale or Hogarth, Gowing's comments are the first to articulate the artist's awareness of his relationship with his servant model; like Hogarth he sought to identify not just with his sitter's subordinate status, but with her personality as a whole.

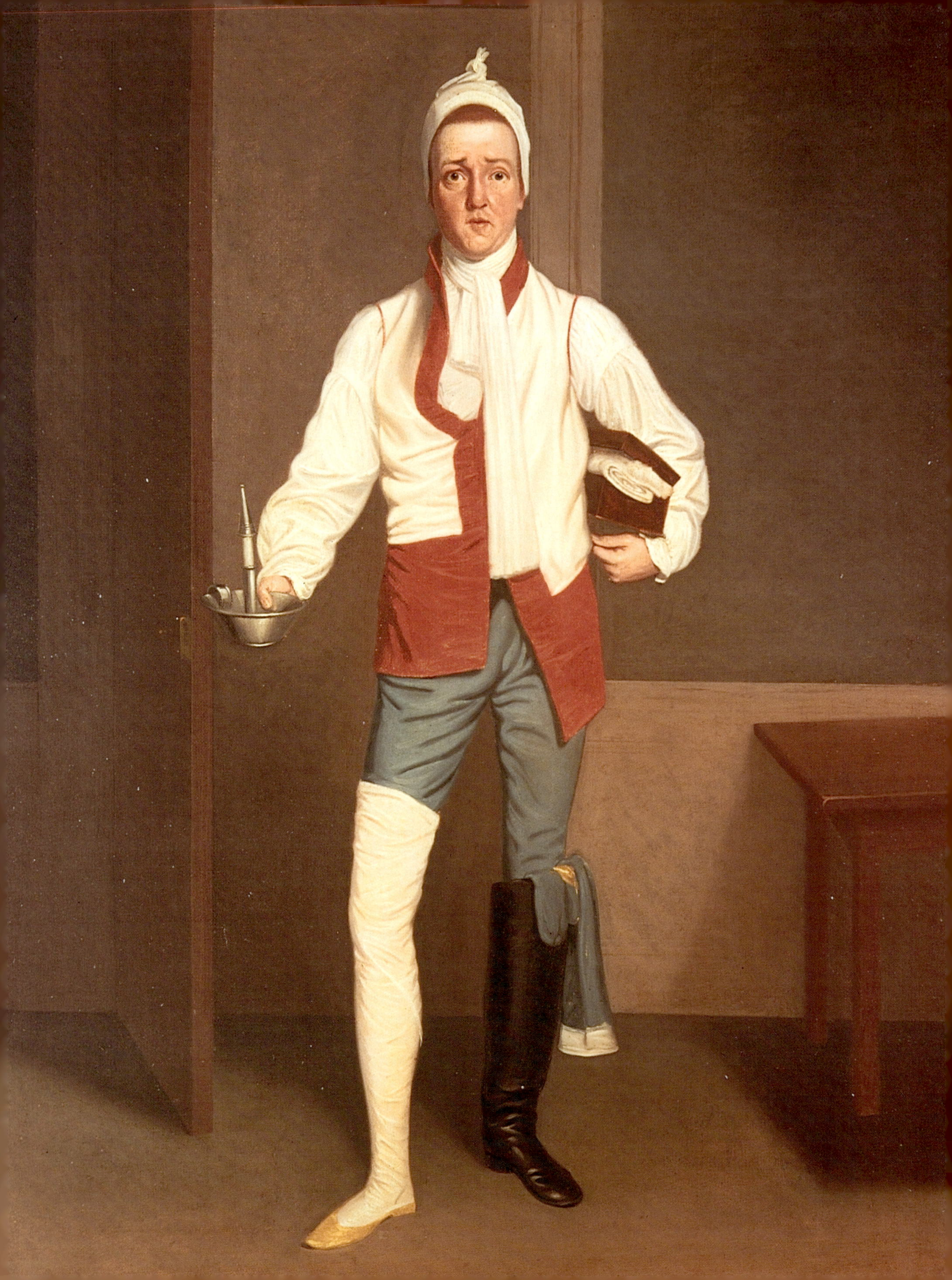

7 THE AMBIGUOUS SERVANT

Anne French

MUCH OF THE DEBATE concerning servants aired in eighteenth-century Britain, both from the employer's viewpoint and, to a lesser extent, that of the employee, was canvassed in literature, on the stage and in the moral narratives of Hogarth, his contemporaries and successors. On the whole, the focus, in tune with the general thrust of the age, was on 'faulty' servants, in particular on their perceived exploitation of their employers and aping of their employers' manners and mores. The ignorant rural footman or manservant, and the Figaro-type servant as in the bumpkin Jacob Gawkey or the aptly named Timothy Sharp, 'schemer general' in David Garrick's *The Lying Valet*, were staple comic ingredients in a theatre which could no longer rely on the multi-layered great household of Shakespeare's day for models. However, in *Pamela* (1740) Samuel Richardson, who had risen from humble origins, explored many of the themes of concern to servants themselves, such as the sexual exploitation of women servants by their masters, the entering of service to improve one's prospects, notably through marriage, the pressures of home circumstances which forced young people into service, and the loss of personal identity involved.

In a number of cases, notably Joseph Highmore's and Philippe Mercier's scenes from *Pamela*, artists seem to have seized independently on the opportunity to capitalise on a novel, play or poem's continuing success, by producing paintings about servants that were usually designed to appeal to a wider market through engraving. There is no record of a major painting on the theme of servanthood belonging to an eighteenth-century collector, although Edward Penny must have exhibited his *A Description of a City Shower* at the Free Society of Artists in 1764 in that hope. Most theatrical paintings featuring servants were painted primarily as records of an actor's performance, or for inclusion in John Bell's *The British Theatre* (1791–7) which, with John Boydell's Shakespeare Gallery, was the other major project of this period to involve artists with the theatre.

OPPOSITE Detail of cat.70 **Charles Matthews as Somno in *The Sleepwalker***
Samuel de Wilde, *c.*1813

This chapter also explores the 'ambiguous' servant – aristocrats or gentry masquerading as employees in portraiture – although the ambiguities of those former servants like the poet and publisher Robert Dodsley, whose abilities enabled them to move out of servitude, are not included, given that these men and women were rarely portrayed during their years in service. Similarly, although it has recently been established that some servants were not only literate but literary, and, again like Dodsley, spoke in their own voice, no visual images survive.

Servants in literature

Richardson's great novel *Pamela, or Virtue Rewarded* (1740), is not only one of the earliest and greatest English novels, it is also, together with the imitations it spawned, notably Fielding's satirical *Shamela* (1741) and *Joseph Andrews* (1742), one of the rare works in the eighteenth-century canon where the servant stands centre stage. As the story of a virtuous maidservant whose epic resistance to the repeated attempts at seduction by her employer, the wealthy squire Mr. B., finally leads to their marriage, and her integration into a higher social group, it represents the rags-to-riches Cinderella story at its most compelling, standing at the head of a central tradition in the novel from Jane Austen's *Pride and Prejudice* to Charlotte Bronte's *Jane Eyre*. An immediate bestseller, combining the 'attractions of a sermon and a striptease',[1] *Pamela* went into six editions in two years, and was translated into five other languages. This was the first great novel of sentiment, appealing specifically to the tastes of the new middle class: its depiction of domestic virtue and the 'social disciplining of the unregenerate Adam' in Mr B. are related to the emergence of the nuclear family, in which the voluntary relationship between a man and woman became central to the concept of marriage.[2] If Richardson's themes were topical, his anti-heroic approach, locating class conflict, romantic love and sexuality firmly within the world of an English gentry household, also appealed to his readership.

Although *Pamela* was read avidly by the middle and upper classes, many of the novel's early readers were probably servants, who had opportunities to read not shared by most working people: more time and opportunity, the presence of books in the house, candle-light and greater spending money, not having to pay for food or lodgings.[3] Pamela herself, as letter writer *par excellence*, is a prime example of the developing literacy of this social group, and the book's popularity with maidservants and the working class is supported by Lady Mary Wortley Montagu's comment that Pamela's 'undeserved' fate was 'the joy of the chambermaids of all nations'.[4] Even as late as 1820, Leigh Hunt's sketch of a maidservant included an old volume of *Pamela* among her possessions.[5]

Pamela's success took Richardson by surprise. Almost immediately, however, as publisher as well as author, he began planning an illustrated edition – a remarkable venture, given that he had just written one of the

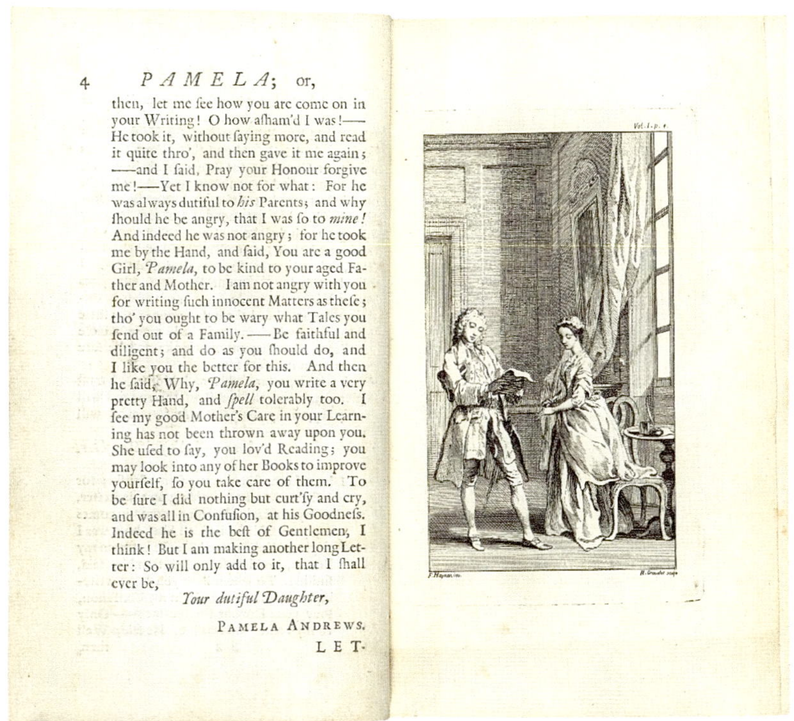
4 *PAMELA*; or,

then, let me ſee how you are come on in your Writing! O how aſham'd I was!——He took it, without ſaying more, and read it quite thro', and then gave it me again; ——and I ſaid, Pray your Honour forgive me!——Yet I know not for what: For he was always dutiful to *his* Parents; and why ſhould he be angry, that I was ſo to *mine!* And indeed he was not angry; for he took me by the Hand, and ſaid, You are a good Girl, *Pamela*, to be kind to your aged Father and Mother. I am not angry with you for writing ſuch innocent Matters as theſe; tho' you ought to be wary what Tales you ſend out of a Family.——Be faithful and diligent; and do as you ſhould do, and I like you the better for this. And then he ſaid, Why, *Pamela*, you write a very pretty Hand, and *ſpell* tolerably too. I ſee my good Mother's Care in your Learning has not been thrown away upon you. She uſed to ſay, you lov'd Reading; you may look into any of her Books to improve yourſelf, ſo you take care of them. To be ſure I did nothing but curt'ſy and cry, and was all in Confuſion, at his Goodneſs. Indeed he is the beſt of Gentlemen, I think! But I am making another long Letter: So will only add to it, that I ſhall ever be,

Your dutiful Daughter,

PAMELA ANDREWS.

LET-

Cat.63 ***Pamela, or Virtue Rewarded***
Samuel Richardson, 1740–41

Following the success of the newly published *Pamela*, Richardson chose to enhance the novel by commissioning twenty-nine engraved plates for a luxury edition, printed 'on a Writing-Paper'. For this he selected the prominent illustrator Gravelot to collaborate with Hayman, whose own reputation as an illustrator was established by the project. This first plate, designed by Hayman, depicts Mr B. reading the letter he discovers Pamela writing.

earliest, and hence experimental, English novels. His first thought was to involve Hogarth, whose 'modern moral subjects' seemed to make him the ideal contributor. However, Richardson decided that Hogarth's two frontispieces fell 'very far short of the Spirit of the Passages they were intended to represent',[6] and they were never published, possibly because Hogarth's satirical approach exposed those ambiguities in his heroine that led some to interpret her a 'hypocritical crafty girl … who understands the art of bringing a man to her lure'.[7] By early 1741 Richardson had embarked instead on a more enterprising project: a lavishly illustrated four-volume edition of the novel, published in May 1742. The designs, 'done by the best hands',[8] were by Hubert-François Gravelot with Francis Hayman (cat.63).

Gravelot had revolutionised British book illustration since his arrival in England in 1732–3 from France, and his light rococo style gave to Richardson's heroine the grace Hogarth's vision of her presumably lacked. The illustrators were, however, constrained by Richardson's own conception of his novel. None of its more dramatic scenes, including the attempted seductions, is included in the twenty-nine plates, most of which illustrate the somewhat tedious second half of the novel following Pamela's marriage.

Perhaps largely because of its cost, this outstanding example of English book illustration was not a commercial success. However, its production, together with Hogarth's recent completion of *Marriage à la Mode*, may have decided Joseph Highmore to produce from 1743 to 1744, quite independently, a series of scenes from *Pamela* for the lucrative print market. Instead of being bound in book form, these represented a self-contained retelling of the story; the originals remained in Highmore's studio as a stimulus to further commissions. It now seems clear that Highmore's graceful rococo compositions, which, like an intimate stage performance, bring together a small number of key characters at moments of tension or drama, paring down the action in the interests of clarity, represent the perfect painted expression of Richardson's novel. However, it was only after the series' completion that the two men met and became friends.

This ambitious venture had no direct successors in terms of painted illustrations to the English novel. However, Highmore's scenes represent a high point in English eighteenth-century art. His decision to telescope the entire two volumes into twelve scenes in which he tried to comprehend Pamela's 'whole story' was in large part responsible for the project's success. Of the scenes depicted, only two come from Volume II, with its account of the virtuous marriage. Instead, Highmore selected those passages in the

Cat.64 **Pamela and Mr B. in the Summerhouse**
Joseph Highmore, *c.*1744

In this second scene from the series, Pamela's would-be seducer first reveals his dishonourable intentions. Pamela is isolated in the enclosed space of a garden building with her tormentor, as the retreating figure of the housekeeper is glimpsed in the distance.

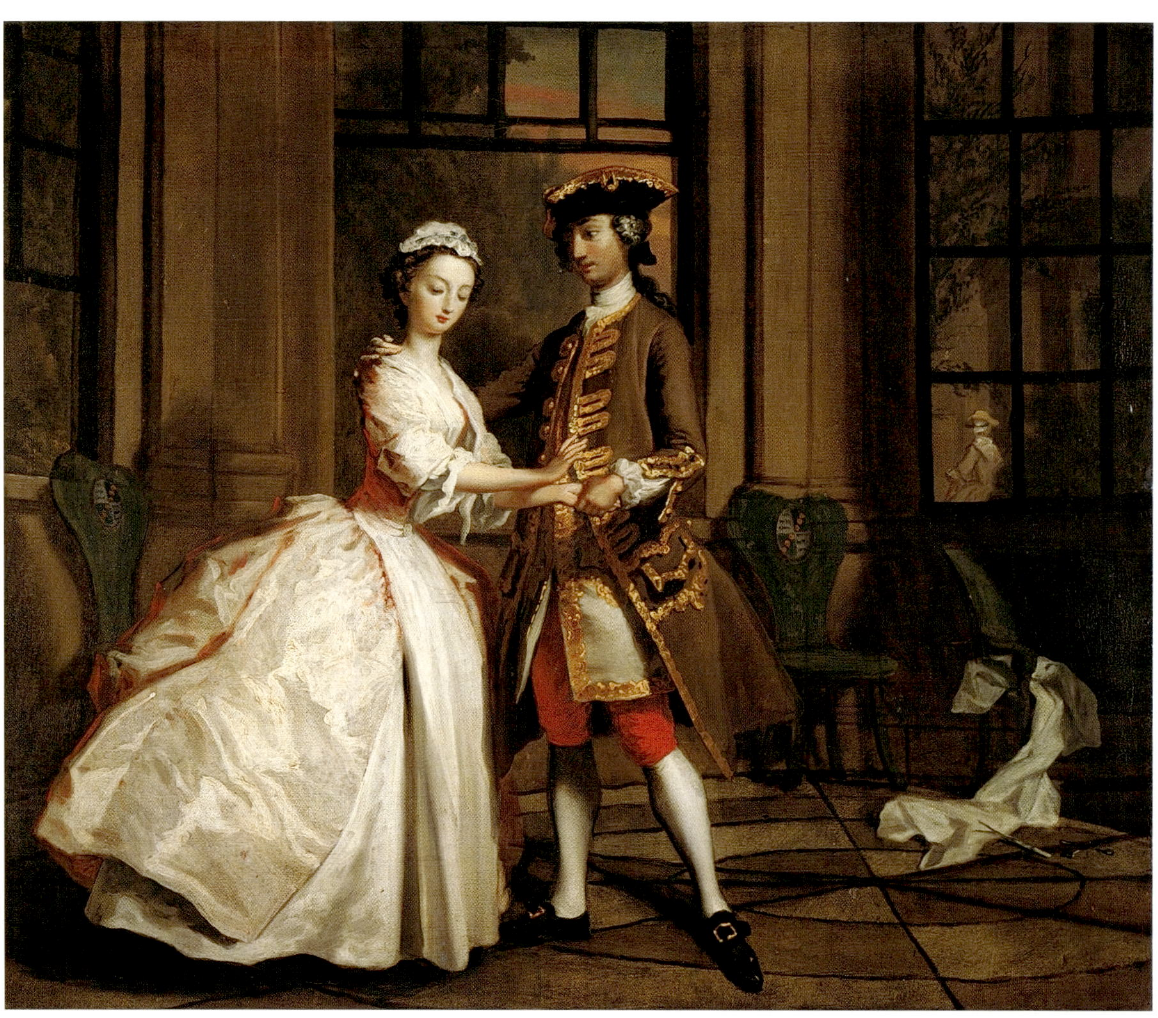

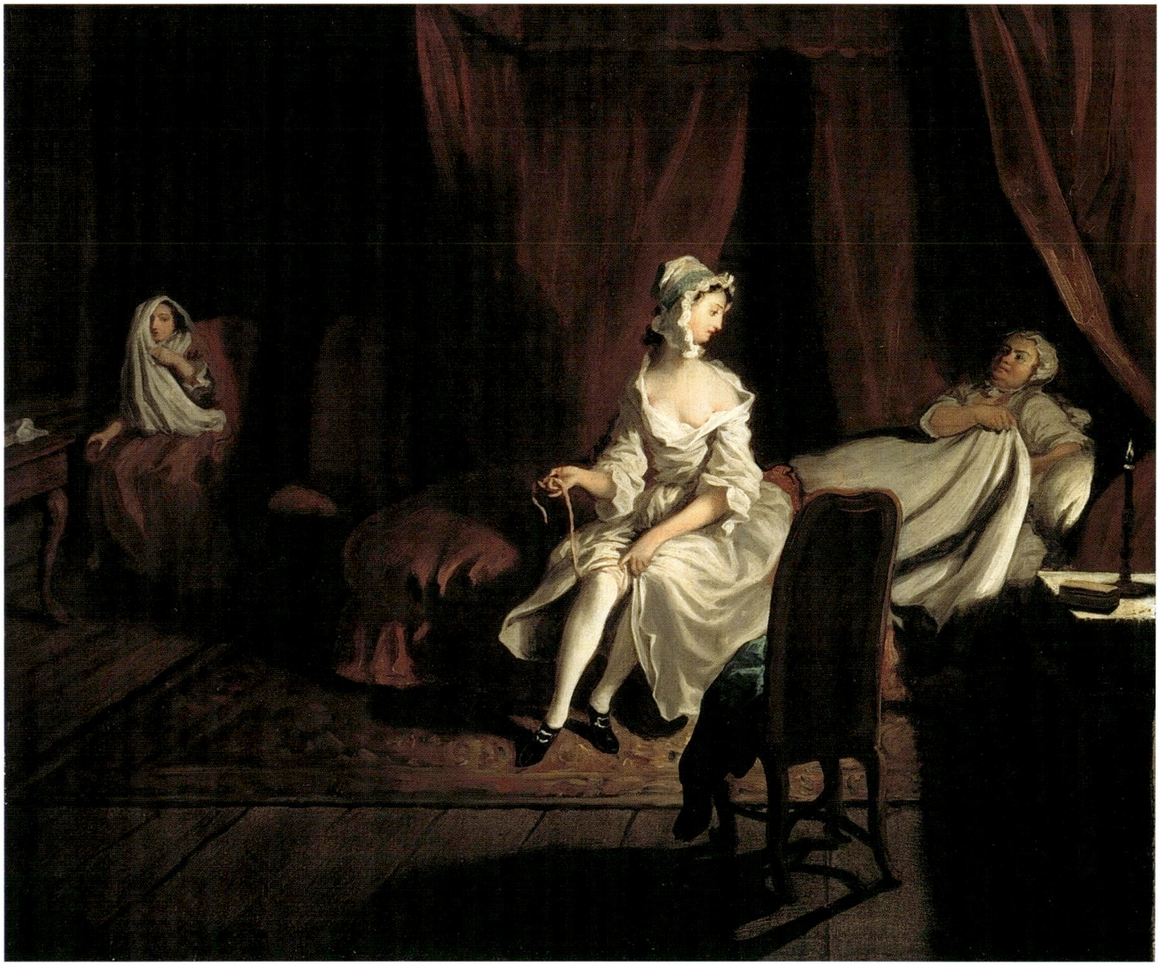

Cat.65 **Pamela in the Bedroom with Mrs Jewkes and Mr B.**
Joseph Highmore, 1743–4

Highmore's seventh episode depicts the novel's principal attempted seduction scene. Disguised as a maid with an apron covering his face, Mr B. watches as Pamela undresses in the room she shares with his co-conspirator Mrs Jewkes. Only a fainting fit saves her from rape. The floral-patterned carpet, four-poster bed and handsome high-backed chair all confirm the scene's setting in the room of an upper servant.

novel charged with sexual tension and hints of future danger (cat.64),[9] including the bedroom scenes, which come closer to attempted rape than to seduction (cat.65). The often concealed presence of Mr B., or one of his co-conspirators, notably the Lincolnshire housekeeper Mrs Jewkes, in many of the paintings, lends an ever-present air of menace which is not entirely removed even after the marriage itself. Only the final scene leaves Pamela secure as wife and mother, the 'painting over the fireplace reflecting her Madonna-like status' as she tells her children a story.[10]

Two other artists interpreted *Pamela* in paint. Francis Hayman's use of scenes from the novel, based on his own engravings, in two of his Vauxhall supper-boxes was an advertisement for his heroine that might have disturbed Richardson himself, who believed the pleasure gardens would carry women 'out of all domestic duty and usefulness'.[11] However, he would have disapproved far more of Philippe Mercier's provocative rendering *c.*1743–5, which shows Pamela rising from bed, semi-clothed, in a composition derived from Italian Renaissance nudes – the visual equivalent to Richard Hurd's comment on *Pamela* in 1742 that 'The too lively representation warms and inflames – the passions kindle at the view …'[12]

Poetry

The only eighteenth-century poem to have inspired a painting in which a servant occupies centre stage is *A Description of a City Shower* by Jonathan Swift (1667–1745), published in *The Tatler* in October 1710. Swift's short poem describes a London shower, not in terms of natural phenomena, but of its impact on Londoners ranging from a laundry-maid to a seamstress, a group of Whigs and Tories and a London beau stranded in his sedan chair. Over fifty years later, in 1764, Edward Penny exhibited a painting at the Free Society of Artists (cat.66) illustrating the lines in which a housemaid bespatters a fashionably dressed gentleman with her mop. Curiously, the maid is not, strictly speaking, a character in the poem at all; instead, the sprinkling she provides becomes a metaphor for the laundry-maid's washing, dampened by the onset of the shower:

> Such is that sprinkling which some careless quean
> Flirts on you from her mop, but not so clean.
> You fly, invoke the gods; then turning, stop
> To rail; she singing, still whirls on her mop.

As the poem goes on to discuss the state of the 'needy' poet's coat, the gentleman in Penny's light-hearted confrontation is presumably Swift himself, which perhaps accounts for Penny's choice of subject. His painting was exhibited in the wake of Swift's *Directions to Servants* (1745), and in these early years of public art exhibitions in London, when Penny exhibited some of his most original genre scenes, he may have felt that dramatising the conflict between this famous author and one of the targets of his ridicule was a suitable and indeed saleable subject for a genre painting. Certainly he ensured that the exhibited title, *A Scene from Jonathan Swift's Description of a City Shower*, reflected its derivation from Swift's poem, while an engraving, published in 1775 as *The Mop Trundler*, also makes explicit this connection.

The *Description of a City Shower* could be interpreted as representing a reversal of roles in which the maid, 'filled with the confidence of working for the worthy classes, is shown displaying great independence'.[13] However, several of Penny's genre scenes, notably *The Marquess of Granby, Giving Alms to a Sick Soldier* or *The Virtuous Comforted by Sympathy and Attention* (which also includes servants), focus on the exercise of charity or virtue by the ruling class, and there is no reason to assume that Penny's sympathies differ markedly from those in the poem itself, which, although in milder form, reflect the prejudice against servants found in Swift's famous *Directions* (cat.107). Penny's painting is probably a straightforward, if

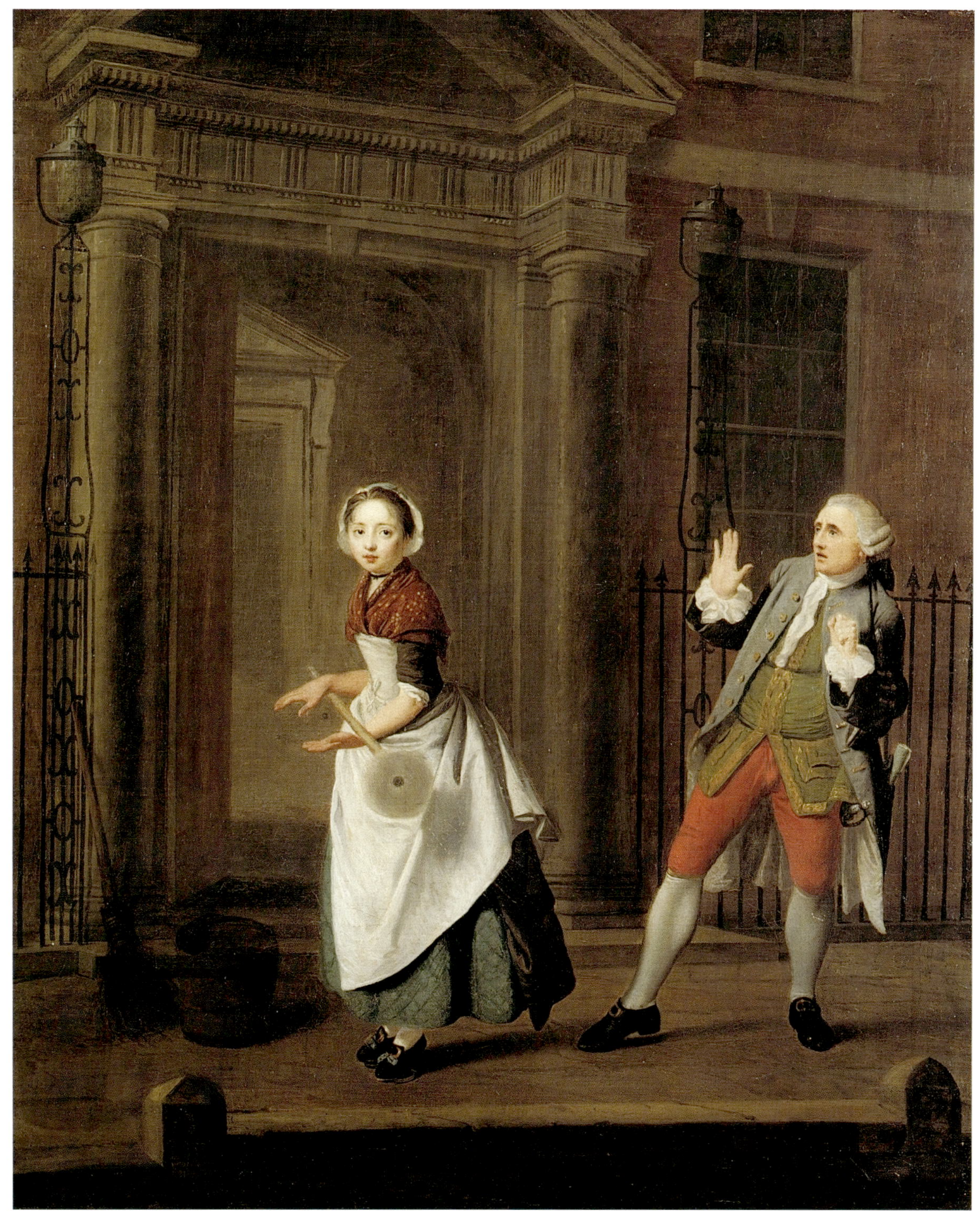

Cat.66 **A Scene from Jonathan Swift's Description of a City Shower**
Edward Penny, 1764

humorous, interpretation of the poem, siding with the bespattered gentleman-poet and his ruined coat, rather than the saucy maid.

The theatre

Servants occupied an important place in English drama from the beginning of professional companies under Elizabeth I. The enterprising manservant appears in the two Dromios in Shakespeare's *A Comedy of Errors*, and disturbingly in Iago in *Othello*, while loyal servants include Emilia in *The Winter's Tale*, the nurse in *Romeo and Juliet* and the Fool in *King Lear*. This 'natural' fool, and clowns such as Touchstone in *As You Like It*, offer close parallels with the slightly later painted images of natural and artificial fools (cats 2, 3). One of the principal themes of *Twelfth Night* is the relationship between a household of servants, including the aspiring steward Malvolio and the maid Maria and their mistress. Later, Jacobean tragedy's exploration of darker themes led to the daring introduction in Middleton and Rowley's *The Changeling* (1621–2) of the manservant Deflores, whose (gratified) sexual passion for his mistress leads to murder.

James Townley's famous farce *High Life Below Stairs*, first performed at Drury Lane in 1759 to an uproar from the servants' gallery, is a classic example of the much more restricted and critical role allocated to the servant in eighteenth-century drama, usually as stage plebian; it is exceptional only in portraying a whole household of servants. Translated into French and German, often attributed to David Garrick and

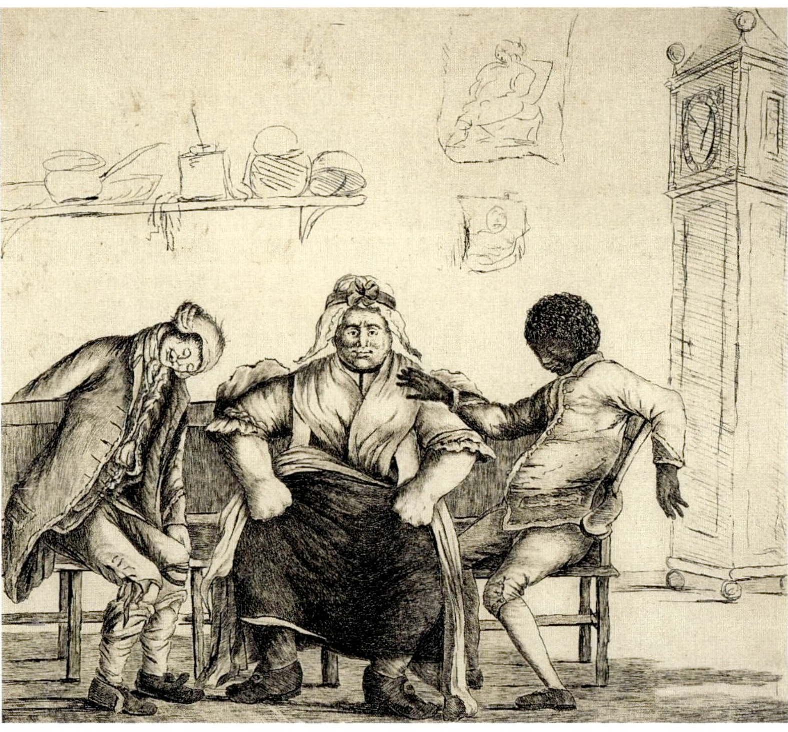

Cat.67 **High Life Below Stairs**
James Bretherton after Thomas Orde-Powlett (1st Lord Bolton), 1774

Orde-Powlett's etching depicts Act I, Scene III of Townley's play. The obstinate cook is seated on a bench in the servants' hall between the coachman and the black servant Kingston, trying to rouse them to answer the door-bell. However, they are both too drunk and sleepy after celebrating the supposed absence of their master Lovel. The cook also refuses to go, on the grounds of job demarcation.

frequently produced, it concerns a man gulled by his servants, who, to expose them, disguises himself as a yokel wishing to enter service. Contrary to his expectations, the servants he trusted, including his butler/steward and housekeeper, are principals in the attempt to defraud him; only one servant is honest, and the play ends with the expulsion of the wrongdoers and his promotion in their place. Much of the criticism is directed at servants' social pretensions, upper servants calling each other by their employers' names ('the Duke' or 'Lady Bab'), and imitating their social mores by drinking wine, taking snuff, conversing in French, and reading novels or plays. Their creation of a hierarchy 'downstairs' is confirmed by the 'Duke's' opening lines: 'What wretches are ordinary servants ... we, who have the honour to serve the nobility, are of another species',[14] while two of the characters are black and are discriminated against by the others. If the play represents employer grievances by now well rehearsed in print, it ends on a note more in accord with Steele and Addison's creation of Sir Roger de Coverly in *The Spectator*: 'If persons of rank would act up to their Standard, it would be impossible that their servants could ape them/But when they affect every Thing that is ridiculous, it will be in the Power of any low Creature to follow their Example.'[15]

The talented amateur Thomas Orde-Powlett (1746–1807) almost certainly sketched this scene from Townley's play (cat.67) while taking part in an amateur production at Cassiobury around 1774; the famous later production of *Lovers' Vows* in Austen's *Mansfield Park* confirms that amateur theatricals were an absorbing country-house activity, and Orde-Powlett's Cambridge contemporary and fellow amateur caricaturist William Henry Bunbury also drew such performances. Orde-Powlett's engraving was presumably made to circulate among friends and others involved in the play's production. However, the below-stairs subject matter perhaps appealed to him; when at Cambridge, he had made informal sketches of local characters, including a *Shoe Black* and a *College Porter*.

Francis Wheatley's *Lady Easy's Steinkerk* (1791) reproduces a scene (cat.69) from a well-known play written nearly a century earlier, *The Careless Husband* (1704), by the actor/manager of Drury Lane Colley Cibber (1671–1757). It was produced for inclusion in John Bell's *The British Theatre* (1791–7), which reprinted established plays alongside contemporary drama, providing engraved frontispieces for each play showing an actor or actress in a central role. Wheatley, who produced six of these scenes, was an obvious choice of illustrator; he also specialised in literary and sentimental genre scenes for London print-sellers, and historical pictures for John Boydell.

22 HIGH LIFE

SCENE, *The Servant's Hall in* LOVEL'S *House.*

KINGSTON *and* COACHMAN, *drunk and sleepy.*

[*Knocking at the Door.*

KINGSTON.

Some body knocks—Coachy, go—go to the Door, Coachy.—

COACHMAN.

I'll not go—do you go—you black Dog.

KINGSTON.

Devil shall fetch me, if I go. [*Knocking.*

COACHMAN.

Why then let 'em stay—I'll not go—Damme—Aye, knock the Door down, and let yourself in. [*Knocking.*

KINGSTON.

Ay, ay, knock again—knock again—

COACHMAN.

Master is gone into *Devonshire*—So he can't be there—So I'll go to sleep.—

KINGSTON.

So will I—I'll go to sleep too.

COACHMAN.

You lie, Devil—You shall not go to sleep till I am asleep—I am King of the Kitchen.

KINGSTON.

No, you are not King; but when you are drunk you are sulky as a Hell.—Here is Cooky coming—She is King and Queen too.

Enter COOK.

COOK.

Some body has knock'd at the Door twenty times, and nobody hears—Why Coachman—*Kingston*—Ye drunken Bears, why don't one of you go to the Door.

COACHMAN.

BELOW STAIRS. 23

COACHMAN.

You go Cook; you go—

COOK.

Hang me, if I go—

KINGSTON.

Yes, yes, Cooky go; *Molly*, *Polly* go.—

COOK.

Out you Black Toad—It is none of my Business, and go I will not. [*Sits down.*

Enter PHILIP *with* LOVEL *disguised.*

PHILIP.

I might have staid at the Door all Night, as the little Man in the Play says, if I had not had the Key of the Door in my Pocket—What is come to you all?

COOK.

There is *John* Coachman, and *Kingston*, as drunk as two Bears.

PHILIP.

Ah, hah! my Lads, what finish'd already? These are the very best of Servants—Poor Fellows, I suppose they have been drinking their Master's good Journey—ha, ha, ha.

LOVEL.

No doubt on't. [*Aside.*

PHILIP.

Yo ho, get to bed, you Dogs, and sleep yourselves sober, that you may be able to get drunk again by-and-by—They are as fast as a Church—*Jemmy.*

LOVEL.

Anon?

PHILIP.

Do you love drinking?

LOVEL.

Yes,—I loves Ale.

PHILIP.

Cat.68 High Life Below Stairs
James Townley, 1768

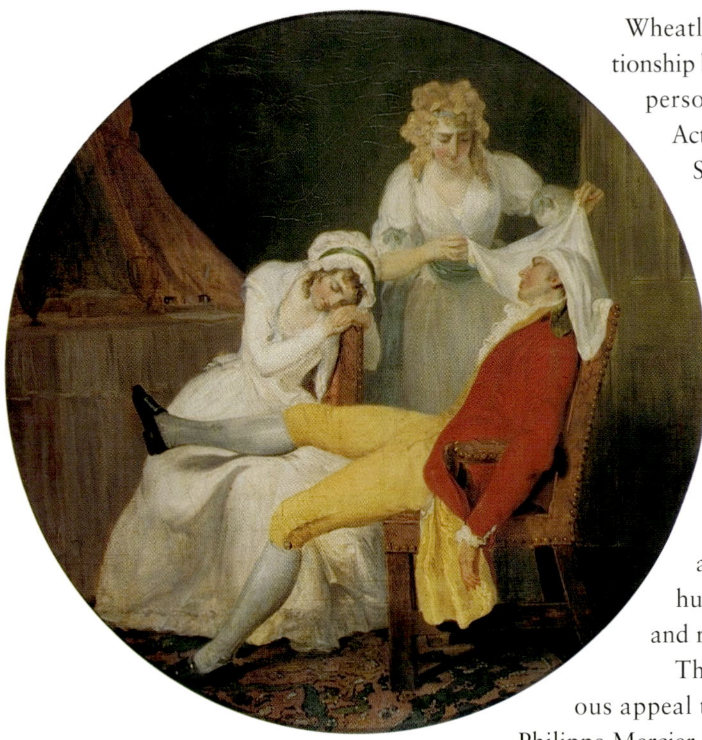

Cat.69 **Lady Easy's Steinkerk**
Francis Wheatley, 1791

This tryst between Sir Charles Easy and his wife's lady's maid takes place in Lady Easy's dressing room. Like many illicit eighteenth-century sexual encounters, when privacy was scarce, this one has been snatched hastily on movable chairs. Servants often witnessed their employers' liaisons in similar situations, and were called as witnesses to adultery in court.

Wheatley's frontispiece depicts the triangular relationship between a lady, her husband and her impudent personal maid at the denouement of the play in Act V, Scene 5, when Lady Easy finds her husband Sir Charles in post-coital slumber next to the maid Mrs Edging. Instead of expressing anger, the devoted wife covers his bare, wigless head with her 'steinkerk' (neckcloth) in a gesture of tenderness, lest 'while thus exposed to th'unwholesome Air/... Heav'n, offended, may o'ertake his crime/And, in some languishing distemper, leave him'. She even shifts the blame on to herself: 'If he should wake offended at my too busy care, let my heart-breaking patience, duty, and my fond affection plead my pardon.' On waking, the husband realises his wife's worth, and remorse and reconciliation follow.

This scene of lovers *in flagrante* had an obvious appeal to artists, and had already been painted by Philippe Mercier (1736).[16] In his much more sexually explicit rendering, master and maid lie slumped in chairs and one of her breasts is suggestively exposed, while Sir Charles's bare head seems to express the full force of his adultery and betrayal; as wigs were *de rigueur* on all social occasions, and men shaved their heads to accommodate them, they looked quite literally naked without them.[17] By contrast, Wheatley's painting confirms the more sanitised taste of later audiences. His lady's maid looks almost coy, and her clothing remains undisturbed, while the fact that both mistress and maid are clad almost identically in simple, Neoclassical gowns, serves to make the husband's adulterous choice seem somehow less shocking. It also reflects the reality that many eighteenth-century lady's maids did indeed look like their mistresses, in view of the widespread practice of giving them cast-off clothes as a perquisite. Contemporary opinion held that it was sometimes impossible to tell mistress and servant apart, and ladies' maids were particular targets: 'For being cloathed above their Equals, they think themselves equal to their Superiors, and begin to act accordingly.'[18] Wheatley's canvas, while reflecting such views, does not appear to offer a judgement on them. However, his more domestic rendering of the scene means that the sense of outrage and guilt in Mercier's interpretation is lacking.

John Bell's *The British Theatre* was also responsible for launching the career of Samuel de Wilde, when Bell selected him as the principal artist for the second part of his venture. In his ninety-three illustrations, de Wilde developed a highly successful format of small, whole-length paintings or watercolours showing single-figure actors in costume, derived from Zoffany, which remained his speciality for the rest of his career, and from around 1790 to 1820 leading actors flocked to his studio near Covent Garden and Drury Lane to sit to him in their most famous roles. A number of De Wilde portraits featuring servants survive in the Garrick Club. Most, like those of Jacob Gawkey, the dishonest steward Item in *The Deserted Daughter* by Thomas Holcroft, or the poetaster-butler Verdun in *Lovers' Vows*, pillory servants for their stupidity or avarice. However, *Thomas Hull as Jarvis in 'The Gamester' by Edward Moore* depicts the loyal man-servant encouraging his master to return to his wife, while Whimsiculo in Thomas John Dibdin's comic opera *The Cabinet* is an enterprising valet who helps his master win the girl of his choice. An even more unusual man-servant is portrayed by De Wilde in *Charles Matthews as Somno in The*

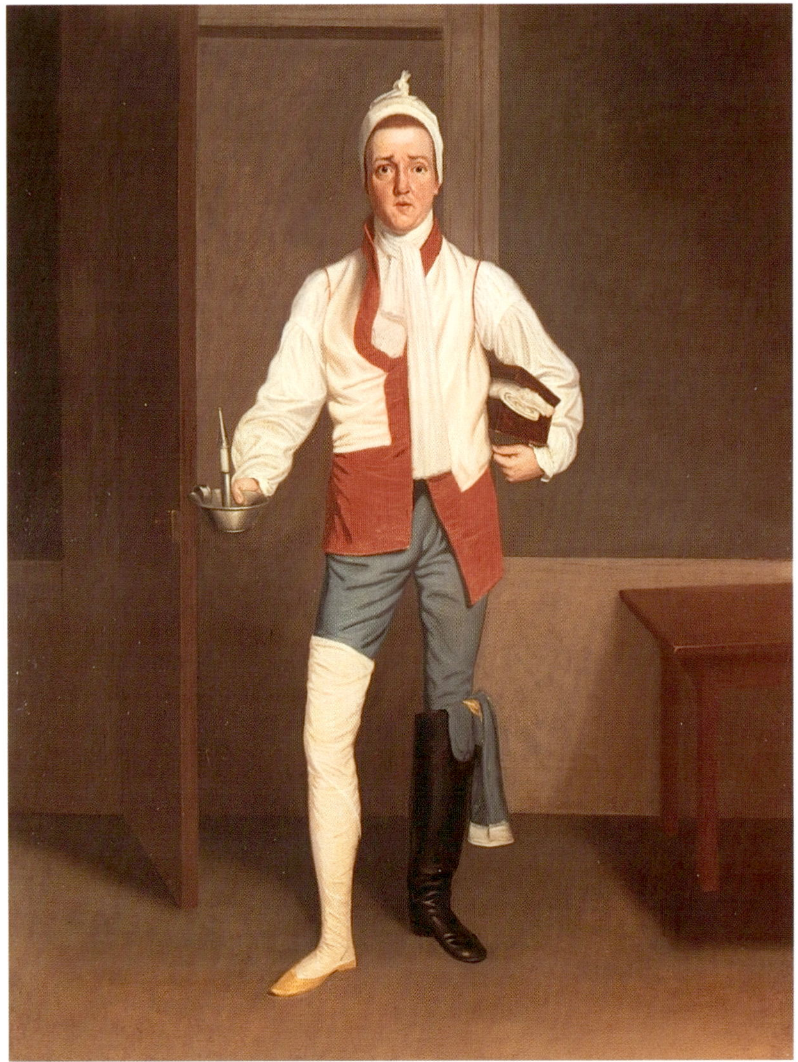

Cat.70 **Charles Matthews as Somno in *The Sleepwalker***
Samuel de Wilde, *c.*1813

In this sleepwalking scene, the aptly named Somno apostrophises his 'sword' while in fact laying a candlestick and dressing box on a table. Contemporary audiences would have recognised this as a mock-heroic rendering of Lady Macbeth's famous sleepwalking scene. Somno's costume in the harlequin mode is deliberately absurd: a white nightcap, differently shod feet, waistcoat askew and stock untied.

Sleepwalker by the Irish dramatist Walley Chamberlain Oulton (1770–1820), first performed at the Haymarket in 1812. Somno, the histrionic manservant of Sir Patrick M'Guire, is a failed actor turned servant who relives his wished-for roles through sleepwalking. De Wilde's portrait of the great Regency comic actor Charles Matthews in this guise, shown at the Royal Academy in 1813, was commissioned by Matthews to record his success in the part, forming part of his famous collection of theatrical portraits. In 1817, Oulton thanked him for 'being awake to all the eccentricities of a sleep walker'.[19]

The moral narrative from Hogarth to Northcote

The moral narrative paintings of Hogarth, offering a visual counterpart to the novels of Fielding, but in fact coming closer to the conventions of the stage, include a number of servants, many of them as involved in the pursuit of Mammon as their employers. These range from the steward in *Marriage à la Mode*, Series II, *After the Marriage* with his sheaf of bills, who belongs to a 'chillingly Puritannical sect,'[20] to the freezing liveried foot-boy who carries the old maid's prayer book as she walks through Covent Garden in *Morning*; despite her apparent piety, she is indifferent to his suffering. Two black servants offer an ironic commentary on their employers: in *Marriage à la Mode*, Series IV, in *The Countess's Levée* the manservant waiting on a seated visitor is pointedly ignored, while in *The Harlot's Progress* II (1731), which shows Moll Hackabout cuckolding her wealthy Jewish protector, the turbanned page boy stands, an innocent amid vice, in a room filled with disorder and signs of infidelity. His inclusion reflects the harlot's doomed attempts at fashion and gentility. The ragged bunter who later waits on Moll before her death represents the most impoverished kind of servant; although the engraving shows a more buxom figure, in the preparatory drawing (fig.21), she represents the extremes of poverty and degradation.

Francis Hayman also included servants in the backgrounds of some of his Vauxhall Gardens supper-box decorations (*c.*1743), where a maid and black page, singly or together, offer a detached and ironic commentary on amorous pursuits and gambling. However, it was Joseph Highmore who first placed the servant centre stage in 1743–4 with his *Pamela* series (pp. 123–5). Returning to this ground fifty years later in *Diligence and Dissipation*, James Northcote sought to capitalise on Highmore's success by producing another series focusing on the maidservant – this time without a literary source (cat.71). Borrowing from Hogarth's *Industry and Idleness* (1747), a narrative contrasting the paths of vice and virtue, Northcote's ten paintings, produced in partnership with the engraver Thomas Gaugain, follow the lives of a virtuous and wanton maidservant in scenes

Fig.21 **A Harlot in Her Garret Attended by Her 'Bunter'**
William Hogarth, *c.*1731

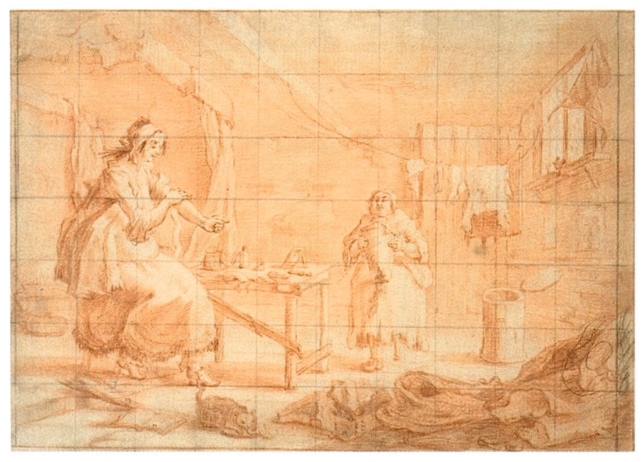

also reflecting the Harlot's or the Rake's Progress. Whereas the good servant listens to the housekeeper's advice, rejects her master's improper advances, reads improving literature, and is eventually rewarded by him with marriage, the wanton thinks only of sexual conquests, make-up, pulp novels and fortune-tellers. After her dismissal from service she becomes a prostitute and is lowered into her grave as the virtuous servant leaves church as a bride.

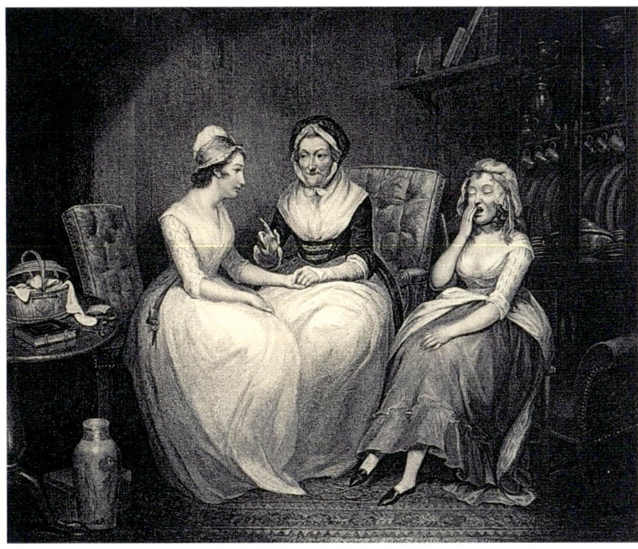

Cat.71 **Good Advice from an Old Servant to the Young Ones**
Gaugain and Hellyer after James Northcote, 1796

In this scene set in her own room, the elderly housekeeper lectures the two maidservants on their duties. The good servant, her breast modestly covered, listens attentively. Beside her is a table with signs of virtuous activity including a sewing box, and probably a Bible. In contrast the wanton yawns while her apron is pushed back immodestly. A dropped mirror testifies to her vanity.

Although Northcote laboured hard with his narrative, ensuring that every detail contributed to the overall moral message, which was reinforced by quotations from the *Book of Proverbs*, the series was not a commercial success, Northcote confirming that 'I never receivd from these pictures more than the value of about 15 pounds'.[21] The originals themselves proved unsaleable, appearing in his studio sale in 1836. Perhaps this was partly because Northcote's classicising style, echoing Reynolds, combined uneasily with his attempt to offer cutting-edge commentary. However, a more fundamental reason was surely that this kind of modern morality tale had now had its day.

Fancy pictures: Mercier to Gainsborough

A very different tradition of genre painting is represented by Philippe Mercier – himself a gentleman servant in the household of Frederick, Prince of Wales – and his successor in this type of painting, Henry Robert Morland. Mercier arrived in London in 1720. With his cosmopolitan training in France and Germany he was well placed to introduce new themes to British painting, including from around 1737 the domestic fancy picture, which shows the influence of Chardin and derives ultimately from Dutch seventeenth-century genre paintings. These scenes of virtuous and industrious domestic life, 'addressed to the individual, like the immaculate sentiments of a Richardson novel',[22] were designed to appeal to bourgeois sentiment and to the expanding print market. They feature girls engaged in occupations such as sewing, preparing oysters, reading by candlelight, cradling a cat or churning butter. Although the models' simple clothes are often suggestive of domestic employment, these fancy pictures were not intended to portray servants as such. Instead, Mercier's treatment of his young and discreetly alluring female models hints at the leisure hours of service, or at rustic occupations such as the dairymaid's, and they share with Pamela herself a refinement that would have appealed equally to 'Mr B.' and a middle-class audience. Positioned halfway between upstairs and downstairs, they form a visual equivalent to the territory occupied by *Pamela*, at

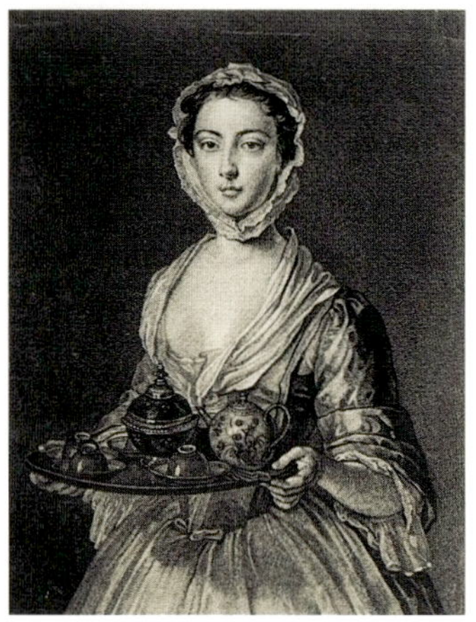

Fig.22 **Molly, Girl with a Tea Tray**
John Faber Junior after a print by Philippe Mercier, 1744

According to an early inscription on a copy of this mezzotint, the sitter is Mercier's maid Hannah, who was considered to be irresistible when determined to move someone. The composition is closer to Mercier's genre paintings than to portraiture. The still-life element of the tea tray brings Mercier's picture even closer than usual to Chardin, and parallels the contemporary *The Chocolate Maid* by Liotard (fig.6).

exactly the same date. In their engraved form, Mercier's fancy pictures are often given generic titles such as *Rural Life*, while four scenes which include a girl blowing bellows are dressed up as *The Four Elements*. Similarly, *Molly, Girl with a Tea Tray*, which comes close in manner to Chardin, is clearly a fancy picture not a portrait, even if the sitter was indeed the Merciers' maid Hannah.

From the early 1760s or just before, Henry Robert Morland began to paint fancy pictures closely based on Mercier, also intended for the print market. Among his ballad sellers and oyster girls are a number of servants, notably *A Lady's Maid Soaping Linen* (*c*.1765–82) and its pendant *A Laundry Maid Ironing*. Clearly these domesticated yet distinctly provocative images were among Morland's most popular sellers, as he exhibited these paintings, or replicas of them at the Free Society of Artists as many as five times from 1768 to 1782, and numerous versions survive. If these pictures present a somewhat fanciful and sanitised view of domestic service, not

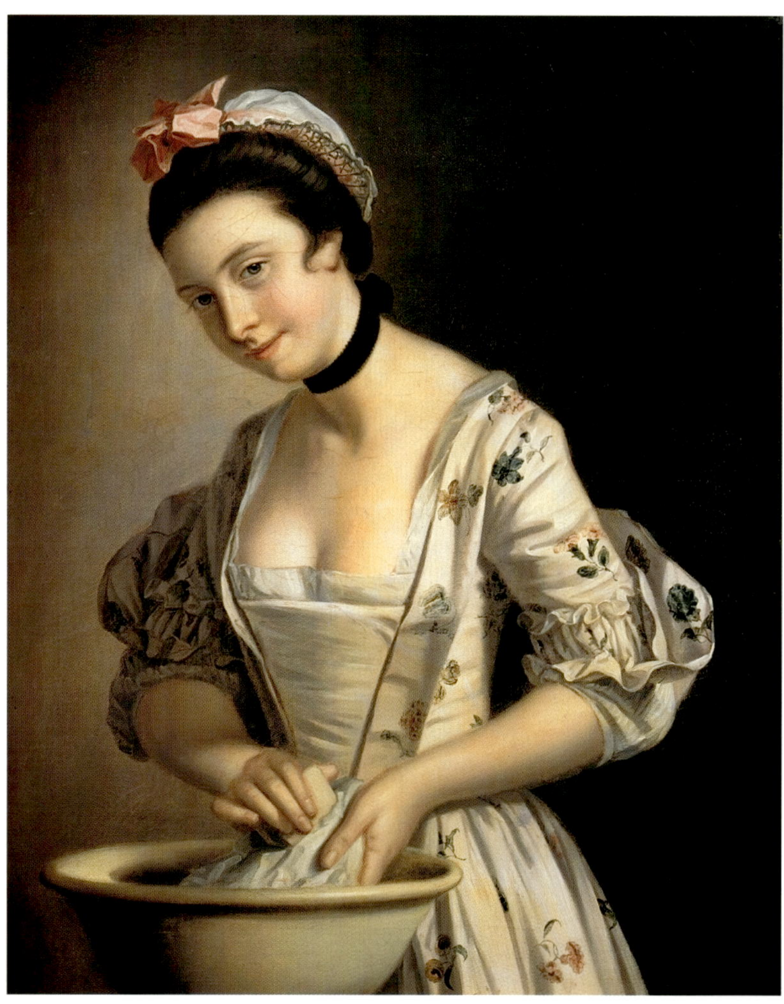

Cat.72 **A Lady's Maid Soaping Linen**
Henry Robert Morland, *c*.1765–82

The notion that this painting and its pendant were portraits representing the famous society beauties the Gunning sisters, has long been discounted. Instead the model was probably Morland's sister, who sat for other of his fancy paintings. Morland's lady's maid is shown washing her mistress's linen with a bar of soap in a glazed earthenware bowl. The pattern and cut of her dress date to the early 1760s.

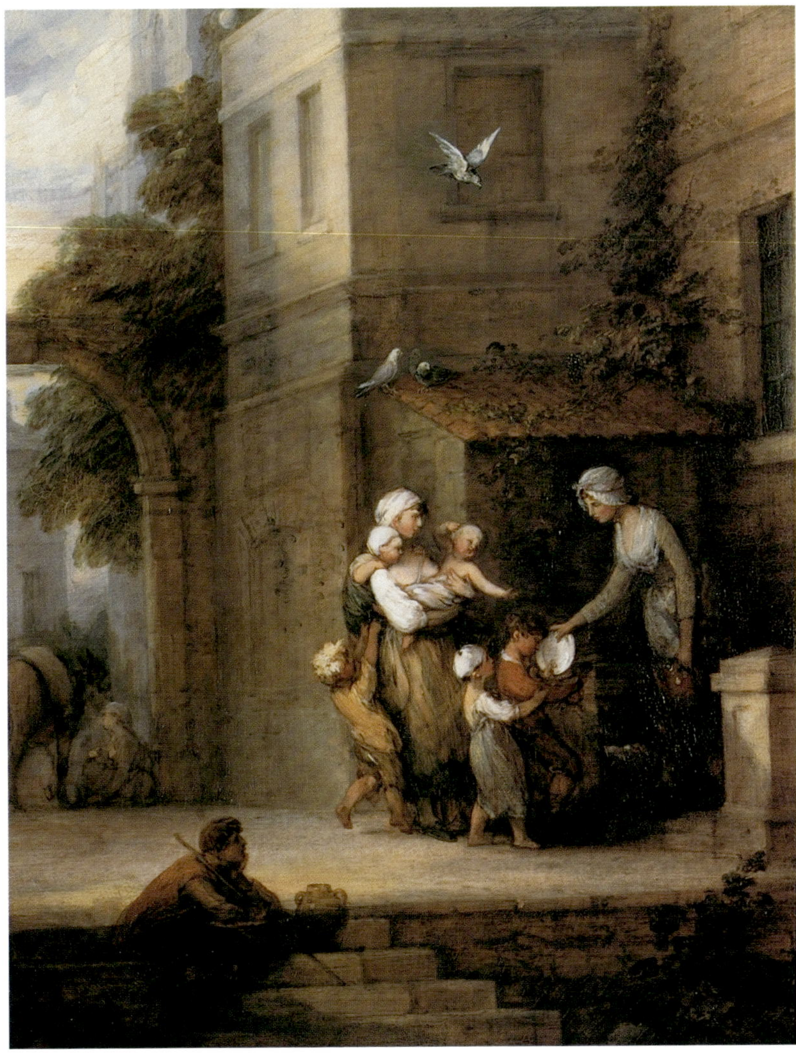

Fig.23 **Charity Relieving Distress**
Thomas Gainsborough, 1784

Gainsborough's painting represents the giving of alms by a maidservant at a somewhat fanciful country mansion to a beggar woman surrounded by children, However, the beggar, her breasts part-exposed, is herself an allegorical figure of charity, and rather than being a realistic depiction of class relations and destitution in the countryside, this is a fancy picture debating the Christian nature of charity.

all details are inaccurate; the lady's maid's painted silk dress might appear too costly for a servant, but documentary evidence confirms that ladies' maids frequently received cast-off dresses from their mistresses, and Richardson's Pamela dresses herself shortly before her marriage in 'a flowered pattern, that was my lady's, and looked as good as new'.[23]

Although themes relating to the rural poor are prefigured in his landscapes, Thomas Gainsborough included fancy pictures in his repertory only from 1781. Many are on subjects linked to servitude, although in only one case is a servant actually portrayed. This is *Charity Relieving Distress* (fig.23), exhibited in 1784, in which a maidservant gives alms at the service door of a country mansion to a beggar and her children. Gainsborough was probably fully conscious of the inversion of roles implied in a maid acting as benefactress, and the painting emphasises the Christian nature of her act, including the 'Holy Spirit, who hovers above the principal group in the form of a white dove'.[24] However, the much later engraving was dedicated to 'the Nobility & Gentry, whose humane exertions are employed in alleviating the distresses of the Poor', and whatever Gainsborough's viewpoint, there can be no doubt that the servant gives alms as her employer's agent. Other famous images dating to the 1780s such as *The Housemaid*, *A Girl with Pigs*, or *A Shepherd* are more problematical as images of servanthood, representing instead rustic figures within pastoral idylls akin to Gainsborough's late cottage door scenes. Even *The Woodman*, gathering firewood in the forest, seems unconnected to the world of paid employment, although Gainsborough's model for the painting was 'a poor smith worn out by labour',[25] and the painting represents a nostalgia for the more communal use of land before the enclosure movement.

Masqueraders

The affinity between society and the theatre in the eighteenth century – 'Life was a stage on which good actors would shine; courtesy books, dancing masters and elocutionists abounded to teach the parts'[26] – perhaps lies behind the fact that a small group of British portraits, mostly dating to the 1720s, shows ladies masquerading as servants. Much of the stimulus towards this type of portrait must have come from the pastoral tradition in British portraiture from Van Dyck onwards which presented ladies as shepherdesses, and from the dream, extending far beyond portraiture, of an idyllic pastoral life manifested in the involvement of the upper classes in activities such as haymaking, the *cottage orné*, and in Marie Antoinette's role-playing as a dairy-maid at Versailles.

Although the wearing of masks and disguises had played an important role in society from earliest times,[27] they came to assume particular importance in eighteenth-century London with the introduction around 1710 of the masquerade, which became the entertainment of the century *par excellence*, not just with the upper classes but much lower down the social scale. Here the social mix and the wearing of disguises allowed for experimentation with roles not permissible in normal social intercourse. Dressing at masquerades as a shepherd or shepherdess was commonplace, and appearances as chimney sweeps are recorded. However, most masqueraders favoured exotic costumes, and the only aristocrat known to have disguised herself as a servant is Georgiana, Duchess of Devonshire in 1786. The motive for dressing-up for masquerades was, however, underpinned by 'the powerful motivating force of conspicuous consumption',[28] and a rather different type of role-playing seems to have led to the commissioning of servant 'masquerader' portraits. Certainly the best-known of these is the portrait of *Catherine, Duchess of Queensberry as a Milkmaid* (*c.*1725–30, cat.130). Although the Duchess was one of the great beauties of her day, she was a noted eccentric, renowned for wearing such simple country clothes and aprons

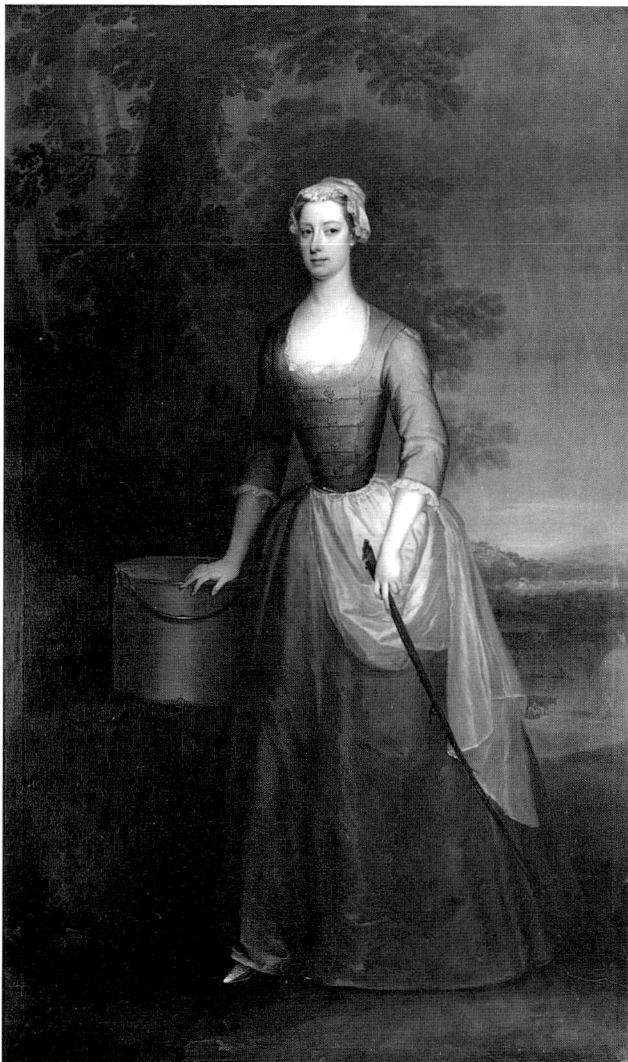

Fig.24 **Miss Mary Warde as a Milkmaid**
Charles Jervas, *c.*1730s

Mary Warde of Squerryes Court in Kent was probably painted as a milkmaid not long after the Duchess of Queensberry established the fashion for sitting for a portrait in this guise. Like the Duchess, she is allocated pastoral props such as the apron, metal pail and broken-off stick used by milkmaids to drive cows. Later in the century Reynolds also painted ladies involved in rustic pursuits, such as feeding poultry.

that she was refused entry to great houses by servants, and it was as a milkmaid that she elected to be painted in a portrait attributed to Charles Jervas. The appearance of a well-known society lady in this guise inevitably spawned a number of derivatives, including Jervas's *Miss Mary Warde as a Milkmaid* (fig.24). A rather different type of masquerading is provided by Bartholomew Dandridge's enchanting *A Young Girl Dressed as a Housemaid* (private collection), which places her in a Palladian interior complete with her bucket, broom and mop.

Although such role-playing in portraiture was an eighteenth-century phenomenon, many of the themes explored in this chapter, notably in Richardson's *Pamela*, would be developed in the nineteenth century, which, both in literature and genre painting, saw a new awareness of the servant as victim (see p.178).

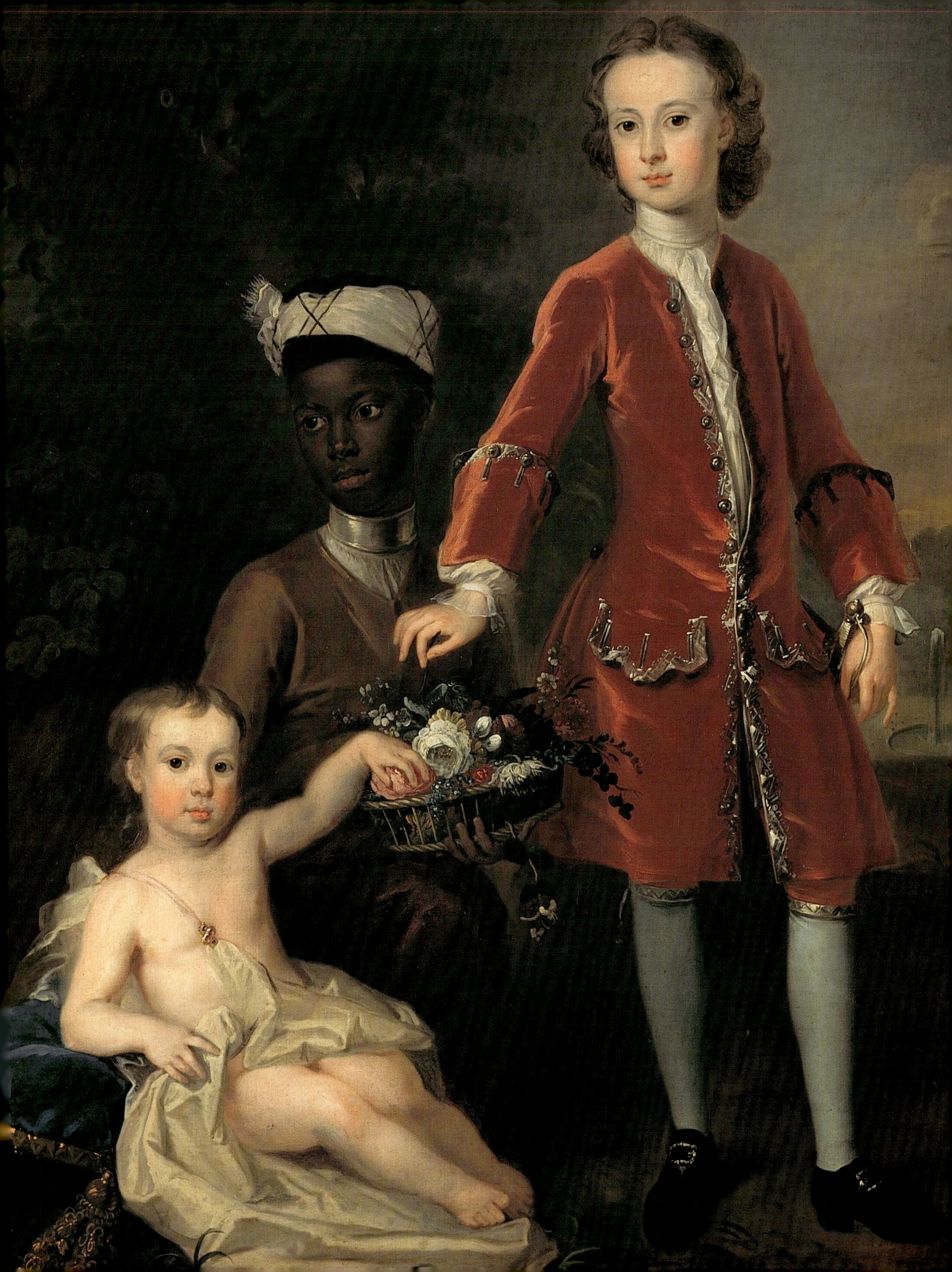

8 BLACK SERVANTS

Giles Waterfield

BLACK SERVANTS OR BLACK SLAVES? 'Black slaves' is a more accuate description of the thousands of Africans working in British households during the seventeenth and eighteenth centuries. Their history has often been forgotten, in spite of eloquent narratives written at the time and since the 1970s. The facts are that the first African slaves were brought to Britain in 1555 by a trader; that in 1563 the slave trade gathered force with John Hawkins's sale of Africans into slavery in the West Indies; that numerous slaves were brought into Britain throughout the eighteenth century by traders and plantation owners, and were bought and sold in London and elsewhere (Wapping was a good spot to buy a man); that in spite of extended arguments about the legality of slavery, and an energetic campaign against the slave trade and slavery in Britain, slavery was not formally abolished in the colonies until 1834 even though slavery was not permitted in Britain after 1772; that as late as 1849 the eminent Thomas Carlyle could publish his *Discourse on the Nigger Question*, attacking black people with virulent prejudice. Though there were free black people in Britain throughout the period, the expression 'black slaves' is all too often the right one.

Historically, being black in white Europe carried a particular status. It meant one was exotic, and in demand. Black people, especially men, were employed at the courts of medieval Europe, particularly as musicians: the German Emperor Frederick II had five black trumpeters, as well as black pages, at his Palermo court in the early thirteenth century. In Britain the earliest recorded black slaves served King James IV of Scotland at the beginning of the sixteenth century, and at the English court black musicians were working for the king from the reign of Henry VII. Royal patronage of 'exotic' foreigners was to be a vigorous tradition up to the end of the nineteenth century. For the nobility it also became fashionable to have an African attendant, a mark of wealth and sophistication: already

OPPOSITE Detail of cat.73 **The Hon. John and the Hon. Thomas Hamilton with a Negro Servant** William Aikman, 1728

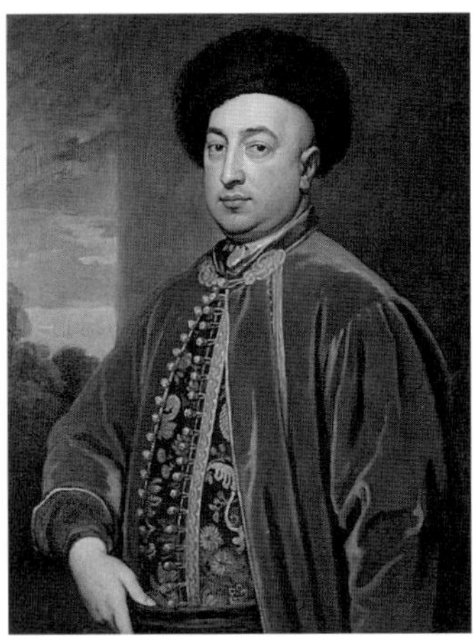

Fig.25 **Mehemet**
Sir Godfrey Kneller, 1715

under Elizabeth I black slaves were owned by such people as the Earl of Derby (as early as 1569) and Lady Ralegh, wife of Sir Walter. Although Elizabeth at the end of her reign issued various proclamations against black people, whose numbers in London were increasing, and ordered them to be deported from the country, she herself appears to have employed black trumpeters and dancers. The tradition of 'exotic' slaves or servants survived at court well into the eighteenth century. George I's Turkish body servant Mehemet, given to the king as a slave (with another slave, Mustafa) but freed, ennobled and promoted to Groom of the King's Chamber and Keeper of the Closet, was magnificently painted by Sir Godfrey Kneller in 1715, the year of his ennoblement. In the portrait, which remains in the Royal Collection, he wears sumptuous costume, a vigorous statement of his status at court, which included the privilege of dressing the king and which was much resented by other courtiers. Mehemet reappears in William Kent's painting of the court on the Grand Staircase at Kensington Palace, of around 1725. Kneller executed a number of other remarkable depictions of black people, often clothed in exotic dress and in such roles as musicians, but there is no condescension in these images. While depictions of black people in Europe in the seventeenth and eighteenth centuries show the sitters in extravagant dress and make no effort to portray them in the context of their own society, Kneller's portraits generally respect their personal individuality and show them as physically impressive.

Servants or slaves?

By the eighteenth century the number of black people in England had risen: it was estimated that in the later eighteenth century the black population, primarily living in London and other seaports, was around 15,000.[1] While some of these people were employed by the nobility, many of them worked for people of lesser wealth (Samuel Pepys had a black 'cookmaid' in 1659). One of their great advantages was that once bought, they did not have to be paid.

The majority of black people worked as domestic servants. Slaves carried to an extreme the peculiarities of the servant's position, particularly the decorative male. Black men were much more in demand than women, as pages, footmen and butlers: it has been estimated that 80 per cent of black people in England during the eighteenth century were male.[2] Boy pages, some as young as five or six, were in favour as personal attendants on great ladies (as illustrated by Hogarth in *Marriage à la Mode* and elsewhere). The future of the black page was unpredictable: when he approached manhood, or insubordination, he might be shipped off to the West Indies, where he would revert to servitude. Such pages were treated as exotic beings, expected to be in constant attendance on their mistresses, dressed in vaguely oriental clothes and given ironically imposing classical names (their own names being ignored) such as Socrates or Pompey, which was the most

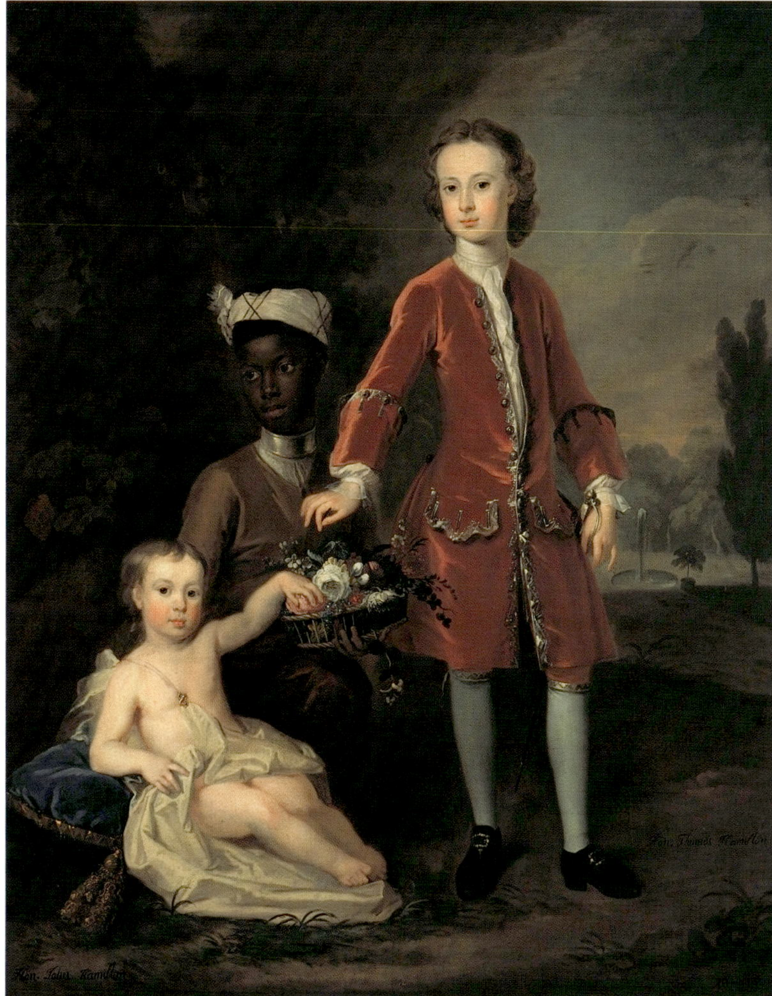

Cat.73 **The Hon. John and the Hon. Thomas Hamilton with a Negro Servant**
William Aikman, 1728

popular choice. But their servitude was affirmed by the metal collars that slaves were often compelled to wear: these were inscribed with the owner's name and were made by the craftsmen who produced dog collars.

Given the nature of the employment of black people, it is not surprising that at least until the late eighteenth century very few were portrayed in the way some of their white equivalents were. They feature primarily as attendants in fashionable portraits. Introducing a black attendant into a portrait of an important person was an extension of the sixteenth-century Italian convention of including a servant, a page, a secretary, a dwarf, or a dog or horse in a portrait as a foil to the principal subject. The idea of the black page as decorative accessory derives from Titian's *Laura Dianti* as well as Veronese's depictions of young black (male) servants in his large-scale biblical paintings: it reflects the employment in Genoa, Florence and other Italian cities of African house servants in the sixteenth century and later.[3] The tradition was developed by Rubens, who sometimes introduced a black page into his large compositions (and carried further by Antoine Watteau in the early eighteenth century.) In a British context, the use of the black attendant was taken up by Van Dyck as in *Princess Henrietta of Lorraine* (1634); and became increasingly popular, notably in the work of William Dobson and Sir Peter Lely. At times the genre also includes Indian servants. The custom became a staple of eighteenth-century portraiture in the work of Godfrey Kneller, Andrea Soldi, William Hogarth and Johann Zoffany among many others. Late in the century the custom was still being energetically applied by Joshua Reynolds.

Early in the eighteenth century the black attendant also takes on a new, more domestic role. Like many white servants, he or she is frequently shown in attendance on a family group or a social gathering, as in Robert West's portrait of *Thomas Smith and His Family* (1733). In West's painting the anonymous black servant stands, in characteristically fanciful dress, on the periphery of the family group. Both British styles of depicting black attendants remained standard conventions until the end of the eighteenth century.

Fig.26 **Thomas Smith and His Family**
Robert West, 1733

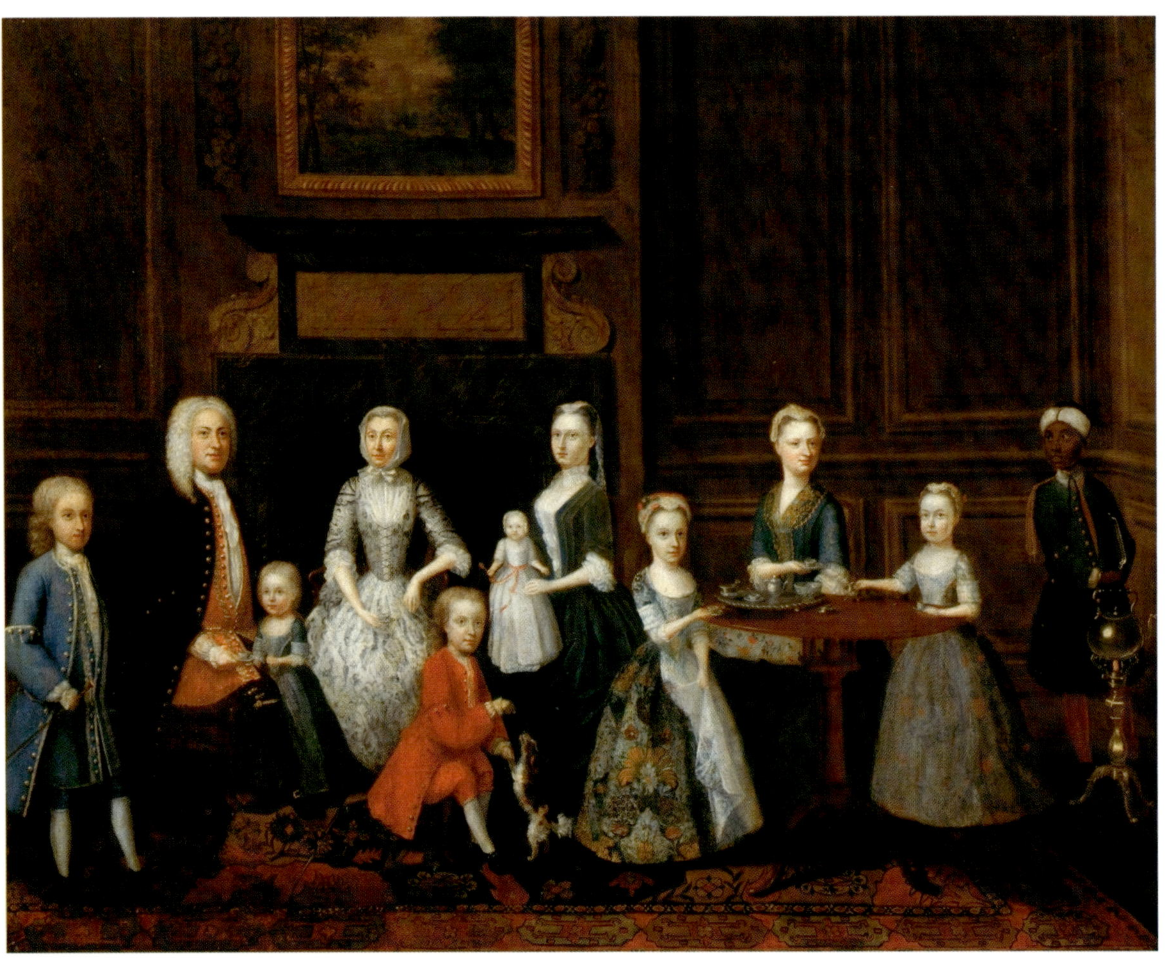

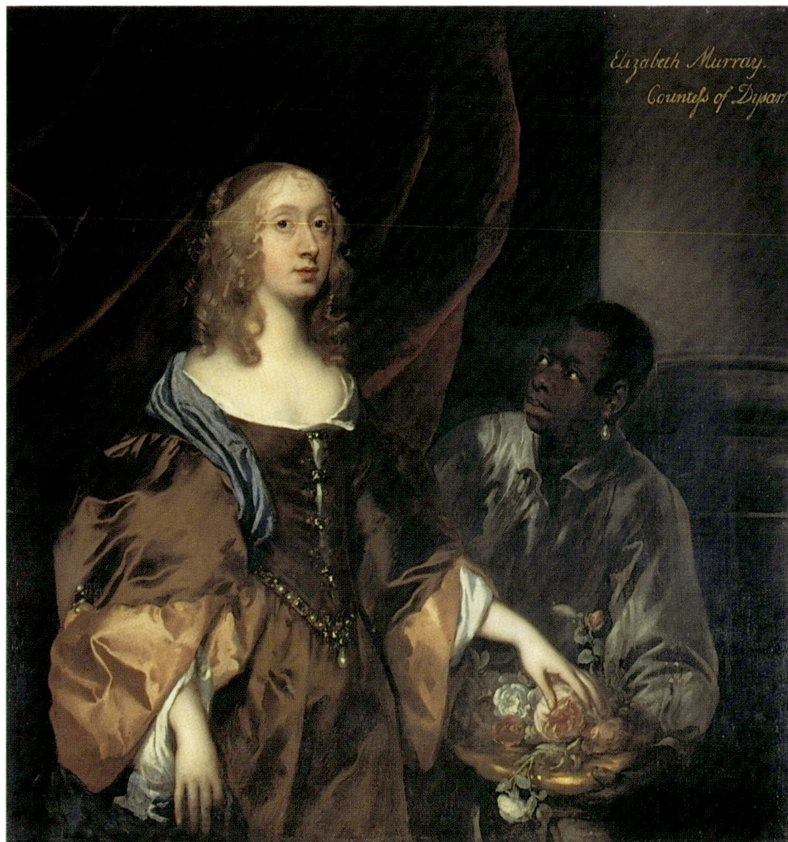

Fig.27 **Elizabeth Murray, Countess of Dysart, and a Black Servant**
Sir Peter Lely, *c.*1651–2

The black person in these portraits is seldom individually identifiable and is often presented as a form of staffage rather than an actual person. Sometimes a reference to Africa or elsewhere arose from the experiences of the sitter, as in Van Dyck's *William Fielding, 1st Earl of Denbigh* with an Indian page, but the connections were not always so specific. One purpose of including a black retainer was to indicate the wealth and status of the principal sitter, since such attendants were relatively expensive, but this tended to be a British convention. Hugh Honour has demonstrated how in North America, at the end of the eighteenth century, where black slaves were extremely common, they were almost never used in this way in portraiture. Thus when John Trumbull was painting George Washington, he introduced a black attendant in a version of the portrait painted in England but not in the versions of the canvas painted across the Atlantic.[4]

Little better than lions, tigers, leopards

It is difficult to determine exactly what was meant by the inclusion of these black attendants, who might also be girls (particularly if they are shown with young girl mistresses) though not grown women. In some instances Indians are shown, as in Lely's *Lady Charlotte Fitzroy*, though the number of Indians, whether slaves or free, in eighteenth-century Britain was relatively small. Whatever their identity, they tend to gaze, as though adoringly, at their master and mistress, who may well be touching them or accepting flowers or fruit from them. Is this a reflection of the view, still current well into the nineteenth century, that black people were inferior to white, so that tribute is being paid to the embodiment of natural superiority? Since in the eyes even of intelligent and literate people in the eighteenth century, Africans were 'the most ignorant and unpolished people in the world, little better than lions, tigers, leopards, and other wild beasts ...' as Lord Chesterfield put it,[5] such paintings can be interpreted as statements of the sitter's ability to dominate the world around them.[6] This is a process which, in the view of David Dabydeen writing of Van Dyck's *Princess Henrietta of Lorraine Attended by a Page*, involved the audience: 'the black is the external spectator internalized, for we too, the spectators are meant to adopt his servile perspective in beholding her image.'[7] For Dabydeen, 'what emerges from such paintings is a sense of the loneliness and humiliation of blacks in white aristocratic society'. While the subservience of the attendant is clear, it may be felt that this is, rather, a pictorial convention, with the black person playing a role comparable to the sitter's child or grandchild or trusted adviser. As Linda Colley has pointed out in *Captives*,[8] her study of the numerous British men and women taken prisoner by the various foreign peoples they were attempting to colonise or suppress, the attitudes towards these peoples held by the small and relatively weak British nation were complex and by no means always triumphalist.

Black servants in art had other roles. David Dabydeen, who in *Hogarth's Blacks* wrote one of the first analyses of depictions of black people in British art, proposed William Hogarth, 'the first English artist to represent on canvas the lives of the common people in a serious and sympathetic way,'[9] as an innovator in his compassionate interest in black people. In the Levée scene of *Marriage à la Mode*, Dabydeen proposes, the black servant's calm dignity exposes the pretentious and licentious absurdity of the other figures, 'symbolising the "natural" as opposed to the "artificial", the "real" as opposed to the ostentatious'.[10] However exotic black people may have appeared to the aristocracy, a comparable attitude seems not to have been current at other social levels. Black people were readily assimilated by working people into whose ranks many of them fled from slavery, as well as in large domestic households.

Not all eighteenth-century black people living in England were condemned to obsurity. This was recognised when in the 1970s Black Studies emerged as a powerful discipline in Britain, partly as a result of contemporary political developments. Accounts of the black presence in Britain were written by such scholars as James Walvin, Folarin Shyllon (sponsored by the Institute for Race Relations) and Peter Fryer. They found in this unhappy story a number of heroes, men whose names were well known in Britain in the late eighteenth century, when attitudes to slavery and the slave trade were changing. Among the most significant of these people were three men who spent at least some of their careers as servants. These were Ignatius Sancho, whose letters were published posthumously in 1782; Ottobah Cuguano, whose *Thoughts and Sentiments* (1787) contrasted English with African society; and Olaudah Equiano, whose autobiography (published in 1787) ran into eight editions in five years. These men were 'lionised by polite society to whom they represented a certain ideal type of African'.[11] They demonstrated to a possibly sceptical public that if properly educated and brought up in the Christian tradition, Africans could become models of behaviour, on the lines determined in western Europe. All these men were depicted in straightforward portraits as individuals, with none of the overtones of subservience apparent in the other images we have considered – Gainsborough's portrait of *Ignatius Sancho* is an important example.

BUST OF A MOOR

Black servants were frequently to be found in noble and royal households from the late seventeenth century. Such exotics were often included as accessory figures in portraits of their masters, but were only rarely portrayed alone. The traditional, though unsubstantiated, identification of this individual as a favourite personal servant of King William III makes this a unique instance of such a portrait in English sculpture.

This bust is incised on the reverse 'J.N. Fecit', which has been read as the signature of John van Nost the Elder, a native of Mechelen (Malines) in present-day Belgium, who is recorded as working in England from 1679 until his death in around 1711. He is best known for carved marble funerary monuments and lead statuary for gardens and public monuments, and as a maker of fine marble chimneypieces. That he was familiar with the technique of *commesso in pietre dure* (hardstone intarsia) employed on the bust is clear from the tabletops with mosaics of coloured marbles which he supplied to Queen Anne and others.

The Moor's feathered turban and jewelled band seem to indicate a high, perhaps royal status, but the collar unmistakably marks him as a slave. The collar originally had a small padlock, whose position is indicated by two tiny stubs of marble where it joins. Such collars were often made of silver and inscribed with the name of the servant's master. Several of the jewels and the buttons of the chemise are also missing, while the pierced earlobes suggest that these were also once ornamented.

JONATHAN MARSDEN

Cat.74
Bust of a Moor
John van Nost the Elder, *c.*1700

Fig.28 **Ignatius Sancho**
Thomas Gainsborough, 1768

One of the best-known members of the eighteenth-century black community in London, Sancho started his career as a servant and (like the founders of Fortnum and Mason) moved on to be a grocer, as well as a literary figure. He was painted at the same time as his employer the Duchess of Montagu, in the dress of a gentleman.

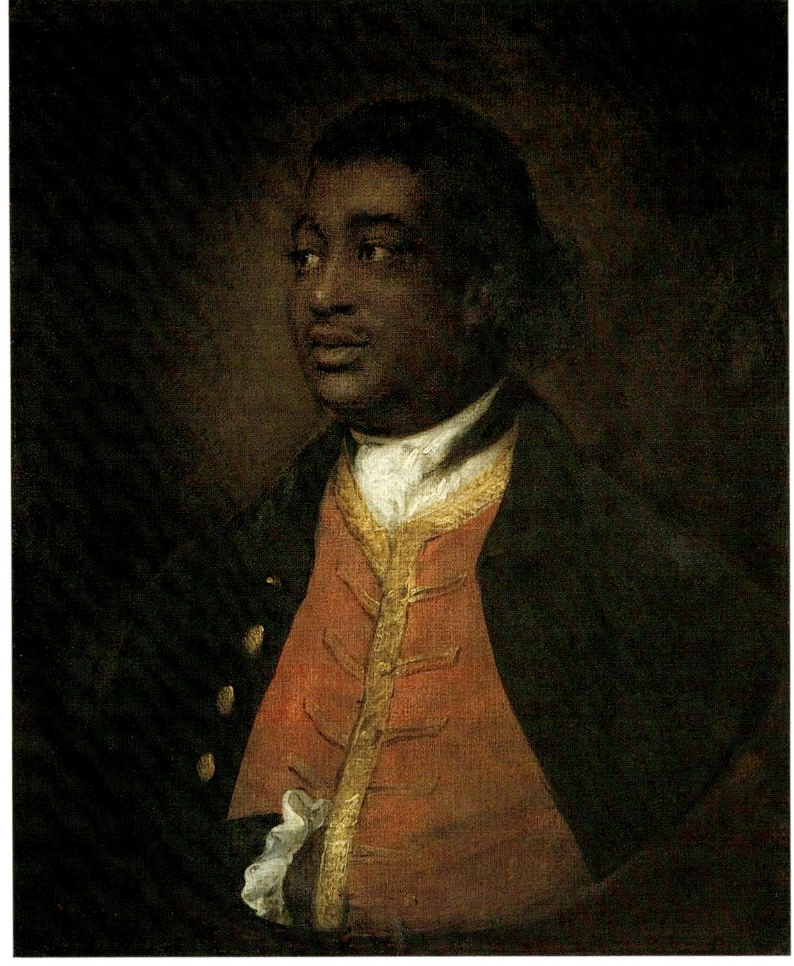

Ignatius Sancho was, like Robert Dodsley, a servant educated and succoured by a noble family. He worked for the family of the Dukes of Montagu from 1749 until 1773, when, with their support, he set up as a grocer in Mayfair. Already as a servant he had become a literary figure, notably as a correspondent of Laurence Sterne, and was perhaps regarded to an extent as an interesting curiosity. His portrait by Gainsborough, dating from 1768 at a time when his mistress was also being painted by that artist, may have been commissioned by his mistress as a gift to her favourite retainer. It shows her servant in the clothes of a gentleman, not at all a usual approach. As the portrait suggests, Sancho is remarkable in having crossed not just one but two powerful cultural barriers.

OPPOSITE Cat.75 **A Gentleman, Possibly William Hickey, and an Indian Servant**
Arthur William Devis, *c.*1785

Son of the more famous Arthur Devis, A.W. Devis lived in Bengal for eleven years, where he enjoyed the patronage of senior members of the colonial administration. The British in India were enabled by their generous salaries to maintain large retinues of servants, and frequently chose to be portrayed accompanied by Indian attendants in native dress.

Indians in British portraiture

It was not only Africans who came to Europe from another continent from the late Middle Ages onwards. Some Asians also found their way to Europe and to Britain, as did a few native Americans. Though some

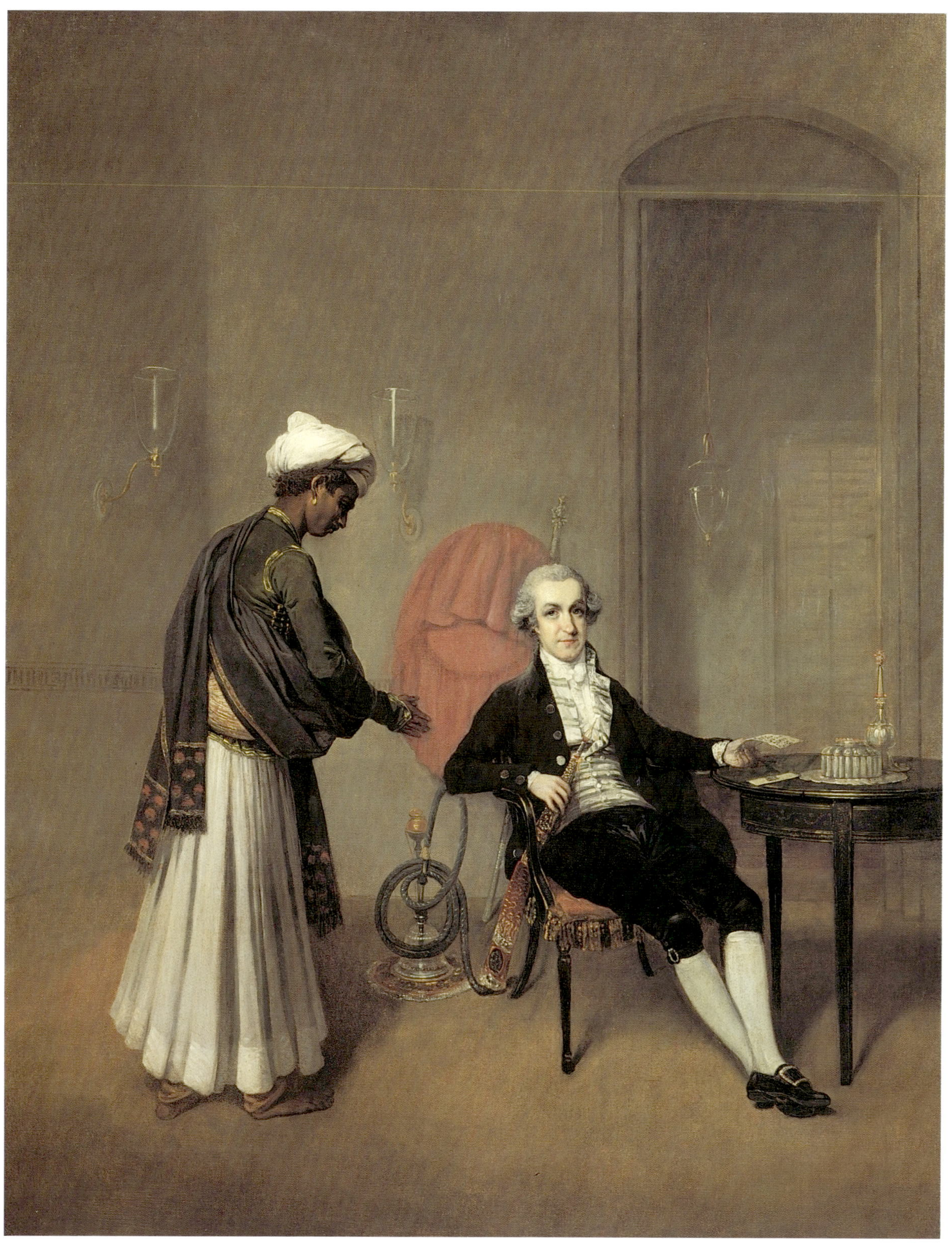

Indians were brought to Britain by their British employers in India in the eighteenth and nineteenth centuries, their numbers were small compared to Africans. The Indian tradition of servant portraiture is quite different from the black African one. There was an active British presence in India from the seventeenth century onwards, and Indian servants are primarily shown not in Britain but in India. They form part of the enormous households which clustered around prominent Europeans, many of them performing for their British employers a range of functions for which there was no parallel at home: as water-coolers, bearers 'to pull the pankhas (ceiling fans)', grass-cutters, the 'gwala, or cowherd'.[12] These images were painted by Indians, by amateur British artists, and by the painters (Zoffany was the most famous) who travelled to India in search of patronage. Such a painting as Arthur William Devis's portrait of *A Gentleman, Possibly William Hickey, and an Indian Servant* (*c*.1785), is characteristic, with the Englishman shown seated at leisure with his servants in dutiful attendance.

In such portraits another difference emerges from the conventional depiction of the African retainer. Africans are never seen in the context of their own continent, which the British had not occupied and about which they knew almost nothing. India was a different matter. British people had been going there since Elizabeth I set up the East India Company in 1600 and had found a society which they could admire and sympathise with. Relations between British employers and their household staffs in India seem

Cat.76 Figures of Bengali Servants
Early nineteenth century

Made by native craftsmen in Bengal, an area where figurative clay modelling flourished from the early eighteenth century, these naturalistically modelled servants are representative of those employed by European colonials. Commissioned groups of figures depicting types of occupation or caste were a common cultural expression of a more widespread imperial endeavour to classify the Indian people, and, as well as being obtained as souvenirs, they were often acquired by museums for educational purposes.

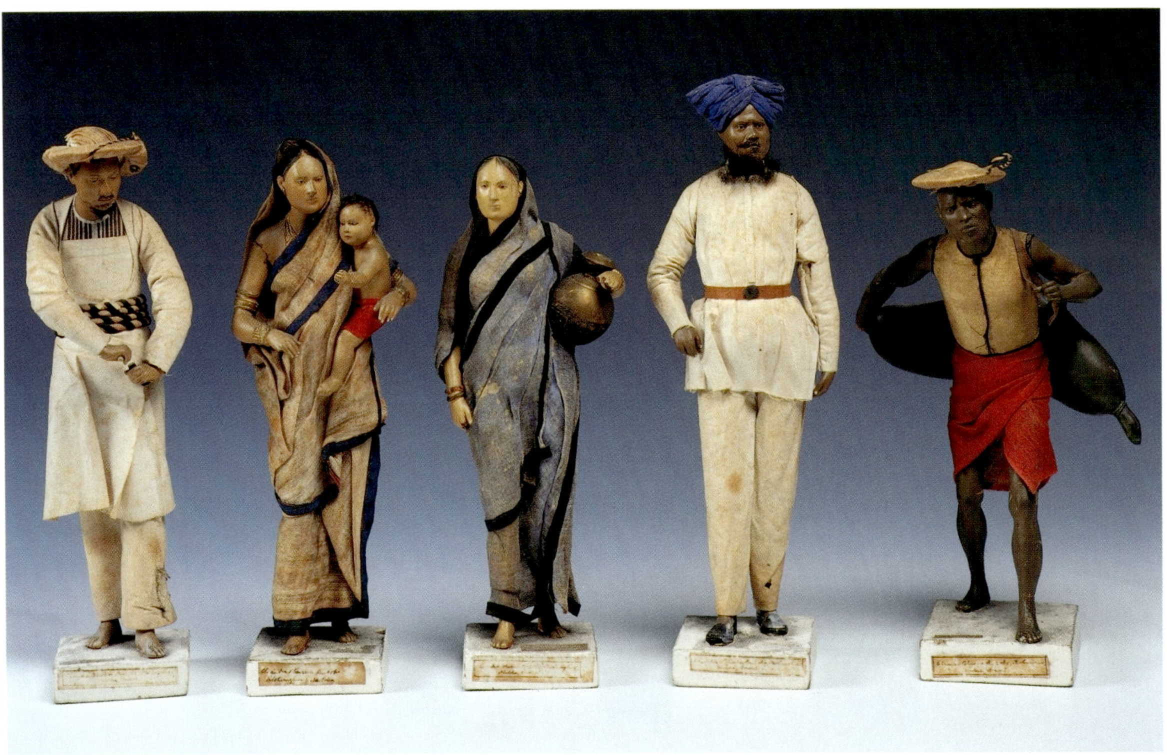

often to have been cordial: some of the most touching memorials of the personal relationships which could develop in these circumstances are the sets of figures made of Indian households when their employers left India for their homeland, a version of the serial portraits we have already seen. Produced from the late eighteenth century onwards, these figures, made of clay and individually clothed and provided with utensils, were intended to recall old friends, when they were thousands of miles away.

In the nineteenth century the situation of black people living in Britain changed drastically. With the abolition of the slave trade in 1807 very few black people entered Britain, and the black people who remained tended to intermarry with the white population. By 1900 black people were even more of a rarity in Britain than they had been in the eighteenth century. To employ a black servant was not unheard of in the late Victorian period, as is indicated by a photograph of the (admittedly somewhat exceptional) Livingstone family with Dr Livingstone's two 'faithful servants from Zanzibar' at Newstead Abbey near Nottingham around 1874,[13] but it was certainly unusual.

By contrast, the number and the visibility of Indian servants rose. Some of these were the employees of prominent Indians, such as Duleep Singh, setting up large households in England. The most prominent, and potentially subversive, examples, however, were the Indian servants of Queen Victoria.

The Queen's Munshi

Victoria was declared Empress of India in 1877, and became fascinated by the country. Though she could not go there, she surrounded herself with a miniature Indian court at home. One of the first Indians to be engaged as a royal servant, in the Golden Jubilee year of 1887, was the twenty-four-year-old Abdul Karim, who was soon followed by other Indian retainers.[14] Abdul Karim, whom the Queen thought intelligent and well-mannered, and no doubt found good-looking as well, was originally expected to wait at table but was soon promoted to be her *Munshi* (teacher) in Hindustani. Not at all an estimable character in the eyes of the royal household, who found him aggressive and repellent, he became a royal favourite. The Queen granted him the use of cottages in the grounds of Osborne House, Balmoral and Windsor, in which he installed a number of ladies variously known as his wife and his aunts. In 1894 he was again promoted, to be the Queen's Indian Secretary. Until Victoria's death he was a prominent figure at court, with influence (or so some of her advisers thought) over the sovereign. The Queen was also served by a substantial group of other Indian servants, who were in regular attendance.

The Munshi's role at Court raises interesting issues in terms of class and race. From the beginning he asserted that he was not from the servant caste, and that his father was a doctor (though actually he was a minor hospital administrator). He aspired to an elevated position at court, and a

Cat.77 **The Munshi Abdul Karim**
Rudolph Swoboda, 1888

This Austrian artist painted a series of portraits of Indians for Queen Victoria in India in 1886–8: these now hang at Osborne House. For the Queen, this image of her much-admired teacher and Indian Secretary was of particular significance. It is one of the most romanticised images of a servant to survive.

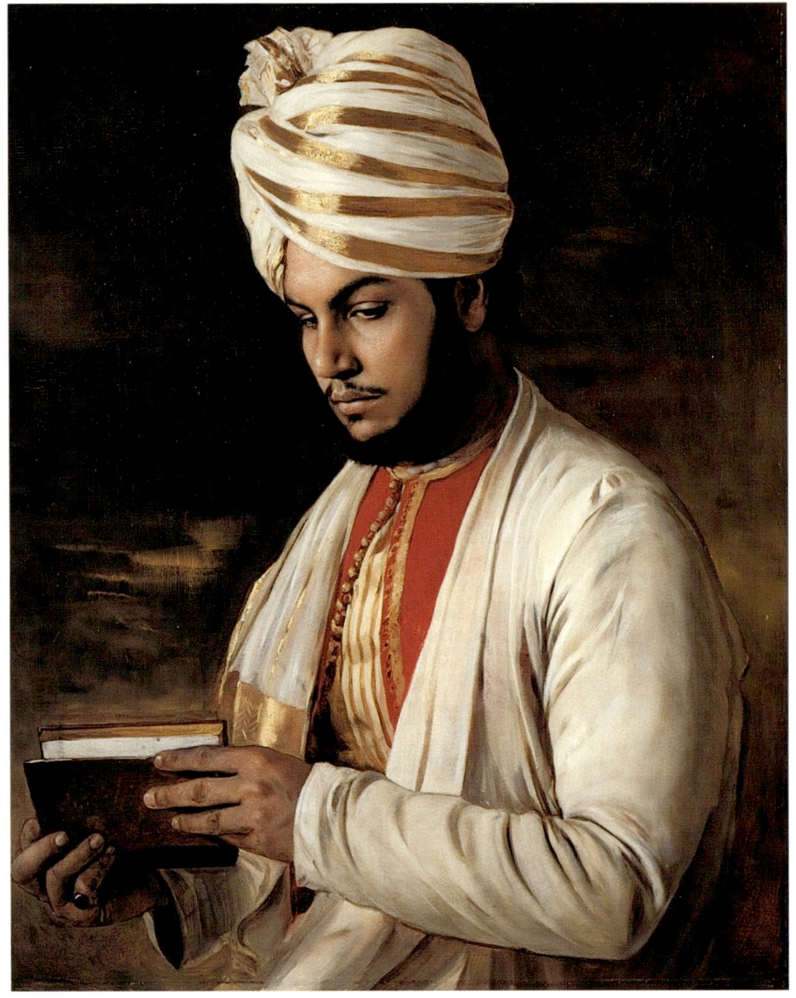

furious row broke out when he insisted on taking his meals with the royal household. Although, on the evidence of recent biographies, the household was hardly made up of inhumane people, they refused to accept him as their equal. It enraged them that he enjoyed privileged access to the monarch and saw himself, and was seen by the Queen, as a gentleman. In their view, he had no right to either privilege. He followed in a long tradition of royal favourites regarded as upstarts by other courtiers, and his non-European origins made it particularly difficult to consign him to any recognised social rank. In addition, India enjoyed a particular status in Britain and it was possible for Indians to reach a high position in society in a way that was inconceivable for Africans – as the example of Indian MPs elected in the 1890s illustrates.

It was these origins that aroused such tension between the Queen and her court. Members of the court found the idea of a non-European holding an important position close to the Queen disconcerting, if not worse.

Victoria was more liberal. As Elizabeth Longford suggested, the Queen was passionately hostile to both class and race discrimination (courtiers were forbidden to call Indians by what was regarded as the denigratory term 'black men'), and was more enlightened in terms of racial inclusiveness than most of her contemporaries. Over the Munshi affair, which lasted for some years, 'it is hard', in Longford's words, 'not to marvel at the old lady who, partly as a protest against prejudice, challenged two Viceroys, two Prime Ministers, two Secretaries of State, many other officials and most of the court.'[15]

Naturally the Queen wanted her favourite to be painted. The Munshi was depicted in two oils, of 1888 and 1889 respectively, by the Viennese artist Rudolph Swoboda, who in India had already executed for the Queen a remarkable series of portraits of Indians in native dress or uniform.[16] In the 1888 portrait the Munshi is shown in rich Indian costume, like a nobleman's, wearing a white and gold turban. He carries a book, a reference to his role as man of learning and tutor to the Queen, and an air of profundity. However unjustified this depiction of the Munshi as noble scholar may have been, the portrait pays respectful and indeed romantic tribute to the Indian origins of the sitter. The portrait now hangs, as it was intended to do, within the set of portraits of royal servants and other Indians in the New Wing corridor at Osborne House, on the way to the Durbar Room created in the 1890s. It contributes to the statement of Imperial inclusiveness sought by the Queen at the end of her reign and gives a powerful indication of the cultural changes that had taken place over the past hundred years. Whether it was the foreignness of the sitter, his very Otherness, that made possible this leap of sympathy in the Queen's mind, is another issue.

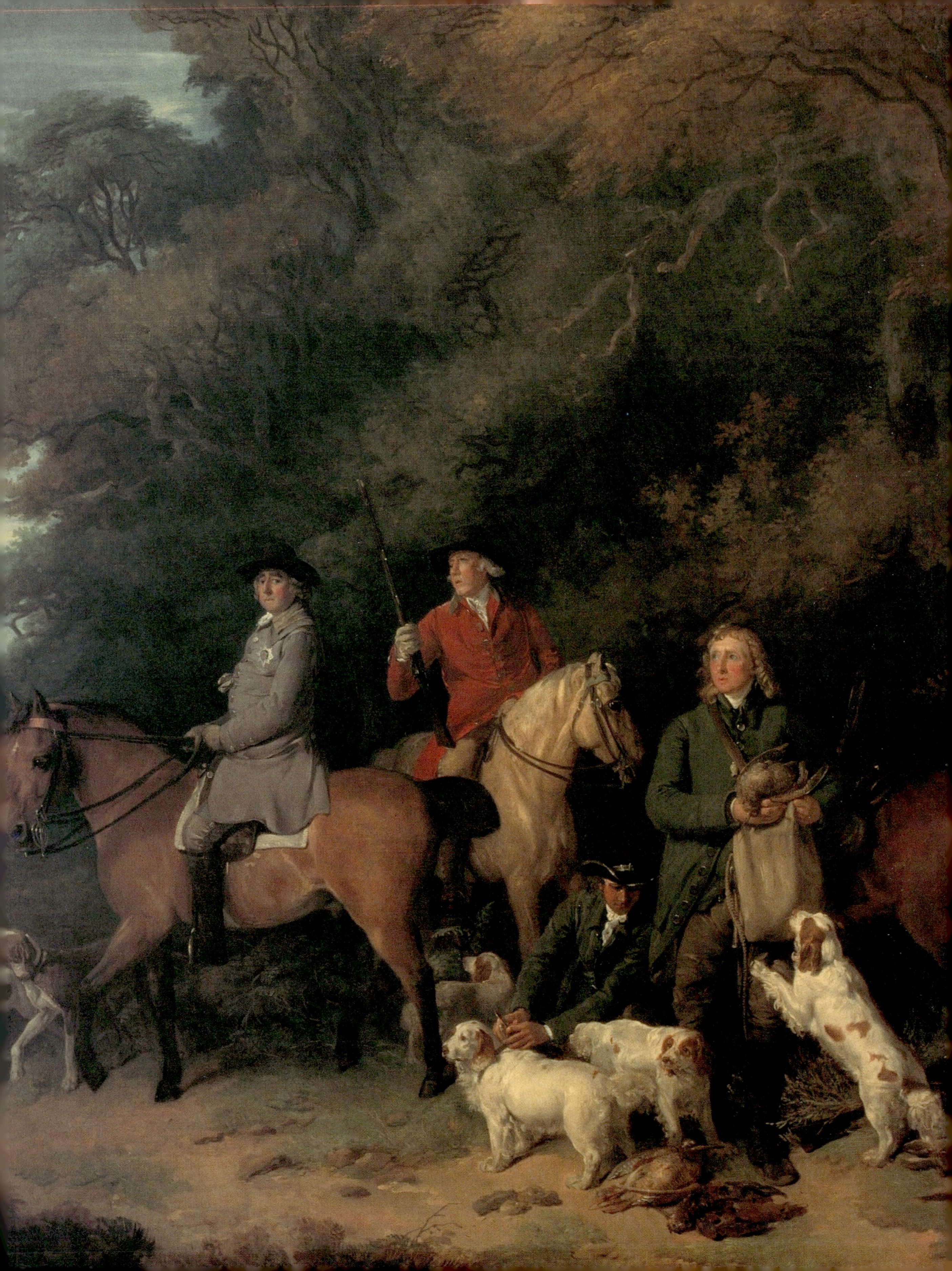

9 IN THE REALM OF NATURE AND BEASTS

Matthew Craske

AS THE TITLE OF THIS BOOK IMPLIES, the popular understanding of a servant in English history is of a 'domestic' who inhabited a world below stairs in a private household. In the eighteenth and early nineteenth centuries, however, the term servant simply denoted a class of engaged labour: the assistant to a blacksmith, the shepherd or ploughman to a tenant farmer might well be 'servants'. A proportion of those servants employed on country estates were not domestics; even a modest gentry household was likely to include a groom, gamekeeper and coachman. Great country establishments had an array of such staff: a postillion, coachmen and grooms, slaughtermen and butchers, ploughmen, shepherds, dairymaids, park-keepers, gamekeepers, under-keepers and gardeners. Satisfying the particular sporting concerns of the wealthy often entailed substantial additions to this retinue: a trainer, sporting grooms and jockeys based in the proximity of a racecourse, a huntsman to the foxhounds, whippers-in and dog-feeders or kennelmen to breed and exercise greyhounds for hare-coursing.

There has been no sustained historical study of this type of servant. Indeed, much of the literature on service concentrates solely on domestics. This is a serious omission for the art historian, since the great majority of our images of eighteenth- and early nineteenth-century servants are of those involved in outdoor activities. So extensive is the painted record that one is obliged to regard the visual arts as a major source of historical information concerning this type of labour. It is essential to take into account the witness of painting when exploring the moral economy that underscored the relationships between landowners, outdoor servants and the animals whose care was the principal duty of the latter.

To a degree, this tradition of images can be understood in terms of practical expediency. It can be observed, for instance, that grooms had good practical reasons for making regular appearances in that most

OPPOSITE Detail of fig.35 **The Return from Shooting**
Francis Wheatley

characteristic of English genres, the equine portrait. In order to be painted, a horse needed to be constrained in the stable with its head held by a groom. A self-portrait by the early nineteenth-century sporting artist John Ferneley (1782–1860) shows him at his easel in a stable interior before just such a horse and groom. Most animal painters, from John Wootton (*c.*1682–1764) onward, simply transposed these figures to an open landscape, understanding that a groom in livery might lend status and a touch of specificity to their image. Wootton occasionally improvised oriental groom's garb to indicate a prestigious Arabian bloodline. It was also difficult to generate an impression of the atmosphere of the hunt without some image of the 'lusty huntsman' with his characteristic cap and horn. These characters made regular appearances within hunting poetry and song, summoning up the essential sights and sounds of the field. When, in the early eighteenth century, English painters took up the tradition of painting the chase from Dutch, Flemish and French artists, they were bound to include the generic image of the huntsman so favoured by their forebears. In this school of imagery, the sight or sound of the huntsman was expected to trigger memories of the sensory pleasures of the hunt.

These figures, however, clearly became more than mere props, functionaries and sensory impressions. Indeed, they developed a complex iconography in late eighteenth- and early nineteenth-century art, at the very time that the white domestic became 'invisible' to painters, to use the phrase of Jean Hecht, the noted historian of service. While domestics were excluded from the group portrait imagery of the elite household, it became increasingly fashionable in portraits of social groups to celebrate the affectionate relationship between a gentleman and his gamekeeper, or the pride of the hunt in its huntsman and whippers-in.

White domestic servants featured regularly in only one form of portrait at this time: the 'small figure conversation piece' which was probably introduced to the English market in about 1710 by Marcellus Laroon (1679–1772), and developed by William Hogarth, Gawen Hamilton and Charles Philips. The adaptation of the conventions of this art form to the culture of hunting gave rise to a genre in which the portrait depiction of outdoor servants first derived, though it was their master, his family and friends rather than servants who were accorded the status of being portrayed as identifiable individuals.

Hunt servants

Hunting artists of this era, in particular John Wootton and Peter Tillemans (1684–1734), seem to have deployed generic conventions in the representation of the outdoor 'conversation' – a form of art in which friends or families were presented in sociable groups within a landscape. Huntsmen and grooms presided over the rituals of the field in a manner similar to that of the butlers and maids of interior conversation pieces presiding over the rituals of the table or of taking tea. Like Hogarth, Wootton included the occasional portrait of a favourite servant. Such is the engaging figure of the liveried park-keeper with a slain deer, surely a portrait of an individual, who is seen in the foreground of a hunting 'conversation' painted for the 4th Earl of Coventry in 1714.

By the 1750s, the genre of the 'small figure' interior conversation piece was on the wane. A new generation of conversation painters emerged, led by Johann Zoffany and Francis Wheatley (1747–1801) in whose art servants appear infrequently. Only in the portraiture of colonial households were servants routinely included in the family 'conversations' of the late eighteenth and early nineteenth centuries. Images of Indians and Africans had the advantage of adding an air of the exotic to the scene. Equally, such figures were difficult for outsiders and posterity to confuse with actual members of the family. Seldom included within group portraits of life-sized subjects, white domestic servants virtually disappear from English group portraiture in the second half of the eighteenth century.

In the realm of the sporting and agricultural artist, however, demand for portrait images of servants significantly accelerated in the same period. By contrast with earlier English sporting painters, George Stubbs (1724–1806) tended to treat grooms, gamekeepers and huntsmen as subjects for portraiture, rather than reduce them to type. Indeed, he began from the 1760s onward to take commissions for works that were intended specifically as portraits of servants. His first commission of this sort around 1765 was for a series of

Fig.29 **Lord Torrington's Hunt Servants Setting Out from Southill**
George Stubbs, *c.*1765

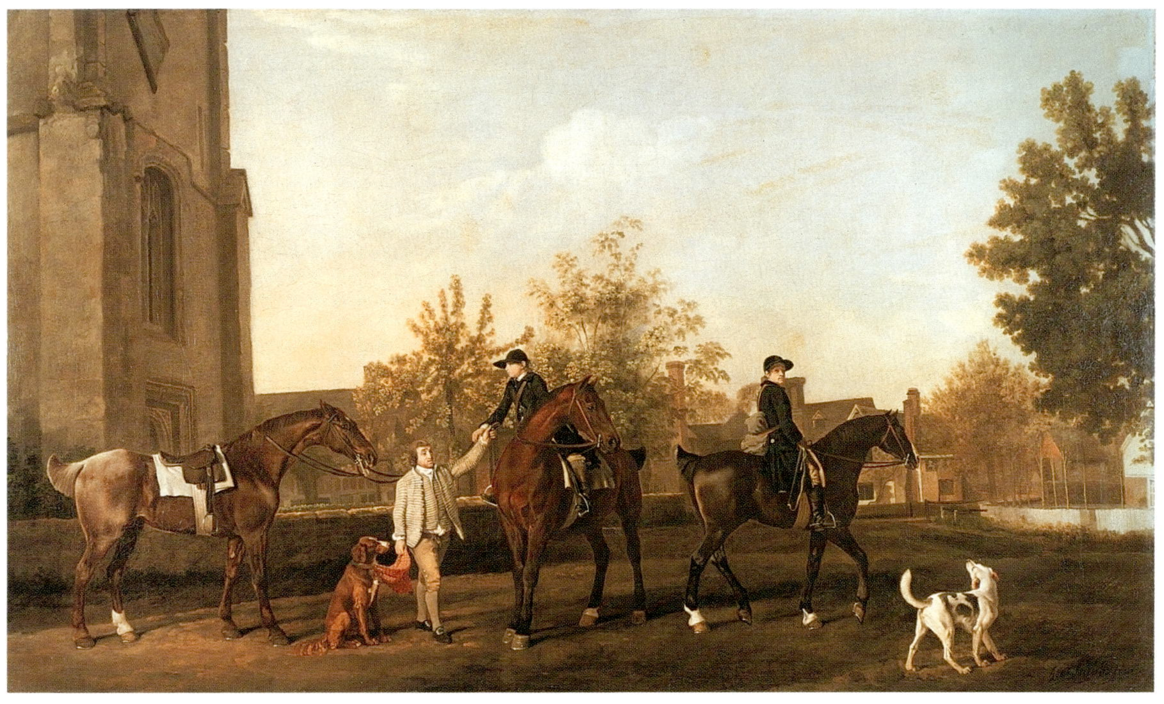

three paintings recording the specific features of Lord Torrington's outdoor servants at work on his Bedfordshire estate, Southill (fig.29). These were the first 'conversation' portraits of outdoor servants; a departure from the previous convention of the conversation form, the 'small figure' rural scene in which images of servants featured though the central emphasis was on the portraits of their employers.

Stubbs was a pioneer of the outdoor servant portrait. No predecessor or competitor granted these figures such careful attention. By the early nineteenth century, however, most important sporting and animal painters took care routinely to record the individual characteristics of outdoor servants. Stubbs's successors to the helm of English animal painting – George Garrard (1760–1826), Benjamin Marshall (1768–1870), John Ferneley, James Ward (1769–1859) and Edwin Landseer (1802–73) – made a regular practice of servant portraiture. Portraits that focused on the figure of an individual and named outdoor servant were rarely seen in the eighteenth century beyond the oeuvre of Stubbs. Such works, however, became

Cat.78 **Freeman, the Earl of Clarendon's Gamekeeper, with a Dying Doe and Hound**
George Stubbs, 1800

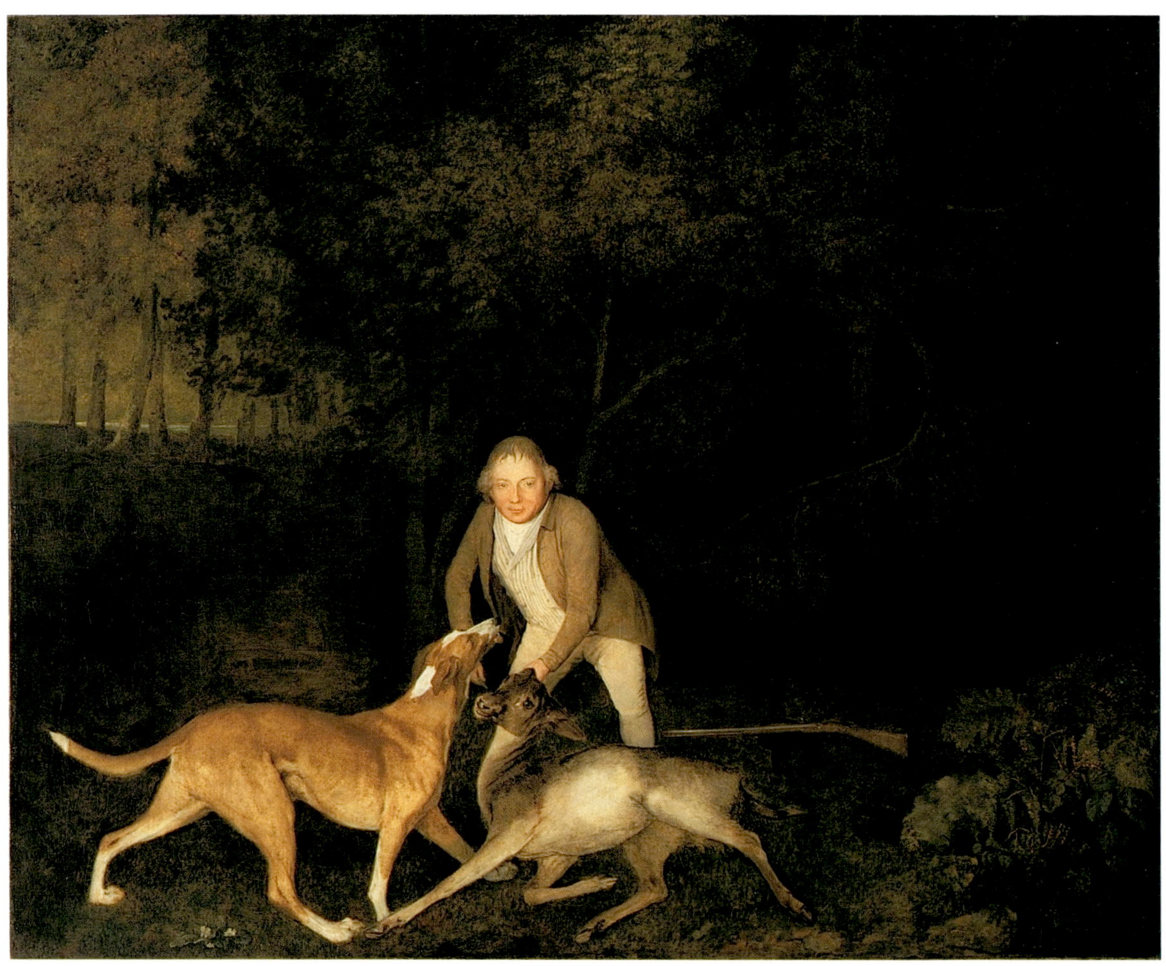

relatively commonplace in the early decades of the succeeding century with the demand for images of figures involved in fox hunting. Unlike Stubbs, some of the artists of the later period sent such images for exhibition in London with the name of the servant appended for addition to the catalogue. Moreover, in reproductive prints such figures were not rendered anonymous, as they had been in engravings after Stubbs's images of Lord Torrington's servants, which were published in 1789 and 1790 under the simple titles *Labourers* and *Gamekeepers*. Rather, it became fashionable to include the name of the servant at the base of the image or within an accompanying key to a group portrait. This tendency applied to images of even the most humble of hunt servants such as earthstoppers, men who blocked foxholes before the hunt, and feeders, those who cooked and served horsemeat to foxhounds.

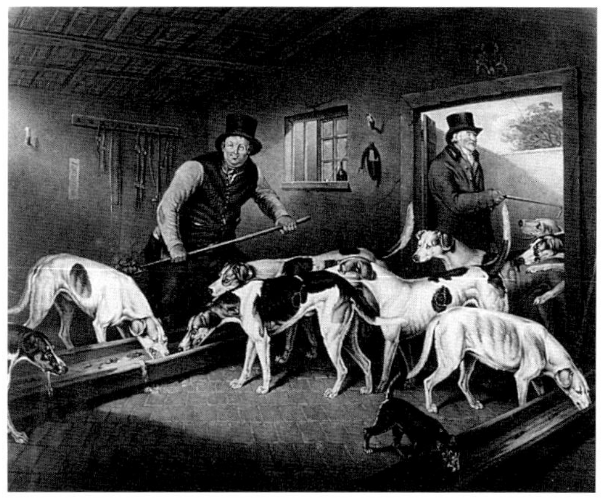

Fig.30 The Raby Pack
William Ward after Henri Bernard Chalon

The upper hunt servants of the great early nineteenth-century hunts were popular subjects for prints which generally feature some note of their names. Few were more commonly portrayed than Tom Oldaker and Thomas Goosey, huntsmen respectively to the Old Berkeley and Belvoir hunts. These men were each the subject of a dozen or more painted portraits. Many of these images were turned into prints for sporting books and magazines or for the collections of subscribers to, or guests of, their hunts.

This increased interest in the individual hunt servant needs to be set within the context of the general appetite for specificity in contemporary English sporting culture. This appetite grew as country sports slowly emerged as a national obsession. Even a cursory glance through the contemporary ephemeral literature of the field – in particular early sporting magazines and serials – reveals extraordinary concern with inside knowledge or gossip, curious anecdotes of idiosyncrasy, technical detail and jargon. As adepts habitually claimed, 'modern' hunting (post-1760) had won the right to be described as a 'science' and as such should be recorded in minute detail. This period marked the development of careful documentation: the hound book focused on seemingly interminable lists of bloodline; the game book recorded the grim statistics of numbers shot; and the hunt diary bore witness to weather conditions, attendance and landmarks traversed. Early nineteenth-century ephemeral literature, in particular 'Nimrod's' *Famous Sporting Tours*, fueled the appetite for detailed, precise and picaresque observation. Nimrod, the greatest of the gentlemen journalists, set the tone for his times by being entirely fascinated with the sporting characters of the day. His reports abound with tales and descriptions of the sporting servants that he met on his trips around Britain. It is possible to verify most of the painted portraits of notable early nineteenth-century English huntsmen from the detailed descriptions provided by Nimrod.

It is not surprising that the artists associated with this culture of minute observation and anecdote were assessed in terms of their attention to detail. It followed that progress in their art was measured in terms of greater improvements in their techniques of achieving verisimilitude.

To conform to such demands for accuracy many sporting painters became enthusiastic participants in the activities that they represented. The slow rise in the social standing of the sporting artist meant that there was an increased tendency in the elite sporting community to befriend and include painters. Some sporting painters of the early eighteenth century did become part of hunting society. Peter Tillemans, for instance, seems to have had a hunting friendship with his most enthusiastic patron, the Suffolk squire Dr Cox Macro. A slow change in emphasis did, however, occur whereby famous sporting painters were more likely to be insiders rather than outside observers of British sporting society. It is clear that men such as Landseer and Ferneley became active participants in the hunting communities that they painted. Like the sporting servant, these painters made the transition from functionary to admired celebrity or treasured companion. There is a strong sense that the attention to the characteristics of hunting servants which is encountered frequently in early nineteenth-century sporting art derives from the painters' familiarity with the personalities of hunting parties of which they were invited members. The capacity of an artist to reflect the insider's respect for the celebrated hunt servant is nowhere better expressed than in the oeuvre of Sir Francis Grant (1803–78). Grant, a gentleman turned painter, was very much part of the national fox-hunting elite in the mid-nineteenth century. His portraits of well-known huntsman servants, perhaps the most striking and dignified images of their type and date, reflect the inside view of these men, the affection and respect due to a familiar and an inferior.

The sporting bond

One major issue dominates the phenomenon of the portrait of the sporting servant: the supposed healthiness, moral and physical, of the masculine bond between master and man that was forged in the realm of nature. A suitable point of departure in this respect is Thomas Rowlandson's famous comparative prints of 1788, *Four O'clock in the Town*, *Four O'clock in the Country* (figs 31, 32) In the first, we witness a young married man being put to bed by his two chambermaids in a fashionable townhouse, as his wife pleads for him to come to bed. The manner in which he is being undressed suggests that he has a more tactile relationship with his maids than with his wife. In the companion print, the same man rises early for the hunt, seen off by his loving wife. Instead of maids, he is attended by his hunt servant who carries his saddle. On the wall, next to the pelt of a fox, hangs a print of a huntsman and hounds. A baby sleeps in the cradle, a sign of the healthy fecundity of his marriage.

Comparison between the servant imagery in these prints is vital to their meaning. In the country, a man is deemed to have his hunt servant as his companion, a relationship that presents no threat to his marriage. Indeed, the world of sport is presented here as one of separate spheres of gender: the woman attends her children in the home, while the man finds his leisure outside the home in the company of other men, including his hunt servants. In the town, a man is prone to fall into the company of female domestics,

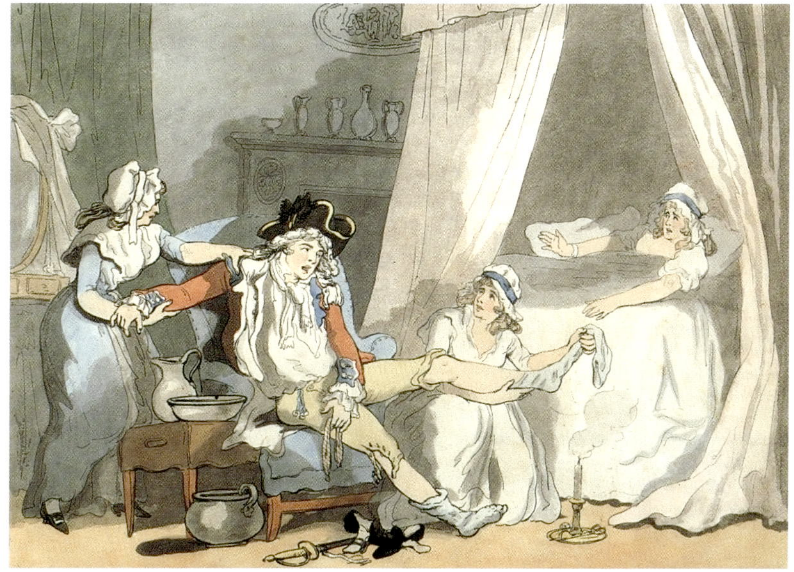

Fig.31 **Four O'clock in the Town**
Thomas Rowlandson, 1788

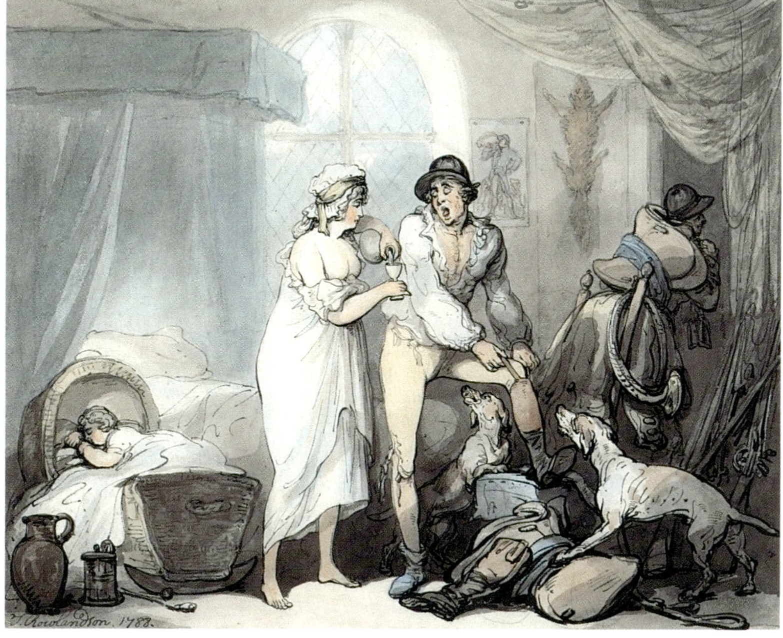

Fig.32 **Four O'clock in the Country**
Thomas Rowlandson, 1788

apparently becoming unhealthily close to them. Mixed up with the affairs of the wife, the female domestic is depicted as a threat to the family. That the wife of the man who is handled by his female domestics has no child is no coincidence.

The development of the moral requirement to separate domestic servants from the family was, if we are to believe the social historical theories of Lawrence Stone and others, a major trend in eighteenth-century English private life. It was, it is argued, in the interest of the formation of a nuclear family that domestics were made invisible: excluded from family conversations, both painted and spoken, summoned by bells only when required, kept to a servants' staircase or confined to entirely separate quarters. Such exclusion ensured that privacy allowed for the development of intimacy among close relations – domestic servants became notorious for interfering in family affairs and overhearing secrets. There was, by contrast, no necessity to exclude the outdoor servant, for he had no claim to be part of the family and no contact with their intimate affairs. Rather, he was part of that life outside the domestic sphere which a virile gentleman of leisure might enjoy without a threat to his family. In this light, we can perhaps understand why, 140 years after the publication of Rowlandson's image, D.H. Lawrence's *Lady Chatterley's Lover* (1928) became such a shocking metaphor for the crumbling virility of the English aristocracy. This tale of the erotic relationship between the aristocratic wife and the estate gamekeeper, a man on friendly terms with the husband, exposed a true taboo. It inverted dangerously the safe old cliché of a gentleman's affair with his maid and subverted the assumption that the manly prowess of the outdoor servant could be safely limited to the realm of masculine sporting society.

D.H. Lawrence keyed into a long tradition of regarding the outdoor servant as a force of nature. As literal outsiders, such men were regarded as emblems of the outdoors and with it all that was natural and healthy. They were, in the ideal, figments of the territory of nature and the kingdom of the animals which they hunted or for which they cared. Their individual characteristics were akin to the craggy irregularities admired in the 'picturesque' landscape. Much of what appealed in prints and paintings of outdoor servants was their enduring natural vitality. There was in such portraiture a strong preference for vibrant men of mature years. The testimony of such images seems to have functioned as an assurance to hunting gentlemen that their own lifestyle was likely to lead to longevity.

The close association between outdoor servant and fine animal, which was so enjoyed by Nimrod, was an important element of outdoor servant portraits. The attachment of a gentleman to his outdoor servants was indistinguishable from that which he expressed towards his animals. Indeed, animal painters were generally commissioned to record these figures. It was an exception when Sir George Beaumont commissioned David Wilkie, an artist who concentrated on human rather than animal nature, to paint a portrait of his head keeper on his estate at Dumnow, Essex, between 1810 and 1811. In hunt literature, such as the journalism of Nimrod or Pearce Egan, the celebrated hunt servant was likely to share the ennobling attributes of the animals: loyalty, vitality, strength, bravery, health or cunning. While numerous early nineteenth-century hunt servants were regarded as famous or celebrated, it was only in as much as they came to rival the thoroughbred animals with which they kept company, in the attentions of elite rural society.

That the status of certain classes of British outdoor servants was markedly enhanced in the late eighteenth and early nineteenth centuries was largely owing to the broader phenomenon of agricultural improvement. It can be no coincidence that all the major kinds of servants who were the subjects of portraits were involved in a common activity: the breeding of domestic animals for higher food yield, finer appearance or athletic performance. This is the common denominator between the huntsman, gamekeeper, shepherd, cowman, coachman, racing groom or trainer. In most surviving portraits of outdoor servants they are seen posed with the animals which they had bred.

In the period between 1770 and 1840 there was a pervasive craze for the breeding of animals amongst England's country nobility and gentry. This encouraged employers to set great store on the engagement of men of sound practical experience who could manage the processes. While landowners stood to gain social kudos among their peers for the production of an improved breed, they relied on the knowledge, hard work and patience of their servants to succeed. Such servants were highly valued, and often highly remunerated, by their employers, who were usually those who commissioned their portraits. In the realm of fox hunting, the prestige associated with breeding hounds was such that skilled servants were often offered inducements to defect. Many noted hunt servants had a host of employers in the course of their careers.

Those servants who stood to gain public celebrity rather than just the respect of their employers were likely to be adepts of the culture of speed that emerged out of improved breeding. Most notable were the late eighteenth- and early nineteenth-century huntsmen who presided over the 'science' of breeding a new type of light and fast foxhound. They were also obliged to ride with the hounds, a matter which, given the pace of the modern hound, increasingly required a mount that was bred for speed. A new vogue for dare-devil riding emerged which centred on the traversal of an improved agricultural landscape: enclosed drained fields allowed for bursts of speed which were punctuated by leaps over hedges and drainage dykes. This culture of terrible tumbles and scrapes, which had its most extreme expression in the Melton Mowbray hunts of the 1820s and 1830s, was immortalised by the highly popular prints and drawings of Henry Alken (1785–1851).

To negotiate such obstacles, the late eighteenth-century huntsman generally abandoned the cumbersome livery of his forebears in favour of light and practical dress and equipment. The curled French horn beloved of seventeenth- and early eighteenth-century sporting artists was widely abandoned in favour of a light, straight instrument that would not be as likely to cause injury in the inevitable heavy falls. The early nineteenth-century world of hunting with hounds celebrated the 'neck or nothing' rider, who risked his life to keep up with the prey. The most famous figure of this type was Dick Christian, a rum character much painted by Ferneley, who retired from life as a hunt servant and set up a private riding school. Christian lived a charmed life; numerous famous hunting servants of this era died or were maimed in the course of their work – the perception of the huntsman as hero clearly affected the manner in which he was depicted, with many artists opting for a glamour and dash otherwise reserved for paintings of cavalry officers.

The development of fox hunting in the period between 1770 and 1830 demonstrates the strong connection between the 'useful' culture of agricultural improvement and a leisure culture based on the swift traversal of the landscape. On occasion, painters provide us with direct comparison between servants operating in different fields of animal management. A remarkable example is found in the work of John Ferneley and his fine portraits of the servants of Sir Robert Palmer, MP for Leicester. The first painting was of John Green the shepherd in 1823, showing off his prize Leicester longwool sheep to his master (fig.33). The second was of Palmer's head groom, John Mentham in 1826, 'on favourite grey horse'. Mentham is literally above the world of agricultural beasts; he rides gallantly through the landscape, which is dominated by an enormous prize Durham ox which he patently ignores, preferring to gaze at the view from his hilltop vantage. These servant portraits demonstrate the contrast, as well as connection, between two spheres: the stolid and useful realm of agricultural improvement and the elegance which attended the world of fine thoroughbred horses. Green is reasonably well dressed in an irregularly buttoned pink cotton waistcoat, an outfit a cut above the smock often seen in the portraits of estate shepherds. He is, however, far from a stylish figure. A sense of panache, however, surrounds Mentham, who is seen in an outfit no less fashionable than that of his master, complete with top hat, cream gaiters and long frock coat. His grey horse seems to be a more spirited mount than that of Sir John.

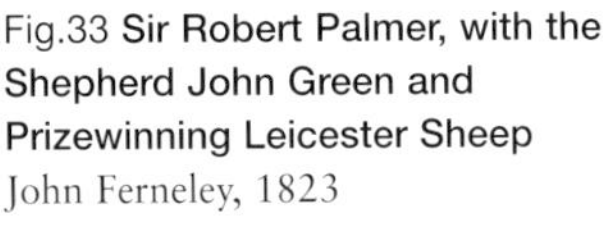
Fig.33 **Sir Robert Palmer, with the Shepherd John Green and Prizewinning Leicester Sheep**
John Ferneley, 1823

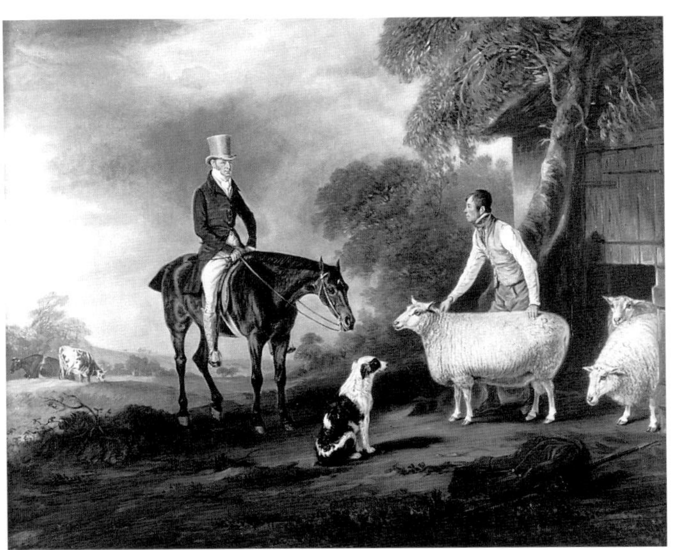

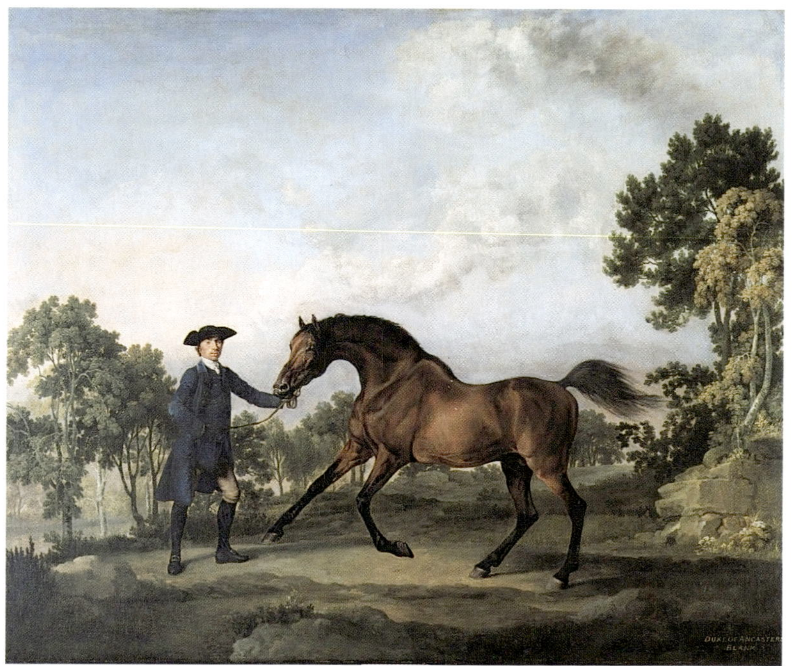

Cat.79 **The Duke of Ancaster's Bay Stallion Blank Held by a Groom**
George Stubbs, *c.*1762–5

This late masterpiece by Stubbs of the famous stallion Blank (son of the Godolphin Arabian) held by his groom was commissioned by Peregrine Bertie, 3rd Duke of Ancaster, King George III's Master of Horse. The Duke was passionate about racing and breeding horses, and married Mary Panton, daughter of the Keeper of the King's Running Horses. Although Blank won only one race at Newmarket, he was immensely successful at stud, the role which is commemorated here. The Duke was a major patron of sporting art, commissioning two other horse portraits with their grooms from Stubbs, and other racing pictures from artists including John Wootton, James Seymour and Francis Sartorius, as well as a set of seventeen portraits of his brood mares. The groom shown here may be Tom Parnell, who appears in the second portrait of this stallion. Like other outdoor servants involved in breeding animals, grooms to famous racehorses were often highly prized servants.

Such conspicuous elegance is regularly encountered in portraits of head grooms of the early nineteenth century. Their splendour was rivalled by two other types of servant also strongly associated with breeding and command of thoroughbred horses: the coachman and attendant groom who brought up reserve horses for gentlemen of the hunt. The latter was a specialist type of servant who emerged only in the last thirty years of the eighteenth century, as the hunt became so fast that a single horse could not be expected to stay the pace for more than a few hours. The need for reserve horses substantially increased the cost of hunting and there was, accordingly, a sense of conspicuous consumption in the dress of the grooms who rode them. In sartorial terms these men seem to have been the élite among the outdoor servants of their times. The most arresting image of such a character is Stubbs's excellent portrait of William Anderson, groom to the Prince of Wales, who, splendid in top hat and red frock coat, brings up the reserve horses (1793).

The sartorial splendour of this servant is rivalled only in Stubbs's art by the image of another of the Prince of Wales's servants, Samuel Thomas, coachman to the Prince of Wales's phaeton (1793). In relishing such care upon rendition of the personal characteristics of a named coachman, Stubbs was, once again, a pioneer. The great majority of portraits of liveried coachmen date from the period between 1810 and 1830. Before this time, there were few even generalised images of these men. The lionisation of liveried coachmen coincided with a wider phenomenon, the craze for coaching, in which gentlemen took up the reins to rival the feats of professional

Fig.34 **Two Coach Horses of Sir John Fleming Leicester with Gaskill, the Coachman, and a Carriage in the Forecourt of Tabley House**
George Garrard, 1871

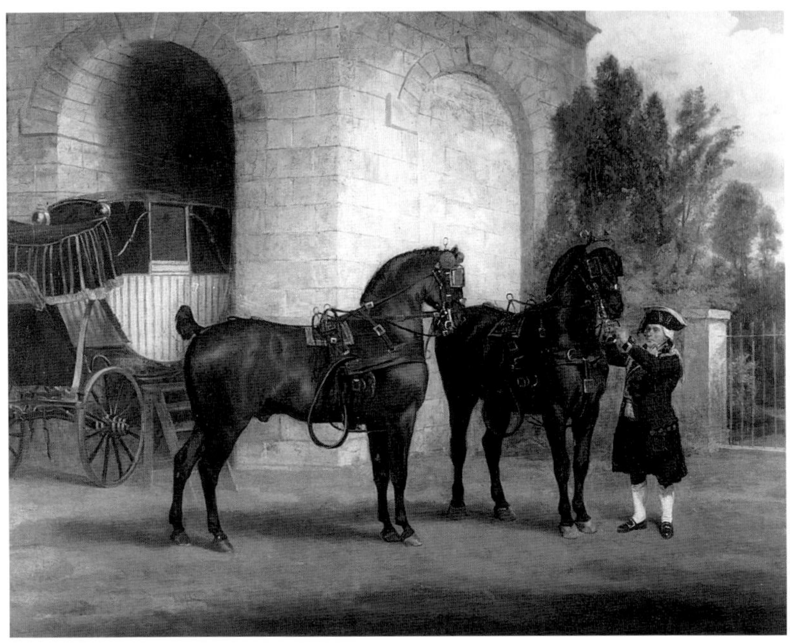

stage-coach drivers. The public admiration was not upon servants to private households but employees – the famous stage-coach drivers who drove the great routes between English cities. The general cult of driving seems to have enhanced the respect in which servant coachmen were held by their employers. So popular did the public coach become as a subject for painting in the early nineteenth century that it developed its own specialist practitioners.

No type of outdoor servant was more valued in old age, if the evidence of portraits is to be believed, than the gamekeeper. Portraits of gamekeepers, singular or in conversation with their masters, were far from scarce in the period between 1780 and 1840. Virtually all are of old men. Stubbs's great portrait of Freeman, Keeper to the Earl of Clarendon on his Watford estate, is a typically venerable figure. Perhaps the definitive aged character was John Crerar, the much-respected keeper of the Duke of Atholl, who was a favourite subject of Edwin Landseer. In accounting for the particularly strong association between gamekeeping, as idealised by painters, and old age, it is important to bear in mind the vigorous moral debates which surrounded the application of game law in this period. Even in sporting magazines, over-zealous keepers were much derided for violent conduct toward poachers or persons who they encountered on their territory. It is significant that very few surviving portraits of named keepers refer, even obliquely, to their function in the control of poaching, that role which has most excited the attention of modern historians. The venerable gamekeepers of the world of sporting painting did not carry the complications of the muscular threat of youth.

The most popular role of the good old keeper was to preside over dead game, attended by the dogs which he was responsible for breeding. Such a character is seen in the fine group portrait by Francis Wheatley of the 2nd Duke of Newcastle riding in the famous woodlands of his estate at Clumber (fig.35). So valued were the Duke's keepers that their names were recorded on the frame. The picture hung, along with another servant portrait, in the hall of the great house seen in the picture. The survival of estate documents means that we have detailed knowledge of these keepers.

Wheatley had good reason to make fine portraits of the keepers at Clumber. By the criteria of the culture of rural 'improvement' these were important men. They presided over that magnificent control of nature for which their master had become famous. No painting better illustrates the ideal of mutual regard between the servant and master which underscored the practice of improvement. Although historians and art historians most associate improvement with the degradation of the rights of the common man, the rise of the portrait of the outdoor servant indicates that there was ample respect for those who administered its processes.

Fig.35 **The Return from Shooting**
Francis Wheatley

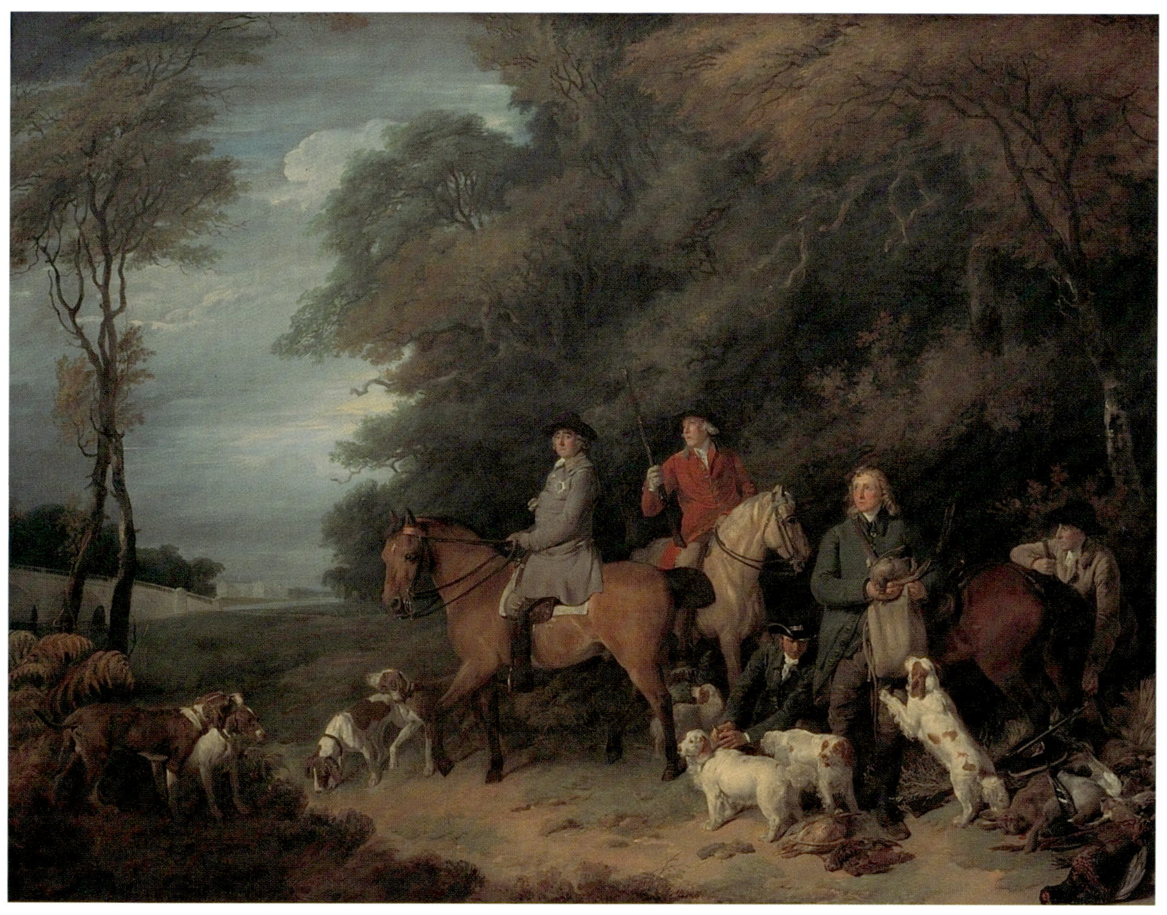

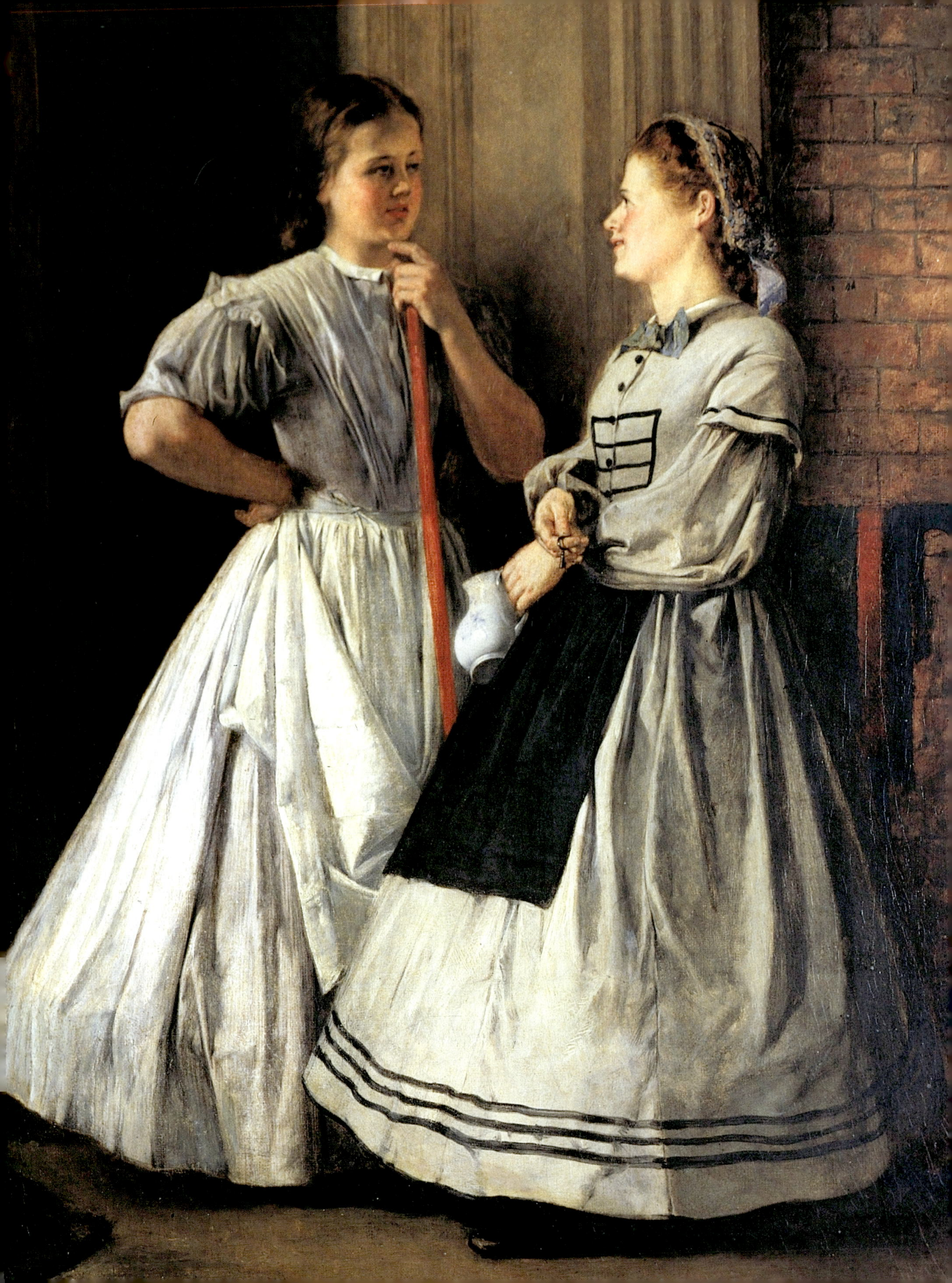

10 SOCIAL CRITIQUE

Giles Waterfield

FROM THE 1830s onwards, society in Britain changed with increasing rapidity. The parliamentary Reform Act of 1832 announced the first redistribution of political power while the population tended increasingly to live in towns rather than in the countryside. An increasingly wealthy and numerous middle class (for the first time generally defined as such) was led by plutocratic industrialists and financiers. But on the surface and in terms of social life, society did not change correspondingly. The aristocracy, tenacious of wealth and power, maintained (at least until the advent of the agricultural depression in the 1870s) large households, both in the country and in London. At the beginning of the nineteenth century the Earl of Bridgewater employed some five hundred men in the gardens and workshops of the enormous Ashridge Park, Hertfordshire, partly to provide employment for local people (in times of economic hardship the numbers increased). In the 1890s the Duke of Westminster, one of the wealthiest men in the country, had a household of over three hundred indoor and outdoor servants at Eaton Hall in Cheshire. Such a scale of establishment was unusual. John Bateman's *The Return of Owners of Land*, effectively a census of landowners, which was first published in 1872–3, estimated that a staff of thirty to fifty indoor servants was appropriate for a nobleman.

At the same time, the character of large households changed substantially. Though upper-class households were not necessarily larger than they had been in the eighteenth century (historians disagree on this point), they came to be organised on more strictly hierarchical lines, with an elaborate chain of command and a complex system of etiquette. Clothing was symptomatic: whereas in the earlier period female servants wore their own clothes (often handed down by their employers), a system of uniform dress for almost all servants became the norm in the later Victorian period. Even in their leisure hours, servants were expected by some employers to dress in a style appropriate to their status, and *Punch* is full

OPPOSITE Detail of cat.84 **Maids of All Work**
John Finnie, 1864–5

of cartoons of employees aping their betters. The rules included (as they had not done in the eighteenth century) such senior figures as the butler, whose dress subtly aped his master's. The occupation of the servant was much discussed, and numerous manuals were produced for employers and staff. *The Complete Servant* (1825) by Samuel and Sarah Adams (both ex-servants), with its stress on the need for loyalty, its recipes and guidance on appropriate behaviour and its demarcation of domestic duties, was one of the earliest, while *Mrs Beeton's Book of Household Management* (1861) was probably the most famous.

For the better employers, educating their staff was regarded as desirable and was supported by a quite considerable literature. Not only were servants' libraries provided in a number of households (such as Cragside, the great house in Northumberland of the philanthropic arms manufacturer Lord Armstrong),[1] but publishers produced prayer books with appropriate prayers for each type of employee and easy-to-read books of an improving nature, offering innocent entertainment for maidservants.

But while the well-being of servants was sometimes regarded as important, many Victorian employers were not anxious to see their staff unless it was essential. As Mark Girouard has pointed out,[2] newly built Victorian houses tended to be organised on the lines recommended by Robert Kerr in his influential book *The Gentleman's House* (1864). Kerr stipulated that the plan of a large new house should ensure that the family and their guests were kept as separate as possible from the staff. 'As regards Privacy,' he wrote, 'in the place of that seclusion which is the privilege of the family, what we have to provide for the servants is that freedom from interruption which is essential to the efficient performance of their work.'[3] Ideally, it was only the upper servants and those who waited at table that the gentry would be obliged to see. While old ideas of mutual respect between employers and servants, and a belief in the continuity of service, survived among liberal employers and in rural communities, it is not surprising that in this business-like context relations between masters and servants cooled, and that the number of servants' portraits diminished.

Nationwide, the number of servants increased very considerably during the second half of the nineteenth century. This rise was most marked among the newly prosperous and confident middle classes, especially in cities: between 1861 and 1891 the figures for domestic servants in London rose continuously from 284,000 in 1861 to 399,200 thirty years later.[4] It was noted in 1871 that, 'wives and daughters at home do now less domestic work than their predecessors: hence the excessive demand for female servants and the consequent rise of wages.' (Census report, 1871) As a result it became a mark of gentility to employ at least one

Cat.80 The Maid of All-Work's Prayer!!
Thomas Rowlandson after Woodward, 1801

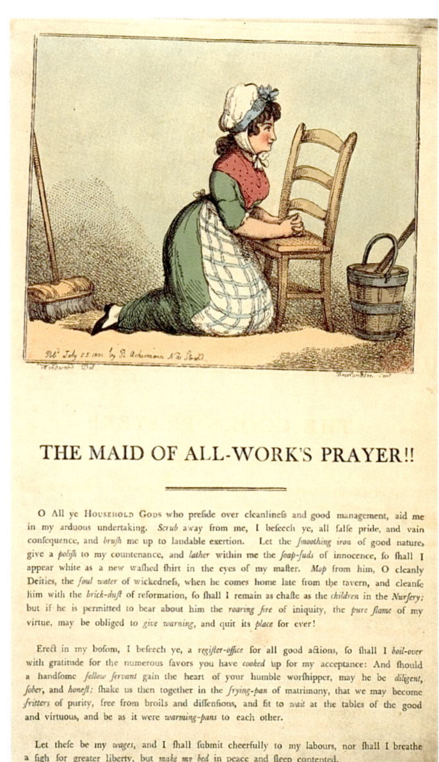

THE MAID OF ALL-WORK'S PRAYER!!

O All ye Household Gods who preſide over cleanlineſs and good management, aid me in my arduous undertaking. *Scrub* away from me, I beſeech ye, all falſe pride, and vain conſequence, and *bruſh* me up to laudable exertion. Let the *ſmoothing iron* of good nature, give a *poliſh* to my countenance, and *lather* within me the *ſoap-ſuds* of innocence, ſo ſhall I appear white as a new waſhed ſhirt in the eyes of my maſter. *Mop* from him, O cleanly Deities, the *foul water* of wickedneſs, when he comes home late from the tavern, and cleanſe him with the *brick-duſt* of reformation, ſo ſhall I remain as chaſte as the *children* in the *Nurſery*; but if he is permitted to bear about him the *roaring fire* of iniquity, the *pure flame* of my virtue, may be obliged to *give warning*, and quit its *place* for ever!

Erect in my boſom, I beſeech ye, a *regiſter-office* for all good actions, ſo ſhall I *boil-over* with gratitude for the numerous favors you have *cooked* up for my acceptance: And ſhould a handſome *fellow ſervant* gain the heart of your humble worſhipper, may he be *diligent*, *ſober*, and *honeſt*; ſhake us then together in the *frying-pan* of matrimony, that we may become *fritters* of purity, free from broils and diſſenſions, and fit to *wait* at the tables of the good and virtuous, and be as it were *warming-pans* to each other.

Let theſe be my *wages*, and I ſhall ſubmit cheerfully to my labours, nor ſhall I breathe a ſigh for greater liberty, but *make my bed* in peace and ſleep contented.

SPRAGG, PRINTER, 27, BOW-STREET, COVENT-GARDEN.

servant, and to expect her (it was almost invariably a woman) to work extraordinarily hard, sometimes sixteen hours a day, with almost no time off. She was not allowed to leave the house without permission or to entertain her friends (though as the memoirs of Hannah Cullwick make clear, these rules were often bent). The majority of servants worked in small households, often on their own. Very often they were young girls working to accumulate a dowry: in 1851, of the million or so servants employed in England, 40 per cent were under nineteen and a further 26 per cent under twenty-four. The tendency of servants to stay only a short time in a domestic situation, leaving to be married or in search of variety and promotion,[5] contributed to the scarcity of servant images.

The nineteenth century saw the further feminisation of domestic service. The number of male servants dropped steadily (in Britain from

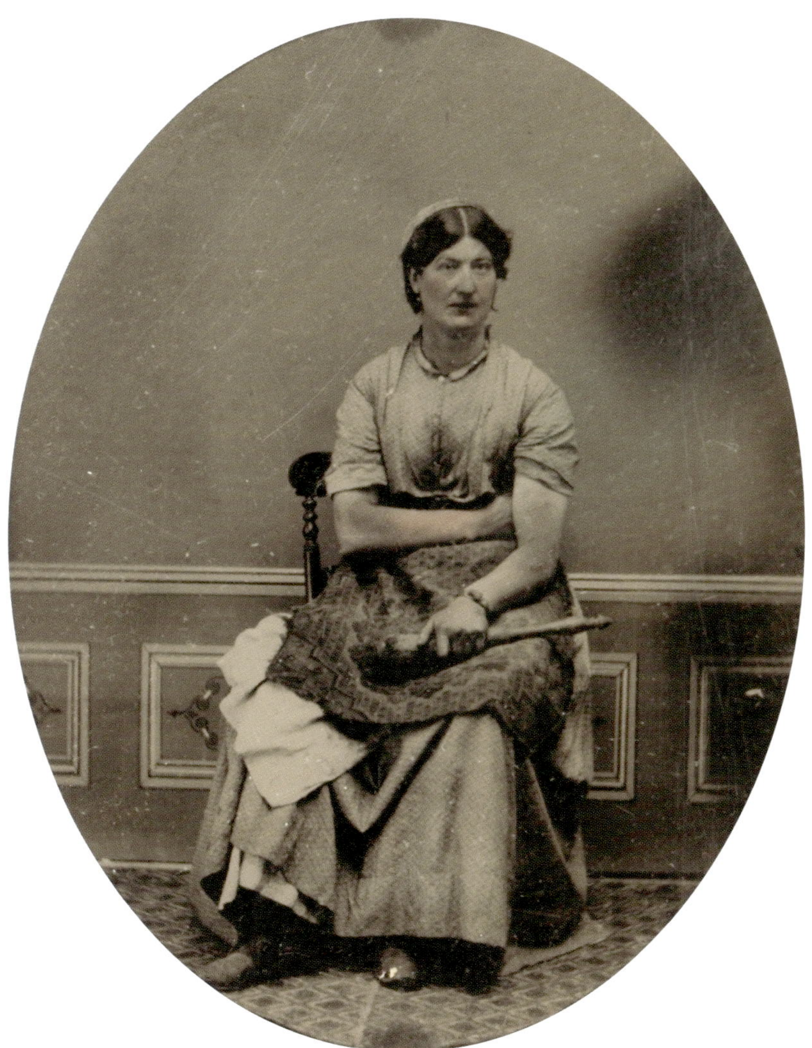

Cat.81 **Hannah Cullwick**
Unknown photographer

Arthur Munby, a Victorian civil servant, was obsessed by working women, the rougher the better. He enjoyed an extended relationship with Hannah Cullwick, a servant who kept a revealing diary of her work. A woman of great character and goodness, Hannah delighted to serve Munby and particularly to carry out tasks signifying submission, such as polishing his boots. Their eventual marriage was not a success. Munby commissioned many photographs of working women. The images of Hannah are among the most haunting, indeed obsessive, images of any master–servant relationship, in which the notion of personal service was expressed in strongly eroticised form.

74,000 in 1851 to 58,000 in 1891) for a number of reasons: the tax on male servants, introduced in 1777, continued through the nineteenth century; employers found men harder to handle than women; better-paid alternative occupations beckoned; and the status of the servant remained equivocal. It was mostly the aristocracy who employed indoor male servants, in a senior position of trust as a steward and butler or as a footman: a tall handsome man commanded a considerably larger wage than a small one.

In this context, the nature of servant portraiture changed. The portrait conventions that had applied since the early seventeenth century – the conversation piece with servant on duty, the great person with attendant – had relegated the servant to a subordinate position but had at least recognised their existence and on occasion their individuality. This convention hardly applies in the Victorian period, where the sitter is generally shown alone or in the company of people at their own social level; the exception is the sporting picture. With the decline of the 'feudal' establishment, the number of 'loyal servant' portraits diminishes. The place of 'loyal servant' portraits is taken by genre paintings, cartoons, and photographs of groups or individuals. In this new framework, depictions of servants take two major forms. On the one hand, they are shown neutrally as supporters of the status quo. But another language emerges, in which the servant – and notably the woman servant – is seen as the victim of thoughtless employers and ultimately of a cruel society.

Royal commissions

The major exception is, perhaps surprisingly, the royal household. Queen Victoria, warm-hearted and passionately fond of recording those around her, commissioned numerous portraits, both of her family and of her staff. The Queen was highly selective in her choice of sitters from her household. She concentrated on two principal acts of patronage in this field: firstly in Scotland, notably in the 1860s, and secondly towards the end of her reign, in studies of Indian servants (see pp.149–51). Both Scotland, with its sublime landscape, its supposed seclusion from the public and its noble Highland retainers, and her Indian servants, represented private Arcadias (a word she herself applied to Scotland). They offered a pastoral existence away from London and official duties, and by extension the modern world. Arcadias have, of course, traditionally been populated, and so were Victoria's.

For the Queen rural Scotland, epitomised by Balmoral Castle, which Prince Albert rebuilt for her, presented an image of an ideal society. On their first visit in 1842 she and Albert approached Scotland through the eyes of a writer they greatly admired, Sir Walter Scott. His romantic vision of Scotland and its inhabitants shaped their view of the country and contributed to her strong sense of Scottish history and of her Scottish lineage. For the Queen there was no race like the Highlanders: 'these dear, good, superior, people wch. I miss dreadfully elsewhere. Shrewd, clever, noble, vy.

independent & proud in their bearing – always answering you & speaking openly & strictly the truth, with gt. freedom, but ever respectful.'[6] The Highlanders depicted for her by a number of artists, notably Edwin Landseer and Kenneth MacLeay, were more than retainers: in these idealised depictions they had a quality, not exactly of the Noble Savage, but of the Noble Rustic. This theme, always latent in the tradition of the servant portrait, had never before been so vigorously developed.

The Queen enjoyed recording her life in Scotland, and this interest encouraged one of her most important acts of patronage after Prince Albert's death. In 1865 Kenneth MacLeay, a Scottish watercolourist and miniaturist who had already drawn some of the royal children, was commissioned to paint watercolours of the Queen's favourite Scottish retainers. Those chosen, all men, included her personal servant John Brown, keepers and foresters, pipers to various members of the royal family, as well as some people who worked in the English palaces but were of Scottish origin. The Scottish element was crucial. Wearing the kilts, which were obligatory costume for all male Scottish retainers of the Queen unless advancing age had affected their legs, these fine men (whose physical appearance was of strong interest to the Queen) are depicted in heroic yet convincing stances. Some are shown in front of English palaces, as though they could impart to these southern places the best qualities of the north. The

BELOW LEFT Cat.82 **John Brown, Personal Servant to Queen Victoria**

BELOW RIGHT Cat.83 **William Ross, Queen Victoria's Piper**
Kenneth MacLeay, 1866

In 1865 Queen Victoria wrote that John Brown became her 'regular attendant out of doors everywhere in the Highlands ... He has all the independence and elevated feelings peculiar to the Highlands, and is singularly straightforward, simple-minded, kind-hearted and disinterested ... and of a discretion rarely to be met with.'

Appointed Piper to Queen Victoria in 1854, William Ross also acted as a footman, sometimes 'in full Highland dress'. Victoria regarded him as 'a very respectable, good man'. Ross belonged to the Queen's intimate circle in the Highlands, where social divisions became relatively relaxed.

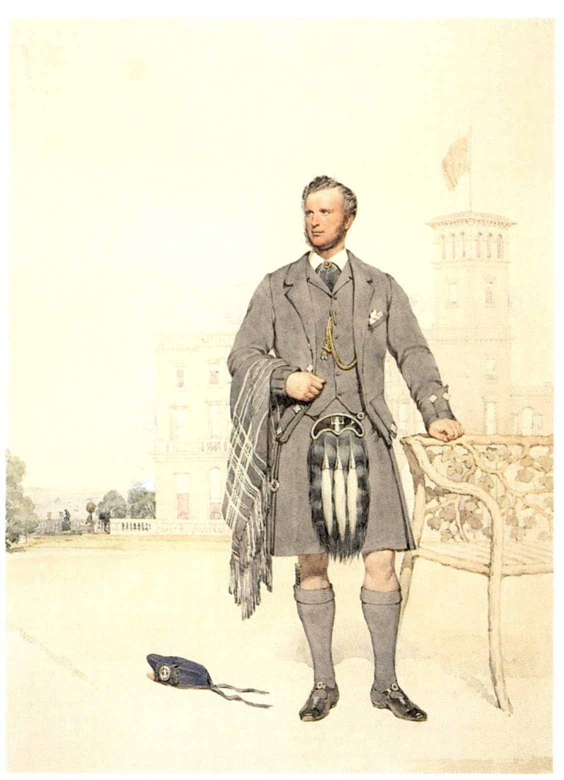

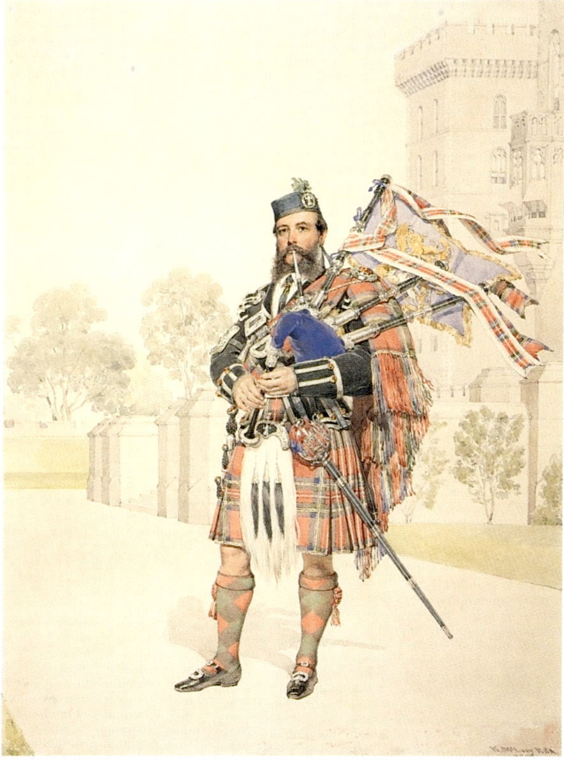

positions some of them held – such as the role of Queen's Piper occupied by William Ross – and the magnificence of their poses and costume, recall (as was no doubt intended) the type of retainer celebrated in the seventeenth century in great Scottish households.

The Queen was unusual in her willingness – not shared by her family – to enjoy her private Scottish idyll in public. She published an intimate account of her experiences in *Leaves from the Journal of Our Life in the Highlands*, issued privately in 1865 and published three years later. As a complement to this immensely popular publication, the MacLeay watercolours were exhibited in London in 1869 and published as part of MacLeay's illustrated volume *The Highlanders of Scotland* in 1870. This imposing work, in which the Queen took a close interest, depicted representatives of the principal clans, with their tartans delineated with minute accuracy. This was probably the first and last time that a project based on a set of servant portraits achieved wide public recognition. It is also significant, as Helen Smailes has pointed out, that this encomium of traditional Highland values appeared at a time of major distress and emigration from the Highlands, problems to which it does not refer.[7]

A rather different form of domestic Arcadia is apparent in the work of Charles Dickens, who provided for an increasingly large and popular readership. In fiction, the established tradition of the loyal but characterful servant better adapted to the contemporary world than the master, was developed in the character of Sam Weller in *The Pickwick Papers*, published in twenty monthly parts between April 1836 and November 1837 (cat.131). The book was illustrated by R. Seymour and particularly by 'Phiz'[8] in a series of memorable plates which contributed to the success of the publication and have not been superseded. Celebrated in the nineteenth century and beyond, and frequently the subject of memorial pottery and similar objects, Weller, faithful servant to the vague but good-hearted Mr Pickwick, is young, impudent and witty, always ready with an entertaining verbal analogy and speaking an ungrammatical but pungent and entertaining English. At a time of violent social upheaval and the threat of revolution, Sam Weller was a comforting creation for a growing middle-class public which was beginning to embark on the employment of servants. For all his impudence, Sam knows his place and is unfailingly loyal: at the end of the book he is prepared to postpone matrimony in order to serve Mr Pickwick in his retirement. He poses no threat to the established order. But the portrait of Sam Weller, inhabitant of the slightly chaotic but essentially Merrie England of the novel, is not typical of the depiction of the Victorian servant in art and literature.

In some versions, the depiction is quite neutral, with maids shown as ornamental figures in genre paintings. W.P. Frith, an immensely successful artist whose works were mobbed at the Royal Academy, offered a studiedly cheerful approach to Victorian genre painting, applying a bland quality to the social issues which other artists addressed with sighs. He

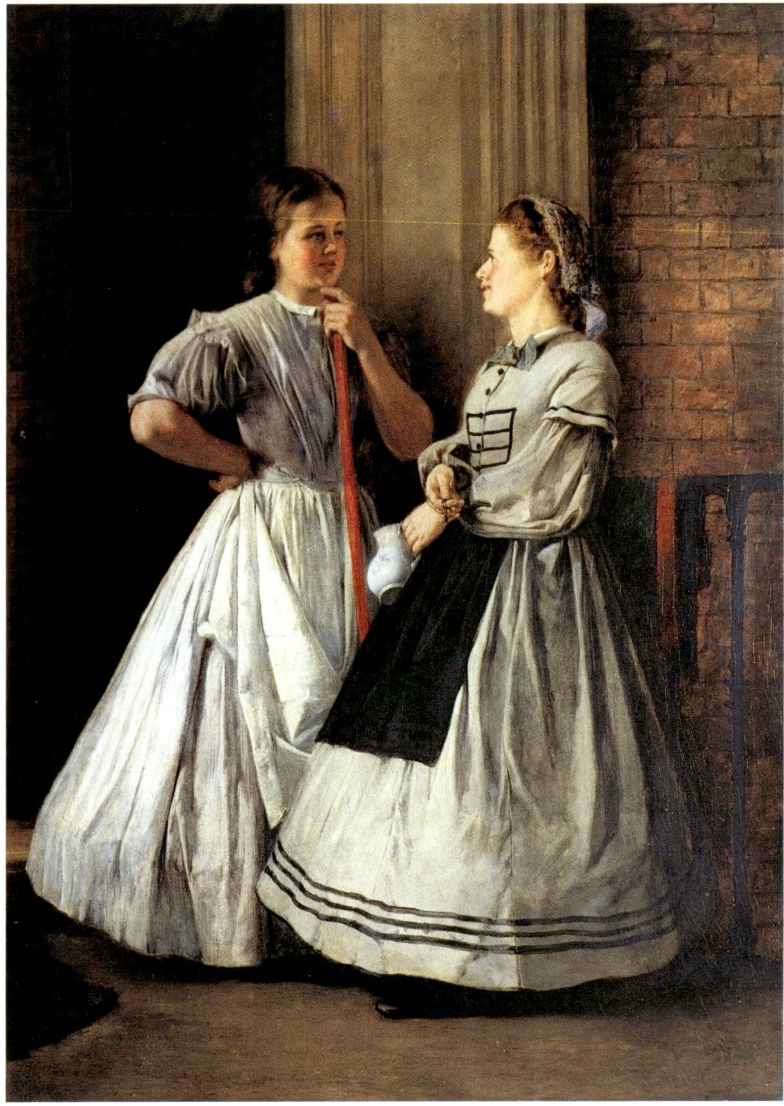

Cat.84 **Maids of All Work**
John Finnie, 1864–5

A Scottish-born artist, Finnie spent most of his career as an art teacher, and specialised in landscape. Here he depicts, in idealistic form, the type of servant who predominated in the nineteenth century as increasing numbers of upwardly mobile employers sought domestic help. Due to their lowly status, such maids were almost never painted.

used pretty maidservants in several paintings, often intended to be reproduced as prints and aimed at a popular audience. A 'little study, done from a good-looking girl who was in my service as housemaid' sold well as a print, under the title of "*Sherry, sir?*".'[9] In a less well-known work, Frith painted a young housemaid knocking at a bedroom door as she delivers a jug of hot water in the morning. Frith records securing 'the services of some of my servants as models' but did not recommend the practice 'because it is apt to "turn their heads" a little, and to make them careless over less agreeable duties.'[10] In this case he uses a favourite commercial model who appears in a number of other works, including a study of a wealthy lady leaving a house in Park Crescent, London.[11] The apparently innocent charm of this image, flavoured with a mild eroticism, recalls Henry

Robert Morland's portrayals of two imaginary maids, but is not intended to present the maid as more than a charming adornment to the house. Equally John Finnie's *Maids of All Work* (1864–5) offers a straightforward depiction of a type of servant that was hardly ever painted, with no consideration of the unpleasant position actually occupied by maids-of-all-work (cat.84).

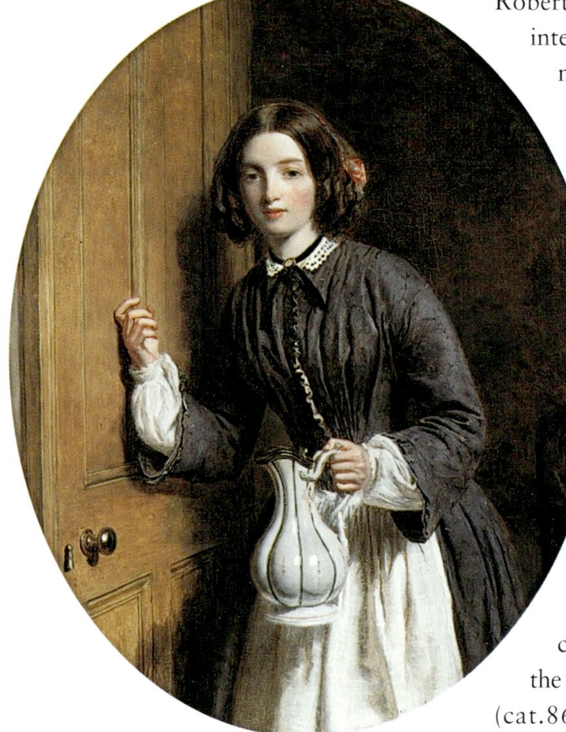

Cat.85 **Servant Girl**
W.P. Frith, nineteenth century

Frith made a number of studies of servants, though he warned in his memoirs against the problems of using actual servants as models. In this mildly titillating painting, there is no suggestion of the extremely long hours worked by servants, whose complaints over their plight were dismissed until late in the nineteenth century.

At the end of the nineteenth century and well into the twentieth, a similar style of dispassionate social observation was employed by the accomplished Yorkshire artist Frederick Elwell. Elwell was an admirer of Chardin,[12] and in their affectionate, calm and visually seductive quality, his paintings are probably the closest English equivalent to the French artist's work. Using models (including his own staff) to depict fictitious servants, he created imaginary domestic scenes in establishments from the mansion to the hotel. His early work sometimes portrayed stereotypes, as in the theatrically set *The Butler Takes a Glass of Port* (1890), in which the butler does exactly what butlers were always accused of doing (cat.86). In later years, Elwell – who was also an admirer of Dutch genre painting, in which work and domesticity play a leading role – frequently returned to images of the servant, but in a calmer more sympathetic way. He sometimes showed entire households, as in *The Squire* (1931), painted shortly before the war put an end to such large establishments (fig.20), or illustrated the running of a household in a style which hardly ever occurs elsewhere. He also painted scenes in the appealing country town of Beverley, Yorkshire, where he spent the latter part of his life. He loved to paint the servants at the Beverley Arms Hotel (where he was a regular patron), at work, or assembled over meals in the hotel kitchen. Though most of his images in this genre are invented compositions, using models to play roles in his fictitious scenes, Elwell did not engage in social criticism but celebrated the dignity of his sitters and their occupations.

Photography and *Punch*

While the scale of domestic households remained at the very least constant in the second half of the nineteenth century, two developments in technology and communications provided a considerable source of material for the study of depiction of servants in the period: photography and *Punch*. As Christopher Simon Sykes has shown in *Country House Camera*, photography encouraged a lively production of domestic images, beginning with the photographs taken by a pioneer, William Fox Talbot, at his house, Lacock Abbey in Wiltshire, from 1835 onwards. By the 1850s photography was becoming an activity for amateurs, who in the early

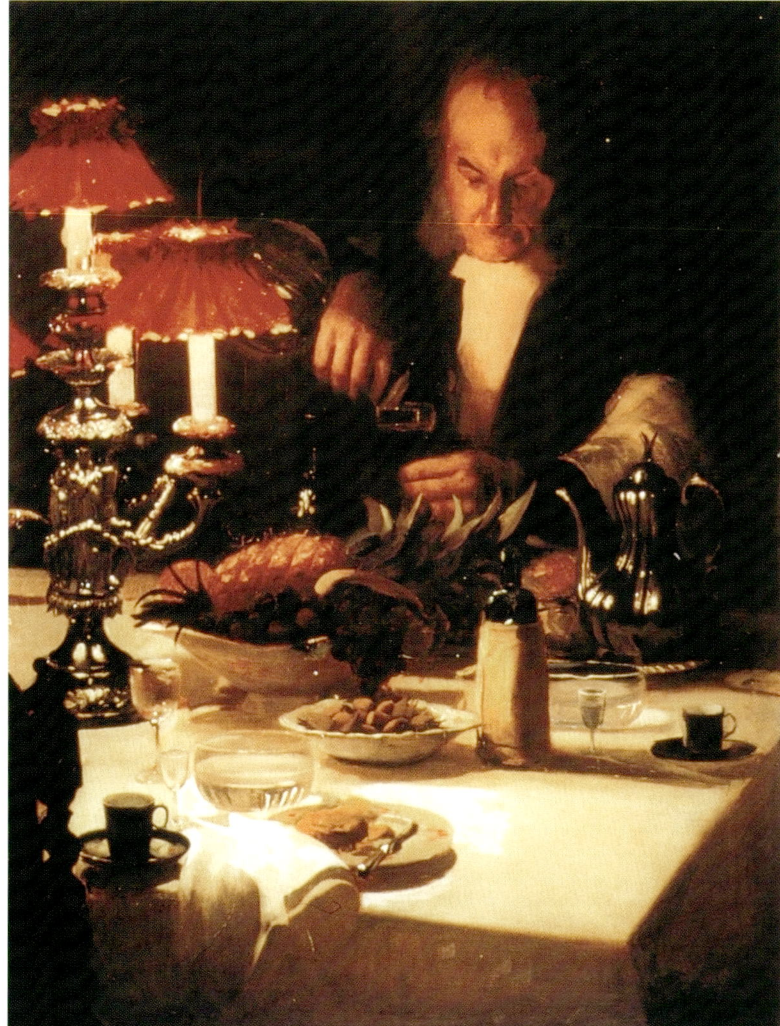

Cat.86 **The Butler Takes a Glass of Port (or All Things Come to the Man Who Waits)**
Frederick Elwell, 1890

days needed to acquire technical expertise. By the early 1850s Lady Lucy Bridgeman, one of the most talented early photographers, was an active recorder of her family and friends. She created a memorable image of a group of the servants, posed and contemplative (as they would need to be, given how long they had to remain immobile) at Weston Park, her family house in Shropshire.[13] This new tradition flourished well into the twentieth century. Sometimes entire households are shown together arranged in ranks, with the senior members of the household in the centre (though very seldom in the company of their employers), sometimes in groups, sometimes on their own, as individuals or in a Victorian version of the servant portrait.

At Petworth House in Sussex, two notable series of photographs were made. Mrs Percy Wyndham, sister-in-law of Lord Leconfield, the then owner of the house, who lived there from 1860 to 1869, assembled photographs of the indoor and outdoor servants in an album she entitled *All*

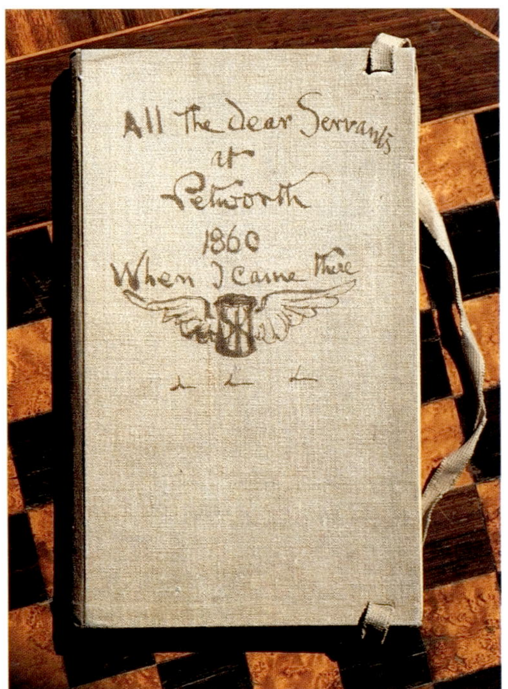

Cat.87 **Our Friends**
Mrs Wyndham, late nineteenth century

Sister-in-law of Lord Leconfield, owner of Petworth House, Mrs Wyndham lived there from 1860 to 1869. A celebrated patron of the arts, Mrs Wyndham was unusual in her close and affectionate interest in the staff, both indoor and outdoor, and in commemorating them in this little album.

the Dear Servants at Petworth. The images (mostly taken by a professional photographer in a studio but in a few instances in the sitter's place of work) include the French chef, the children's nurse, the stud groom and the dairymaid, the coachman and the laundry-maid, Mrs Wyndham's maid and Lord Leconfield's valet (who married one another), and many others, giving a vivid impression of a tightly knit community. The photographs are accompanied by notes written by Mrs Wyndham, illustrating her affectionate acquaintance with the individuals and placing the album squarely in the tradition of serial images of loyalty. The photographic tradition in country houses continued at least until the Second World War and is not dead yet: since the 1970s the present Duchess of Buccleuch has assembled photographs of the staff at Bowhill and Boughton, the family's houses in the Borders and Northamptonshire respectively. While sets of photographs such as these show less commitment, in terms of money or time, to the commemoration of the household than do painted versions, they celebrate the same virtues and aspirations.

There is, as we have seen, another, less contented aspect to the depiction of working people, and servants in particular, in the Victorian period. The 1830s and 1840s was a period of major social upheaval and of critical examination of the unregulated new industrial society which had developed over the previous fifty years. Social reformers such as the 7th Earl of Shaftesbury sought to introduce legislation protecting factory workers, particularly women and children, and Charles Dickens and other writers vigorously attacked a great number of other social ills. A closely connected group of writers and artists began to produce works of art that aimed to spell out the problems of the unfortunate, including servants and most particularly women. While these artists criticised the organisation of society only by implication, they repeatedly questioned the human effects of arbitrary differences between rich and poor and the general esteem for rank and wealth.

Unhappy governesses

In this context, one recurring theme was the suffering undergone by governesses. These unhappy individuals (as they often were) became a favourite subject of novelists and journalists in the 1840s and 1850s.[14] Not a regular feature of households in the seventeenth century, governesses became more numerous in the late eighteenth century, possibly because George II and George III employed them. By the early Victorian period, employing a governess was a regular practice for the expanding middle classes, demonstrated by numerous manuals on handling one's governess aimed at middle-class employers unfamiliar with the rules. Anna Jameson, one of the ablest writers on art and public affairs at the time, lamented the unhappy position in which these women were placed in *The Relative Social Position of Mothers and Governesses* (1846). Tutors were much less numerous and generally had an easier time. The role of the governess was not easy: generally paid less than a good cook, she was entrusted with the despised role of educating girls destined for the marriage market, in whom excessive intelligence or learning were thought unattractive. Required to be ladylike in their manners and dress, they occupied a socially ambiguous position, neither a member of the gentry nor a servant, symbolically served after all the other women at dinner (if invited at all) and often despised by both gentry and servants. These mid-century publications were harshly critical of the conditions in which governesses lived, and of their employers' attitudes. Two highly successful novels in which governesses played leading parts appeared in 1847: W.M. Thackeray's *Vanity Fair*, in which the governess is a brilliant minx (a not infrequent literary stereotype) and Charlotte Brontë's *Jane Eyre* (cat.126) The book was inspired by Brontë's own experiences as a governess, which she enjoyed as little as did her sister Anne, who published her own version, *Agnes Grey*, in the same year. The heroine of *Jane Eyre* is shown to be as good a person as, indeed considerably better than the fashionable people who treat her with contempt. In the end, she triumphs.

It is striking that no depictions (other than a few photographs) appear to exist of actual governesses: the loyalty motif which encouraged serial portraits did not apply to those who questioned Victorian preconceptions by being ladies who worked. The visual images relating to governesses are to be found, rather, in genre painting, from the 1840s onwards. The most famous governess image was painted, in several versions, by the Royal Academician and arts administrator Richard Redgrave, who took a particular interest in depictions of oppressed women during the 1840s.[15] According to his daughter, he 'longed to fight for the oppressed and to help the weak, and could only do it with his brush.'[16] In 1843 Redgrave exhibited at the Royal Academy *The Poor Teacher*, and a further version, *The Governess*, was commissioned for the collector John Sheepshanks, who gave it to the Victoria & Albert Museum (fig.36). Redgrave's image achieved huge critical and popular success. He created a potent image of a beautiful young woman, probably ill, in mourning, who is condemned by poverty to a life of lonely drudgery. In the Victoria & Albert's version, she is contrasted (at Sheepshanks's request) with her happy pupils who play outside in the sun, in bright clothes, oblivious to her suffering. This image of a servant – albeit someone who is not quite a servant – as victim, introduces a new motif, touched with feeling, into the servant portrait tradition.

Redgrave's concerns were shared by a number of painters including Augustus Egg, Emily Mary Osborn and Rebecca Solomon. In the eyes of some contemporaries – notably Thackeray – they worked on the borderline between compassion and sentimentality, sometimes exploiting their

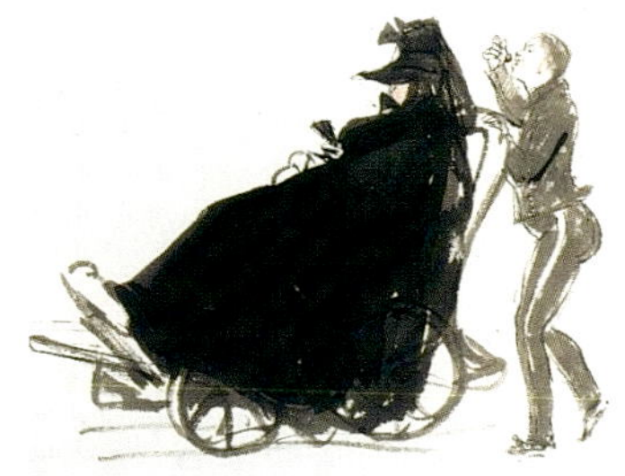

Cat.88 **Lady Holland in a Bath Chair with a Page**
Sir Edwin Landseer

The famous hostess Elizabeth, Lady Holland (1770–1845) gathered around her a powerful circle of statesmen and intellectuals, whose patronage was key to the professional and social success of Sir Edwin Landseer. As a frequent guest at Holland House and other aristocratic homes, Landseer was a prolific caricaturist, capturing informal moments such as Lady Holland being pushed in her bath chair by a page.

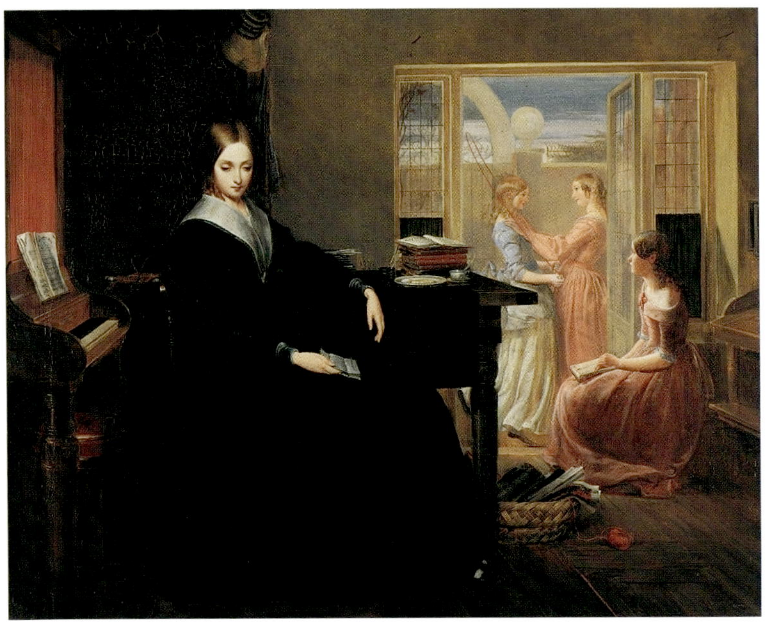

Fig.36 **The Governess**
Richard Redgrave, 1844

This is one of the most potent Victorian images of a suffering woman. In its compassionate approach it is comparable to another work of 1844 by Redgrave, *The Seamstress*. The painting was accompanied in the Royal Academy catalogue in 1845 by the text 'She sees no kind domestic visage here.'

Emily Mary Osborn (far right) specialised in depicting young women in distress. Mrs Jameson wrote of the relationship between mistress and governess: 'equal, perhaps, by nature and by education, they are divided by position, by prejudices of caste, by pride ... by acquired habits of thought; and looking in each other's faces every day, they remain to the end strangers.'

tear-inducing material in a style reminiscent of the contemporary theatre. Thus, the memory of Redgrave's painting – and its success – is apparent in *The Governess* (1860) by Emily Mary Osborn (cat.89), one of many professional women artists working in Victorian London, who took a particular interest in the theme of oppressed womanhood. Her painting makes a more satirical statement than Redgrave's, contrasting the beautiful young governess with her ugly, vulgar and wealthy employer, who castigates the governess for some supposed offence, and her richly dressed and nastily sniggering children. For contemporaries, such paintings were disturbing because they pointed out the governess's ambiguous social position: as the *Art Journal* remarked in 1860, the picture illustrated 'a too prevalent vice ... the practice of treating educated women as if they were menial servants ...'[17] The picture was well received. The first version was bought by Prince Albert in September 1860 as a Christmas present for the Queen[18] and hung at Osborne House until, at a time when Victorian paintings had gone hopelessly out of fashion, it was destroyed by Queen Mary in 1924.

It was not only beautiful young governesses who served as victims in Victorian genre paintings; in an emerging feminist discourse, maidservants also featured in this role. Genre paintings showing the hardships suffered by servants form a recurring Victorian theme. They should be seen in the context of depictions of other victimised groups such as seamstresses, whose plight was famously depicted in Thomas Hood's *Song of the Shirt*, first printed in *Punch* in 1843. The contrast between the lavish hospitality enjoyed by the wealthy and the efforts required of the invisible servant class is underlined in Frederic Hardy's *After the Party* (1876). Here the little maidservant, sleeping amidst the debris of a party which has left piles of plates and glasses around her, is woken by another maid, while (reflected in the mirror) a male servant looks on (cat.90). The thoughtlessness of her employers, at a time when in some circles concern over the life led by servants was growing, is the sub-text of this superficially charming image.

The concern with social issues is reflected in a magazine which enjoyed huge success in the middle and late nineteenth century. *Punch* first appeared in 1841, the inspiration of a group of journalists who devised a new magazine formula by combining text and illustrations (largely satirical), and

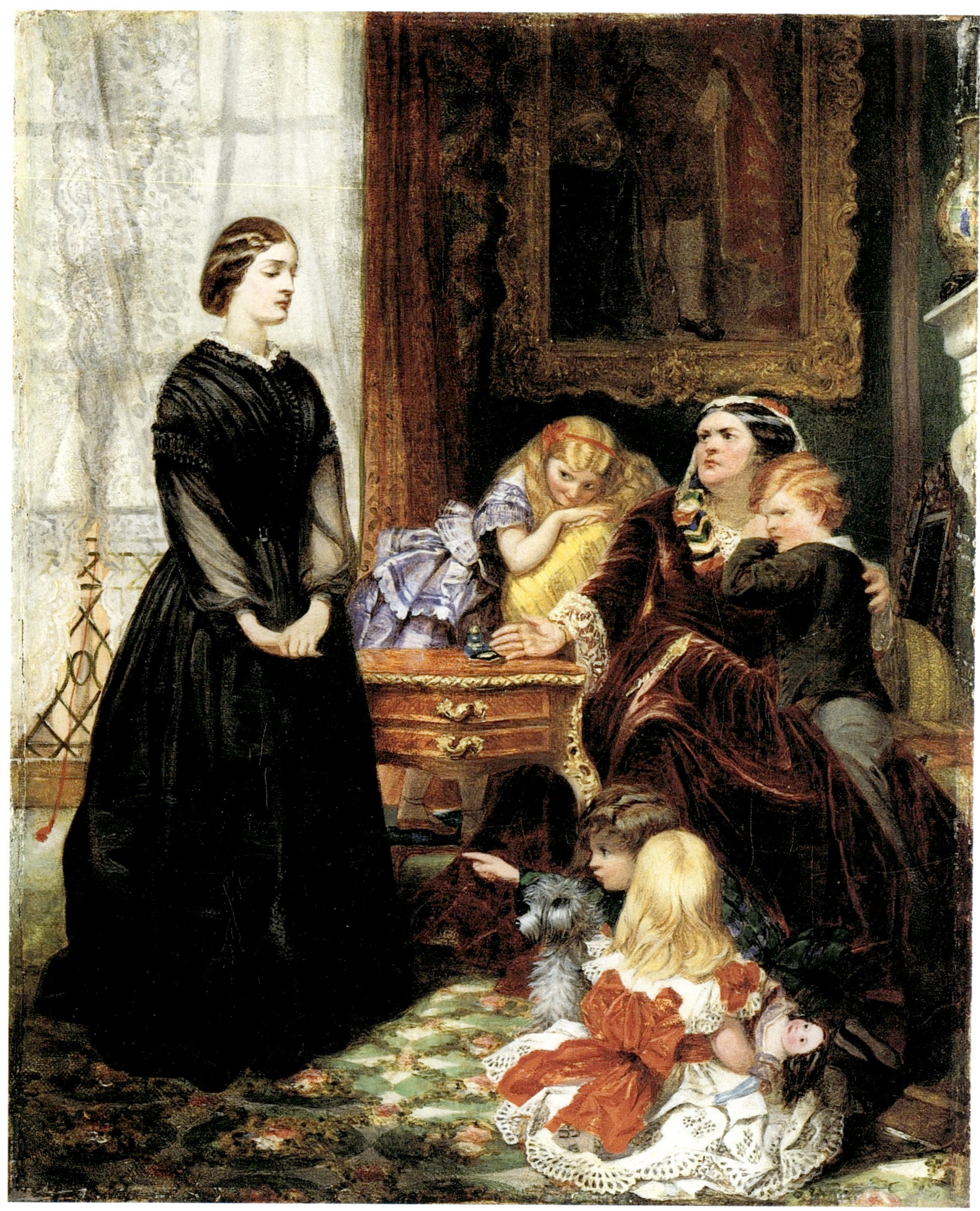

Cat.89 **The Governess**
Emily Mary Osborn, 1860

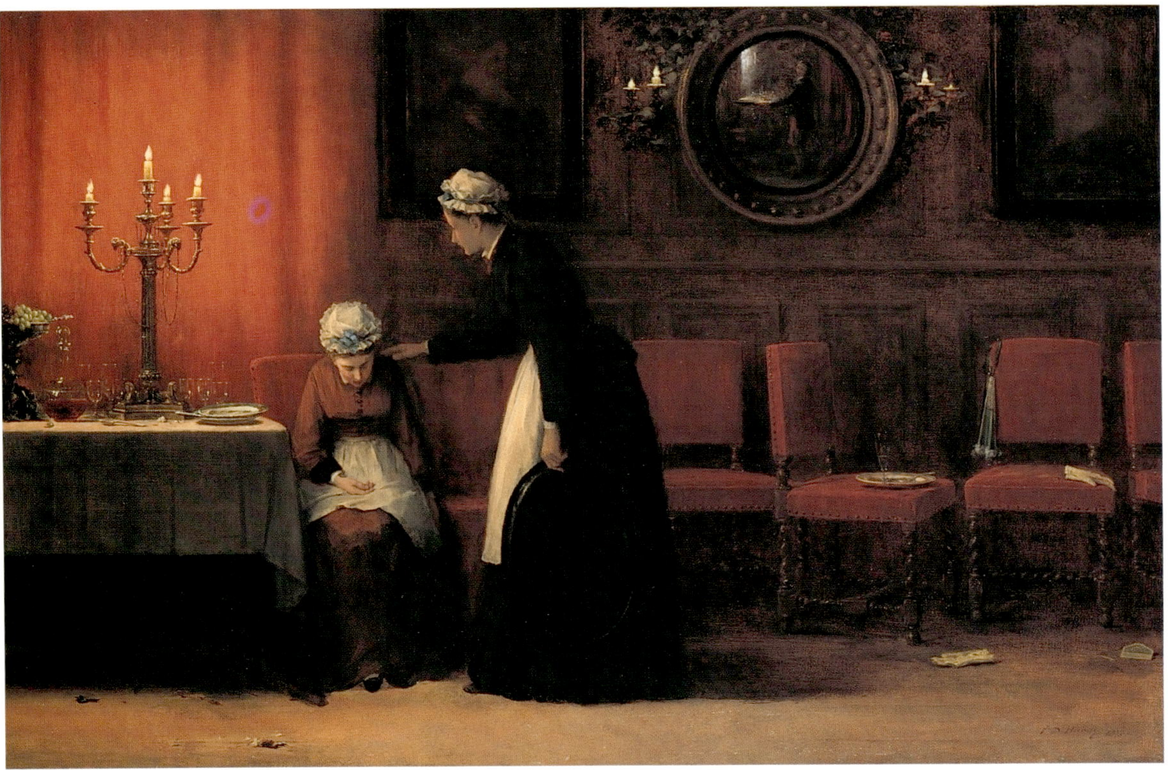

Cat.90 **After the Party**
Frederic Hardy, 1876

Hardy was a member of the tightly knit Cranbrook Colony of artists in Kent, which included several highly successful genre painters. He specialised in interiors with a strong human interest. Here an exhausted maid is woken by a colleague in the early hours, with another (male) servant seen in the mirror.

mixing sharp social and political criticism with knockabout humour in a style not dissimilar to *Private Eye*'s. It soon gained a large readership and was conscious of its own significance as a record of the time: as a magazine commented thirty years later, the paper would be seen by future historians 'as testifying to the temper in which [events] were at any time viewed by the English middle class'.[19] It reached a new family audience, partly by avoiding the salacious humour of some of its predecessors.

Punch's relatively frequent depictions of servants are revealing of Victorian attitudes to the domestic worker. In the 1840s and 1850s its drawings were dominated by the prolific illustrator John Leech (a close friend of Thackeray, who shared his enjoyment of satirising contemporary society, including the foibles of servants). Leech was certainly not motivated by social concern in his depiction of the servant class. In his series *Servantgalism* (which began in 1853 and ran until 1858) and in the following series *Flunkeiana*, which targeted the absurdities of menservants, he is fairly unsympathetic to his subjects, even though their employers (generally shown as middle rather than upper class) are not very flatteringly depicted either. Certain themes appear repeatedly: servants make absurd demands at interview; they complain of hard work while sitting comfortably by the kitchen fire; they expect to be paid more than 'the hinferior order of the clergy'; they protest at having to clean the boots or find the other servants 'so 'orrid vulgar, and hignorant'; and repeatedly object to the low quality of the food supplied by their employers. With the exception of the occasional servant girl, shown as pretty in contrast to an ugly mistress, Leech uses a regular vocabulary to depict his servants. They are shown as physically unattractive, often pretentiously dressed, stupid, ignorant and tiresome. Their inferior abilities, as well as their inferior status, are underlined by their ungrammatical English, full of dropped or superfluous aspirates (whereas Pamela speaks correct English). For the reader at the time, even the servant reader, such humour, and other versions of it in the paper, was seen as 'fun'. As a writer to *Punch* pointed out in 1860: 'You are always chaffing us poor servants ... To judge from what you say of us, one would think that there were no such things as good servants or bad masters and mistresses.'[20]

Leech was succeeded by the brilliant Anglo-French draughtsman and writer George du Maurier. Du Maurier moved away in the 1870s from Leech's bourgeois subjects to elegant satires of high society, in which the world-weariness and self-confidence of the aristocracy are contrasted with the pretensions of the *nouveaux riches*. Servants feature frequently in these images, but generally in a supporting role, for example in the form of loftily superior menservants, unconscious performers of *faux pas* or symbols of the pretentious wealth of the *nouveaux riches*. During the last third of the century *Punch* continued to offer numerous caricatures of servants, still often shown as ignorant, demanding and so forth. But there is a parallel development: from the 1870s onwards the paper begins to question the thoughtlessness and even the cruelty of employers. In an 1871 cartoon a child asks her mother if she can have her dog vaccinated. The mother (who is being attended by her lady's maid at the dressing-table) replies that only human beings are vaccinated. The child answers 'Why Lady Fakeaway's had all her servants vaccinated, Mamma!'[21] A new mood is emerging.

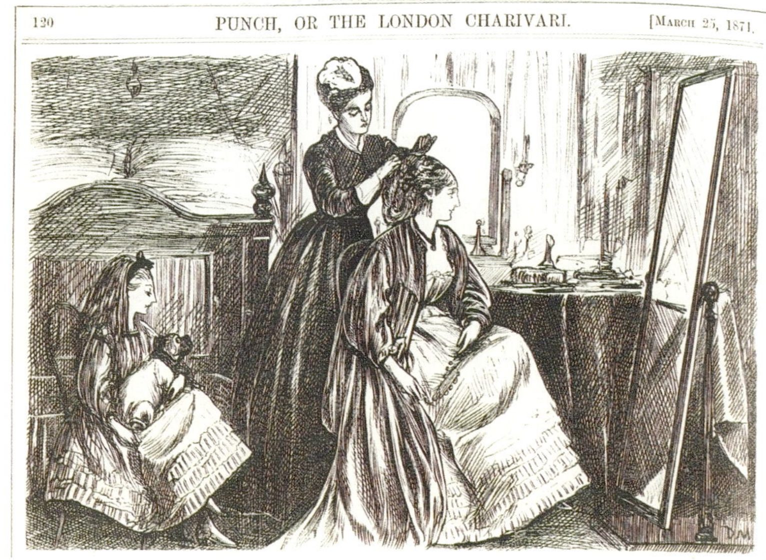

Cat.91 **'Train up a Child'**
Punch, 25 March 1871

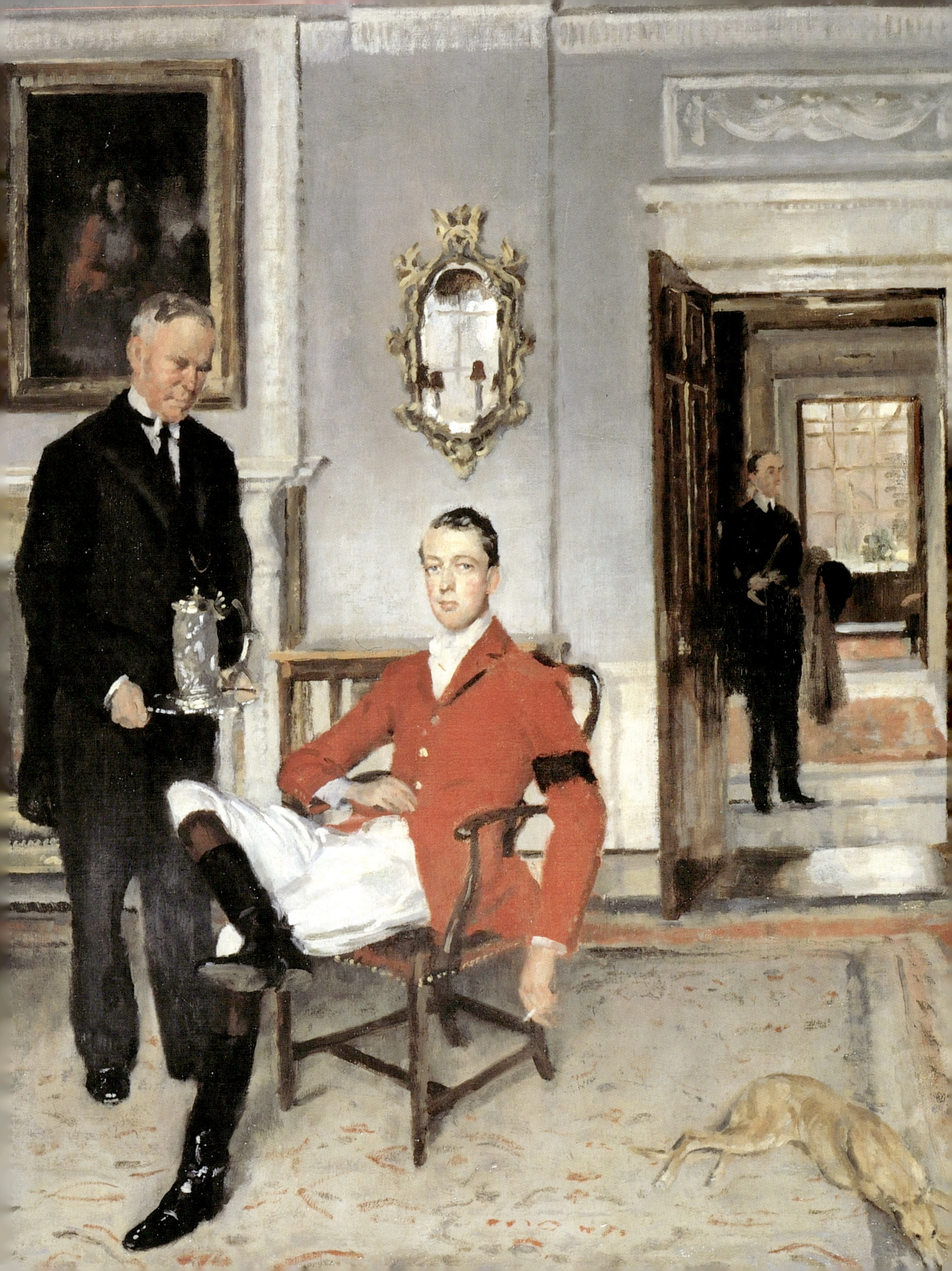

11 THE TRADITION DISINTEGRATES

Giles Waterfield

DOMESTIC SERVICE by no means disappeared in the twentieth century. More accurately, the traditional servant faded away. The First World War liberated women by allowing them, for the first time, to take on a large range of previously unavailable jobs, as munitions workers, bus drivers and agricultural workers. After the war many were unwilling to return to domestic service, which now seemed a demanding and unattractive way of life carrying a social stigma. The supply of fresh country girls declined severely with rural depopulation, and in schools in poorer areas – traditionally a source of servants – only the least able were directed towards private service. In spite of these shifts, in 1921 there were still around 1.1 million servants in Britain; by 1931 the Depression had driven many women back into what remained a relatively stable means of employment, so that numbers had risen to around 1.3 million. Service remained a primarily female occupation, as it had been for many years; men represented a small proportion of these figures, fewer than 80,000 in 1931.[1]

Where did these servants work? In 1931 three-quarters of employers had only one servant,[2] but larger households continued to exist. This was not so often the case in London, where large houses were often abandoned or households reduced, although some private houses continued to function on luxurious Edwardian lines. Bill Brandt's evocative photographs of impeccably uniformed housemaids, published in *Picture Post* in 1939 (cat.116), hardly convey social tension. On the other hand many country houses remained generously staffed. As Nancy Mitford remarked in her playfully snobbish essay on the English aristocracy *Noblesse Oblige* (1956), even after the Second World War in some great houses 'several men-servants wait on one young woman at dinner'.[3] The prosperous artists and writers of the Bloomsbury Group continued in the inter-war period to be looked after by cooks and maids, whom they often recorded in paintings, diaries and letters. Virginia Woolf's cook, with whom the

OPPOSITE Detail of cat.95 **Sir Richard Sykes, 7th Bt. of Sledmere**
Simon Elwes, 1936

writer had a stormy relationship for many years, was one of the most famous examples, while Dora Carrington, intimate friend of Lytton Strachey, several times painted Annie Stiles, the maid at Tidmarsh. Such arrangements survived the Second World War. In 1960 Nellie Hudson, who worked as

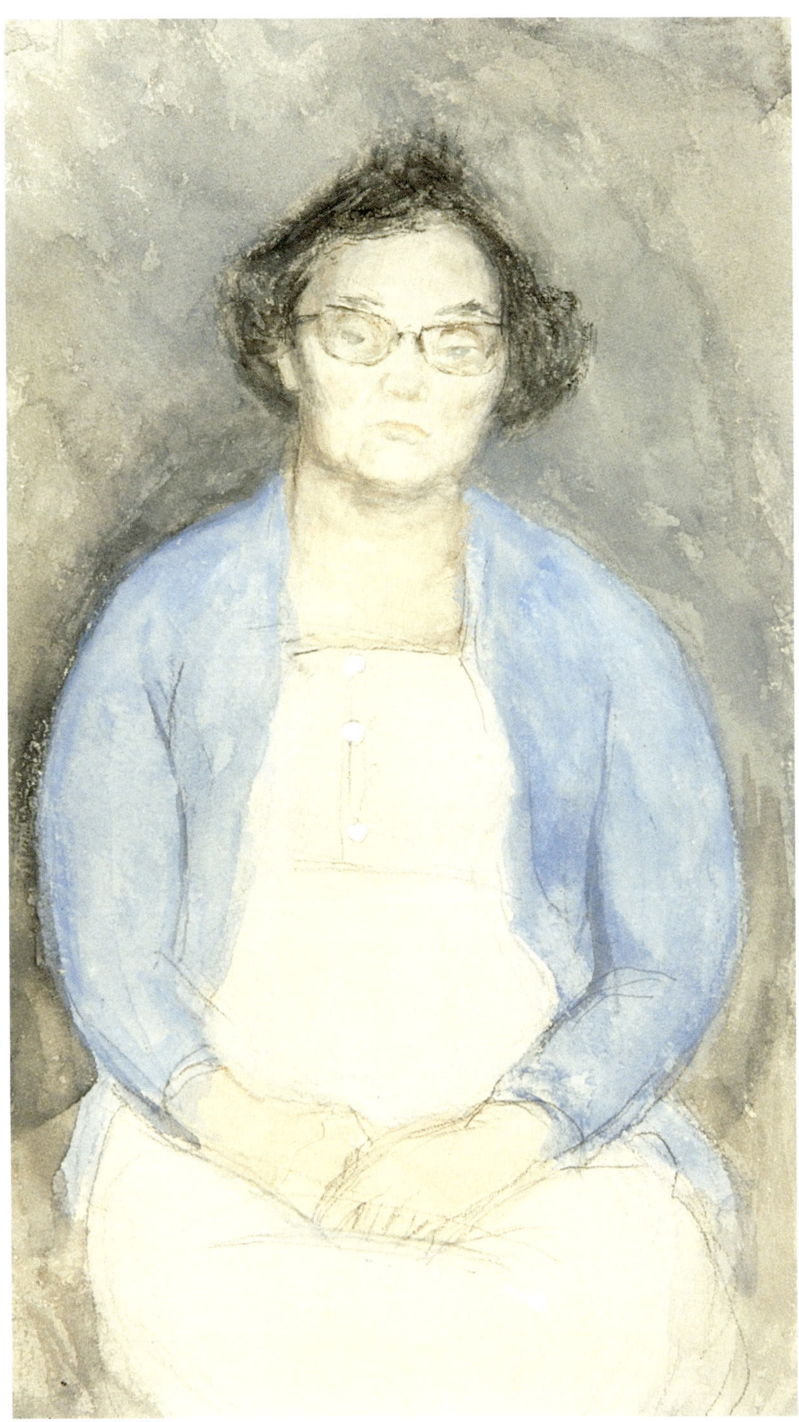

Cat.92 **Miss Hudson**
Mary Potter, 1960

Nellie Hudson worked for many years for Benjamin Britten and Peter Pears at the Red House in Aldeburgh. She was the niece of the miller at Snape, and proved the perfect housekeeper. Taken aback at first to find that her employers mixed with actors and opera singers, she became a fixed part of the establishment.

housekeeper for twenty-five years to the composer Benjamin Britten and his partner, the tenor Peter Pears, was painted in watercolour by a friend of Britten's, Mary Potter, a professional artist whom he had encouraged to resume painting when her children had grown up.[4] Britten and Pears were also painted by her, but in oils. Up to 1939 the prosperous middle classes regarded life without servants as intolerable, and were still able, with difficulty, to find such help. At the lower end of the market, however, women who had slaved as maids-of-all-work found better things to do.

The precarious state of the domestic economy between the wars is conveyed by the writer Monica Dickens, who as a young woman chose to

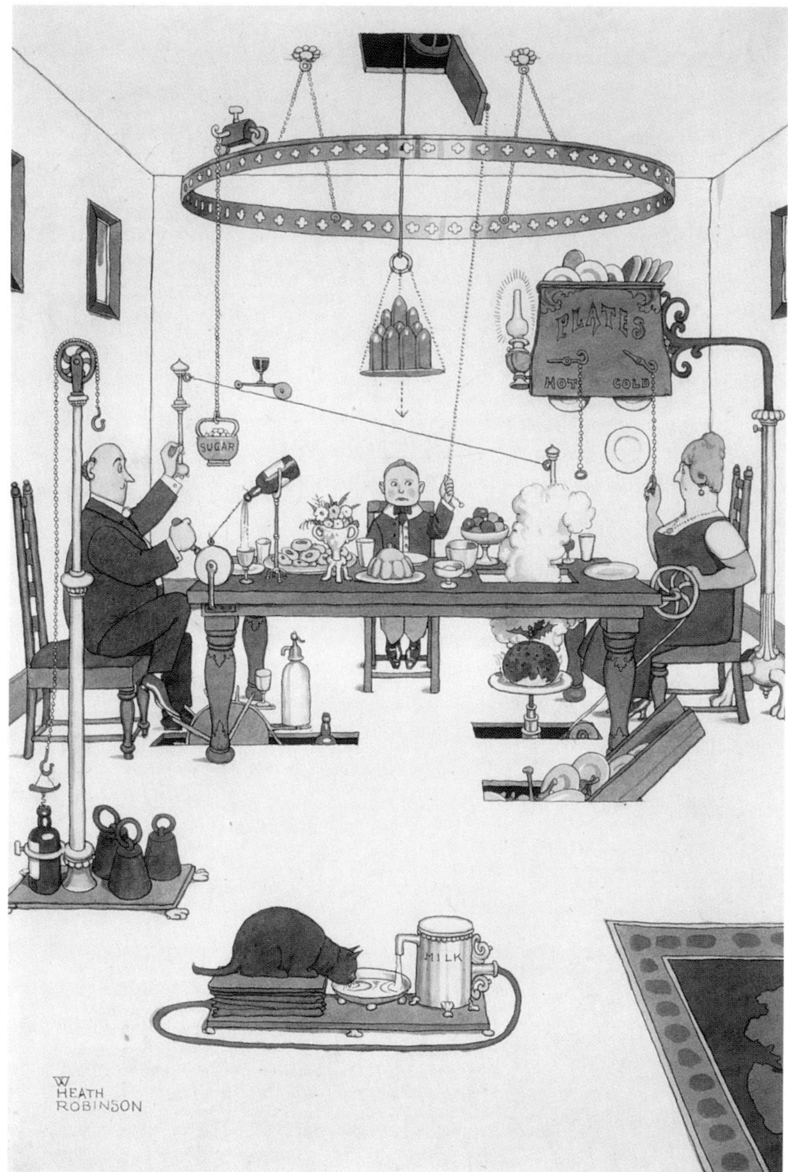

Cat.93 **How to Dispense with Servants in the Dining Room**
William Heath Robinson, 1921

As the 'servant problem' became acute in the twentieth century, various solutions were put forward to assist those who had never had to look after themselves domestically before. Heath Robinson neatly satirises the despair felt by the newly servantless middle classes.

work as a cook. As she remarked in her memoirs, although she had little training, 'In those two years, I had about twenty jobs. They were easy to get in the late Thirties. Fewer people wanted to be servants, but until the war forced everyone to learn how to take care of themselves, just as many people still wanted them.'[5] Various solutions were proposed. In 1920 Randal Phillips wrote *The Servantless House*, in which he suggested how a middle-class house might be pleasantly run by judicious modification of furniture and fixtures. A playful approach was taken by the versatile illustrator William Heath Robinson, now most famous as the depicter of absurd practical devices. In *How to Dispense with Servants in the Dining Room*, published in the Christmas number of the *Sketch* in 1921 under the title 'Heath Robinson Patents for Doing Away with Servants', he showed how a family (and their cat) could serve themselves at table by means of a complicated pulley system (cat.93). Amusing as the sketch is, from an artist regarded by his biographer as 'a great satirical commentator',[6] there is an edge to this depiction of a family which submits to the tyranny of complex machinery rather than simply serving themselves.

During and after the Second World War, the situation continued to change. During the war itself the employment of large numbers of servants came to be regarded as unpatriotic, and was in any case difficult as younger people were called up. This problem, as it was seen to be even in government circles, continued with peace in 1945. In the later 1940s, domestic service was an even more unpopular activity than it had been before the war. The traditional servants who survived tended to be older people, supplemented from the 1940s onwards by waves of foreign immigrants in search of a living; this was in striking contrast to the nineteenth century when foreign employees – other than French chefs and ladies' maids – were looked on with suspicion. As more women sought full-time careers, various alternative forms of domestic assistance developed, from au pairs to cleaning agencies. Bridget Hill, the Marxist historian whose strongly disapproving studies of servanthood are among the most illuminating accounts of this history, wrote in 1996 of the considerable number of women still in domestic service, and still as exploited as their predecessors a hundred years earlier.[7]

Given the transitory nature of domestic employment in the twentieth century, it is not surprising that servant portraits became infrequent apart from artists painting their employees, and that many of the most interesting depictions of servants, and their way of life, are found in literature. Several of the images produced have an ambiguous quality, as though servanthood opened for consideration complex issues about human identity in society. Take, for example, *He Gained a Fortune but He Gave a Son*, or in other terms a portrait of Henry Moat, by Christopher Nevinson, a Futurist regarded as dangerously avant-garde in the conservative art world of early twentieth-century Britain (cat.94). Moat had entered the

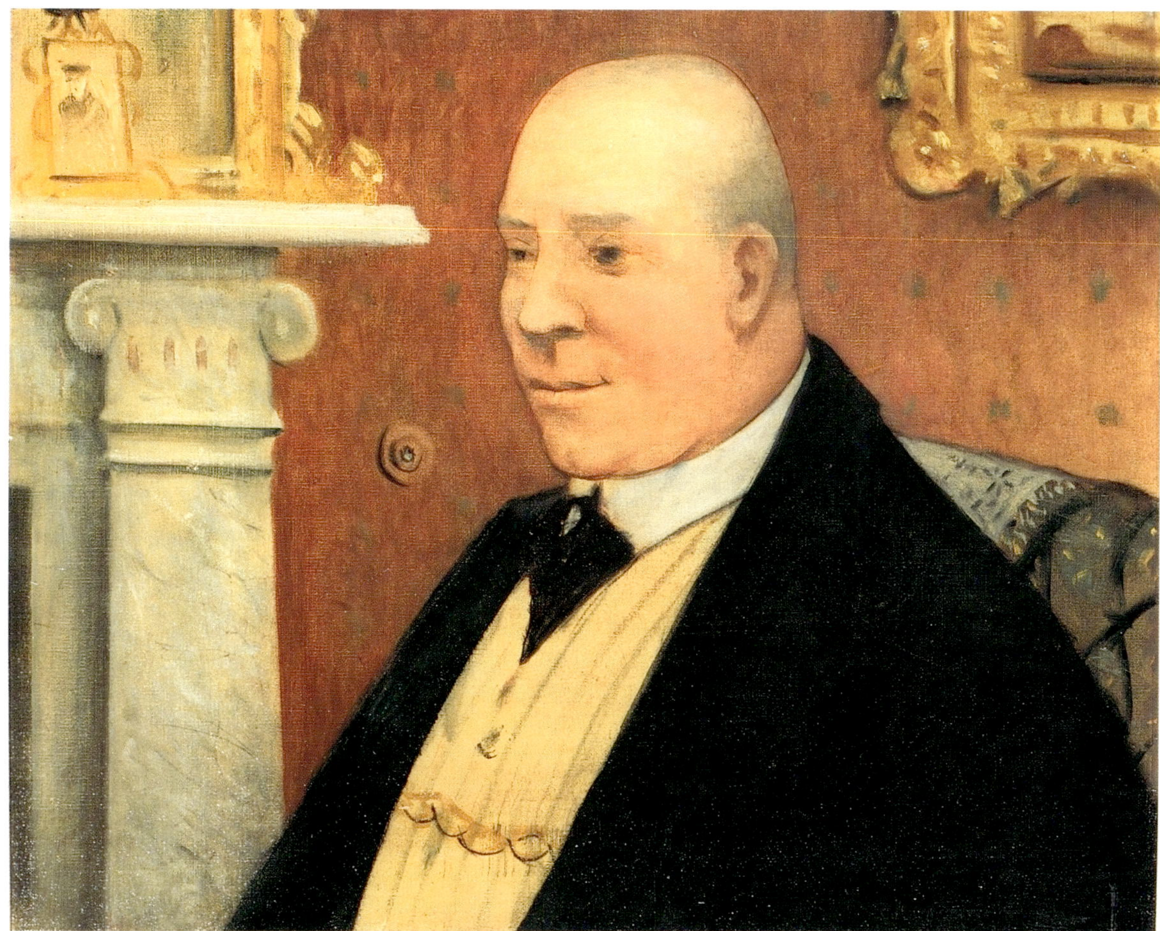

Cat.94 **Henry Moat, Butler to the Sitwells (or He Gained a Fortune but He Gave a Son)**
Christopher Richard Nevinson, 1918

In his autobiography *Left Hand Right Hand!* Osbert Sitwell describes Henry Moat, who used regularly to resign from service: 'He and my father, though mutually critical and at the same time appreciative, never failed to gravitate towards each other again, as if influenced by the working of some natural law. My father always referred to Henry as "the Great Man", and Henry for his part, mixed with feelings of the utmost disrespect, cherished towards him sentiments approaching veneration.'

service of the Sitwell family of Renishaw Hall in Derbyshire as a footman in 1893 and remained as butler until his retirement in 1936. The mutual dependency of Sir George Sitwell and his butler, comparable to Virginia Woolf's relationship with her cook, was a not unusual phenomenon, but was perhaps particularly strong in the twentieth century at a time when traditional social barriers were weakening.

The Nevinson portrait is not straightforward. Nevinson was a friend of the young Sitwells, and the choice of their butler as his sitter may have been a private joke. Moat acts as the model (though it is not known whether he actually sat) for a fictitious war profiteer, inscrutably gloomy but comfortably dressed and seated in a handsome interior. Behind him on the mantelpiece is a photograph of the son he has supposedly lost in war and, ironically prominent on the wall, is the bell-push which the real Moat frequently complained of having to answer. The picture is far removed in manner from Nevinson's early work: as a recent critic has remarked, the artist here subordinated 'all form of artistic experimentation and innovativeness to the function of conveying a moral message'.[8] Though the moralistic

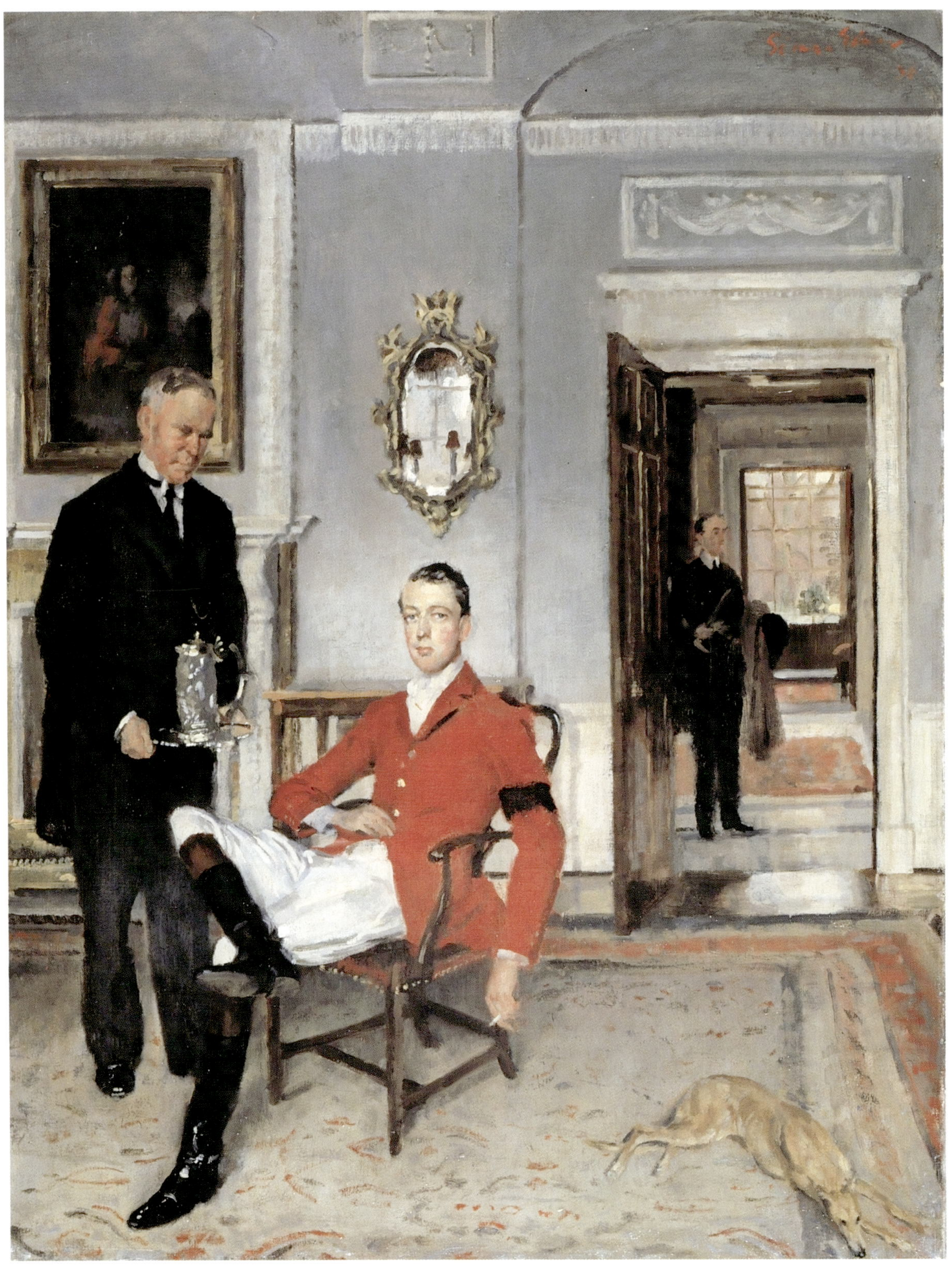

element – the attack on the widely disliked war profiteers – seems direct (though unusual), the picture gains an ironic complexity in the choice of a well-known servant as a player in this fiction. The element of performance which was an essential part of a butler's life is suggested by Moat's involvement in this opaque, and variously titled, painting.

A similar element of ambiguous play-acting underlies a painting of Sir Richard Sykes by his brother-in-law Simon Elwes, a successful society portraitist who regularly showed images of members of the royal family at the Royal Academy. Sir Richard, who had inherited a baronetcy and the fine house and estate of Sledmere in Yorkshire in his early teens, was well known among his friends for his extravagant way of life, largely supported by the Sledmere Stud. During his time at Sledmere, jazz and cocktails and amateur film-making replaced the sober godliness of an earlier Sykes generation,[9] though by the late 1930s Sir Richard's financial position was perilous. In 1936 Elwes painted Sykes in the dining-room at Sledmere wearing hunting pink, as though he had just come in from hunting (he was Master of the Middleton Hunt). This is not strictly speaking a servant portrait since Sykes is the principal sitter, but his status is underlined by the attentive butler (Mr Cassidy, who worked for many years for the family) with a footman seen through the door, suggesting aristocratic arrogance succoured by traditional deference. When this image of hauteur was shown at the Royal Academy in 1936, at a time of social and political tension, it was greeted with some hostility by the press. The artist regarded it as a *jeu d'esprit*, a caricature of how his dashing relation might be viewed, but the sitter was not pleased: he hated the painting. In this curious survival of the long-established trope of master with attendants, the tradition is slyly undermined.[10]

OPPOSITE Cat.95 **Sir Richard Sykes, 7th Bt. of Sledmere**
Simon Elwes, 1936

This portrait received a mixed reception at the Royal Academy in 1936, where it was the artist's diploma piece. Anthony Blunt in *The Spectator* complained 'As usual, the Academy is dominated by Society portraits. At the present time it must be almost impossible to make a serious work of a Society portrait ... they use every device towards the end not of direct rendering but of simple flattery ... the finest specimen of all, is, without doubt, Simon Elwes's portrait of Sir Richard Sykes complete with pink coat, butler, and family seat.'

Servants and literature

As they had done for many years, servants played an important role in twentieth-century literature in Britain. From the early years of the twentieth century, when an emergent Socialist ideology and the feminist movement questioned old assumptions about a natural class order, the traditional class system came increasingly under fire in literature. This was not a new phenomenon but as Bruce Robbins has pointed out in *The Servant's Hand*, the servant in literature traditionally embodied qualities not readily found in their real-life counterparts. In the twentieth century the theme of the ambiguous master–servant relationship became more pronounced, sometimes in apparently playful forms of literature.

One of the most interesting expressions of the Saturnalian theme of the master–servant reversal was created by J.M. Barrie, author of *Peter Pan*, in *The Admirable Crichton*, first performed in London in 1902 (cat.113). It tells the story of an aristocratic family shipwrecked on a remote island, where the butler Crichton proves he has all the necessary qualities of leadership and takes charge of the shipwrecked party. The play caused a sensation,' as the drama critic and historian W.A. Darlington put it, 'by reason ... of its implied social criticism. People discussed its subversive ideas with enormous solemnity.'[11] Many of the stage directions are acidly outspoken: 'It would not be good taste to describe Crichton, who is only a servant: if to the scandal of all good houses he is to stand out as a figure in the play, he must do it on his own ...'[12] The figure of Crichton is more complex than the play's apparent good humour might suggest: 'devotedly attached to his master' and proud to be a butler in London, on the island he becomes 'a strong and perhaps rather sinister figure'.[13] The review that Barrie was most pleased with, according to his biographer, was written by A.B. Walkley, critic of *The Times*, which praised the 'subtlety and complexity of the ideas ... a piece of hard logic, of close-packed thought ... something Voltaire could never have succeeded in writing.'[14]

From 1915 to 1971, the humorous writer P.G. Wodehouse published innumerable short stories and novels on the theme of Bertie Wooster, a cheerful and good-natured but idiotic young man about town, and his 'gentleman's gentleman' Jeeves (cat.118). Bertie (always the narrator) is repeatedly shown mired in problems from which only his impeccably educated and unruffled attendant can release him. Though the tone is humorous, the implication is clear: Jeeves is altogether his master's superior.

The subversive role of the servant is carried further in a post-war novel, subsequently a film. In 1948 Robin Maugham published *The Servant*, a novella about a rich and aimless young man called Tony. He employs a manservant, Barrett, who insinuates himself into his employer's favour, banishes his girl friend and ultimately takes control of his life. Barrett is presented by Maugham, if only by implication, as a caricatured homosexual with 'a prissy, affected voice ... In the middle of his sallow face were stuck a pair of rosebud lips, which gave him the look of a dissolute cherub. His lids were heavy and looked oily ...'[15] This repulsive depiction, and the ease with which Tony allows himself to be subjugated, offer a demonised version of the theme of the servant taking control of his master, given an additional twist by the suggestion of sexual dominance. The possibilities of this narrative were richly realised in Joseph Losey's sinister 1963 film – 'stinking of moral corruption' as Harold Pinter, who wrote the screenplay, put it[16] – with Dirk Bogarde terrifyingly menacing in the role of the manservant.

What these various depictions of servants suggest is that the type of the servant, particularly the manservant, had by the middle of the twentieth century developed into a potent symbol of insubordination and even anarchy in the traditional social order. In the most extreme view, he (or she) was qualified by their intimate position within the enemy camp to act as an agent of class conflict. In spite of the light-hearted nature of much of the material, these novels and films (and many other novels – D.H. Lawrence's *Lady Chatterley's Lover* (1932), Daphne du Maurier's

Rebecca (1938) and the work of Henry Green and Ivy Compton-Burnett) reflect a period when old antagonisms were emerging into a public arena.

The change in the style of servant's memoirs in the twentieth century makes this point forcefully. The new pattern was, arguably, established by a cuckoo in the nest, a writer who did not come from the usual social background for domestic service but played at servanthood. In the late 1930s the young ex-debutante and budding journalist Monica Dickens, a member of a prosperous family with an odious butler, decided, having nothing in particular to do, to enter domestic service. In *One Pair of Hands* (1939), she described her experiences as cook to a succession of vapid and demanding people in London, as well as in a country house. Though she found some of her employers sympathetic, her new role in service put her mentally on the other side of the green baize door: after her first dinner party as a cook, she found that she and the other servants 'had been welded together in the common cause of us against them … Ignoring the washing-up, we had a charming little supper round the kitchen table, tearing apart the hostess and guests piece by piece, as I had torn those doomed pheasants with my hands when carving did not work.'[17] This wittily subversive book belongs in the tradition of George Orwell's *Down and Out in Paris and London* (1933), in which another questing member of the privileged classes assumes an 'inferior' social position, to study society from beneath.

With the disappearance of deference went the old reticence, just as limited literacy, which had kept most servants of an earlier generation quiet, receded. After the Second World War, when domestic service was beginning to seem a curiosity, such publications flourished. In 1950 a scandal erupted when Marion Crawford, governess to Princess Elizabeth and Princess Margaret, published *The Little Princesses*, her memoir of life in the royal household. While the book is loyal and affectionate by present-day standards, the breach of confidence involved was widely regarded as outrageous. It contributed, however, to an increasingly vigorous trend. For example, in 1968 Margaret Powell, born in 1910 in Hove, issued *Below Stairs*, her first account of her life in service (cat.129). She described how in the 1920s, as a young girl of great academic promise, she was forced by family poverty to go into service in Brighton and then London. The book's success encouraged her to write several more works in similar vein.

In the late twentieth century the theme of the servant as the (often silent) subverter of the traditional social order has continued in a range of publications, even though inaccuracies of detail sometimes appear. In 1989 Kazuo Ishiguro offered a variation on the theme in his prize-winning novel *Remains of the Day*, in which a butler who places loyalty to his master and to professional standards above personal affection and truth, becomes a symbol of a misguided and even corrupted society (cat.115). This symbolism evidently transcended nation and period: the book has been translated into numerous languages, and the film (directed by James Ivory in 1993) enjoyed

BELOW LEFT Cat.96 **Joseph Jacklin, Odd-Job Man**
Richard Foster, 1970

This portrait of Joseph Jacklin, who was odd-job man at Deene Park until he died, is one of a set of small monochrome oil sketches recording employees who had served there for at least thirty years. Inspired by a visit to Erddig, the commission represents a revival of the tradition of serial portraits celebrating loyal service.

BELOW RIGHT Cat.97 **Jack Elliott, Chauffeur/Carpenter**
Richard Foster, 1970

As the son of a house carpenter at Deene Park, Jack Elliott represents continuity through the generations as well as faithful service. Like the other seven sitters in this series, he is depicted without reference to his roles as chauffeur and later carpenter. The artist focuses instead on individual characterisation of these valued servants.

equal success. In Robert Altman's film *Gosford Park* (2001), scripted by Julian Fellowes, the servants in a large Edwardian household offer an ironic counterpoint to the house party.

The country house revival

As we have seen, many if not most of the servants' portraits discussed in this book are associated with country houses, the most palpable symbol of the aristocracy's and gentry's way of life. Though the story of the changing attitudes to these houses has recently been told (as by Peter Mandler in *The Fall and Rise of the Stately Home*),[18] it is worth considering how this story affects our narrative. When the ownership of large country houses was embarked on by the National Trust for England and Wales in the 1930s, the houses were regarded primarily as architectural and artistic ensembles (much as Nikolaus Pevsner's early volumes in the *Buildings of England* series hardly mention patrons). In this view the ways houses were built, used and serviced were of no interest: the relics of domestic service would be disposed of when ownership passed to the National Trust, since service areas were not put on view.

In the 1960s and 1970s this attitude changed. Social history was becoming increasingly popular as a subject for academic research. To many historians at the time, it seemed that political history was being replaced by the

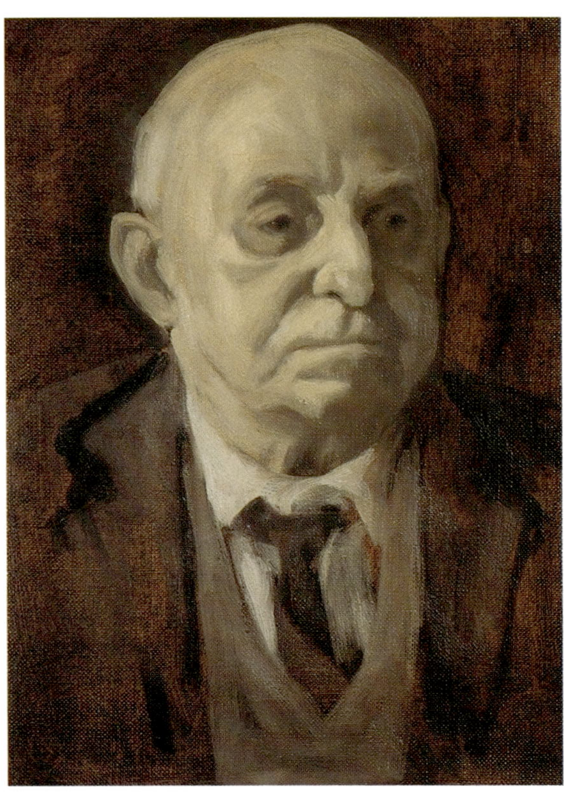

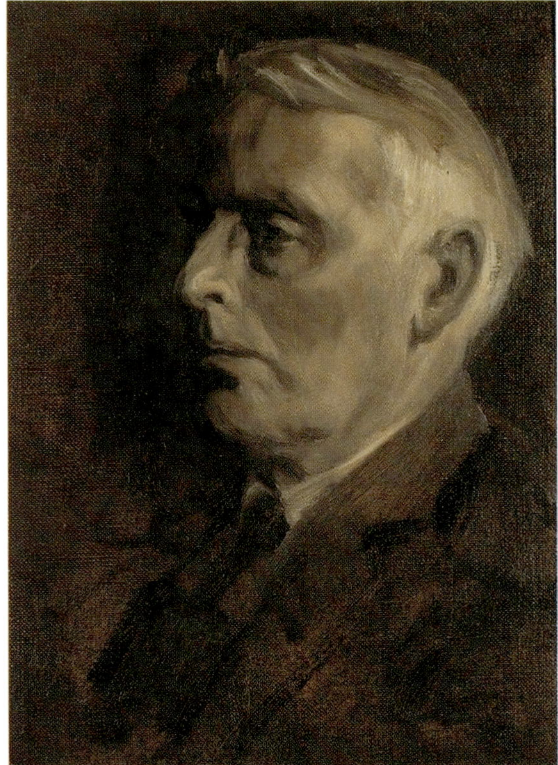

history of society. In this atmosphere, the literature on household management and on servants, which was distinguished but small, expanded. A steady flow of books emerged, mostly written by women and inspired by a range of attitudes to domestic service, from neutral (though seldom nostalgic) to strongly critical. They included E.S. Turner's popular but well-researched *What the Butler Saw* (1962), Theresa McBride's *The Domestic Revolution: The Modernisation of Household Service in England and France* (1976), several books and articles by Leonore Davidoff and Pamela Horn, Jessica Gerard's illuminating *Country House Life: Family and Servants 1815–1914* (1994), and Bridget Hill's lapidary collection of essays, published as *Servants: English Domestics in the Eighteenth Century* (1996).

The most influential book, which worked brilliantly at both academic and popular levels, was Mark Girouard's *Life in the English Country House* (1978). As the author put it, 'most people know comparatively little about how [English country houses] operated or what was expected of them when they were first built'.[19] Girouard of course discusses domestic employment within these great houses at some length. A huge success, the book's publication coincided – to their mutual benefit – with a television series which innovatively examined the life of an early twentieth-century household from top to bottom. *Upstairs Downstairs*, devised by Jean Marsh and Eileen Atkins and first shown in 1971, neatly, and with minute attention to detail, interwove the lives of a prosperous upper middle-class London family with those of their servants. The series did not make moral judgements about the society it portrayed but it showed the servants – in a way not previously seen on television – as rounded human beings, quite as sympathetic as their employers. It was based on thorough and first-hand knowledge of how domestic service worked. Originally, it was intended to show rather less sympathy for the employers.

Interest in the details of running households had already been stimulated in 1973 when Erddig, in Wales, was opened to the public by the National Trust. Those responsible for organising its presentation, notably Merlin Waterson, sought, as no one previously had, to make the everyday life of the house and the servants central. It was considered revolutionary that at Erddig, for the first time, paying visitors entered the building through the service block rather than the front door. Waterson's work reached a wide public through his history of the house in *The Servants' Hall* (1980), which was probably the first detailed study of a household seen through the lives of staff. The public loved Erddig, a house which they could be easily identified with. It did not present the formidable problems of envisaging the remote way of life and the aristocratic culture presented by state rooms to which visitors had previously been limited. It is from Erddig and these pioneering publications that the present book derives.

The interest taken by social historians in country houses was fuelled not only by the National Trust's activities but by increasing confidence among

HOLKHAM

One of the most ambitious and organised commissions for a series of portraits of employees in modern times was initiated by the Earl of Leicester (then Viscount Coke) in 1993, when he commissioned Andrew Festing to begin a series of paintings of the staff on his Holkham Hall estate in Norfolk. The first painting was inspired by the imminent retirement of three senior staff members, and the artist was asked to paint all the heads of department with Lord Leicester in the estate office at Holkham. Festing has since painted three other group portraits, including the maintenance personnel, the house staff and the gardeners. When the series is completed, the six portraits – which will all hang as a group in the Old Kitchen, now the visitors' tea-room – will depict all 280 people working on this flourishing estate, which has experienced a major revival in recent years. While Festing's image lies within the long tradition of group portraits (though it would be hard to find precise analogies), it is hardly a servant portrait. Although it is clear from the grouping of the figures which one is the Earl, he is shown not as a person on a different plane but as the head of an efficient organisation, a managing director rather than a nobleman. The portrait makes it clear that all those depicted have an important part to play in the survival and success of the estate. While a hierarchy is still apparent, this is perhaps an image for the twenty-first century, a statement of mutual endeavour rather than accepted hierarchy.[20]

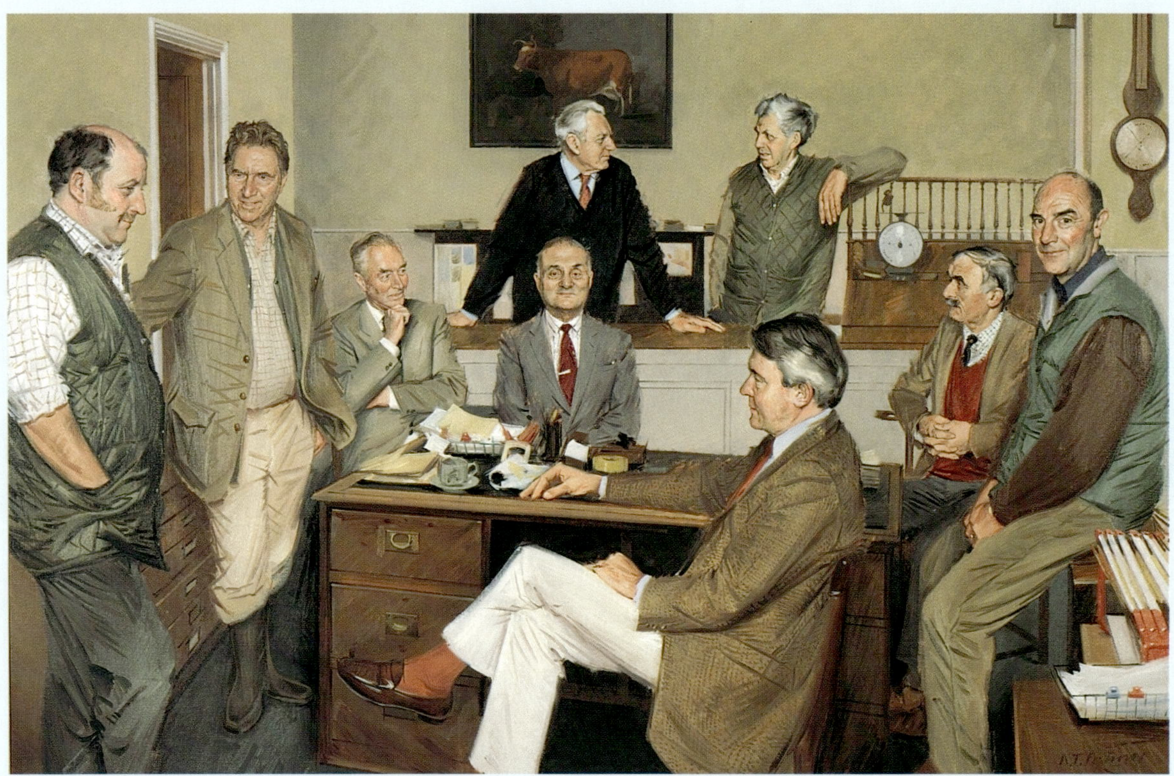

Cat.98 **Viscount Coke with Heads of Department at Holkham**
Andrew Festing, 1993

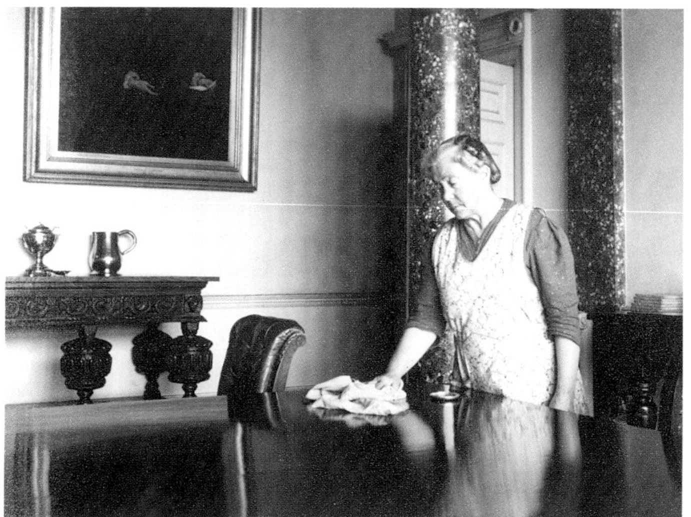

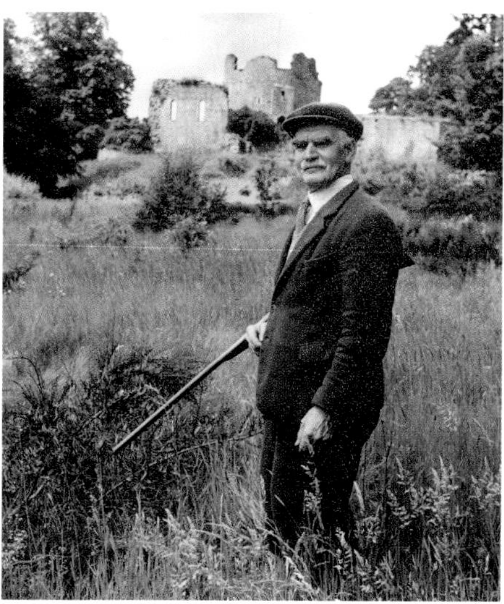

Cat.99 **Hawarden Castle Estate Staff**
J. Burge, *c.*1953

traditional owners in the viability of houses which had often been regarded as white elephants. From the 1960s until the 1990s, numerous houses and gardens in private hands were restored and opened to the public. (In return for grants to repair historic houses, the Historic Buildings and Monuments Act of 1953 stipulated that the public be granted a measure of access.) This confidence is reflected in a modest revival of portraits of loyal and long-serving members of staff commissioned by grateful employers: Henry Coleman, the butler at Chatsworth, was painted by the mercurial artist Derek Hill, who also portrayed Alphonse Gaffka, the estate carpenter, in his workshop at Buscot Park in Oxfordshire; Syd Terry, handyman at Antony House in Cornwall, painted by Peter Kuhfeld; Mr and Mrs Fobbester, cook and butler at Ragley Hall in Warwickshire, included in an enormous mural by Graham Rust in the South Staircase Hall. Mutual loyalty and respect between employee and employer are, as they had been for many years, the leitmotifs of these depictions.

The confidence, both social and economic, that supports the commissioning of such portraits may not last for much longer. Domestic service in the early twenty-first century has expanded considerably compared with the situation fifty years ago, particularly as a result of the infinitely greater number of women and mothers in full- or part-time employment. But this is domestic service of a quite different type to that which was practised in the nineteenth or early twentieth century. It is more casual, temporary and egalitarian, and altogether less likely to lead to commemoration in the form of paintings or even photographs. What is certain is that at a time when domestic service in the old manner is practically extinct, the complex attitudes involved in the master–servant relationship remain of universal interest.

Illustrated Exhibition Items

Cat.1 **The Trusty Servant**
William Cave,1809
Oil on canvas, 1970 x 1510mm (77½ x 59⅝")
THE WARDEN AND FELLOWS OF WINCHESTER COLLEGE
© THE WARDEN AND FELLOWS OF WINCHESTER COLLEGE

Cat.2 **Tom Derry, Jester to Anne of Denmark**
Attributed to Marcus Gheeraerts the Younger, 1614
Oil on panel, 714 x 579mm (28⅛ x 22¾")
SCOTTISH NATIONAL PORTRAIT GALLERY, EDINBURGH

Cat.3 **Thomas Skelton, 'The Fool of Muncaster'**
Unknown artist, *c.*1659–65
Oil on canvas, 2006 x 1143mm (79 x 43")
MUNCASTER CASTLE

Cat.4 **A Sleeping Dwarf: Richard Gibson**
Sir Peter Lely, late 1640s
Oil on canvas, 737 x 622mm (29 x 24½")
BERKELEY WILL TRUST

Cat.5 **The Life of James Allan, the Celebrated Northumberland Piper**
Frontispiece by A. Dick to book by Andrew Wight, 1818
Book, 210 x 130mm (8¼ x 5⅛")
DUKE OF NORTHUMBERLAND, ALNWICK CASTLE

Cat.6 **Alistair Mor Grant, the Champion of the Laird of Grant**
Richard Waitt, 1714
Oil on canvas, 2184 x 1613mm (86 x 63½")
THE REIDHAVEN TRUST

Cat.7 **Nic Ciarain, the Henwife of Castle Grant**
Richard Waitt, 1726(?)
Oil on canvas, 762 x 635mm (30 x 25")
PRIVATE COLLECTION

Cat.8 **A 'Gillee Wet Feit' or Errand Runner**
Attributed to Paul Sandby, *c.*1749
Sketchbook, 168 x 260mm (6⅝ x 10¼")
THE NATIONAL GALLERY OF SCOTLAND, EDINBURGH

Cat.9 **The Accomplisht Cook**
Robert May, 1685
Book, 190 x 150mm (7½ x 5⅞") 1st Edition
THE BRITISH LIBRARY

Cat.10 **Fulke Harold, Gardener**
John Ellys, *c.*1736–44
Oil on canvas, 737 x 584mm (29 x 23")
HOUGHTON COLLECTION
© NORFOLK MUSEUMS SERVICE

Cat.11 **Robert Pointer, Coachman [to Mr Boulton]**
Richard Earlom after Samuel de Wilde, 1811
Coloured mezzotint, 485 x 352mm (19⅛ x 13⅞")
THE BRITISH MUSEUM, LONDON

Cat.12 **Servant to the Duke of Cumberland**
Paul Sandby, *c.*1750s
Pen and watercolour, 120 x 60mm (4¾ x 2⅜")
THE ROYAL COLLECTION
ROYAL COLLECTION © 2003, HER MAJESTY QUEEN ELIZABETH II

Cat.13 **The Dudmaston Gamekeeper with Spaniel and Dead Partridge**
English School, *c.*1720
Oil on canvas, 1220 x 990mm (48 x 39")
DUDMASTON, THE WOLRYCHE-WHITMORE COLLECTION (THE NATIONAL TRUST)
© NATIONAL TRUST PHOTOGRAPHIC LIBRARY/JOHN HAMMOND

Cat.14 **Study for a Portrait of Mr Gretton of Trinity College, Cambridge, Tutor to Governor Holdsworth**
John Downman, 1778
Charcoal touched with red and black chalk, 370 x 540mm (14½ x 21¼")
THE BRITISH MUSEUM, LONDON

Cat.15 **The Experienced English Housekeeper**
Elizabeth Raffald, 1784
Book, 210 x 140mm (8¼ x 5½")
THE BRITISH LIBRARY

Cat.16 **Mrs Garnett**
Thomas Barber, *c.*1800
Oil on canvas, 895 x 690mm (35¾ x 27⅛")
KEDLESTON HALL, THE SCARSDALE COLLECTION (THE NATIONAL TRUST, ACQUIRED WITH THE AID OF A GRANT FROM THE NHMF)
© NATIONAL TRUST PHOTOGRAPHIC LIBRARY/JOHN HAMMOND

Cat.17 **Isabel Smith, called Munia, Nurse to the Angerstein Family**
Sir Thomas Lawrence, *c.*1800
Pencil on paper, 356 x 302mm (14 x 11⅞")
TATE. BEQUEATHED BY MISS MAY ROWLEY 1965

Cat.18 **Catherine Hughes, Nanny to the Williams Family of Bodelwyddan**
George Hargreaves, 1824(?)
Ivory miniature, 85 x 66mm (3⅜ x 2½")
CHARLECOTE PARK, THE LUCY COLLECTION (THE NATIONAL TRUST)

Cat.19 **The Wolryche Fool as an Older Man**
George Alsop, mid-eighteenth century
Oil on canvas, 735 x 610mm (28⅞ x 24")
DUDMASTON, THE WOLRYCHE-WHITMORE COLLECTION (THE NATIONAL TRUST)
© NATIONAL TRUST PHOTOGRAPHIC LIBRARY/JOHN HAMMOND

Cat.20 **Edward Prince, Carpenter**
John Walters, 1792
Oil on canvas, 1230 x 1016mm (44½ x 37¼")
ERDDIG, THE YORKE COLLECTION (THE NATIONAL TRUST)
© NATIONAL TRUST PHOTOGRAPHIC LIBRARY/JOHN HAMMOND

Cat.21 **Thomas Rogers, Estate Carpenter**
William Jones, 1830
Oil on canvas, 1105 x 940mm (43½ x 37")
ERDDIG, THE YORKE COLLECTION (THE NATIONAL TRUST)
© NATIONAL TRUST PHOTOGRAPHIC LIBRARY/JOHN HAMMOND

Cat.22 **Two Servants (Daniel Taylor and Elinor Low)**
Arnold Almond, 1783
Oil on canvas, 350 x 440mm (13¾ x 17⅜")
PRIVATE COLLECTION

Cat.23 Mary Hayes, Housemaid
Arnold Almond, 1783
Oil on canvas, 290 x 240mm (11⅜ x 9½")
PRIVATE COLLECTION

Cat.24 John Holt, Gardener
Arnold Almond, 1783
Oil on canvas, 290 x 240mm (11⅜ x 9½")
PRIVATE COLLECTION

Cat.25 A Gardener at Bramham Park
George Garrard, *c.*1822
Oil on canvas, 445 x 362mm (17½ x 14¼")
LEEDS MUSEUMS AND GALLERIES (TEMPLE NEWSAM HOUSE)
© LEEDS MUSEUMS AND GALLERIES (TEMPLE NEWSAM HOUSE)

Cat.26 Mrs Brown, the Housekeeper at Bramham Park
George Garrard, 1822
Oil on canvas, 464 x 362mm (18¼ x 14¼")
LEEDS MUSEUMS AND ART GALLERIES (TEMPLE NEWSAM HOUSE)
© LEEDS MUSEUMS AND ART GALLERIES /BRIDGEMAN ART LIBRARY

Cat.27 Bridget Holmes
John Riley, 1686
Oil on canvas, 2247 x 1490mm (88½ x 58⅝")
THE ROYAL COLLECTION
ROYAL COLLECTION © 2003, HER MAJESTY QUEEN ELIZABETH II

Cat.28 Jonathan Ritson, Woodcarver
George Clint, *c.*1830
Oil on canvas, 380 x 305mm (15 x 12")
PETWORTH, THE EGREMONT COLLECTION (THE NATIONAL TRUST, ACCEPTED IN LIEU OF TAX BY HM GOVERNMENT IN 1989, AND ALLOCATED TO THE NATIONAL TRUST)
© NATIONAL TRUST PHOTOGRAPHIC LIBRARY/DERRICK E. WITTY

Cat.29 Robert Shaw, Keeper of the Forest of Bowland
James Northcote, *c.*1806
Oil on canvas, 737 x 635mm (29 x 25")
THE PARKER FAMILY
© ROBERT PARKER

Cat.30 Peter Mathieson, Coachman to Sir Walter Scott with Donald the Pony
G.D., 1851
Oil on canvas, 593 x 470mm (23⅜ x 18½")
ABBOTSFORD COLLECTION
© ABBOTSFORD COLLECTION

Cat.31 Thomas Hudson, Keeper at Bowhill
William Douglas, 1810
Oil on panel, 590 x 460mm (23¼ x 11⅛")
THE DUKE OF BUCCLEUCH AND QUEENSBERRY, KT

Cat.32 Joseph Florance
John Ainslie, 1817
Oil on canvas, 900 x 720mm (35½ x 28⅜")
THE DUKE OF BUCCLEUCH AND QUEENSBERRY, KT

Cat.33 Joseph Paxton
Octavius Oakley, *c.*1850
Watercolour, 467 x 349mm (18⅜ x 13¾")
NATIONAL PORTRAIT GALLERY, LONDON
© NATIONAL PORTRAIT GALLERY, LONDON

Cat.34 The Scullion at Christ Church
John Riley, *c.*1680s
Oil on canvas, 997 x 605mm (39¾ x 23¾")
THE GOVERNING BODY OF CHRIST CHURCH, OXFORD

Cat.35 Thomas Hodges, College Servant
L.L., 1768
Oil on canvas, 770 x 650mm (30⅜ x 25½")
THE WARDEN AND SCHOLARS OF NEW COLLEGE, OXFORD

Cat.36 The Arts Club's Woman Chef
Francis Edwin Hodge, 1935
Oil on canvas, 890 x 710mm (35 x 28")
THE ARTS CLUB, LONDON

Cat.37 Will They Never Go Home?
From Boodle's (1762–1962)
Roger Fulford, 1962
Book, 245 x 190mm (9⅝ x 7½")
GILES WATERFIELD

Cat.38 William Banning, Head Gate Porter at the Bank of England 1763–77
Unknown artist, *c.*1760
Line engraving, 330 x 400mm (13 x 15¾")
THE GOVERNOR AND COMPANY OF THE BANK OF ENGLAND

Cat.39 One of the Porters of the Royal Academy (John Withers?)
John Russell, *c.*1792
Pastel on paper, 770 x 600mm (30¼ x 23⅝")
THE COURTAULD INSTITUTE GALLERY, LONDON

Cat.40 Samuel Barnetson, Parlour Messenger
Thomas Monnington, 1937
Chalk, 274 x 230mm (10¾ x 9")
THE GOVERNOR AND COMPANY OF THE BANK OF ENGLAND

Cat.41 The Master Cook, 1st Battalion Welsh Guards Sergeant J.W. Isaacs
Rex Whistler, 1940
Oil on canvas, 393 x 305mm (15½ x 12")
PROPERTY OF REGIMENTAL HEADQUARTERS WELSH GUARDS
© PROPERTY OF REGIMENTAL HEADQUARTERS WELSH GUARDS

Cat.42 Thomas Allen, a Greenwich Pensioner and Servant to Lord Nelson
John Burnet, *c.*1832
Oil on canvas, 305 x 230mm (12 x 9")
NATIONAL MARITIME MUSEUM, LONDON
© NATIONAL MARITIME MUSEUM, LONDON

Cat.43 The Allees and Arcades behind the House
Balthasar Nebot, 1738
Oil on canvas, 675 x 900mm (26⅝ x 34⅞")
BUCKINGHAMSHIRE COUNTY MUSEUM COLLECTIONS
© BUCKINGHAMSHIRE COUNTY MUSEUM

Cat.44 Register Office for the Hiring of Servants
Thomas Rowlandson, *c.*1800–05
Pen, ink and watercolour over graphite on wove paper, 235 x 349mm (9¼ x 13¾")
YALE CENTER FOR BRITISH ART, PAUL MELLON COLLECTION

Cat.45 The Great Law of Subordination Consider'd
Daniel Defoe, 1724
Book, 200 x 130mm (7⅞ x 5⅛")
THE BRITISH LIBRARY

Cat.46 Loo in the Kitchin or High Life Below Stairs
Woodward after I.R.Cruikshank, 1799
Etching with hand colouring, 340 x 471mm (13⅜ x 18½")
LEWIS WALPOLE LIBRARY, YALE UNIVERSITY

Cat.47 The Passage to the Gothic Room at Stowe House
J.C. Nattes, 1807
Pen and ink, 211 x 227mm (8¼ x 8⅞")
BUCKINGHAMSHIRE COUNTY MUSEUM COLLECTIONS
© BUCKINGHAMSHIRE COUNTY MUSEUM

Cat.48 **Fish Nell, John Sutherland, Laundryman and 'Dummy' King (Servants at Dalkeith House)**
Attributed to John Ainslie, 1832
Oil on canvas, 460 x 360mm (18⅛ x 14⅛")
THE DUKE OF BUCCLEUCH AND QUEENSBERRY, KT

Cat.49 **The Footman's Guide**
Illustration from book by James Williams, 1840
Book, 170 x 100mm (6¾ x 4")
THE BRITISH LIBRARY, LONDON

Cat.50 **The Housekeeper's Room (Morning Orders)**
Frederick Elwell, 1911
Oil on panel, 1130 x 920mm (44½ x 36¼")
FERENS ART GALLERY: HULL CITY MUSEUMS & ART GALLERY

Cat.51 **William, 4th Lord Byron and Household at Newstead Abbey**
Peter Tillemans, 1726
Oil, 240 x 680 (9½ x 22¾")
LORD BYRON

Cat.52 **Susan Gill, Maid to the Beale Family**
Charles Beale II, 1680s
Red chalk, 268 x 430mm (10½ x 17")
THE BRITISH MUSEUM, LONDON

Cat.53 **A Servant Girl Asleep**
Charles Beale II, 1680
Red chalk with touches of black chalk, 243 x 188mm (9½ x 7⅜")
THE BRITISH MUSEUM, LONDON

Cat.54 **Heads of Six of Hogarth's Servants**
William Hogarth, *c.*1750–55
Oil on canvas, 630 x 755mm (24¾ x 29¾")
TATE. PURCHASED 1982

Cat.55 **The Artist in His Studio with his Man, Gibbs**
George Morland, *c.*1802
Oil on canvas, 635 x 762mm (25 x 30")
NOTTINGHAM CITY MUSEUMS AND GALLERIES

Cat.56 **James Richards**
Heneage Legge, 1815
Pencil on paper, 485 x 410mm (19⅛ x 16⅛")
DARTMOUTH HEIRLOOMS TRUST. DEPOSITED AT THE STAFFORDSHIRE RECORD OFFICE

Cat.57 **Woodward**
Heneage Legge, 1820
Pencil on paper, 410 x 305mm (16⅛ x 12")
DARTMOUTH HEIRLOOMS TRUST. DEPOSITED AT THE STAFFORDSHIRE RECORD OFFICE

Cat.58 **A Cowper Brewer**
Francis Hawksworth Fawkes, *c.*1820s
Album of caricatures, 228 x 279mm (9 x 11")
PRIVATE COLLECTION

Cat.59 **Cut-outs: Family Servant, Mr Swift, known as 'Horrible Dick;' Lady's Maid, Miss Morpline; Family Embroiderer, Miss Collins**
Susan and Marion Drummond, *c.*1830–32
Watercolour
VICTORIA & ALBERT MUSEUM

Cat.60 **Idleness**
Patrick Allan-Fraser, *c.*1871
Oil on canvas, 500 x 642mm (19⅝ x 25¼")
THE TRUSTEES OF PATRICK ALLAN-FRASER OF HOSPITALFIELD

Cat.61 **The Kitchen**
Harold Gilman, *c.*1908
Oil on canvas, 610 x 457mm (24 x 18")
NATIONAL MUSEUMS & GALLERIES OF WALES

Cat.62 **Mrs Roberts**
Sir Lawrence Gowing, 1944
Oil on canvas, 406 x 508mm (16 x 20")
TATE. PRESENTED BY THE CONTEMPORARY ART SOCIETY 1945

Cat.63 **Pamela, or Virtue Rewarded**
Samuel Richardson, 1740–41
Book, 205 x 280mm (8⅛ x 11")
ROBERT HARDING

Cat.64 **Pamela and Mr B. in the Summerhouse**
Joseph Highmore, *c.*1744
Oil on canvas, 629 x 756mm (24¾ x 29¾")
THE SYNDICS OF THE FITZWILLIAM MUSEUM, CAMBRIDGE

Cat.65 **Pamela in the Bedroom with Mrs Jewkes and Mr B.**
Joseph Highmore, 1743–4
Oil on canvas, 630 x 760mm (24¾ x 29⅞")
TATE. PURCHASED 1921

Cat.66 **A Scene from Jonathan Swift's Description of a City Shower**
Edward Penny, 1764
Oil on canvas, 765 x 640mm (30⅛ x 25¼")
MUSEUM OF LONDON, PURCHASED WITH THE ASSISTANCE OF THE MGC/V&A PURCHASE FUND GRANT AND THE NATIONAL ART COLLECTIONS FUND

Cat.67 **High Life Below Stairs**
James Bretherton after Thomas Orde-Powlett (1st Lord Bolton)
Etching, 1774. 270 x 295mm (10⅝ x 11⅝")
THE BRITISH MUSEUM, LONDON

Cat.68 **High Life Below Stairs**
James Townley, 1768
Book, 210 x 130mm (8¼ x 5⅛")
THE BRITISH LIBRARY

Cat.69 **Lady Easy's Steinkerk**
Francis Wheatley, 1791
Oil on canvas, 614 x 614mm (24⅛ x 24⅛")
VICTORIA & ALBERT MUSEUM

Cat.70 **Charles Matthews as Somno in The Sleepwalker**
Samuel de Wilde, *c.*1813
Oil on canvas, 770 x 583mm (30¼ x 23")
THE GARRICK CLUB

Cat.71 **Good Advice from an Old Servant to the Young Ones**
Gaugain and Hellyer after James Northcote, 1796
Line engraving, 467 x 540mm (18⅜ x 21¼")
THE BRITISH MUSEUM, LONDON

Cat.72 **A Lady's Maid Soaping Linen**
Henry Robert Morland, *c.*1765–82
Oil on canvas, 743 x 616mm (29¼ x 24¼")
TATE. PURCHASED 1984

Cat.73 **The Hon. John and the Hon. Thomas Hamilton with a Negro Servant**
William Aikman, 1728
Oil on canvas, 1570 x 1280mm (61¾ x 50⅜")
THE MELLERSTAIN TRUST

Cat.74 **Bust of a Moor**
John van Nost the Elder, *c.*1700
Marble, 985 x 600 x 400mm (38¾ x 23⅝ x 15¾")
THE ROYAL COLLECTION

Cat.75 **A Gentleman, Possibly William Hickey, and an Indian Servant**
Arthur William Devis, *c.*1785
Oil on canvas, 1060 x 835mm (41¾ x 32⅞")
YALE CENTER FOR BRITISH ART, PAUL MELLON COLLECTION

Cat.76 **Figures of Bengali Servants**
Early nineteenth century
Clay and textile, 241mm (9½") high
HOBHOUSE LTD

Cat.77 **The Munshi Abdul Karim**
Rudolph Swoboda, 1888
Oil on canvas, 767 x 640mm (30¼ x 25¼")
THE ROYAL COLLECTION

Cat.78 **Freeman, the Earl of Clarendon's Gamekeeper, with a Dying Doe and Hound**
George Stubbs, 1800
Oil on canvas, 1015 x 1270mm (40 x 50")
YALE CENTER FOR BRITISH ART, PAUL MELLON COLLECTION

Cat.79 **The Duke of Ancaster's Bay Stallion, Blank, Held by a Groom**
George Stubbs, *c.*1762–5
Oil on canvas, 1020 x 1270mm (40⅛ x 50")
PRIVATE COLLECTION

Cat.80 **The Maid of All-Work's Prayer!!**
Thomas Rowlandson after Woodward, 1801
Coloured etching, 490 x 705mm (19⅜ x 27¾")
THE BRITISH MUSEUM, LONDON

Cat.81 **Hannah Cullwick**
Unknown photographer
Photograph, 295 x 210 (11⅝ x 8¼") (estimated)
THE MASTER AND FELLOWS, TRINITY COLLEGE, CAMBRIDGE

Cat.82 **John Brown, Personal Servant to Queen Victoria**
Kenneth MacLeay, 1866
Watercolour, 525 x 398mm (20¾ x 15¾")
THE ROYAL COLLECTION

Cat.83 **William Ross, Queen Victoria's Piper**
Kenneth MacLeay, 1866
Watercolour, 527 x 410mm (20¾ x 16⅛")
THE ROYAL COLLECTION

Cat.84 **Maids of All Work**
John Finnie, 1864–5
Oil on canvas, 580 x 425mm (22⅞ x 16¾")
THE GEFFRYE MUSEUM, LONDON

Cat.85 **Servant Girl**
W. P. Frith, nineteenth century
Oil on canvas, 500 x 410mm (19⅝ x 16⅛")
PRIVATE COLLECTION

Cat.86 **The Butler Takes a Glass of Port (or All Things Come to the Man Who Waits)**
Frederick Elwell, 1890
Oil on canvas, 940 x 740mm (37 x 29⅛")
BEVERLEY ART GALLERY, EAST RIDING OF YORKSHIRE COUNCIL

Cat.87 **Our Friends**
Mrs Wyndham, 1860s
Album, 210 x 145mm (8¼ x 5¾") (estimated)
LORD EGREMONT

Cat.88 **Lady Holland in a Bath Chair with a Page**
Sir Edwin Landseer
Pen, sepia ink and wash on paper, 178 x 203mm (7 x 8")
ABERCORN HEIRLOOMS SETTLEMENT

Cat.89 **The Governess**
Emily Mary Osborn, 1860
Oil on canvas, 349 x 292mm (13¾ x 11½")
YALE CENTER FOR BRITISH ART, PAUL MELLON FUND

Cat.90 **After the Party**
Frederic Hardy, 1876
Oil on canvas, 692 x 1089mm (22¼ x 42⅞")
PRIVATE COLLECTION

Cat.91 **'Train up a Child'**
Punch, 25 March 1871
NATIONAL PORTRAIT GALLERY, LONDON

Cat.92 **Miss Hudson**
Mary Potter, 1960
Pencil and watercolour, 220 x 128mm (8⅝ x 5")
PRIVATE COLLECTION

Cat.93 **How to Dispense with Servants in the Dining Room**
William Heath Robinson, 1921
Pen and black ink and watercolour, 449 x 322mm (17⅝ x 12⅝")
THE BRITISH MUSEUM, LONDON

Cat.94 **Henry Moat, Butler to the Sitwells (or He Gained a Fortune But He Gave a Son)**
Christopher Richard Nevinson, 1918
Oil on canvas, 400 x 506mm (15¾ x 19⅞")
UNIVERSITY OF HULL ART COLLECTION

Cat.95 **Sir Richard Sykes, 7th Bt. of Sledmere**
Simon Elwes, 1936
Oil on canvas, 775 x 725mm (30½ x 28½")
ROYAL ACADEMY OF ARTS, LONDON

Cat.96 **Joseph Jacklin, Odd-Job Man**
Richard Foster, 1970
Oil on canvas, 254 x 191mm (10 x 7½")
BRUDENELL COLLECTION–DEENE PARK

Cat.97 **Jack Elliott, Chauffeur/Carpenter**
Richard Foster, 1970
Oil on canvas, 254 x 191mm (10 x 7½")
BRUDENELL COLLECTION–DEENE PARK

Cat.98 **Viscount Coke with Heads of Department at Holkham**
Andrew Festing, 1993
Oil on canvas, 1180 x 1830mm (46½ x 72")
THE EARL OF LEICESTER AND TRUSTEES OF THE HOLKHAM ESTATE

Cat.99 **Hawarden Castle Estate Staff**
J. Burge, *c.*1953
Photograph album, 300 x 250mm (11⅞ x 9⅞")
SIR WILLIAM GLADSTONE

Unillustrated Exhibition Items

Cat.100 **Chronique d'Angleterre: Lancaster Dines with the King of Portugal, 1386**
Jean de Wavrin, late fifteenth century
Manuscript on vellum, 470 x 350mm (18½ x 13¾")
THE BRITISH LIBRARY

Cat.101 **Footman with Silver at Bramham Park**
Oil on canvas, 445 x 357mm (17½ x 14")
TRUSTEES OF BRAMHAM SETTLED ESTATE

Cat.102 **Advantages of a Modern Education**
Charles Williams, 1825
Coloured etching, 423 x 575mm (16⅝ x 22⅝")
VICTORIA & ALBERT MUSEUM
© V&A PICTURE LIBRARY

Cat.103 **Steward to Lord Plymouth**
J. Cooke, early nineteenth century
Watercolour with body colour on paper, 525 x 431 (20⅝ x 17")
VISCOUNT WINDSOR

Cat 104 **Crude Ditties**
Philip Yorke I, 1795
Book, 170 x 110mm (6¾ x 4⅜")
THE BRITISH LIBRARY

Cat.105 **Faithful Servants**
Arthur Joseph Munby, 1891
Book, 200 x 140mm (7¾ x 5½")
THE BRITISH LIBRARY

Cat.106 **Mary Bygrave, Housekeeper to the British Museum**
British School(?), 1844
Oil on canvas, 395 x 285mm (15½ x 11¾")
THE BRITISH MUSEUM, LONDON

Cat.107 **Directions to Servants in General; and in Particular to the Butler, Cook, Footman, Coachman, Groom, House-Steward and Land-Steward, Porter, Dairy-Maid, Chamber-maid, Nurse, Laundress, House-keeper, Tutoress or Governess**
Jonathan Swift, 1768
Book, 218 x 140 (8⅝ x 5½")
THE PROVOST AND FELLOWS OF ETON COLLEGE

Cat.108 **A Girl Peeling Apples**
Late seventeenth or early eighteenth century
Dummy board, 1190 x 780 x 40mm (46⅞ x 30¾ x 1½")
DYRHAM PARK, THE BLATHWAYT COLLECTION (THE NATIONAL TRUST)

Cat.109 **Servants in Livery Outside a London House**
Photograph, *c.*1911
TATTON PARK, THE EGERTON COLLECTION (THE NATIONAL TRUST)

Cat.110 **Servitude**
Robert Dodsley, 1729
Book, 195 x 120mm (7⅝ x 4¾")
THE BRITISH LIBRARY

Cat.111 **Ignatius Sancho**
Francesco Bartolozzi after Thomas Gainsborough, published 1802
Engraving, second state
NATIONAL PORTRAIT GALLERY, LONDON

Cat.112 **The Fruit Sellers**
W. H. Fox Talbot, *c.*1860
Photograph
THE W. H. FOX TALBOT TRUST COLLECTION, FOX TALBOT MUSEUM, LACOCK ABBEY (ON LOAN TO THE NATIONAL TRUST)

Cat.113 **The Admirable Crichton, illustrated by Hugh Thomson**
J.M. Barrie, 1914
Book, 270 x 220 (10⅝ x 8⅝")
THE BRITISH LIBRARY

Cat.114 **The Servantless House**
R. Randal Phillips, 1920
Book, 220 x 150 (8⅝ x 6")
THE BRITISH LIBRARY

Cat.115 **The Remains of the Day**
Kazuo Ishiguro, 1989
Book, 225 x 140 (8⅞ x 5½")
THE PROVOST AND FELLOWS OF ETON COLLEGE

Cat.116 **The Perfect Parlourmaid**
Bill Brandt, 29 June 1939
Photograph from *Picture Post*, 267 x 348mm (10½ x 13¾")
NATIONAL PORTRAIT GALLERY, LONDON

Cat.117 **The Butler and Footmen**
1912
Photograph, 284 x 231mm (11⅛ x 9")
POLESDEN LACY, THE MCEWAN COLLECTION (THE NATIONAL TRUST)

Cat.118 **Carry on Jeeves**
P.G. Wodehouse, 1924
Book, 190 x 135mm (7½ x 5⅜")
THE BARRY PHELPS' WODEHOUSE COLLECTION, DULWICH COLLEGE, LONDON
© ESTATE OF P.G.WODEHOUSE

Cat.119 **William Hayes, Porter in Grosvenor Square**
Arnold Almond, 1783
Oil on canvas, 290 x 240mm (11½ x 9½")
PRIVATE COLLECTION

Cat.120 **Samuel Potter, Labourer**
Arnold Almond, 1783
Oil on canvas, 290 x 240mm (11½ x 9½")
PRIVATE COLLECTION

Cat.121 **Carpenter's Tools Used by Thomas Rogers and Stamped with his Name**
Saw, chisels and wheelwright's gouge
Saw: 680 x 160mm (26¾ x 6¼"); chisels: 350 x 33mm (13¾ x 1"); wheelwright's gouge: 455 x 35mm (18 x 1¼")
KEVIN HUW JONES, GREAT GREAT GREAT GRANDSON OF THOMAS ROGERS

Cat.122 **Housekeeper's Account Book at Erddig, 1798–1806**
Book, 410 x 175mm (16⅛ x 6⅞")
ERDDIG, THE YORKE COLLECTION (THE NATIONAL TRUST)

Cat.123 **Livery for Footman for 3rd Earl of Ashburnham**
Fabric and gold textile, 1829
Coat: 1310 x 410mm (63⅜ x 16⅛");
Waistcoat: 790 x 300mm (31 x 11¾");
Breeches: 790 x 400 (31 x 15¾")
TIM KNOX AND TODD LONGSTAFFE-GOWAN

Cat.124 **The Steward and Housekeeper with Housemaids**
Artist unknown, 1912
Photograph, 284 x 231mm (11⅛ x 9")
POLESDEN LACEY, THE MCEWAN COLLECTION (THE NATIONAL TRUST)

Cat.125 **The Fool's Glass**
*c.*1710
Glass, 280mm (11") high
DUDMASTON, THE WOLRYCHE-WHITMORE COLLECTION (THE NATIONAL TRUST)

Cat.126 **Jane Eyre**
Charlotte Brontë, 1847
Book, 205 x 140mm (5½ x 1⅛")
THE BRITISH LIBRARY

Cat.127 **Directions to Footmen**
Thomas Rowlandson, 1807
Coloured etching, 350 x 240mm (13¾ x 9½")
THE BRITISH MUSEUM, LONDON

Cat.128 **Stories for Young Servants**
Anna Butler, 1876
Book, 150 x 110mm (6 x 4⅜")
THE BRITISH LIBRARY

Cat.129 **Below Stairs**
Margaret Powell, 1968
Book, 223 x 145mm (8¾ x 5¾")
GILES WATERFIELD

Cat.130 **Catherine, Duchess of Queensberry as a Milkmaid**
Charles Jervas, *c.*1725–30
Oil on canvas, 1270 x 1010mm (50 x 39¾")
NATIONAL PORTRAIT GALLERY, LONDON

Cat.131 **The Pickwick Papers**
Charles Dickens, 1836
Book, 225 x 140mm (9 x 5½")
THE CHARLES DICKENS MUSEUM, LONDON

Cat.132 **Daily Prayers for Servants**
Unknown author, 1853
Book, 145 x 90mm (5¾ x 3½")
THE BRITISH LIBRARY

Cat.133 **Letter to Walter Francis, 5th Duke of Buccleuch**
Joseph Florance, 22 July 1827
Paper, 295 x 210mm (11⅝ x 8¼")
THE DUKE OF BUCCLEUCH AND QUEENSBERRY, KT

Comparative images provided as figure references

Fig.1 **A Lady Writing a Letter with her Maid**
Jan Vermeer, 1670
Oil on canvas, 711 x 605mm (28 x 23¾")
THE NATIONAL GALLERY OF IRELAND
© COURTESY OF THE NATIONAL GALLERY OF IRELAND

Fig.2 **Interior with a Sleeping Maid and her Mistress**
Nicolaes Maes, 1655
Oil on wood, 700 x 533mm (27½ x 21")
© THE NATIONAL GALLERY, LONDON

Fig.3 **An Old Peasant Caresses a Kitchen Maid in a Stable**
David Teniers the Younger, *c.*1650
Oil on wood, 432 x 649mm (17 x 25½")
© THE NATIONAL GALLERY, LONDON

Fig.4 **Thomas Wentworth, 1st Earl of Strafford with Sir Philip Mainwaring**
Sir Anthony van Dyck, *c.*1639–40
Oil on canvas, 1232 x 1397mm (48½ x 55")
PRIVATE COLLECTION
THE BRIDGEMAN ART LIBRARY/PHOTOGRAPH: MARK FIENNES

Fig.5 **The Governess**
Jean-Baptiste-Siméon Chardin, 1739
Oil on canvas, 467 x 375mm (18⅜ x 14¾")
© NATIONAL GALLERY OF CANADA, OTTAWA/PURCHASED 1956

Fig.6 **Chocolate Maid**
Jean-Etienne Liotard, *c.*1744–5
Oil on vellum, 825 x 525mm (32½ x 20⅝")
© STAATLICHE KUNTSAMMLUNGEN DRESDEN/PHOTOGRAPH: KLUT

Fig.7 **Henry VIII with a harp as David, with Will Somers**
Unknown artist, 1540
Vellum, 139 x 203mm (5½ x 8")
THE BRITISH LIBRARY

Fig.8 **The Blind Harpist, John Parry**
William Parry, *c.*1760–80
Oil on canvas, 8480 x 7390mm (333 x 290")
© NATIONAL MUSEUMS & GALLERIES OF WALES

Fig.9 **Lord Warkworth and his Tutor, Jonathan Lippyeatt**
Nathaniel Dance, 1763
Oil on canvas, 952 x 698mm (37½ x 27½")
DUKE OF NORTHUMBERLAND, SYON HOUSE
© COURTAULD INSTITUTE OF ART

Fig.10 **Cookmaid with Dead Birds**
Sir Nathaniel Bacon
Oil on canvas, 1511 x 2051mm (59½ x 80¾")
REPRODUCED BY PERMISSION OF THE EARL OF VERULAM
PHOTOGRAPHIC SURVEY, COURTAULD INSTITUTE OF ART

Fig.11 **Jonathan Jackman, Gardener at Wicken Park**
Johann Zoffany, 1780
Oil on canvas, 622 x 495mm (24½ x 19½")
COURTESY OF MRS R. H. COBHAM/NATIONAL PORTRAIT GALLERY

Fig.12 **The Servants' Hall at Erddig, Wrexham**
© NATIONAL TRUST, ERDDIG

Fig.13 **Brass Rubbing at Hunsdon Church, Hertfordshire, commemorating the 'Parke and Hovse Keper' James Gray**
Unknown artist, 1591
THE CONWAY LIBRARY, COURTAULD INSTITUTE OF ART

Fig.14 **William Simpson, a waiter at Ye Olde Cheshire Cheese**
Thomas Charles Wageman, 1829
COURTESY OF COUNTRY LIFE

Fig.15 **Edward Wise, College Butler at Eton College**
British School, *c.*1680s
Oil on canvas, 756 x 622mm (29¾ x 24½")
BY PERMISSION OF THE PROVOST AND FELLOWS OF ETON COLLEGE
PHOTOGRAPHIC SURVEY, COURTAULD INSTITUTE OF ART

Fig.16 **Alice George**
William Sonmans, late 1700s
Oil on canvas, 749 x 610mm (29½ x 24")
THOMAS PHOTOS/OXFORDSHIRE COUNTY COUNCIL PHOTOGRAPHIC ARCHIVE

Fig.17 **Richard Cadman**
John Ward, 1964
Pencil, red ink and coloured washes, 460 x 635mm (18⅛ x 25")
THE PRESIDENT AND FELLOWS OF TRINITY COLLEGE, OXFORD

Fig.18 College Staff at Girton College, Cambridge
Unknown photographer, 1907
THE MISTRESS AND FELLOWS, GIRTON COLLEGE, CAMBRIDGE

Fig.19 View of the South Front of Belton House, Lincolnshire
Unknown artist, *c.*1720
Oil on canvas, 2370 x 3130mm
(93⅜ x 123")
BELTON HOUSE COLLECTION
NATIONAL TRUST PHOTOGRAPHIC LIBRARY/GRAHAM CHALLIFOUR

Fig.20 The Squire (or Family Prayers)
Frederick Elwell, 1931
Oil on canvas, 1143 x 1092mm (45 x 43")
ART GALLERY & MUSEUM, KELVINGROVE
© GLASGOW MUSEUMS

Fig.21 A Harlot in her Garret Attended by Her 'Bunter'
William Hogarth, *c.*1731
Red chalk touched with black, squared, 250 x 359mm (9⅞ x 14⅛")
TRUSTEES OF THE BRITISH MUSEUM, LONDON

Fig.22 Molly, Girl with a Tea Tray
John Faber Junior after a print by Philippe Mercier, 1744
Mezzotint, with engraved lettering, 333 x 226mm (13⅛ x 8⅞")
© THE BRITISH MUSEUM (BEQUEATHED BY WILLIAM, 2ND BARON CHEYLESMORE (1843–1902)

Fig.23 Charity Relieving Distress
Thomas Gainsborough, 1784
Oil on canvas, 980 x 762mm (38½ x 30")
PRIVATE COLLECTION

Fig.24 Miss Mary Warde as a Milkmaid
Charles Jervas, *c.*1730s
Oil on canvas, 2350 x 1422mm
(92½ x 55")
J. ST. A. WARDE ESQ., SQUERRYES COURT
PHOTOGRAPHIC SURVEY, COURTAULD INSTITUTE OF ART

Fig.25 Mehemet
Sir Godfrey Kneller, 1715
Oil on canvas, 910 x 716mm
(35⅞ x 28⅛")
THE ROYAL COLLECTION
THE ROYAL COLLECTION © 2003, HER MAJESTY QUEEN ELIZABETH II

Fig.26 Thomas Smith and His Family
Robert West, 1733
Oil on canvas, 593 x 892mm
(23⅜ x 35⅛")
UPTON HOUSE (BEARSTED COLLECTION)
NATIONAL TRUST/NTPL/ANGELO HORNAK

Fig.27 Elizabeth Murray, Countess of Dysart, and a Black Servant
Sir Peter Lely, *c.*1651–2
Oil on canvas
VICTORIA & ALBERT MUSEUM
© VICTORIA & ALBERT IMAGES

Fig.28 Ignatius Sancho
Thomas Gainsborough, 1768
Oil on canvas, 737 x 622mm (29 x 24½")
© NATIONAL GALLERY OF CANADA, OTTAWA, PURCHASED 1907

Fig.29 Lord Torrington's Hunt Servants Setting Out from Southill
George Stubbs, *c.*1765
Oil on canvas, 597 x 1054mm (23½ x 41½")
PRIVATE COLLECTION

Fig.30 The Raby Pack
William Ward after Henri Bernard Chalon
Mezzotint
© THE BRITISH MUSEUM, LONDON

Fig.31 Four O'clock in the Town
Thomas Rowlandson, 1788
Coloured etching with aquatint, 229 x 305mm (9⅛ x 12")
PRIVATE COLLECTION
THE BRIDGEMAN ART LIBRARY

Fig.32 Four O'clock in the Country
Thomas Rowlandson, 1788
Watercolour on paper, 240 x 300mm
(9½ x 12")
NEWPORT MUSEUM AND ART GALLERY, SOUTH WALES
THE BRIDGEMAN ART LIBRARY

Fig.33 Sir Robert Palmer, with the Shepherd John Green and Prizewinning Leicester Sheep
John Ferneley, 1823
Oil on canvas, 860 x 1090mm (33⅞ x 42⅞")
© LEICESTER CITY MUSEUMS SERVICE

Fig.34 Two Coach Horses of Sir John Fleming Leicester with Gaskill, the Coachman, and a Carriage in the Forecourt of Tabley House
George Garrard, 1871
Oil on canvas, 685 x 890mm (27 x 35")
UNIVERSITY OF MANCHESTER, TABLEY HOUSE COLLECTION
PHOTOGRAPHIC SURVEY, COURTAULD INSTITUTE OF ART

Fig.35 The Return from Shooting
Francis Wheatley
Oil on canvas
PRIVATE COLLECTION
BRIDGEMAN ART LIBRARY

Fig.36 The Governess
Richard Redgrave, 1844
Oil on canvas, 915 x 715mm (36 x 28⅛")
VICTORIA & ALBERT MUSEUM
V&A PICTURE LIBRARY

Acknowledgements

We would like to thank the many owners, curators, conservators, librarians, record office staff and scholars with have assisted us with the preparation of this catalogue, and in particular Gene Adams, David Alexander, Clare Baxter, Betty Beesley, Michael Blackwell, Douglas Brine, Michelle Brown, Ann Bukantas, David Burton, Juliet Carey, Hugh Cheape, Margie Christian, Rosalys Coope, John Cornforth, Jeremy Cragg, Matthew Craske, Richard and Elizabeth Dalkeith, Lucy Dixon, Elizabeth Einberg, Liz Emerson, Andrew Festing, Peter Funnell, Christopher Gibbs, Sir James and Lady Graham, Richard Green, Margaret Gray, James Holloway, Holger Hoock, Valerie Hunter, Haidee Jackson, Beryl Jones, Rica Jones, Nicola Kalinsky, Susanna Kerr, John Keyworth, Helen Kirk, Tim Knox, Alastair Laing, Alison Light, Christopher Lloyd, James Lomax, Clare Van Lonen, Jean Marsh, Jonathan Marsden, Dame Jean Maxwell-Scott DCVO, Kate Mayne, Charles Noble, Julia Nurse, Sheila O'Connell, Martin Olin, Mr and Mrs Christopher Parker, Robert Parker, Thea Randall, Margret Ribbert, David Solkin, Lindsay Stainton, Merlin Waterson, Lady Willoughby d'Eresby and Viscount Windsor.

We should also like to express our gratitude to the staff of the National Portrait Gallery, to Peter Mandler for his valuable comments on the draft, and to our editors, Anjali Bulley and Marilyn Inglis, and designer Karen Stafford. Above all, we are indebted to our researcher Kate Newman for her unfailing intelligence, efficiency and energy throughout the work on exhibition and catalogue. Anne French would also like to thank her family for their patience and restraint over the past year.

Notes

Introduction

1. Marcia Pointon, *Hanging the Head* (Yale University Press, New Haven & London 1993) p.16
2. Jean Hecht, *The Domestic Servant Class in Eighteenth-Century England* (Routledge & Kegan Paul, London 1956) p.3
3. Jonas Hanway, *Letters on the Importance of the Rising Generation of the Labouring Part of our Fellow subjects* (A. Millar, T. Cadell, C. Marshe, G. Woodfall, London 1767) ii p.158, quoted in Bridget Hill, *Servants. English Domestics in the Eighteenth Century* (Clarendon Press, Oxford 1996) p.6
4. Bridget Hill, *Women, Work and Sexual Politics in Eighteenth-Century England* (Basil Blackwell, Oxford 1989) p.125
5. Margaret Powell, *Below Stairs* (Peter Davis, London 1968) passim
6. Frederick Gorst, *Of Carriages and Kings* (W.H. Allen, London 1956) p.112
7. Phillis Cunnington, *Costume of Household Servants From the Middle Ages to 1900* (A.&C. Black, London 1974) pp.69–71
8. *The Diaries of Hannah Cullwick, Victorian Maidservant* (ed. Liz Stanley, Virago Press, London 1984) passim
9. See Powell, Chapter 12
10. Giovanni de Rosselli, *Opera noua chiamato Epulario* (Iacomo Pentio, Venice 1517)
11. Sarah Maza, *Servants and Masters in Eighteenth-Century France* (Princeton University Press, Princeton 1983) passim

chapter 1

1. Mark Girouard, *Life in the English Country House* (Yale University Press, New Haven & London 1978) p.15
2. John Southworth, *The English Medieval Minstrel* (The Boydell Press, Suffolk 1989) p.53
3. See, for example, *A pleasant history of the life and death of Will Somers*, 1676, or *Archy's Dreame, Sometimes Jester to his Majestie, but exiled the court*, 1641
4. Quoted in Karen Hearn (ed.) *Dynasties, Painting in Tudor and Jacobean England 1530–1630* (Tate Publishing, London 1995) p.194
5. Enid Welsford, *The Fool, His Social and Literary History* (Faber & Faber, London 1968) p.179
6. The Royal Collection, see Oliver Millar, *Tudor, Stuart and Early Georgian Pictures in the Royal Collection* (Phaidon, London 1963) no.125
7. Christopher Brown and Hans Vlieghe, *Van Dyck, 1599–1641* (Royal Academy, London 1999) p.246
8. Quoted in Oliver Millar, *Sir Peter Lely, 1618–80* (National Portrait Gallery, London 1978) p.44
9. For this portrait see E.W. Ives, 'Tom Skelton – A Seventeenth-Century Jester' in *Shakespeare Survey, An Annual Survey of Shakespearian Study & Production*, **13**, 1960, pp.90–105
10. Op. cit., p. 94
11. Millar, p.44
12. Millar, p.43
13. Southworth, p.8
14. Op. cit., p.22
15. Victoria Percy and Gervase Jackson-Stops, 'A Jovial Heap of Contradictions', The Travel Journal of the 1st Duchess of Northumberland – I, *Country Life*, Jan.31, 1974, p.192
16. *The Life of James Allan, The Celebrated Northumberland Piper* (Mackenzie & Dent, Newcastle upon Tyne 1818) p.315
17. For the identification of this portrait as Turnbull, see the Business Minutes of the 4th Duke of Northumberland, Alnwick Castle Archives, 8 July, 1850, pp.263–4
18. Peter Lord, *The Visual Culture of Wales: Imaging the Nation* (Cardiff 2000) pp.126–7
19. Hugh Cheape, 'The Piper to the Laird of Grant', *Proceedings of the Society of Antiquaries of Scotland*, Vol. 125, 1995, p.1164; We are indebted to his discussion of these portraits and that of James Holloway (note 20 below)
20. James Holloway, *Patrons and Painters: Art in Scotland, 1650–1760* (Scottish National Portrait Gallery, Edinburgh 1989) p.72
21. Duncan MacMillan, *Scottish Art 1460–1990* (Mainstream, Edinburgh 1990) p.88
22. Cheape, p.1164
23. Holloway, p.69
24. Holloway, p.21

chapter 2

1. Jean Hecht, *The Domestic Servant Class in Eighteenth-Century England* (Routledge & Kegan Paul, London 1956) p.70
2. Bridget Hill, *Servants, English Domestics in the Eighteenth Century* (Clarendon Press, Oxford 1996) p.156
3. Hecht, p.46
4. Op. cit., p.47
5. Op. cit., p.53, p.55
6. Op. cit., p.61
7. Op. cit., p.64
8. Von Archenholz, 1784, quoted in Lawrence Stone, *The Family, Sex and Marriage in England 1500–1800* (abridged edition, Penguin Books, London 1979) p.272
9. Karen Hearn (ed.) *Dynasties, Painting in Tudor and Jacobean England 1530–1630* (Tate Publishing, London 1995) p.220
10. Mary Webster, *Johann Zoffany, 1733–1810* (National Portrait Gallery, London 1976) p.70.
11. J.C. Ibbetson in a letter to William Danby dated 21 October, 1802, Cunliffe-Lister papers, Bradford Art Gallery, quoted in James Mitchell, *Julius Caesar Ibbetson (1759–1817): 'the Berchem of England'* (John Mitchell & Son, London 1999) p.82
12. Sale, Christie's, London, 29.11.1977 (101), cat.53

13. Daphne Foskett, *Collecting Miniatures* (The Antique Collectors' Club, 1979) p.97, p.400
14. Ronald Paulson, *Hogarth: His Life, Art, and Times* (Yale University Press, New Haven & London 1971) v.I, p.215
15. David H. Solkin, *Painting for Money, the Visual Arts and the Public Sphere in Eighteenth-Century England* (Yale University Press, New Haven & London 1993) pp.66–72
16. Op. cit., p.86
17. Op. cit., p.105

chapter 3

1. Peter Lord, *The Visual Culture of Wales: Imaging the Nation* (University of Wales Press, Cardiff 2000) p.175. For a full discussion of these portraits see Merlin Waterson, *The Servants' Hall, A Domestic History of Erddig* (Routledge & Kegan Paul, London 1980) passim
2. Alastair Laing, *In Trust for the Nation, Paintings from National Trust Houses* (The National Trust, London 1995) p.72
3. See Philip Yorke's poems for this and other information on the sitters
4. Waterson, p.170
5. For a discussion of these portraits, see James Lomax, 'The Servants' Gallery: Six portraits of early nineteenth-century Domestics from Bramham Park', *Leeds Museums & Galleries Review*, No.2, 1999, pp.41–2
6. For this portrait, see Christopher Lloyd, *The Queen's Pictures: Royal Collectors Through the Ages* (National Gallery, London, 1991) p.112
7. Jacob Simon, 'The Account Book of James Northcote', The Walpole Society, LVIII, 1995–6, p.82
8. Ibid.
9. Walter Scott, *Familiar Letters* (David Douglas, Edinburgh 1894) I, p.449, letter to Lord Montagu, 21 May 1891
10. J.G. Lockhart, *The Life of Sir Walter Scott, Bart.* (A.&C. Black, Edinburgh 1836–8) I, p.342
11. Walter Scott, *Familiar Letters*, I, p.405, letter to the Duke of Buccleuch, 22 January 1817
12. A. Francis Steuart, *Catalogue of the Pictures at Dalkeith House* (2nd ed., privately printed, Dalkeith 1911), pp.58–9. The reference to Major Scott's possible paternity is made in a manuscript quotation to the Drumlanrig Castle copy
13. For Ainslie see David and Francina Irwin, *Scottish Painters at Home and Abroad 1700–1900* (Faber & Faber, London 1975) pp.216–17
14. *Blackwood's Magazine*, April 1817
15. Walter Scott, *Guy Mannering* (Constable & Co., London 1895) vol.I, p.220

chapter 4

1. Judy Egerton, *Wright of Derby* (Tate Gallery, London 1990) no.140
2. Thomas Cocke and Elizabeth Sheldon, 'Refurbishing a Faithful Retainer' *Country Life*, 15 November 1979, pp.12–15
3. See Nicholas Tyacke (ed.), *The History of the University of Oxford*, vol.4, *Seventeenth-Century Oxford* (Clarendon Press, Oxford 1997) pp.38–9 and passim
4. Phillis Cunnington, *Costume of Household Servants* (A.&C. Black, London 1974) fig.23
5. From the 1833 catalogue, quoted in Tancred Borenius, *Pictures by the Old Masters in the Library of Christ Church Oxford* (Oxford University Press, Oxford 1916) p.110
6. Information from Dr Timothy Connor, Eton College
7. Mrs Reginald Lane Poole, *Catalogue of Portraits in the Possession of the University, Colleges, City, and County of Oxford* (Clarendon Press, Oxford 1925) III, Part ii, p.218
8. Peter Laslett, *The World We Have Lost* (Methuen, London 1985) pp.109–10, and information from Dr C.S.L. Davies, Wadham College
9. Lane Poole, 1925, II, pp.161–2. We are grateful to Dr Michael Burden of New College for his help over this portrait
10. L.G. Sutherland and L.G. Mitchell (eds), *The History of the University of Oxford: The Eighteenth Century* (Clarendon Press, Oxford 1986) p.430
11. Christopher Platt, *The Most Obliging Man in Europe: Life and Times of the Oxford Scout* (George Allen & Unwin, London 1986) and see also Brian Harrison (ed.), *The History of the University of Oxford*: vol. VIII, *The Twentieth Century* (1994) pp.205–8
12. Information from Clare Hopkins, Archivist at Trinity College, Oxford.
13. Bernard Denvir, *A Most Agreeable Society: A hundred and twenty-five years of the Arts Club* (The Arts Club, London 1989). p.23
14. *Francis Hodge: Memorial Exhibition catalogue*, 20–31 December 1949, Royal Institute Galleries, 195 Piccadilly, London
15. For example, Percy Colson, *White's 1693–1950* (William Heinemann, London 1951) p.132: 'No history of White's would be complete which did not mention its hall porters.'
16. The house has several paintings by Jan Siberechts painted between 1675 and 1678, showing the porter wearing a livery robe to the ground and holding a staff in his right hand
17. see David Solkin (ed.), *Art on the Line: The Royal Academy Exhibitions at Somerset House 1780–1836* (Yale University Press, New Haven & London 2001) p.62–3
18. David M. Wilson, *The British Museum: A History* (The British Museum Press, London 2002). p.30–1
19. Information from original label, now in Department of Prints and Drawings, the British Museum, and unpublished notes kindly provided by Marjorie Caygill. See also David M. Wilson, 2002, plates 16–17 and passim
20. Photographs of the servants at the Royal Military Academy,

Woolwich, and at the Royal Military College, Sandhurst, do exist. We are grateful to Lt. Col. Stephens of the Welsh Guards, Angela Weight of the Imperial War Museum, and Dr J. Thwaites, Curator of the Sandhurst Collection at the Royal Military Academy, Sandhurst, for their guidance
21. *Pulling Off the Padre's Boots*, Imperial War Museum, LD113
22. See *Rex Whistler1905–44*, Arts Council exhibition 1960, Introduction by Laurence Whistler, p.7
23. Jenny Spencer-Smith, *Rex Whistler's War* (Catalogue, National Army Museum, London, May–Sept 1994) p.76 and passim
24. Hilda Gamlin, *Nelson's Friendships* (Hutchinson, London 1899) II p.295
25. For the final picture, see C.M. Kauffmann, *Catalogue of Paintings in the Wellington Museum* (HMSO, London 1982) no.24

chapter 5

1. W.H. Dilworth, quoted in Kathleen Williams, *Swift: The Critical Heritage* (Routledge & Kegan Paul, London 1970) p.175
2. See Peter Earle, *A City Full of People: Men and Women of London 1650–1750* (Methuen, London 1994) and (for example) Lawrence Stone, *Road to Divorce* (OUP, Oxford 1990) and *Uncertain Unions* (OUP, 1992) and *Broken Lives* (OUP, 1993)
3. John Macdonald, *Memoirs of an Eighteenth-Century Footman: John Macdonald Travels (1745–1779)*, introduced by John Beresford (George Routledge & Sons, London).
4. John Burnet (ed.), *Useful Toil* (Allen Lane, London 1974).
5. John Wilkins, *Autobiography of an English Gamekeeper* (T. Fisher Unwin, London 1892)
6. Wilkins, p.6
7. Eric Horne, *What the Butler Winked At* (T. Werner Laurie, London 1923) p.14
8. Alan and Mary McQueen Simpson, (eds), *I too am here*, selections from the letters of Jane Welsh Carlyle (Cambridge University Press, Cambridge, 1977)
9. Earle, p.85
10. Op. cit., p.189
11. Horne, p.55
12. Daniel Defoe, *The Great Law of Subordination Considered; or the Insolence and Unsufferable Behaviour of Servants in England duly enquired into* (S. Harding, W. Lewis, T. Worrall, A. Bettesworth, W. Meadows & T. Edlin, London 1724), p.8
13. Parts of Swift's *Journal to Stella* were first published in the 1760s; the full version only in 1948. Harold Williams (ed.) (Clarendon Press, Oxford 1948)
14. Title page to Swift's *Directions to Servants* (R. Dodsley & M. Cooper, London 1745)
15. Thorstein Veblen, *The Theory of the Leisure Class* (George Allen & Unwin, London, 1924) p.63
16. For the Ashburnham liveries and for liveries in general, see Tim Knox, 'Enter a Footman in Plush Breeches', *Country Life*, vol excii, 5 March 1998, pp.50–53
17. Jean Rennie, *Every Other Sunday* (Coronet Books, London 1955) p.42
18. Frederick Gorst, *Of Carriages and Kings* (W.H. Allen, London 1956) pp.159–60

chapter 6

1. For these see Tabitha Barber, *Mary Beale (1632/3–1699) Portrait of a Seventeenth-century Painter, Her Family and Her Studio* (The Geffrye Museum, London 1999) pp.70–76; E. Walsh, 'Charles Beale 3d Book. 1680', *The Connoisseur*, CXLIX, pp.248–52; Lindsay Stainton & Christopher White, *Drawing in England from Hilliard to Hogarth* (British Museum, London 1987) pp.214–17; Edward Croft-Murray and Paul Hulton, *Catalogue of British Drawings*, (Trustees of the British Museum, London 1960) pp.148–68
2. Elizabeth Walsh and Richard Jeffree, *The Excellent Mary Beale*, 1975, p.12
3. Elizabeth Walsh and Richard Jeffree, 'Mrs Mary Beale, Printress', *The Connoisseur*, CXXXI, no.530, March 1953, p.4
4. Barber, p.33
5. Op. cit., p.37
6. Ibid.
7. Quoted in Barber, p.54
8. Elizabeth Embery and Judy Egerton, *The Age of Hogarth* (Tate Gallery Publications, London 1988) p.132
9. See F. Antal, *Hogarth and his Place in European Art* (Routledge & Kegan Paul, London 1962) and Neil McWilliam, *Hogarth* (Studio Editions, London,1993)
10. David H. Solkin, *Painting for Money* (Yale University Press, New Haven & London 1993) p.240
11. Antal, p.174
12. John Barrell, *The Dark Side of the Landscape: the Rural Poor in English Painting 1730–1840* (Cambridge, 1980) p.95
13. J.T. Nettleship, *George Morland* (Seely & Co., London 1898) pp.15–16
14. 'Drawings of estate and household servants by children of 3rd Earl of Dartmouth', D1501/H/2/3-27, Staffordshire Record Office; nos. 4, 5 and 6 are not of servants.
15. Sandwell estate rental & current account, D564/5/1/2 (1814–15); D564/5/1/7 (1819–20); Staffordshire Record Office; We are indebted to Mrs Randall, County Archivist, for drawing these records to our attention and for discussions concerning these drawings.
16. William Payne, *Hospitalfield, Patrick Allan-Fraser and his art collection*, (National Galleries of Scotland, 1990) pp.10–11
17. *Harold Gilman 1876–1919*, exhibition catalogue, The Arts Council, 1981, p.4
18. Leeds Museums and Galleries
19. *Gilman*, 1981, loc. cit.
20. Accessible versions at Tate, Walker Art Gallery, Liverpool
21. The largest version is at Tate
22. Tate
23. Williamson Art Gallery, Birkenhead

24. Beaverbrook Collection, Fredricton, New Brunswick. Information on this kindly provided by Rachel Brodie Venart; other twentieth-century servant images by Richard Shone
25. Jane Hill, *The Art of Dora Carrington* (The Herbert Press, 1995) p.61
26. Quoted on the Tate website, home page/contents page/artists A to Z
27. Susan Compton (ed.) *British Art in the 20th Century* (Royal Academy of Arts, London 1987) p.247
28. *Lawrence Gowing*, Arts Council touring exhibition, March–August 1983, pp.19, 21

chapter 7

1. Ian Watt, *The Rise of the Novel* (Chatto & Windus, London 1957; reprinted 1970) p.179
2. Op. cit., p.166
3. Op. cit., p.48
4. Bridget Hill, *English Domestics in the Eighteenth Century*, p.209
5. E.S. Turner, *What the Butler Saw* (Michael Joseph, London 1962) p.101
6. Catherine Gordon, *British Paintings of Subjects from the English Novel* (Garland Publishing Inc., New York & London 1988) p.32
7. Watt, p.175
8. Samuel Richardson, quoted in Gordon, p.33
9. Gordon, pp.43–8
10. Elizabeth Einberg, *Manners & Morals, Hogarth and British Painting 1700–1760* (Tate Gallery, London 1987) p.159
11. Gordon, p.39
12. Op. cit., p.57
13. Mireille Galinau & John Hayes, *London in Paint* (Museum of London, London, 1996) p.106
14. James Townley, *High Life Below Stairs* (J. Newbery, London 1759) pp.7–8
15. Op. cit., p.35
16. York City Art Gallery
17. See Marcia Pointon, *Hanging the Head* (Yale University Press, New Haven & London 1993) pp.119–120
18. Anon, *The Servants Calling* (London 1725) p.21
19. Geoffrey Ashton, *Pictures in the Garrick Club* (Garrick Club, London 1997) p.260
20. David Bindman, *Hogarth* (Thames & Hudson, London 1981) p.114
21. Jacob Simon, 'The Account Book of James Northcote', *Walpole Society*, 1995–6, p.64
22. John Ingamells and Robert Raines, *Philippe Mercier 1689–1760* (City Art Gallery York & Kenwood, 1969) p.9
23. Moira Thunder, 'Pattern Drawing for, Manufacturing, Uses and Abandonment of English Woven Silks', *Making & Unmaking in the Design Professions* (Design History Society 2000) pp.206–7
24. Michael Rosenthal & Martin Myrone (eds), *Gainsborough* (Tate Publishing, London 2002) p.232
25. Op. cit., p.230
26. Quoted in Celina Fox and Aileen Ribeiro, *Masquerade* (Museum of London, 1983) p.4
27. Op. cit. p.1
28. Op. cit, p.2

chapter 8

1. Population figs
2. Ref. proportion of black servants
3. See Paul Kaplan, 'Titian's *Laura Dianti* and the Origins of the Motif of the Black Page in Portraiture', *Antichita Viva* No.1 (1982), pp.11–18 and No.4 (1982) pp.10–18; and *Anthony Van Dyck* (National Gallery of Art, Washington 1990–91) p.176
4. Hugh Honour, *The Image of the Black in Western Art*, Vol.IV, part 1, *Slaves and Liberators* (Harvard University Press, Cambridge, Mass. 1989) p.46
5. Quoted in David Dabydeen, *Hogarth's Blacks* (Manchester University Press, Manchester 1987) p.30
6. The history of philosophical attitudes to the 'problem' of blackness has recently been examined by David Bindman in *Ape to Apollo: Aesthetics and the Idea of Race in the 18th Century* (Reaktion Books, London 2002)
7. Dabydeen, 1987, p.32.
8. Linda Colley, *Captives* (Yale University Press, New Haven 2002)
9. Dabydeen, 1987 p.11
10. Dabydeen, 1987 p.81
11. James Walvin, *The Black Presence: A Documentary History of the Negro in England, 1555–1860* (Orbach & Chambers, London 1971) p. 16.
12. See Stuart Cary Welch, *Room for Wonder* (The American Federation for Arts, New York 1978) pp.70–1
13. Rosalys Coope, *The Webb Family and its Ownership of Newstead Abbey, Notts., 1860–1925*, p.138
14. Information from Oliver Millar, *The Victorian Pictures in the Collection of her Majesty the Queen* (Cambridge University Press, Cambridge 1992) pp.241ff, and from manuscript notes by Edward Sibbick on Osborne collection (held in the archives at Osborne House)
15. Elizabeth Longford, *Victoria R.I.* (Weidenfeld & Nicolson, London 1964) p.535
16. See Saloni Mathur, *An Indian Encounter: Portraits for Queen Victoria* (National Gallery Company, London 2002).

chapter 10

1. See Felicity Stimpson, 'Servants' Reading: An Examination of the Servants' Library at Cragside', *Library History*, vol. 19, March 2003, pp.3–11
2. Mark Girouard, *The Victorian Country House* (Yale University Press, New Haven 1979) pp.28–30
3. Robert Kerr, *The Gentleman's House* (John Murray, London, 2nd ed. 1865) p.199
4. Charles Booth (ed.), *Life and Labour of the People in London* (Macmillan & Co., London 1896) vol. VIII, p.210
5. Theresa McBride, *The Domestic Revolution: The Modernisation of Household Service in England*

and France 1820–1920 (Croom Helm, London 1976) p.74
6. Quoted in Delia Millar, *Queen Victoria's Life in the Scottish Highlands depicted by her water-colour artists* (Philip Wilson, London 1985) p.113
7. Helen Smailes, *Kenneth Macleay 1802–1878* (National Galleries of Scotland, Edinburgh 1992) p.15
8. Actually an illustrator called H.K. Browne
9. W. P. Frith, *A Victorian Canvas* (ed. Neville Wallis) (Geoffrey Bles, London 1957) p.81
10. W. P. Frith, *My Autobiography and Reminiscences* (Richard Bentley & Son, London 1887) vol. II, p.249
11. Private Collection
12. Wendy Lancaster (Anne Bukantas, ed.) *Fred Elwell, R.A. A Life in Art* (Highgate Publications, Beverley 1993)
13. Christopher Simon Sykes, *Country House Camera* (Weidenfeld & Nicolson, London 1980) p.23
14. See Susan Casteras, *Images of Victorian Womanhood in English Art* (Associated University Presses, London and Toronto 1987)
15. See (eds.) Susan Casteras and Ronald Parkinson, *Richard Redgrave 1804–1888* (Yale University Press, New Haven & London 1988), p.43
16. F.M. Redgrave, Richard Redgrave CB R.A.: A memoir compiled from his Diary (London,1891)
17. *Art Journal* 1860. Quoted in draft catalogue entry, Yale Center for British Art, New Haven
18. Catalogue, Osborne House (1876) p.418, no.785
19. *The Athenaeum*, 17 July 1875, p.79, quoted in Richard Altick, *Punch: the Lively Youth of a British Institution 1841–1851* (Ohio State University Press, Columbus 1997) p.6
20. *Punch*, vol. 39, 4 August 1860, p.151
21. *Punch*, vol. 60, 25 March 1871, p.120

chapter 11

1. Pamela Horn, *Life Below Stairs in the 20th Century* (Sutton Publishing, Stroud 2001) pp.35–6
2. Ibid.
3. Alan S.C. Ross, Nancy Mitford (ed.), *Noblesse Oblige* (Hamish Hamilton, London 1956) p.52
4. Humphrey Carpenter, *Benjamin Britten: A Biography* (Faber and Faber, London 1992) p. 379
5. Monica Dickens, *An Open Book* (Heinemann, London 1978) p.39
6. John Lewis, *Heath Robinson* (Constable, London 1972) p.210
7. Bridget Hill, *Servants: English Domestics in the Eighteenth Century* (Clarendon Press, Oxford 1996) pp.258–9
8. Michael Walsh, *C.R.W. Nevinson: This Cult of Violence* (Yale University Press, New Haven and London 2002) pp.173–4
9. C.S. Sykes, *The Visitors' Book* (Weidenfeld & Nicolson, London 1978) passim
10. We are grateful to Sir Tatton Sykes and Christopher Simon Sykes for their help over this portrait
11. W.A. Darlington, *J.M. Barrie* (Black & Son, London 1938) p.90
12. J.M. Barrie, *The Admirable Crichton* (Hodder & Stoughton, 1951) p.11
13. Ibid. p.119
14. Quoted in Cynthia Asquith, *Portrait of Barrie* (James Barrie, London 1954) p.37
15. Robin Maugham, *The Servant* (The Falcon Press, London 1948) p.16
16. Harold Pinter, *Collected Screenplays* (Faber and Faber, London 2000) p.ix
17. Dickens, 1978, p.37
18. Peter Mandler, *The Fall and Rise of the Stately Home* (Yale University Press, New Haven & London 1997).
19. Mark Girouard, *Life in the English Country House* (Yale University Press, New Haven & London 1978)
20. We are grateful to Lord Leicester for his help over these pictures.

Select Bibliography

Note: This list may exclude key primary source material included in the illustrations lists and in the endnotes on pages 196–208.

BURNETT, JOHN (ed.), *Useful Toil: Autobiographies of working people from the 1820s to the 1920s* (Allen Lane, London, 1974)

CHEAPE, HUGH, 'The Piper to the Laird of Grant', *Proceedings of the Society of Antiquaries of Scotland*, Volume 125 (1995), pp.1163–1173

The Diaries of Hannah Cullwick, Victorian Maidservant (ed. Liz Stanley) (London 1984)

CUNNINGTON, PHILLIS, *Costume of Household Servants From the Middle Ages to 1900* (London 1974)

Dabydeen, David, *Hogarth's Blacks* (Manchester University Press, Manchester 1987)

DAWES, DAVID, *Not in Front of the Servants: Domestic Service in England 1850–1939* (London 1973)

DAVIDOFF, LEONORE and HALL, CATHERINE, *Family Fortunes: Men and Women of the English Middle Class, 1780–1850* (Hutchinson, London 1987)

EARLE, PETER, *A City Full of People: Men and Women of London 1650–1750* (Methuen, London 1994)

GATHORNE-HARDY, JONATHAN, *The Rise and Fall of the British Nanny* (Hodder and Stoughton, London 1972)

GERARD, JESSICA, *Country House Life: Family and Servants, 1815–1914* (Blackwell, Oxford, 1994)

GERZINA, GRETCHEN, *Black London: Life before Emancipation* (John Murray, London 1995)

GIROUARD, MARK, *Life in the English Country House, A Social and Architectural History* (Yale University Press, New Haven & London 1978)

HECHT, JEAN, *The Domestic Servant Class in Eighteenth-Century England* (Routledge & Kegan Paul, London 1956)

HILL, BRIDGET, *Servants: English Domestics in the Eighteenth Century* (Clarendon Press, Oxford 1996)

HORN, PAMELA, *The Rise and Fall of the Victorian Servant* (Gill & Macmillan, Dublin 1975)

HORN, PAMELA, *Life Below Stairs in the 20th Century* (Sutton Publishing, Stroud 2001)

HUGGETT, FRANK, *Life Below Stairs* (Book Club Associates, London 1977)

HUGHES, KATHRYN, *The Victorian Governess* (Hambledon Press, London 1993)

LOMAX, JAMES, 'The Servants' Gallery: Six portraits of early nineteenth-century Domestics from Bramham Park' (*Leeds Museums & Galleries Review*, No 2, 1999, pp.41–2)

MCBRIDE, THERESA, *The Domestic Revolution: The Modernisation of Household Service in England and France 1820 –1920* (Croom Helm, London 1976)

O'LEARY, ELIZABETH, *At Beck and Call: The Representation of Domestic Servants in Nineteenth-Century American Painting* (Smithsonian Institution Press, Washington & London 1996)

POWELL, MARGARET, *Below Stairs* (Peter Davies, London 1968)

RENTON, ALICE, *Tyrant or Victim?: A History of the British Governess* (Weidenfeld & Nicolson, London 1991)

ROBBINS, BRUCE, *The Servant's Hand* (New York 1986)

SOUTHWORTH, JOHN, *The English Medieval Minstrel* (The Boydell Press, Suffolk 1989)

SOUTHWORTH, JOHN, *Fools and Jesters at the English Court* (Sutton Publishing, Gloucestershire 1998)

STRAUSS, RALPH, *Robert Dodsley, Poet, Publisher & Playwright* (John Lane, The Bodley Head, London; John Lane Company, New York 1910)

SYKES, CHRISTOPHER SIMON, *Country House Camera* (Book Club Associates, 1980)

TURNER, E. S., *What the Butler Saw* (Michael Joseph, London 1962)

WALVIN, JAMES, *The Black Presence: A Documentary History of the Negro in England, 1555–1860* (Orbach & Chambers, London 1971)

WATERSON, MERLIN, *The Servants' Hall: a Domestic History of Erddig* (Routledge & Kegan Paul 1980)

WELSFORD, ENID, *The Fool, His Social & Literary History* (Faber & Faber, London 1935)

WOOLGAR, CHRISTOPHER M., *The Great Household in Late Medieval England,* (Yale University Press, New Haven & London 1999)

Index

Figures in italics refer to captions

Adams, Samuel and Sarah: *The Complete Servant* 101, 168
Agasse, J.L. 66
Aikman, William 40, 49, 51, *139*, *141*
Ainslie, John 51, 54, 58, 73, *74*, *93*, *99*
Aken, Joseph van *55*
Alken, Henry 161
Allan-Fraser, Patrick *105*, *115*, 115-16
Allen, James (piper) 29, *29*
Allen, Thomas (servant) 91, *91*
Almack, William 78
Almond, Arnold 38, 41, 64–5, *64*, *65*
Alsop, George 51, *59*, 60
Ancaster, Peregrine, 3rd Duke of *163*
Angerstein family 50
Ardizzone, Edward 89
Armstrong, Archibald (jester) 24, 26
Ashridge Park, Hertfordshire 167
Aylesford, Heneage Finch, 4th Earl of 111

Baccelli, Giovanna 38, 65
Bacon, Sir Nathaniel 16, 46, *46*, 48
Bank of England 84–5, *86*, *89*
Banning, William (gate porter) 85, *86*, 87
Barber, Thomas *45*, 45–6, 51
Barlow, Francis 48–9
Barnetson, Samuel (messenger) *89*
Barrie, J.M.: *The Admirable Crichton* 189–90
Beach, Thomas 51
Beale, Charles, II 49, 105–8, *106*, *107*
Beale, Mary 105, 106, *106*
Bell, John: *The British Theatre* 129, 130
Bell, Vanessa 118
Belton House, Lincolnshire 87, *87*
Bengali servants (clay models) *148*
Bone, Muirhead 83
Boucher, François 17
Bowhill, Selkirkshire 71, 72
Bramham Park, Yorkshire 38, 42, 45, 49, 50, 51, 52, 54, 66–7
Brandt, Bill 183
Bretherton, James *128*, 129
Bridgeman, Lady Lucy 175
Bridgewater, Francis Egerton, Earl of 167
British Museum 87–8
Britten, Benjamin *184*, 185
Brontë, Charlotte: *Jane Eyre* 177
Brown, John (gilly) 8, 171, *171*
Brown, Mrs (housekeeper) 66, *67*
Brudenell family 58
Buccleuch family 39, 58, 71–5, 176
Burge, J. *195*
Burnet, John 91, *91*
Bygrave, Mary (housemaid) 88
Byron, William, 4th Lord *103*

Cadman, Richard (college scout) 83, *83*
Carlyle, Jane 95
Carlyle, Thomas 139
Carrington, Dora 119, 184
Cave, William 9, *9*, 79
Chardin, Jean-Baptiste 17, *18*, 133, 134
Charles I 24, *25*, 28
Christian, Dick (huntsman) 162
Ciarain, Nic (henwife) *21*, *33*, 35
Clint, George *70*
Cotes, Francis 46
Cowley, Abraham 107
Crawford, Marion: *The Little Princesses* 191
Crerar, John (gamekeeper) 164
Cuguano, Ottobah 145
Cullwick, Hannah (maid) 12, 94, 169, *169*
Cumberland, William, Duke of 38, *42*
Cummings (Cummines) (pipers) 33

Dalkeith House, Scotland 54, 58, 71, 72, 73, *93*, *99*
Dance, Nathaniel *44*
Dandridge, Bartholomew 137
Dartmouth family 111–13
Debenham, Sir Ernest 58
Deene Park 58, *192*
Defoe, Daniel 14, 29, 97, 97–8, 100
Devis, Arthur *55*
Devis, Arthur William *146*, 148
Devonshire, Georgiana, Duchess of 136
Dickens, Charles 172, 176
Dickens, Monica 12, 103, 185–6, 191
Dinsdale, Jenkin (servant) 42, 50
Dobson, William 142
Dodsley, Robert (footman) 8, 12, 93, 122
Dorset, John Sackville, 3rd Duke of 64, 65
Douglas, William *72*, 73
Downman, John 44, *44*
Draper, Alice (chef) 77, 84, *85*
Drumlanrig Castle, Dumfriesshire 58, 71, 73
Drummond Sisters, the *115*
Dudmaston, Shropshire *37*, *43*, 49, 51, 58–60, 67
Du Maurier, George 181
Durie (Derry), Tom (jester) 24, *25*
Dyck, Sir Anthony van 16, 17, *17*, 24–5, 27, 44, 53–4, 142, 143, 144
Dysart, Elizabeth Murray, Countess of *143*

Earlom, Richard *41*
Eaton Hall, Cheshire 167
Ebrell, Jane ('spider-brusher') 60, 62
Egg, Augustus *116*, 177
Ehrenstrahl, David von 17
Elizabeth I 24, 140, 148
Elliott, Jack (carpenter) *192*
Elliott, Richard 42
Ellys, John *40*, 54
Elvedon, Norfolk 4
Elwell, Frederick 101, *101*, *102*, 174, *175*
Elwes, Simon *183*, 189, *189*
English Lady's Bedchamber, An 45
Equiano, Olaudah 145
Erddig, Wales 7, 26, 43, 49, 50, 51, 52, 54, 58, 60–3, *61*, *62*, 66, 193

Faber, John, Jr 110, *134*
Farnley Hall, Yorkshire 113–15
Fawkes, Francis Hawksworth 113–15, *114*
Fawkes, Walter 113
Ferneley, John 154, 156, 162, *162*
Festing, Andrew 58, 194, *194*
Fielding, Henry *96*, *108*, 122
Finnie, John *167*, *173*, 174
Florance, Joseph (chef) 39, 73–5, *74*
Foster, Richard 58, *192*
Fox, George Lane 67, *114*, 115
Frederick II, Emperor 139
Frith, W.P. 8, *116*, 172–3, *174*
Fulford, Roger 84, *86*
Fyt, Jan 48

Gainsborough, Thomas 8, 38, 49–50, 51, 71, 62, *135*, 135–6, 145, 146, *146*
Gardiner, William (groom) 53, 65
Garnett, Mrs (housekeeper) *45*, 45–6
Garrard, George 51, 54, 58, *66*, 66–7, *67*, 156, *164*
Gaugain, Thomas 132, *133*
George, Alice (laundress) 81, *81*
Gertler, Mark 119
Gheeraerts the Younger, Marcus 24
Gibbs (manservant) 42, *110*, 110–11
Gibson, Richard (dwarf) 25, *27*, 27–8
Gill, Susan (maid) 106, *106*
Gilman, Harold 117, *117*
Girouard, Mark: *Life in the English Country House* 193
Girton College, Cambridge: staff 83, *84*
Gooch, Thomas 52
Goosey, Thomas (huntsman) 157
Gorst, Frederick 103
Gowing, Sir Lawrence 109, *118*, 119
Grant, Alastair Mor *30*, 33, 54
Grant, Alexander 33–4, 35, 58
Grant, Duncan 117, 118
Grant, Sir Francis 72–3, 158
Gravelot, Hubert 123, *123*
Gray, James (huntsman) *69*
Green, John (shepherd) 162, *162*
Gretton, Mr (tutor) 44, *44*
Griffith, George (huntsman) *43*, 59
Gunstone, Richard (college steward) 83

Hamilton, Gawen 55, 154
Hamilton, Hugh Douglas 47, 51
Hamilton, The Hon. John and Thomas *139*, *141*
Hardy, Frederic 178, *180*
Hargreaves, George *53*
Harold, Fulke (gardener) 13, *40*, 54
Hawarden Castle, Wales 60, *195*
Hayes, Mary (housemaid) *65*
Hayman, Francis 55, 123, *123*, 125, 132
Hecht, Jean: *The Domestic Servant Class...* 8, 154
Henry VII 23, 139
Henry VIII 23–4, *24*, 30
Higgens, Grace (housekeeper) 118
Highmore, Joseph 121, 123–5, *124*, *125*, 132
Hill, Bridget: *Servants...* 8, 37, 38, 186, 193
Hill, Derek 195

Hobbes, Thomas 44
Hodge, Francis Edward *77*, 84, *85*
Hodges, Thomas (college servant) 82 , *82*
Hogarth, William 8, 14, 43, 48, 51, 52, 55, 108, *108*, 109–10, 123, 132, *132*, 140, 142, 144, 154
Holkham Hall, Norfolk 58, 194, *194*
Holland, Elizabeth, Lady *177*
Holmes, Bridget (maid) 13, 49, 52, 53, *57*, 67, *68*, 68–70
Horne, Eric: *What the Butler Winked At* 95, 96
Hoskyns, John 9
Houghton Hall, Norfolk 13, *40*, 54
Hudson, Jeffrey (dwarf) 24–5
Hudson, Nellie (housekeeper) *184*, 184–5
Hudson, Thomas (keeper) *72*, 73
Hughes, Catherine (nanny) 52, *53*
Humphrey, Ozias 53
Hunsdon Church, Hertfordshire *69*

Ibbetson, Julius Caesar 42, 50
Isaacs, Sergeant J.W. *90*, 90–1
Ishiguro, Kazuo: *Remains of the Day* 191–2
Ives, Ben (servant) *108*, 109

Jacklin, Joseph (odd-job man) *192*
Jackman, Jonathan (gardener) 50, *50*
James II 69, *80*, 81
Jameson, Anna 176–7, *178*
Jaxon (Jackson), Su (servant) 106, *107*
'Jeeves' 42, 190
Jervas, Charles 136–7, *137*
Jones, William 30, 51, 62, 63, *63*

Karim, The Munshi Abdul 149–51, *150*
Kerr, Robert: *The Gentleman's House* 168
Kneller, Sir Godfrey 49, 95, 140, *140*, 142
Knole, Kent 38, 41, 42, 45, 49, 53, 58, 64–5, 66
Kuhfeld, Peter 195

Landseer, Edwin 8, 156, 164, 171, *177*
Langford, Mrs (charwoman) 118
Laroon, Marcellus 55, 154
'Lascelles the Footman Painter' 67
Lawrence, D.H. 160, 190
Lawrence, Sir Thomas *47*, 50
Lee, Margaret (housekeeper) 46

Leech, John 180–1
Legge, Charlotte 111, 113
Legge, Heneage 111, 112, *112*, 113, *113*
Leicester, Earl of 58, 194, *194*
Lely, Sir Peter 27, *27*, 30, 142, 143, *143*
Leslie, C. R. 72
Lindo, Francis 29, 51
Linsell, Charles 39
Liotard, Jean-Etienne 17, *19*
Lippyeatt, Jonathon *44*
Livingstone family 149
Locatelli, John Baptiste 65
Longhi, Pietro 17
Low, Elinor (servant) *64*, 65

Macdonald, John (footman) 10, 93, 95
MacLeay, Kenneth 171, *171*, 172
Maes, Nicolaes 7, *15*, 15–16
Marshall, Benjamin 156
Mathieson, Peter *71*, 72
Matthews, Charles *121*, *131*, 131–2
Maugham, Robin: *The Servant* 190
Maver, David 116
May, Robert: *The Accomplisht Cook* 39, *39*
Medina, Sir John de 40, 49, 51, 54
Mehemet (servant) 140, *140*
Meller, John 60, 62
Mentham, John (groom) 162
Mercier, Philippe 110, 121, 125, 130, 133–4, *134*
Mitford, Nancy: *Noblesse Oblige* 183
Moat, Henry (butler) 186–7, *187*, 189
Monnington, Thomas *89*
Montagu, Mary, Duchess of 38, 49–50
Morland, George 42, *110*, 110–11
Morland, Henry R. 17, 93, 133, *134*, 134–5, 173–4
Morris, Richard (servant) 95–6
Mounter, Mrs (landlady) 117–18
Mulready, William 111–12, *112*
Muncaster Castle, Cumbria 26
Mytens, Daniel 24

Nattes, J.C. *98*
Nebot, Balthasar *94*
Nevinson, Christopher 186–7, *187*, 189
Newcastle, Henry Clinton, 2nd Duke of *153*, 165, *165*
Newdigate, Lady Barbara (*née* Legge) 111, 112
'Nimrod's' *Famous Sporting Tours* 157, 160, 161
Northcote, James 51, 67, *70*, 70–1,

132–3, *133*
Northumberland, Elizabeth Seymour, 1st Duchess of 28–9
Nost, John van 145, *145*

Oakley, Octavius *75*
Oldaker, Tom (huntsman) 157
O'Leary, Elizabeth: *At Beck and Call* 7
Orde-Powlett, Thomas *128*, 129
Orwell, George: *Down and Out in Paris and London* 191
Osborn, Emily Mary 177, 178, *178*, *179*
Oudry, Jean-Baptiste 17
Oulton, Walley C. *131*, 131–2

Palmer, Sir Robert 162, *162*
Parry, John 30, *30*
Parry, William 30, *30*
Paxton, Joseph 8, 75, *75*
Pembroke, Philip, 4th Earl of 25
Pennington family 26
Penny, Edward 121, 126, *127*, 128
Petworth House, Sussex 175–6, *176*
Philips, Charles *55*, 154
Pointer, Robert (coachman) *41*
Potter, Mary *184*, 185
Potter, Samuel (labourer) *65*
Powell, Margaret 12, 191
Prince, Edward (carpenter) 43, 60, *61*, 62, 63
Prowse, Mrs Elizabeth 50, *50*
Punch 57, 167–8, 174, 178, 180–1, *181*

Queensberry, Catherine, Duchess of 136–7, *137*

Raffald, Elizabeth: *The Experienced English Housekeeper* 45
Redgrave, Richard 177–8, *178*
Reynolds, Sir Joshua 30, 44, 51, *70*, 142
Richards, James (servant) 112, *112*
Richardson, Samuel: *Pamela* 12, 17, 121, 122–6, *123*, *124*, *125*, 133, 135, 137
Riley, John 49, *57*, 67, 68, *68*, 69, 70, 79, *80*, 107
Ritson, Jonathan (woodcarver) *70*
Roberts, Ellen *118*, 119
Robinson, William Heath *185*, 186
Rogers, Thomas (carpenter) 63, *63*
Romney, George 51
Ross, William (piper) *171*, 172
Rowlandson, Thomas *96*, 158–60, *159*, *168*
Rubens, Sir Peter Paul 16, 48, 141–2
Russell, John 51, 87, *88*
Rust, Graham 195

Sancho, Ignatius 38, 49–50, 145, 146, *146*
Sandby, Paul *34*, 38, 42, *42*, 110
Sartorius, Francis *163*
Schwanfelder, Charles Henry 42
Scott, Sir Walter 71–2, 73, 170
Seymour, James *163*
Shakespeare, William 19, 24, 128
Shaw, Robert (keeper) 67, *70*, 70–1
Sheppard, Anne (dwarf) 27
Sickert, Walter 117, 118
Simpson, William (waiter) 78, *78*
Sitwell family 187
Skelton, Thomas (fool) 26, *26*
Slack, John 51
Smith, Isabel (nursemaid) *47*, 50
Smith, Thomas *55*, 142, *142*
Snijders, Frans 48, 70
Soldi, Andrea 142
Solomon, Rebecca 177
Somers, Will (fool) 24, *24*
Sonmans, William 49, 81, *81*
Stowe House *98*
Strafford, Thomas Wentworth, Earl of 17, *17*, 44, 53–4
Stubbs, George 8, 41, 51, 66, *155*, 155–6, *156*, 157, 163, *163*, 164
Swift, Jonathan 14, 93, 96, 98, 99, 126
Swoboda, Rudolph *150*, 151
Sykes, Sir Richard *183*, 189, *189*

Talbot, William Fox 174
Taylor, Daniel (servant) *64*, 65
Teniers, David, the Younger 16, *16*
Thackeray, W.M.: *Vanity Fair* 177
Tillemans, Peter *103*, 154, 158
Titian 16, 17, 25, 141
Townley, James: *High Life Below Stairs* *128*, 128–9, *129*
Troy, Jean-François de 17
Trumbull, John 143
Turnbull, Joseph 29

Upstairs Downstairs 8, 193

Vermeer, Jan *13*, 15, 117
Veronese, Paolo 15, 141
Victoria, Queen 149, 150–1, 170–2, 178

Wageman, Thomas Charles 78, *78*
Waitt, Richard *21*, 30, *31*, *33*, 33–5, 49, 51, 54
Walpole, Sir Robert 13, *40*
Walters, John 51, 52, 60, *61*, 61–2
Ward, James 156
Ward, John 83, *83*
Ward, William *157*
Warde, Mary 137, *137*
Warkworth, Lord *44*
Waterson, Merlin: *The Servants' Hall* 7, 60, 62, 66, 193
Welbeck Abbey, Nottinghamshire 103
Wells, H. G.: *Tono-Bungay* 94
Wentworth Woodhouse 51, 53
West, Robert *55*, 142, *142*
Westminster, Duke of 167
Wheatley, Francis 129–30, *130*, *153*, 155, 165, *165*
Whistler, Rex 89–91, *90*
Widdas, John 51, 66
Wilde, Samuel de *41*, *121*, 130–2, *131*
Wilkie, David 160–1
Wilkins, John: *The Autobiography of an English Gamekeeper* 94
Williams, James *100*
Williams, William (blacksmith) 60–1, 62
Windsor Castle 13, 38, 53
Wise, Edward (Eton butler) 81, *81*
Wodehouse, P.G. 42, 190
Wolryche, Sir John 58–9
Wolryche Fool, the *59*, 60
Woodforde, Parson James 83, 95
Woodward, George *97*
Woodward, Thomas (servant) 113, *113*
Woolf, Virginia 183–4
Wootton, John 154, 155, *163*
Wright, Joseph 50, 78
Wyndham, Mrs Percy 175–6, *176*
Wynn, Sir Watkin Williams 30, *30*

Yorke, Philip, I 60, 61, *61*, 62
Yorke, Simon, II 62, 63
Yorke family 7, 60–3, 66

Zoffany, Johann 8, 50, *50*, 51, *55*, 131, 142, 148, 155